Anonymous

The Christian Hymnal

A Selection of Psalms and hHymns, with Music, for Use in Public Worship

Anonymous

The Christian Hymnal
A Selection of Psalms and hHymns, with Music, for Use in Public Worship

ISBN/EAN: 9783337022228

Printed in Europe, USA, Canada, Australia, Japan

Cover: Foto ©Thomas Meinert / pixelio.de

More available books at **www.hansebooks.com**

THE

CHRISTIAN HYMNAL.

A SELECTION OF

PSALMS AND HYMNS,

With Music,

FOR USE IN PUBLIC WORSHIP.

"Sing praises unto our King: sing praises."

HARTFORD, CONN.:
BROWN & GROSS.
1877.

Entered, according to Act of Congress, in the year 1877, by
HAMERSLEY & CO.,
in the Office of the Librarian of Congress, at Washington.

ELECTROTYPED BY
J. M. ARMSTRONG, MUSIC TYPOGRAPHER,
PHILADELPHIA.

THE CHRISTIAN HYMNAL is just what it purports to be;—a *selection* of Psalms and Hymns, set to music, for use in Public Worship.

The editors entered upon the work of preparing this book with the conviction that a large number of hymns that increase the bulk and expense of many Hymn Books, might well enough be omitted from a Church Hymnal. Careful inquiry has satisfied them that most ministers, in their public use of hymns, move within even narrower limitations than this volume makes.

They have aimed to distinguish between *devotional* and *didactic* hymns, and to retain the more precious and familiar of the one class, and to exclude, for the most part, those of the other class.

In the first general division of the book, will be found the Psalms most commonly chanted in morning and evening worship, set to a variety of plain chants which any congregation may readily learn. Here, too, will be found the Gloria in Excelsis, the Te Deum, Tersanctus, Kyrie Eleison, and other ancient, unmetrical hymns of great value, and several chants for special services, together with the Lord's Prayer, the Commandments, Offertory Sentences, and the Catholic Creeds.

In the second general division will be found nearly five hundred hymns, arranged in topical order, and set to music which is, in the main, quite suitable for congregational use. Much noble music, and several fine hymns, have been taken from the "Hymnary," by J. Barnby, and from "Church Hymns," by Arthur Sullivan. A topical index, an index of first lines of hymns with the names of authors, and an index of tunes with the names of authors, complete this portion of the book. It has been deemed unnecessary to number the verses of the hymns, except in cases where it was not practicable to print the first verse under the tune as well as in it. Where tunes have been used more than once, (such as St. Ann's, Avon, etc.,) different arrangements have purposely been employed.

The editors have thought best to add to the Hymnal thirty-two Lessons for Responsive Readings, selected from Holy Scripture, and chiefly from the Psalter. After due deliberation, it has seemed to them best to copy literally both the text and the verse-divisions of our common and familiar version of the Scriptures.

With these brief explanations, we now submit this book, which for three years has been growing up in our hands, to the judgment of our brethren in the ministry and in the Churches of Christ.

               NATHANIEL J. BURTON.
               EDWIN POND PARKER.
Hartford, Jan. 1st, 1877.   JOSEPH H. TWICHELL.

THE LORD'S PRAYER.

{ OUR Father which art in Heaven, hallowed | be Thy | Name ;
{ Thy Kingdom come, Thy will be done on | earth, as it | is in | Heaven.

{ Give us this day our | daily | bread ;
{ And forgive us our debts as | we for- | give our | debtors :

{ And lead us not into temptation, but deliver | us from | evil ;
{ For Thine is the Kingdom, and the power, and the | glory, for- | ever. A- | men.

DE PROFUNDIS.

OUT of the depths have I cried unto | Thee, O | Lord ;
    Lord, hear my voice, let Thine *ears* be attentive to the | voice of my | suppli- | cations.

If Thou, Lord, shouldest mark iniquities, O Lord, | who shall | stand ?
But there is forgiveness with *Thee,* | that Thou | mayest be | feared.

I wait for the Lord, my soul doth wait, and in His | word do I | hope ;
My soul waiteth for the Lord *more* than | they that | watch for the | morning.

Let Israel hope in the Lord ; for with the Lord is mercy, and | plenteous re- | demption,
And He shall redeem Israel from | all his in- | iqui- | ties.

VENITE EXULTEMUS DOMINO.

(No. 1.)

O COME, let us sing un- | to the Lord;
    Let us heartily rejoice in the | strength of | our sal- | vation.
Let us come before His presence | with thanks- | giving;
And show ourselves | glad in | Him with | psalms.

For the Lord is a | great | God;
And a great | King a- | bove all | gods.
In His hands are all the corners | of the | earth;
And the strength of the | hills is | His— | also.

The sea is His, | and He | made it;
And His hands pre- | pared the dry— | land.
O come let us worship, | and fall | down;
And kneel be- | fore the | Lord our | Maker:

For He is the | Lord our | God;
And we are the people of His pasture and the | sheep of | His— | hand.
O worship the Lord in the | beauty of | holiness;
Let the whole earth | stand in | awe of | Him:

For He cometh, for He cometh, to | judge the | earth;
And with righteousness to judge the world, and the | people | with His | truth.

Glory be to the Father, and | to the | Son,
And | to the | Holy | Ghost;
As it was in the beginning, is now, and | ever shall | be,
World | without | end. A- | men.

CHANTS. 3

JUBILATE DEO.

O BE joyful in the Lord, | all ye | lands;
    Serve the Lord with gladness, and come before His | presence | with a | song.
Be ye sure that the Lord | He is | God;
It is He that hath made us, and not we ourselves; we are His people and the | sheep of | His— | pasture.

O go your way into His gates with thanksgiving, and into His | courts with | praise;
Be thankful unto Him, and | speak good | of His | name.
For the Lord is gracious, His mercy is | ever- | lasting,
And His truth endureth from gener- | ation to | gener- | ation.

Glory be to the Father, and | to the | Son,
And | to the | Holy | Ghost;
As it was in the beginning, is now, and | ever shall | be,
World | without | end. A- | men.

CHANTS.

CHANTS.

BENEDICTUS.

No. 1.

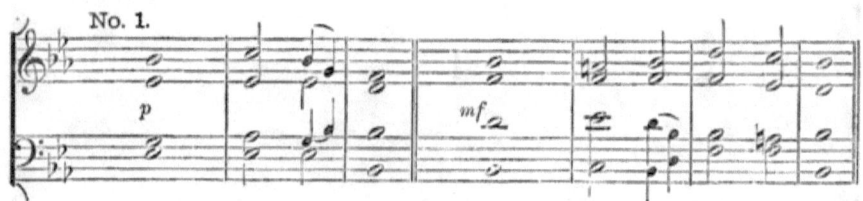

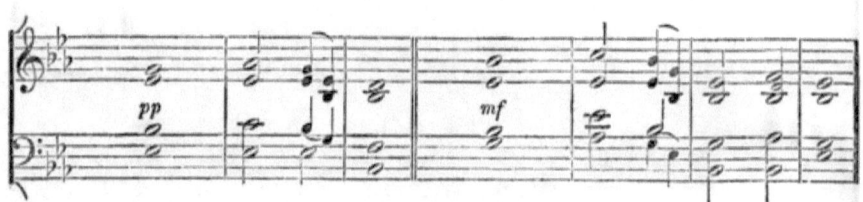

B LESSED be the Lord | God of | Israel;
   For He hath visited | and re- | deemed His | people;
And hath raised up a mighty sal- | vation | for us,
In the | house of His | servant | David.

As He spake by the mouth of His | holy | prophets,
Which have | been since the | world be- | gan :
That we should be saved | from our | enemies,
And from the | hand of | all that | hate us.

Glory be to the Father, and | to the | Son,
And | to the | Holy | Ghost :
As it was in the beginning, is now, and | ever shall | be,
World | without | end. A- | men

No. 2.

CHANTS.

DEUS MISEREATUR.

No. 1.

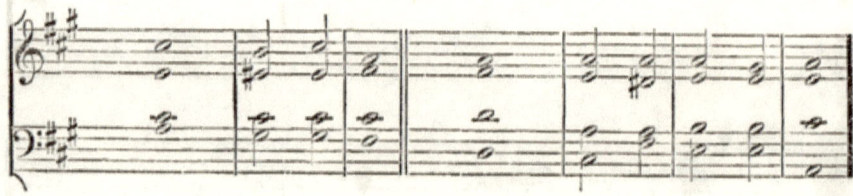

GOD be merciful unto | us, and | bless us;
    And shew us the light of His countenance, and be | merciful | unto | us;
That Thy way may be | known upon | earth,
Thy saving | health a- | mong all | nations.

Let the people praise | Thee, O | God,
Yea, let | all the | people | praise Thee:
O let the nations rejoice | and be | glad;
For Thou shalt judge the folk righteously, and govern the | nations | upon | earth.

Let the people praise | Thee, O | God;
Yea, let | all the | people | praise Thee.
Then shall the earth bring | forth her | increase,
And God, even our own | God shall | give us His | blessing.

God shall | bless | us;
And all the ends of the | world shall | fear | Him.

Glory be to the Father, and | to the | Son,
And | to the | Holy | Ghost;
As it was in the beginning, is now, and | ever shall | be,
World | without | end.   A- | men.

BENEDIC ANIMA MEA.

No. 1.

PRAISE the Lord, | O my | soul,
  And all that is within me | praise His | holy | Name;
Praise the Lord, | O my | soul,
And for- | get not | all His | benefits.

Who forgiveth | all thy | sin,
And | healeth all | thine in- | firmities;
Who saveth thy life | from de- | struction,
And crowneth thee with | mercy and | loving | kindness.

O praise the Lord, ye angels of His, ye that ex- | cel in | strength,
Ye that fulfil His commandment, and hearken unto the | voice— | of His | word;
O praise the Lord, all | ye His | hosts,
Ye servants of | His that | do His | pleasure.

O speak good of the Lord, all ye works of His, in all places of | His do- | minion;
Praise thou the | Lord,— | O my | soul!

Glory be to the Father, and | to the | Son,
And | to the | Holy | Ghost;
As it was in the beginning, is now, and | ever shall | be,
World | without | end. A- | men.

BONUM EST CONFITERI.

It is a good thing to give thanks un- | to the | Lord ;
And to sing praises unto Thy | name, O | Most — | Highest :
To tell of Thy loving-kindness early | in the | morning ;
And of Thy | truth in the | night — | season.

Upon an instrument of ten strings, and up- | on the | lute ;
Upon a loud instrument, | and up- | on the | harp :
For Thou, Lord, hast made me glad | through Thy | works ;
And I will rejoice in giving praise for the oper- | ations | of Thy | hands.

Glory be to the Father, etc.

MAGNIFICAT.

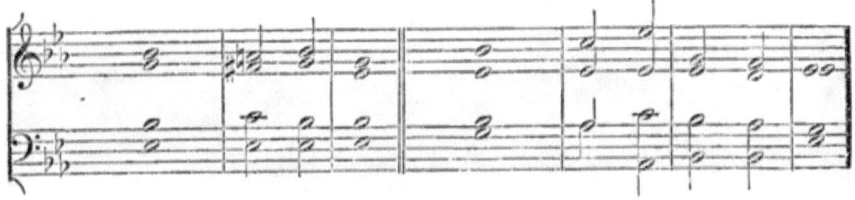

MY soul doth magni- | fy the | Lord,
And my spirit hath re- | joiced in | God my | Saviour.
For He hath regarded the low estate of | His hand- | maiden :
For behold, from henceforth all gener- | ations shall | call me | blessed.

For He that is mighty hath done to | me great | things,
And | holy | is His | name :
And His mercy is on | them that | fear Him,
From gener- | ation to | gener- | ation.

He hath showed strength | with His | arm,
He hath scattered the proud in the imagi- | nation | of their | hearts :
He hath put down the mighty | from their | seats,
And exalted | them of | low de- | gree.

He hath filled the hungry | with good | things,
And the rich He | hath sent | empty a- | way.
He hath holpen His servant Israel, in remembrance | of His | mercy ;
As He spake to our fathers, to Abraham, | and to his | seed for- | ever.

Glory be to the Father, and | to the | Son,
And | to the | Holy | Ghost ;
As it was in the beginning, is now, and | ever shall | be,
World | without | end.   A- | men.

LITANY CHANT.

O SAVIOUR of the world, the | Son Lord | Jesus,
    Stir up Thy strength and help us, we | hum— | bly be- | seech Thee ;
By Thy cross and precious blood Thou | hast re- | deemed us,
Save us and help us, we | hum— | bly be- | seech Thee.

Thou didst save Thy disciples when | ready to | perish,
Save us and help us, we | hum— | bly be- | seech Thee :
Let the pitifulness of | Thy great | mercy
Loose us from our sins, we | hum— | bly be- | seech Thee.

Make it appear that Thou art our Saviour and | mighty De- | liverer,
Save us that we may praise Thee, we | hum— | bly be- | seech Thee ;
Draw near according to Thy promise, from the | throne of Thy | glory,
Look down and hear our crying, we | hum— | bly be- | seech Thee

Come again and dwell with us, O | Lord Christ | Jesus,
Abide with us forever, we | hum— | bly be- | seech Thee ;
And when Thou shalt appear in | power and | glory,
May we be made like unto Thee | in Thy | glorious | Kingdom.

BENEDICITE OMNIA.

O ALL ye works of the Lord, | bless ye the | Lord;
   Praise Him, and | magni-fy | Him for- | ever.

O ye Angels of the Lord, | bless ye the | Lord;
Praise Him, and | magni-fy | Him for- | ever.

O ye Heavens, | bless ye the | Lord;
Praise Him, and | magni-fy | Him for- | ever.

O all ye Powers of the Lord, | bless ye the | Lord;
Praise Him, and | magni-fy | Him for- | ever.

O ye Mountains and Hills, | bless ye the | Lord;
Praise Him, and | magni-fy | Him for- | ever.

O all ye Green Things upon the Earth, | bless ye the | Lord;
Praise Him, and | magni-fy | Him for- | ever.

O ye Children of Men, | bless ye the | Lord;
Praise Him, and | magni-fy | Him for- | ever.

O ye Priests of the Lord, | bless ye the | Lord;
Praise Him, and | magni-fy | Him for- | ever.

O ye Servants of the Lord, | bless ye the | Lord;
Praise Him, and | magni-fy | Him for- | ever.

O ye Spirits and Souls of the Righteous, | bless ye the | Lord;
Praise Him, and | magni-fy | Him for- | ever.

O ye holy and humble Men of heart, | bless ye the | Lord;
Praise Him, and | magni-fy | Him for- | ever.

Glory be to the Father, and | to the | Son,
And | to the | Holy | Ghost,
As it was in the beginning, is now, and | ever shall | be,
World | without end. | A- | men.

GLORIA IN EXCELSIS.

(No. 1.)

GLORY be to | God on | high,
    And on earth | peace, good- | will towards | men.
We praise Thee, we bless Thee, we | worship | Thee,
We glorify Thee, we give thanks to | Thee for | Thy great | glory.

(No. 2.)

O Lord God, | Heavenly | King,
God, the | Father | Al— | mighty.
O Lord, the only-begotten Son, | Jesus | Christ,
O Lord God, Lamb of | God, Son | of the | Father;

(No. 3.)

That takest away the | sins of the | world,
Have mercy | upon | us.
Thou that takest away the | sins of the | world,
Have mercy | upon | us.
Thou that takest away the | sins of the | world,
Re- | ceive our | prayer.
Thou that sittest at the right hand of | God the | Father,
Have mercy | upon | us.

(No. 1.)

For Thou | only art | holy,
Thou | only | art the | Lord.
Thou only, O Christ, with the | Holy | Ghost,
Art most high in the | glory of | God the | Father.   Amen.

ALLELUIA CHANT.

The Holy City shall take | up your | strain,
And with glad songs resounding | wake a- | gain an | endless | Alleluia.
In blissful antiphons, ye | thus re- | joice,
To render to the Lord, with | thankful | voice, an | endless, | endless | Alleluia.

While Thee, by whom were | all things | made,
We praise forever, and tell out in | sweetest | lays, an | endless | Alleluia;
Almighty Christ! to Thee our | voices | sing
Glory forevermore! to | Thee we | bring, an | endless, | endless | Alleluia.

TE DEUM LAUDAMUS.

TE DEUM LAUDAMUS. (No. 1.)

WE praise | Thee, O | God : ‖ we acknowledge | Thee to | be the | Lord.
All the earth doth | worship | Thee : ‖ the | Father | ever- | lasting.

To Thee all angels | cry a- | loud ; ‖ the heavens, and | all the | powers | therein.
To Thee, Cherubim and | Sera- | phim ‖ con- | tin-ual- | ly do | cry ;

(No. 2.)

Holy ! | Holy ! | Holy ! ‖ Lord | God of | Sabaoth ;
Heaven and | earth are | full ‖ of the | majesty | of Thy | glory.

The glorious company of the A- | postles | praise Thee. ‖ The goodly fellowship | of the | Prophets | praise Thee.
The noble army of | Martyrs | praise Thee. ‖ The Holy Church, throughout all the world, | doth ac- | knowledge | Thee,

The Father of an | infinite | Majesty ; ‖ Thine adorable, | true, and | only | Son ;
Also the | Holy | Ghost, ‖ the | Com- | fort- | er.

(No. 3.)

Thou art the King of | glory, O | Christ. ‖ Thou art the everlasting | Son— | of the | Father.
When Thou tookest upon Thee to de- | liver | man, ‖ Thou didst humble Thyself to be | born | of a | Virgin.

When Thou hadst overcome the | sharpness of | death, ‖ Thou didst open the kingdom of | Heaven to | all be- | lievers.
Thou sittest at the right | hand of | God, ‖ In the | glory | of the | Father.

We believe that Thou shall come to | be our | judge. ‖ We therefore | pray Thee, | help Thy | servants,
Whom Thou hast redeemed with Thy | precious | blood ; ‖ Make them to be numbered with Thy saints, in | glory | ever- | lasting.

(No. 1.)

O Lord, save Thy people, and | bless Thine | heritage ; ‖ Govern them, and | lift them | up for- | ever.
Day by day we | magnify | Thee, ‖ And we worship Thy Name ever, | world with- | out— | end.

Vouchsafe, O Lord, to keep us this day | without | sin. ‖ O Lord, have mercy upon us, have | mercy | upon | us.
O Lord, let Thy mercy | be up- | on us, ‖ as our | trust is | in— | Thee.

O Lord, in Thee | have I | trusted ; ‖ Let me | never | be con- | founded.

TRISAGION OR SANCTUS.

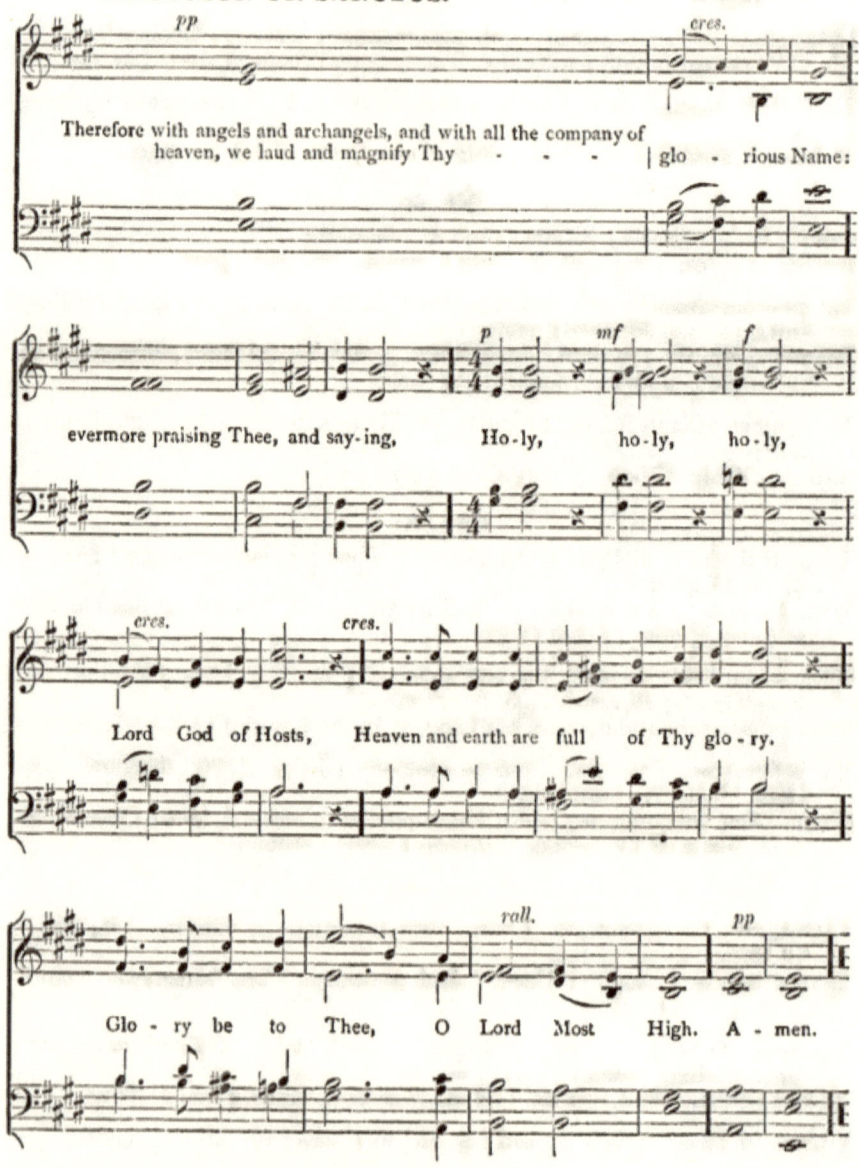

TRISAGION.

PASSION CHANT.

HE is despised and re- | jected of | men ;
   A man of sorrows, | and ac- | quainted with | grief:
And we hid as it were our | faces | from Him ;
He was despised, and | we es- | teemed Him | not.

Surely He hath borne our griefs, and | carried our | sorrows:
Yet we did esteem Him stricken, | smitten of | God, and af- | flicted.
But He was wounded for | our trans- | gressions,
He was | bruised for | our in- | iquities ;

The chastisement of our peace | was up- | on Him ;
And with | His stripes | we are | healed.
All we like sheep have | gone a- | stray ;
We have turned every | one to | his own | way ;

And the Lord hath | laid on | Him
The in- | iquity | of us | all.
And the pleasure of the Lord shall prosper | in His | hand.
He shall see of the travail of His soul, and | shall be | satis- | fied.

Glory be to the Father, and | to the | Son,
And | to the | Holy | Ghost ;
As it was in the beginning, is now, and | ever shall | be,
World | without | end. A- | men.

EASTER CHANT.

CHRIST, our Passover, is sacri- | ficed | for us.
    Therefore | let us | keep the | feast,
Not with the old leaven, neither with the leaven of | malice and | wickedness;
But with the unleavened bread of sin- | ceri- | ty and | truth.

Christ, being raised from the dead, | dieth no | more;
Death hath no more do- | minion | over | Him.
For in that He died, He died unto | sin— | once:
But in that He liveth, He | liveth | unto | God.

Likewise reckon ye also yourselves to be dead indeed | unto | sin,
But alive unto God through | Jesus | Christ our | Lord.
Now is Christ risen | from the | dead,
And become the first- | fruits of | them that | slept.

For since by | man came | death,
By man came also the resur- | rection | of the | dead.
For as in Adam | all— | die,
Even so in Christ shall | all be | made a- | live.

Glory be to the Father, and | to the | Son,
And | to the | Holy | Ghost;
As it was in the beginning, is now, and | ever shall | be,
World | without | end. A- | men.

THE COMMANDMENTS.

God spake these words, and said,

I AM THE LORD THY GOD, WHICH HAVE BROUGHT THEE OUT OF THE LAND OF EGYPT, AND OUT OF THE HOUSE OF BONDAGE.

I.
Thou shalt have no other gods before me.

II.
Thou shalt not make unto thee any graven image, or any likeness of anything that is in heaven above, or that is in the earth beneath, or that is in the water under the earth: thou shalt not bow down thyself to them, nor serve them; for I the Lord thy God am a jealous God, visiting the iniquity of the fathers upon the children, unto the third and fourth generation of them that hate me; and showing mercy unto thousands of them that love me, and keep my commandments.

III.
Thou shalt not take the name of the Lord thy God in vain, for the Lord will not hold him guiltless that taketh his name in vain.

IV.
Remember the Sabbath day to keep it holy; six days shalt thou labor and do all thy work; but the seventh day is the Sabbath of the Lord thy God: in it thou shalt not do any work, thou, nor thy son, nor thy daughter, thy man-servant, nor thy maid-servant, nor thy cattle, nor the stranger that is within thy gates. for in six days the Lord made heaven and earth, the sea, and all that in them is, and rested on the seventh day; wherefore the Lord blessed the Sabbath day and hallowed it.

V.
Honor thy father and thy mother, that thy days may be long in the land which the Lord thy God giveth thee.

VI.
Thou shalt not kill.

VII.
Thou shalt not commit adultery.

VIII.
Thou shalt not steal.

IX.
Thou shalt not bear false witness against thy neighbor.

X.
Thou shalt not covet thy neighbor's house, thou shalt not covet thy neighbor's wife, nor his man-servant, nor his maid-servant, nor his ox, nor his ass, nor anything that is thy neighbor's.

KYRIE ELEISON.

No. 1.

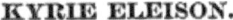

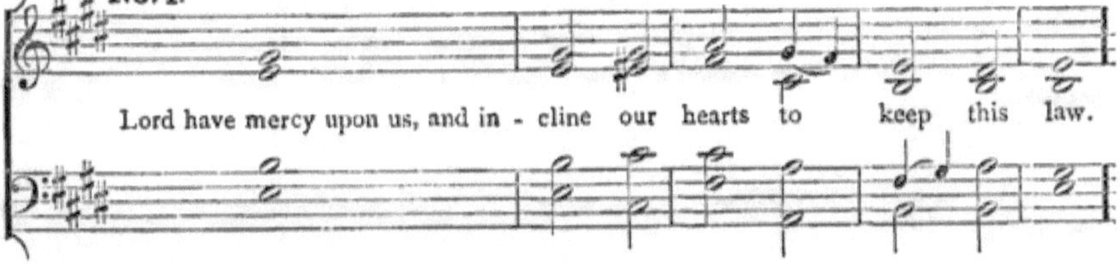

After Tenth Commandment.

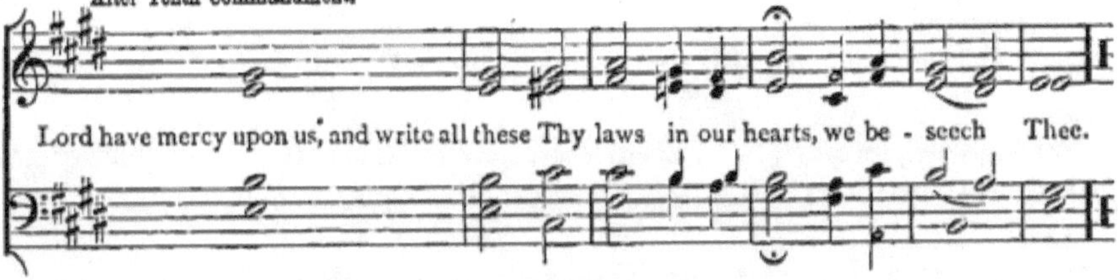

No. 2.

After Tenth Commandment.

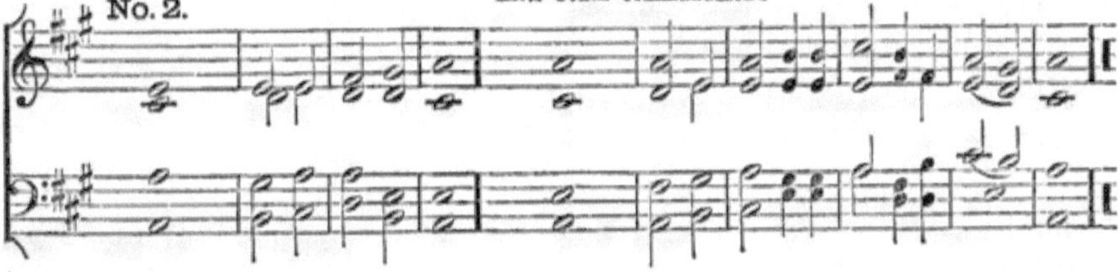

No. 3.

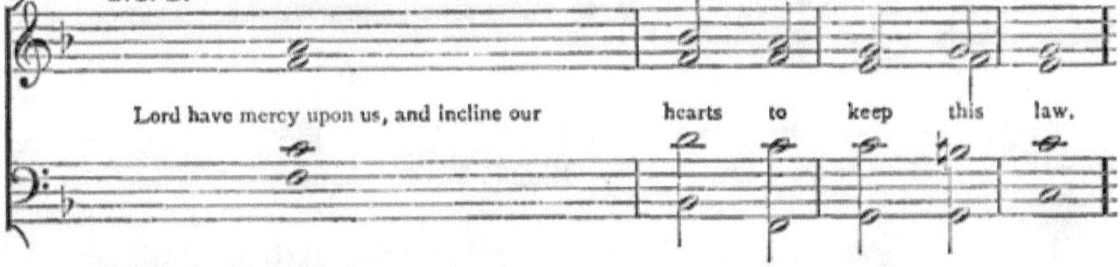

After Tenth Commandment.

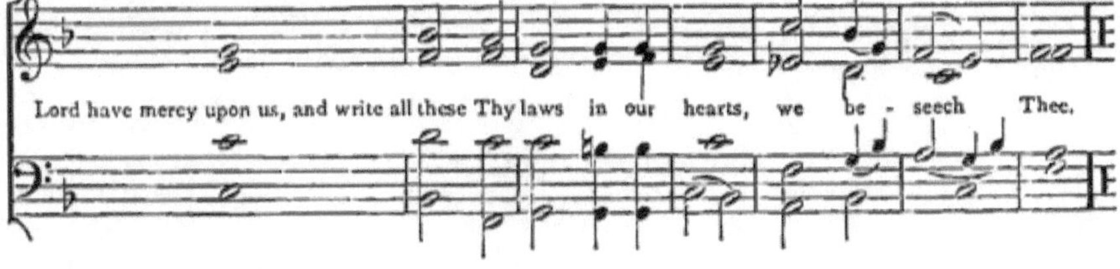

Lay not up for yourselves treasures upon earth, where moth and rust doth corrupt, and where thieves break through and steal; but lay up for yourselves treasures in Heaven, where neither moth nor rust doth corrupt, and where thieves do not break through nor steal: for where your treasure is, there will your heart be also.

Blessèd is he that considereth the poor; the Lord will deliver him in time of trouble.

Therefore all things whatsoever ye would that men should do to you, do ye even so to them; for this is the law and the prophets.

Remember the words of the Lord Jesus, how He said: It is more blessèd to give than to receive.

But this *I say*, He which soweth sparingly shall reap also sparingly; and he which soweth bountifully shall reap also bountifully.

Every man according as he purposeth in his heart, *so let him give;* not grudgingly, or of necessity; for God loveth a cheerful giver.

And let us not be weary in well doing: for in due season we shall reap, if we faint not.

As we have therefore opportunity, let us do good unto all *men*, especially unto them who are of the household of faith.

Charge them that are rich in this world, that they be not highminded, nor trust in uncertain riches, but in the living God, who giveth us richly all things to enjoy.

That they do good, that they be rich in good works, ready to distribute, willing to communicate.

Laying up in store for themselves a good foundation against the time to come, that they may lay hold on eternal life.

But whoso hath this world's good, and seeth his brother have need, and shutteth up his bowels *of compassion* from him, how dwelleth the love of God in him?

BURIAL CHANT.

LORD, Thou hast | been our | refuge,
    From one gene- | ration | to an- | other;
Before the mountains were brought forth, or ever the earth and the | world were | made,
Thou art God from everlasting, and | world— | without | end.

Thou turnest | man to de- | struction,
Again Thou sayest, Come a- | gain, ye | children of | men;
For a thousand years in Thy sight are | but as | yesterday,
Seeing that is past as a | watch— | in the | night.

As soon as Thou scatterest them, they are even | as a | sleep;
And fade away | suddenly | like the | grass;
In the morning it is green, and | groweth | up,
In the evening it is cut | down, dried | up, and | withered.

The days of our age are threescore | years and | ten,
And though men be so strong that they | come to | fourscore | years,
Yet is their strength then but | labor and | sorrow;
So soon passeth it a- | way, and | we are | gone.

For when Thou art angry, all our | days are | gone,
We bring our years to an end, as it | were a | tale that is | told:
So teach us to | number our | days,
That we may apply our | hearts— | unto | wisdom.

Glory be to the Father, and | to the | Son,
And | to the | Holy | Ghost;
As it was in the beginning, is now, and | ever shall | be,
World | without | end. A- | men.

THE APOSTLES' CREED.

I believe in God, the Father Almighty, Maker of heaven and earth; and in Jesus Christ, his only Son, our Lord, who was conceived by the Holy Ghost, born of the Virgin Mary, suffered under Pontius Pilate, was crucified, dead, and buried. He descended into hell [Hades]; the third day he rose from the dead, he ascended into heaven, and sitteth on the right hand of God, the Father Almighty: from thence he shall come to judge the quick and the dead. I believe in the Holy Ghost, the Holy Catholic Church; the Communion of Saints; the Forgiveness of Sins; the Resurrection of the Body, and the Life Everlasting. Amen.

THE NICENE CREED.

I believe in one God, the Father Almighty, Maker of heaven and earth, and of all things visible and invisible: And in one Lord, Jesus Christ, the only begotten Son of God, begotten of his Father before all worlds; God of God, Light of Light, very God of very God, begotten, not made, being of one substance with the Father; by whom all things were made; who, for us men, and for our salvation, came down from heaven, and was incarnate by the Holy Ghost of the virgin Mary, and was made man, and was crucified for us under Pontius Pilate. He suffered and was buried; and the third day He rose again, according to the Scriptures; and ascended into heaven, and sitteth on the right hand of the Father. And He shall come again with glory to judge both the quick and the dead; whose kingdom shall have no end.

And I believe in the Holy Ghost, the Lord and Giver of life, who proceedeth from the Father and the Son; who, with the Father and the Son, is worshipped and glorified; who spake by the prophets.

And I believe one Catholic and Apostolic Church.

I acknowledge one baptism for the remission of sins; and I look for the resurrection of the dead, and the life of the world to come. Amen.

THE LORD'S PRAYER.

Our Father which art in heaven, hallowed be Thy Name; Thy Kingdom come; Thy will be done in earth as it is in heaven. Give us this day our daily bread. And forgive us our debts as we forgive our debtors. And lead us not into temptation, but deliver us from evil. For Thine is the Kingdom, and the power, and the glory forever. Amen.

THE LORD'S DAY AND HOUSE.

SANCTUARY. 8s & 7s.

Zi-on, ope thy gates of beau-ty, Let my soul thy bless-ing share,
With thy saints in joy-ful du-ty, Wor-ship God in song and prayer.
Oh, how bless-ed is this place, Full of glo-ry, full of grace.

1

ZION, ope thy gates of beauty,
Let my soul thy blessing share,
With thy saints in joyful duty,
Worship God in song and prayer.
Oh, how blessed is this place,
Full of glory, full of grace.

While Thy praise, O God, is chanted,
While is sown Thy precious seed,
May my humble prayers be granted,
May Thy word my spirit feed.
When I speak, O Lord, give ear,
When Thou speakest, let me hear.

Now I humbly come before Thee,
Come Thou graciously to me;
Where we find Thee, and adore Thee,
There a heaven on earth must be.
To my heart, oh, enter Thou,
Let it be Thy temple now.

THE LORD'S DAY AND HOUSE.

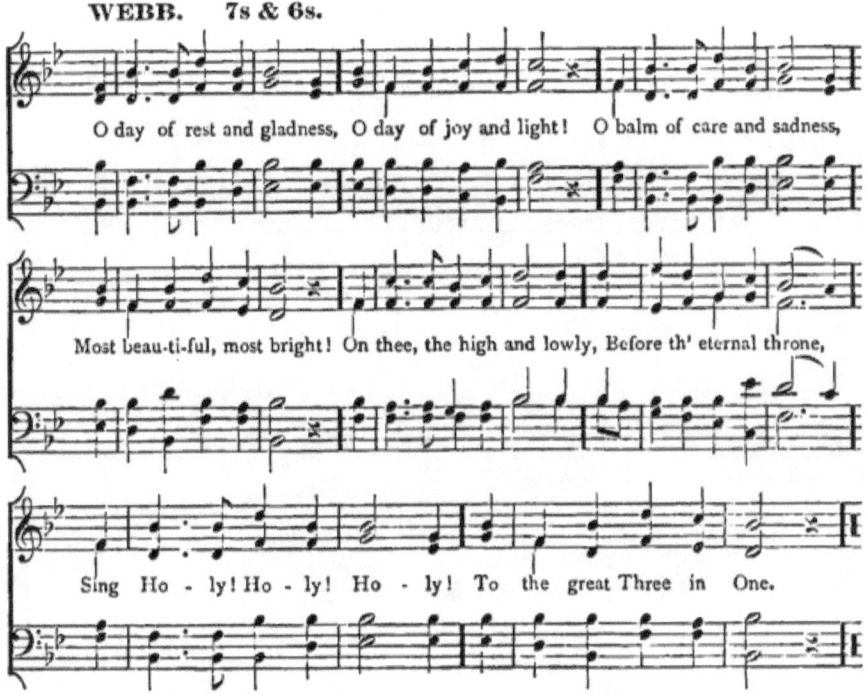

WEBB. 7s & 6s.

O day of rest and gladness, O day of joy and light! O balm of care and sadness, Most beau-ti-ful, most bright! On thee, the high and lowly, Before th' eternal throne, Sing Ho-ly! Ho-ly! Ho-ly! To the great Three in One.

2

O DAY of rest and gladness,
   O day of joy and light!
O balm of care and sadness,
   Most beautiful, most bright!
On thee, the high and lowly,
   Before th' eternal throne,
Sing Holy! Holy! Holy!
   To the great Three in One.

On thee, at the creation,
   The light first had its birth:
On thee, for our salvation,
   Christ rose from depths of earth;
On thee, our Lord, victorious,
   The Spirit sent from heaven,
And thus on thee, most glorious,
   A triple light was given.

Thou art a cooling fountain
   In life's dry dreary sand;
From thee, like Pisgah's mountain,
   We view our promised land:
A day of sweet refection,
   A day of holy love,
A day of resurrection
   From earth to things above.

New graces ever gaining
   From this our day of rest,
We reach the rest remaining
   To spirits of the blest:
To Holy Ghost be praises,
   To Father and to Son;
The church her voice upraises
   To Thee, blest Three in One.

THE LORD'S DAY AND HOUSE.

NEWTON. 7s.

Safe - ly through an - oth - er week God has brought us on our way;

Let us now a bless-ing seek, Wait - ing in His courts to - day;

Day of all the week the best, Em - blem of e - ter - nal rest.

3

SAFELY through another week
   God has brought us on our way;
Let us now a blessing seek,
   Waiting in His courts to-day;
Day of all the week the best,
Emblem of eternal rest.

While we pray for pardoning grace
   Through the dear Redeemer's Name,
Show Thy reconciled face,
   Take away our sin and shame,
From our worldly cares set free,
May we rest this day in Thee.

Here we come Thy Name to praise;
   Let us feel Thy presence near;
May Thy glory meet our eyes
   While we in Thy house appear:
Here afford us, Lord, a taste
Of our everlasting feast.

May Thy gospel's joyful sound
   Conquer sinners, comfort saints;
Make the fruits of grace abound;
   Bring relief for all complaints:
Thus let all our Sabbaths prove,
Till we rest in Thee above.

STEPHENS. C. M.

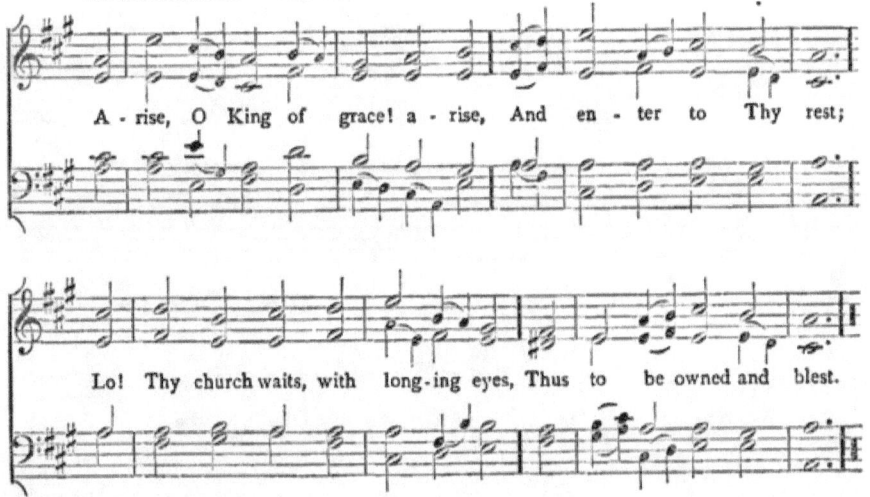

Arise, O King of grace! arise, And enter to Thy rest;
Lo! Thy church waits, with longing eyes, Thus to be owned and blest.

4

ARISE, O King of grace! arise,
　And enter to Thy rest;
Lo! Thy church waits, with longing eyes,
　Thus to be owned and blest.

Enter, with all Thy glorious train,
　Thy Spirit and Thy word;
All that the ark did once contain
　Could no such grace afford.

Here, mighty God! accept our vows
　Here let Thy praise be spread:
Bless the provisions of Thy house,
　And fill Thy poor with bread.

Here let the son of David reign,
　Let God's Anointed shine;
Justice and truth His court maintain,
　With love and power divine.

5

THIS is the day the Lord hath made,
　He calls the hours his own:
Let heaven rejoice, let earth be glad,
　And praise surround the throne.

To-day He rose and left the dead,
　And Satan's empire fell;
To-day the saints His triumph spread,
　And all His wonders tell.

Hosanna to th' anointed King,
　To David's holy Son:
Help us, O Lord! descend, and bring
　Salvation from the throne.

Hosanna, in the highest strains,
　The church on earth can raise!
The highest heavens, in which He reigns,
　Shall give Him nobler praise.

　　To Father, Son, and Holy Ghost,
　　　One God whom we adore,
　　Be glory as it was, is now,
　　　And shall be evermore.

WAREHAM. L. M.

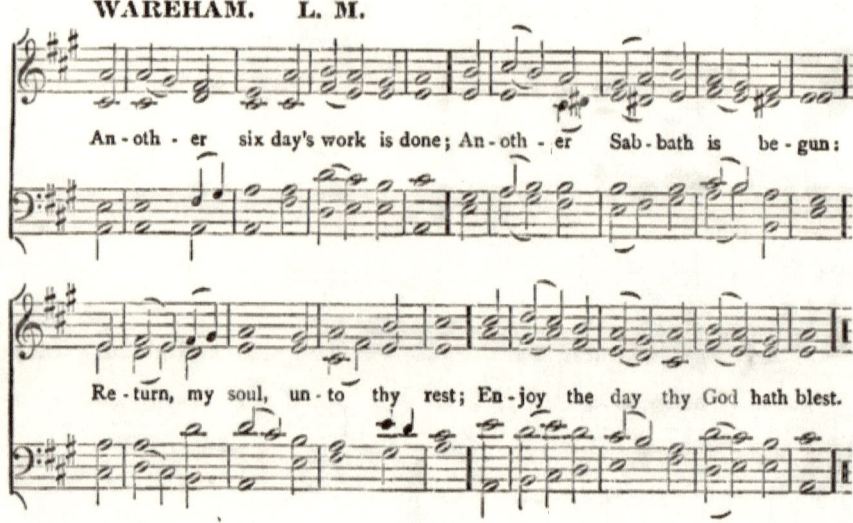

Another six day's work is done; Another Sabbath is begun: Return, my soul, unto thy rest; Enjoy the day thy God hath blest.

6

ANOTHER six day's work is done;
Another Sabbath is begun:
Return, my soul, unto thy rest;
Enjoy the day thy God hath blest.

Oh, that our thoughts and thanks may
As grateful incense to the skies! [rise,
And draw from heaven that calm repose,
Which none but he who feels it knows.

That heavenly calm within the breast!
It is the pledge of that dear rest
Which for the church of God remains,—
The end of cares, the end of pains.

In holy duties let the day,
In holy pleasures, pass away.
How sweet a Sabbath thus to spend,
In hope of one that ne'er shall end!

7

O CHRIST! with each returning morn
Thine image to our hearts be borne;
And may we ever clearly see
Our God and Saviour, Lord, in Thee!

All hallowed be our walk this day;
May meekness form our early ray,
And faithful love our noontide light,
And hope our sunset, calm and bright.

May grace each idle thought control,
And sanctify our wayward soul;
May guile depart, and malice cease,
And all within be joy and peace.

Our daily course, O Jesus, bless;
Make plain the way of holiness:
From sudden falls our feet defend,
And cheer at last our journey's end.

To Father, Son, and Holy Ghost,
The God whom earth and heaven adore,
Be glory, as it was of old,
Is now, and shall be evermore.

WINCHESTER. L. M.

Thine earth-ly Sab-baths, Lord, we love,— But there's a no-bler rest a-bove: To that our long-ing souls as-pire, With cheer-ful hope and strong de-sire.

8

THINE earthly Sabbaths, Lord, we love,—
But there's a nobler rest above:
To that our longing souls aspire,
With cheerful hope and strong desire.

No more fatigue, no more distress,
Nor sin nor death shall reach the place;
No groans shall mingle with the songs
Which warble from immortal tongues.

No rude alarms of raging foes;
No cares to break the long repose
No midnight shade, no clouded sun;
But sacred, high, eternal noon!

O long-expected day, begin,
Dawn on these realms of woe and sin!
Fain would we leave this weary road,
And sleep in death to rest with God.

9

THOU glorious Sun of Righteousness,
On this day risen to set no more,
Shine on us now to heal and bless
With brighter beams than e'er before.

Shine on the temples of Thy grace,
In spotless robes Thy priests be clad;
Unveil the brightness of Thy face,
And make Thy chosen people glad.

Shine too on those for whom we mourn,
Who know not yet Thy healing ray;
Quicken their souls, and bid them turn
To Thee, the Life, the Truth, the Way.

Shine till Thy glorious beams shall chase
The blinding mist from every eye,
Till every earthly dwelling-place
Shall hail the Dayspring from on high.

Shine on, shine on, Eternal Sun!
Pour richer floods of life and light,
Till that bright Sabbath be begun,
That glorious day which knows no night!

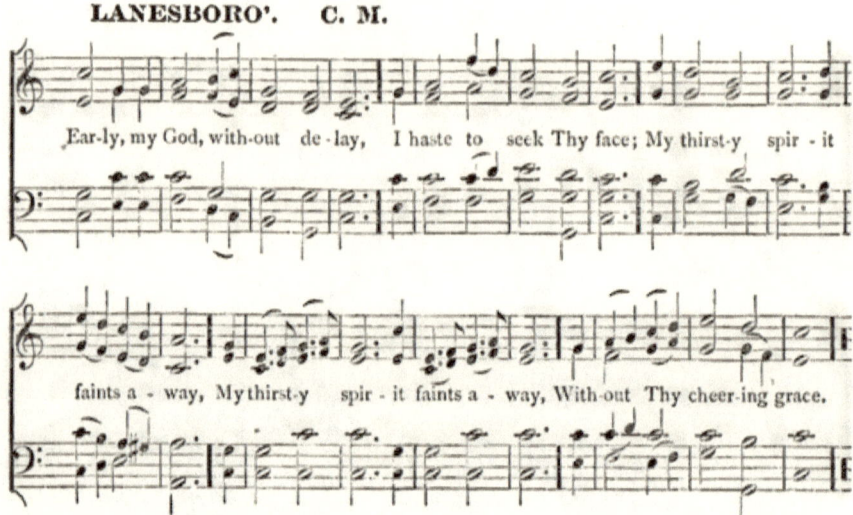

LANESBORO'. C. M.

Early, my God, without delay, I haste to seek Thy face; My thirsty spirit faints away, My thirsty spirit faints away, Without Thy cheering grace.

10

EARLY, my God, without delay,
   I haste to seek Thy face:
My thirsty spirit faints away
   Without Thy cheering grace.

So pilgrims on the scorching sand,
   Beneath a burning sky,
Long for a cooling stream at hand,
   And they must drink or die.

I've seen Thy glory and Thy power
   Through all Thy temple shine;
My God, repeat that heavenly hour,
   That vision so divine.

Not life itself, with all its joys,
   Can my best passions move,
Or raise so high my cheerful voice,
   As Thy forgiving love.

Thus, till my last expiring day,
   I'll bless my God and King;
Thus will I lift my hands to pray,
   And tune my lips to sing.

11

WITH joy we hail the sacred day
   Which God has called His own;
With joy the summons we obey
   To worship at His throne.

Thy chosen temple, Lord, how fair!
   Where willing votaries throng
To breathe the humble, fervent prayer,
   And pour the choral song.

Spirit of grace! oh, deign to dwell
   Within Thy church below;
Make her in holiness excel,
   With pure devotion glow.

Let peace within her walls be found;
   Let all her sons unite
To spread with grateful zeal around
   Her clear and shining light.

THE LORD'S DAY AND HOUSE.

COVENTRY. C. M.

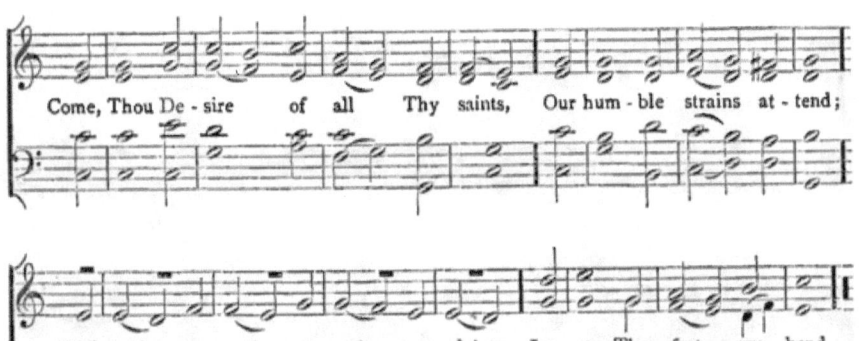

Come, Thou Desire of all Thy saints, Our humble strains attend;
While with our praises and complaints, Low at Thy feet we bend.

12

COME, Thou Desire of all Thy saints,
  Our humble strains attend ;
While with our praises and complaints,
  Low at Thy feet we bend.

How should our songs, like those above,
  With warm devotion rise !
How should our souls, on wings of love
  Mount upward to the skies !

Come, Lord ! Thy love alone can raise
  In us the heavenly flame ;
Then shall our lips resound Thy praise,
  Our hearts adore Thy name.

Dear Saviour, let Thy glory shine,
  And fill Thy dwellings here,
Till life and love and joy divine
  A heaven on earth appear.

Then shall our hearts enraptured say
  Come, great Redeemer ! come,
And bring the bright, the glorious day
  That calls Thy children home.

13

AGAIN our earthly cares we leave,
  And to Thy courts repair ;
Again with joyful feet we come,
  To meet our Saviour here.

Great Shepherd of Thy people, hear !
  Thy presence now display ;
We bow within Thy house of prayer !
  Oh ! give us hearts to pray.

The clouds which veil Thee from our
  In pity, Lord, remove ;   [sight,
Dispose our minds to hear aright
  The message of Thy love.

Show us some token of Thy love,
  Our fainting hopes to raise ;
And pour Thy blessing from on high,
  To aid our feeble praise.

To Father, Son, and Holy Ghost,
  One God whom we adore,
Be glory as it was, is now,
  And shall be evermore.

GREENWOOD. S. M.

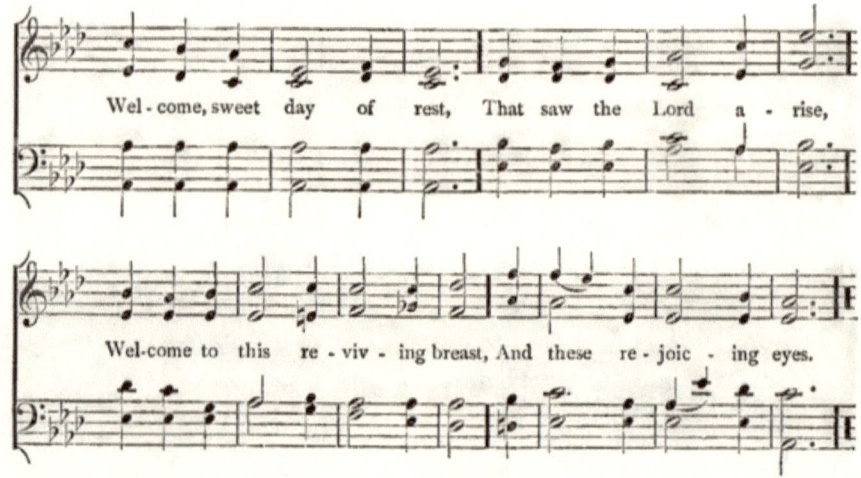

Wel-come, sweet day of rest, That saw the Lord a-rise,
Wel-come to this re-viv-ing breast, And these re-joic-ing eyes.

14

WELCOME, sweet day of rest,
　That saw the Lord arise,
Welcome to this reviving breast,
　And these rejoicing eyes.

The King Himself comes near,
　And feasts His saints to-day;
Here we may sit, and see Him here,
　And love and praise and pray.

One day, amid the place
　Where God, my God, hath been,
Is sweeter than ten thousand days
　Within the tents of sin.

My willing soul would stay
　In such a frame as this,
And sit and sing herself away
　To everlasting bliss.

15

SWEET is the work, O Lord,
　Thy glorious name to sing;
To praise and pray—and hear Thy word,
　And grateful offerings bring.

Sweet—at the dawning light,
　Thy boundless love to tell;
And when approach the shades of night,
　Still on the theme to dwell.

Sweet—on this day of rest,
　To join in heart and voice,
With those who love and serve Thee best,
　And in Thy name rejoice.

To songs of praise and joy
　Be every Sabbath given,
That such may be our blest employ
　Eternally in heaven.

　　The Father and the Son,
　　　And Spirit we adore;
　　We praise, we bless, we worship Thee,
　　　Both now and evermore.

THE LORD'S DAY AND HOUSE.

STATE STREET. S. M.

With joy, we lift our eyes To those bright realms above, That glorious temple in the skies, Where dwells eternal love.

16

With joy, we lift our eyes
  To those bright realms above,
That glorious temple in the skies,
  Where dwells eternal love.

Before Thy throne we bow,
  O Thou Almighty King!
Here we present the solemn vow,
  And hymns of praise we sing.

While in Thy house we kneel,
  With trust and holy fear,
Thy mercy and Thy truth reveal,
  And lend a gracious ear.

Grant us Thy peace, O God,
  Fair love and saintly might,
And for this dim and fleeting day,
  Give us immortal light.

17

We love the place, O God,
  Wherein Thine honor dwells;
The pleasure of Thy blest abode,
  All earthly joy excels.

We love the house of prayer,
  Wherein Thy servants meet,
For Thou, O Lord, art ever there,
  Thy chosen flock to greet.

We love the word of life,—
  The word that tells of peace,
Of comfort in our daily strife,
  Of joys that never cease.

Lord Jesus! give us grace
  On earth to love Thee more,
In heaven to see Thy glorious face,
  And with Thy saints adore.

  To God, the Father, Son,
    And Spirit, glory be,
  As was, and is, and shall remain
    Through all eternity!

THE LORD'S DAY AND HOUSE.

WARWICK. C. M.

Lord, in the morn-ing Thou shalt hear My voice as-cend-ing high;

To Thee will I di-rect my prayer, To Thee lift up mine eye:—

18

LORD, in the morning Thou shalt
  My voice ascending high; [hear
To Thee will I direct my prayer,
  To Thee lift up mine eye :—

Up to the hills where Christ is gone,
  To plead for all His saints,
Presenting at His Father's throne
  Our songs and our complaints.

Thou art a God before whose sight
  The wicked shall not stand;
Sinners shall ne'er be Thy delight,
  Nor dwell at Thy right hand.

But to Thy house will I resort,
  To taste Thy mercies there;
I will frequent Thy holy court,
  And worship in Thy fear.

O may Thy Spirit guide my feet
  In ways of righteousness!
Make every path of duty straight
  And plain before my face.

19

TO our Redeemer's glorious Name
  Awake the sacred song;
O may His love, immortal flame!
  Tune every heart and tongue.

His love, what mortal thought can reach,
  What mortal tongue display!
Imagination's utmost stretch
  In wonder dies away.

Dear Lord, while we adoring pay
  Our humble thanks to Thee,
May every heart with rapture say,
  "The Saviour died for me."

O may the sweet, the blissful theme,
  Fill every heart and tongue;
Till strangers love Thy charming Name,
  And join the sacred song.

To Father, Son, and Holy Ghost,
  One God whom we adore,
Be glory as it was, is now,
  And shall be evermore.

20
Lord of the worlds above,
  How pleasant and how fair
The dwellings of Thy love,
  Thine earthly temples are!
To Thine abode my heart aspires,
With warm desires to see my God.

  Oh happy souls that pray
    Where God appoints to hear!
  Oh happy men that pay
    Their constant service there!
They praise Thee still, and happy they
That love the way to Zion's hill.

  They go from strength to strength,
    Through this dark vale of tears;
  Till each arrives at length;
    Till each in heaven appears:
Oh glorious seat, when God our King
Shall thither bring our willing feet!

21
Welcome, delightful morn,
  Thou day of sacred rest!
I hail thy kind return;—
  Lord, make these moments blest:
From the low train of mortal toys,
I soar to reach immortal joys.

  Now may the King descend
    And fill His throne of grace;
  Thy sceptre, Lord, extend,
    While saints address Thy face:
Let sinners feel Thy quickening word,
And learn to know and fear the Lord.

  Descend, celestial Dove,
    With all Thy quickening powers;
  Disclose a Saviour's love,
    And bless the sacred hours:
Then shall my soul new life obtain,
Nor Sabbaths be enjoyed in vain.

THE LORD'S DAY AND HOUSE.

DALSTON. S. P. M.

How pleased and blest was I To hear the peo-ple cry, "Come, let us seek our God to-day!" Yes, with a cheer-ful zeal, We haste to Zi-on's hill, And there our vows and hon-ors pay.

22

How pleased and blest was I
To hear the people cry,
"Come, let us seek our God to-day!"
Yes, with a cheerful zeal,
We haste to Zion's hill,
And there our vows and honors pay.

Zion, thrice happy place,
Adorned with wondrous grace,
And walls of strength embrace thee round!
In thee our tribes appear
To pray, and praise, and hear
The sacred gospel's joyful sound.

May peace attend thy gate,
And joy within thee wait
To bless the soul of every guest :
The man who seeks thy peace,
And wishes thine increase,
A thousand blessings on him rest !

My tongue repeats her vows,
"Peace to this sacred house!"
For here my friends and kindred dwell ;
And since my glorious God
Makes thee His blest abode,
My soul shall ever love thee well

To Father, Spirit, Son,
Jehovah, Three in One,
Be endless praise and glory given :
Thy name, Almighty King !
Let all creation sing,
With all their powers, on earth, in heaven.

23 Holy, holy, holy! All the saints adore Thee,
  Casting down their golden crowns around the glassy sea;
Cherubim and seraphim falling down before Thee,
  Which wert, and art, and evermore shalt be.

3.
Holy, holy, holy! though the darkness hide Thee,
  Though the eye of sinful man Thy glory may not see,
Only Thou art holy; there is none beside Thee
  Perfect in power, in love, and purity.

4.
Holy, holy, holy! Lord God Almighty!
  All Thy works shall praise Thy Name, in earth and sky and sea:
Holy, holy, holy! merciful and mighty!
  God in Three Persons, Blessed Trinity!

MORNING AND EVENING.

HERALD. L. M.

When streaming from the eastern skies, The morning light salutes mine eyes;
O Sun of righteousness Divine, On me with beams of mercy shine.
Chase the dark clouds of guilt away, And turn my darkness into day.

24

When streaming from the eastern skies,
The morning light salutes mine eyes;
O Sun of righteousness Divine,
On me with beams of mercy shine.
Chase the dark clouds of guilt away,
And turn my darkness into day.

And when, to heaven's all glorious King,
My morning sacrifice I bring,
And, mourning o'er my guilt and shame,
Ask mercy in my Saviour's name,
Then, Jesus! cleanse me with Thy blood,
And be my Advocate with God.

When each day's scenes and labors close,
And wearied nature seeks repose,
With pard'ning mercy richly blest,
Guard me, my Saviour! while I rest;
And, as each morning sun shall rise,
Oh! lead me onward to the skies.

And, at my life's last setting sun,
My conflicts o'er, my labors done,
Jesus! Thy heavenly radiance shed,
To cheer and bless my dying bed;
And, from death's gloom, my spirit raise,
To see Thy face, and sing Thy praise.

MORNING AND EVENING.

HEBRON. L. M.

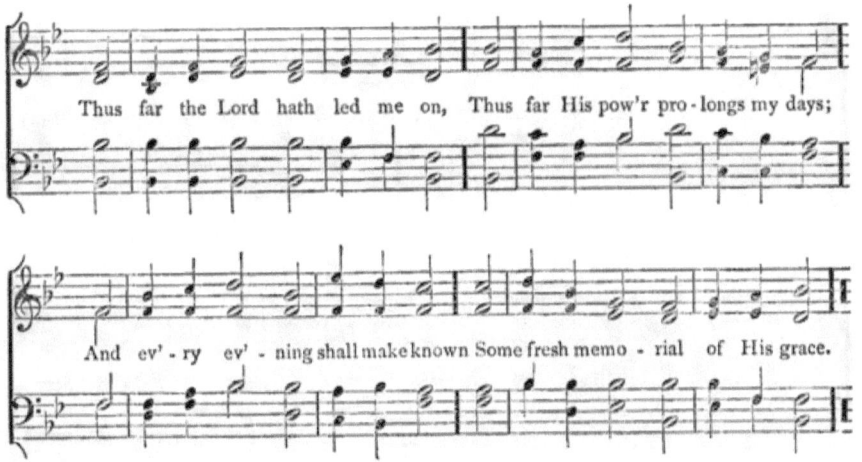

Thus far the Lord hath led me on, Thus far His pow'r pro-longs my days;
And ev'-ry ev'-ning shall make known Some fresh memo-rial of His grace.

25

THUS far the Lord hath led me on,
Thus far His power prolongs my days;
And every evening shall make known
Some fresh memorial of His grace.

Much of my time has run to waste,
And I perhaps am near my home;
But He forgives my follies past,
And gives me strength for days to come.

I lay my body down to sleep:
Peace is the pillow for my head,
While well-appointed angels keep
Their watchful stations round my bed.

Faith in His Name forbids my fear;
Oh may Thy presence ne'er depart;
And, in the morning, make me hear
The love and kindness of Thy heart

Thus, when the night of death shall come,
My flesh shall rest beneath the ground;
And wait Thy voice to rouse my tomb,
With sweet salvation in the sound.

26

MY God, how endless is Thy love!
Thy gifts are every evening new;
And morning mercies from above
Gently distil like early dew.

Thou spread'st the curtains of the night,
Great Guardian of my sleeping hours;
Thy sovereign word restores the light,
And quickens all my drowsy powers.

I yield my powers to Thy command;
To Thee I consecrate my days;
Perpetual blessings from Thy hand
Demand perpetual songs of praise.

To Father, Son, and Holy Ghost,
The God whom earth and heaven adore,
Be glory as it was of old,
Is now, and shall be evermore!

MORNING HYMN. L. M.

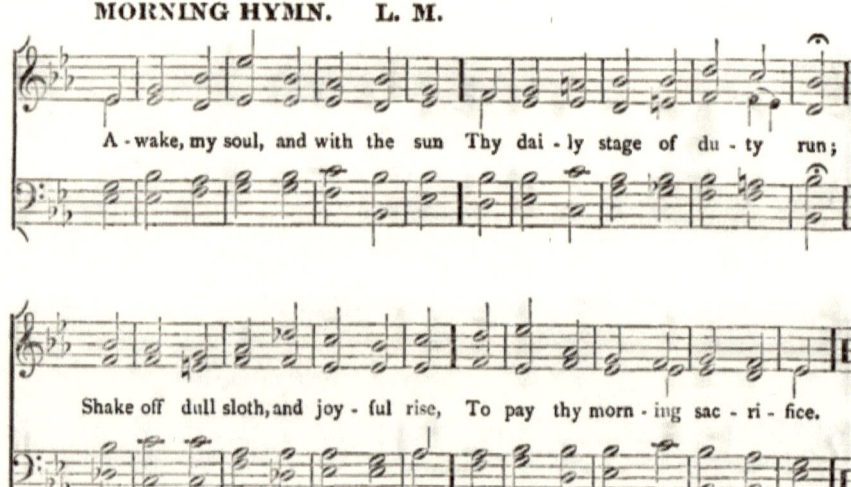

A-wake, my soul, and with the sun Thy dai-ly stage of du-ty run;
Shake off dull sloth, and joy-ful rise, To pay thy morn-ing sac-ri-fice.

27

AWAKE, my soul, and with the sun
 Thy daily stage of duty run;
Shake off dull sloth, and joyful rise,
To pay thy morning sacrifice.

Wake, and lift up thyself, my heart,
And with the angels bear thy part,
Who all night long, unwearied, sing
High praise to the eternal King.

All praise to Thee, who safe hast kept,
And hast refreshed me while I slept;
Grant, Lord, when I from death shall
I may of endless light partake. [wake,

Lord, I my vows to Thee renew;
Disperse my sins as morning dew; [will,
Guard my first springs of thought and
And with Thyself my being fill.

28

MY opening eyes with rapture see
 The dawn of Thy returning day,
My thoughts, O God, ascend to Thee,
While thus my early vows I pay.

I yield my heart to Thee alone.
 Nor would receive another guest;
Eternal King! erect Thy throne,
 And reign sole monarch in my breast.

O bid this trifling world retire,
 And drive each carnal thought away;
Nor let me feel one vain desire, [day.
 One sinful thought, through all the

Then, to Thy courts when I repair,
 My soul shall rise on joyful wing,
The wonders of Thy love declare,
 And join the strains which angels sing.

EVENING HYMN. L. M.

Glo-ry to Thee, my God, this night, For all the bless-ings of the light:
Keep me, O keep me, King of kings Be-neath Thine own Al-might-y wings.

29

GLORY to Thee, my God, this night,
For all the blessings of the light;
Keep me, O keep me, King of kings,
Beneath Thine own Almighty wings.

Forgive me, Lord, for Thy dear Son,
The ill that I this day have done;
That with the world, myself, and Thee,
I, ere I sleep, at peace, may be.

Teach me to live, that I may dread
The grave as little as my bed;
Teach me to die, that so I may
Rise glorious at the awful day.

Oh may my soul on Thee repose;
And may sweet sleep mine eyelids close,
Sleep, that may me more vigorous make
To serve my God when I awake.

When in the night I sleepless lie,
My soul with heavenly thoughts supply;
Let no ill dreams disturb my rest,
No power of darkness me molest.

30

DISMISS us with Thy blessing, Lord!
Help us to feed upon Thy word;
All that has been amiss, forgive,
And let Thy truth within us live.

Though we are guilty, Thou art good;
Wash all our works in Jesus' blood;
Give every burdened soul release,
And bid us all depart in peace.

Praise God from whom all blessings flow;
Praise Him, all creatures here below;
Praise Him above, ye heavenly host;
Praise Father, Son, and Holy Ghost!

MORNING AND EVENING.

STANLEY. C. M.

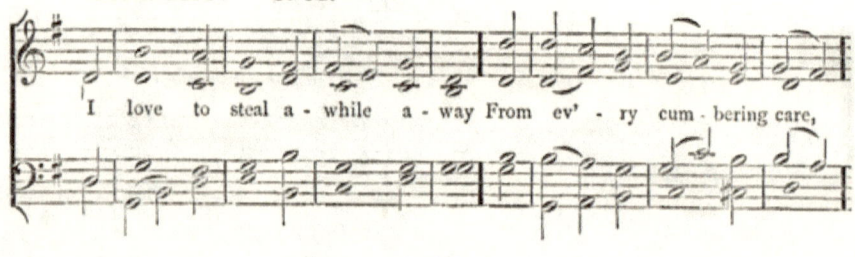

I love to steal awhile away From ev'-ry cum-bering care, And spend the hours of set-ting day In hum-ble, grate-ful prayer.

31

I LOVE to steal awhile away
  From every cumbering care,
And spend the hours of setting day
  In humble, grateful prayer.

I love, in solitude, to shed
  The penitential tear;
And all His promises to plead
  Where none but God is near.

I love to think on mercies past,
  And future good implore;
And all my cares and sorrows cast
  On Him whom I adore.

I love, by faith, to take a view
  Of brighter scenes in heaven;
The prospect doth my strength renew,
  While here by tempests driven.

Thus, when life's toilsome day is o'er,
  May its departing ray
Be calm as this impressive hour,
  And lead to endless day.

32

THE Lord be with us as we bend
  His blessing to receive;
His gift of Peace upon us send,
  Before His courts we leave.

The Lord be with us as we walk
  Along our homeward road;
In silent thought or friendly talk,
  Our hearts be still with God.

The Lord be with us till the night
  Shall close the day of rest;
Be He of every heart the light,
  Of every home the guest.

And when our nightly prayers we say,
  His watch He still shall keep,
Crown with His grace His own blest day,
  And guard His people's sleep.

To Father, Son, and Holy Ghost,
  One God whom we adore,
Be glory as it was, is now,
  And shall be evermore!

ST. ANDREW. 8s.

In-spir-er and Hear-er of prayer, Thou Shepherd and Guardian of Thine,
My all to Thy cov-e-nant care, I, sleep-ing or wak-ing, re-sign.

33

INSPIRER and Hearer of prayer,
  Thou Shepherd and Guardian of Thine,
My all to Thy covenant care,
  I, sleeping or waking, resign.

If Thou art my Shield and my Sun,
  The night is no darkness to me;
And, fast as my minutes roll on,
  They bring me but nearer to Thee.

A Sovereign Protector I have,
  Unseen, yet forever at hand;
Unchangeably faithful to save,
  Almighty to rule and command.

His smiles and His comforts abound,
  His grace, as the dew, shall descend;
And walls of salvation surround
  The soul He delights to defend.
        D

C. M. (Stanley.)

34

AND now the wants are told, that brought
  Thy children to Thy knee;
Here lingering still, we ask for naught,
  But simply worship Thee.

For Thou art God, the One, the Same,
  O'er all things high and bright;
And round us, when we speak Thy Name,
  There spreads a heaven of light.

O Thou above all blessing blest,
  O'er thanks exalted far;
Thy very greatness is a rest
  To weaklings as we are.

And when we feel the praise of Thee
  A task beyond our powers;
We say, "A perfect God is He,
  And He is fully ours."

DAY-SPRING. S. M.

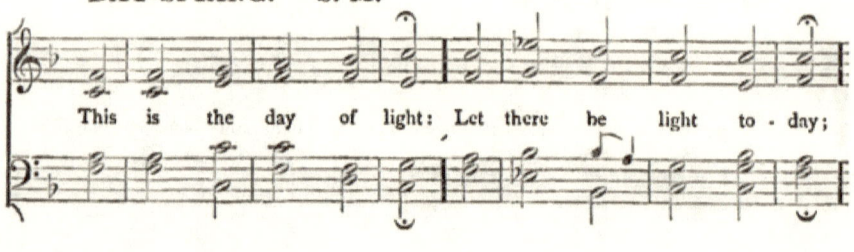

This is the day of light: Let there be light to-day;

O Day-Spring, rise upon our night, And chase its gloom away.

35

THIS is the day of light:
   Let there be light to-day;
O Day-Spring, rise upon our night,
   And chase its gloom away.

This is the day of rest:
   Our failing strength renew;
On weary brain and troubled breast
   Shed Thou Thy freshening dew.

This is the day of peace:
   Thy peace our spirits fill;
Bid Thou the blasts of discord cease,
   The waves of strife be still.

This is the day of prayer:
   Let earth to heaven draw near:
Lift up our hearts to seek Thee there;
   Come down to meet us here..

This is the first of days:
   Send forth Thy quickening breath,
And wake dead souls to love and praise,
   O Vanquisher of death!

36

STILL with Thee, O my God!
   I would desire to be;
By day, by night, at home, abroad,
   I would be still with Thee:

With Thee, when dawn comes in,
   And calls me back to care;
Each day returning to begin
   With Thee, my God! in prayer:

With Thee, when day is done,
   And evening calms the mind;
The setting, as the rising, sun
   With Thee my heart would find.

With Thee, when darkness brings
   The signal of repose,
Calm in the shadow of Thy wings,
   Mine eyelids I would close.

With Thee, in Thee, by faith
   Abiding I would be;
By day, by night, in life, in death,
   I would be still with Thee.

37

THE day is past and gone,
  The evening shades appear;
Oh, may we all remember well
  The night of death draws near.

Lord, keep us safe this night,
  Secure from all our fears,
May angels guard us while we sleep,
  Till morning light appears.

And when our days are past,
  And we from time remove,
Oh, may we in Thy bosom rest,
  The bosom of Thy love.

38

O LORD, accept our praise,
  As, with adoring eye,
From this dim earth we upward gaze
  To Thy bright home on high.

Thou wilt once more appear;
  Lord, give us daily grace
To tread our lowly pathways here,
  Until we see Thy face.

Give us, O Lord, each day,
  Fresh gleams of heavenly light,
To cheer us on our toilsome way,
  And brighten all our night.

39

LORD, at this closing hour,
  Establish every heart
Upon Thy word of truth and power,
  To keep us when we part.

Peace to our brethren give,
  Fill all our hearts with love;
In faith and patience may we live,
  And seek our rest above.

Through changes bright or drear
  We would Thy will pursue;
And toil to spread Thy Kingdom here,
  Till we its glory view.

To God the only wise,
  In every age adored,
Let glory from the church arise,
  Through Jesus Christ our Lord.

EVENTIDE. 10s.

1. A-BIDE with me! Fast falls the e-ven-tide; The dark-ness deep-ens; Lord with me a-bide! When oth-er help-ers fail, and com-forts flee, Help of the help-less, oh a-bide with me!

40

2.
Swift to its close ebbs out life's little day;
Earth's joys grow dim, its glories pass away;
Change and decay in all around I see;
O Thou who changest not, abide with me!

3.
I need Thy presence every passing hour;
What but Thy grace can foil the tempter's power?
Who like Thyself my Guide and Stay can be?
Through cloud and sunshine, oh abide with me!

4.
I fear no foe, with Thee at hand to bless;
Ills have no weight, and tears no bitterness:
Where is death's sting? where, grave, thy victory?
I triumph still, if Thou abide with me!

5.
Hold Thou Thy cross before my closing eyes;
Shine through the gloom, and point me to the skies;
Heaven's morning breaks, and earth's vain shadows flee:
In life, in death, O Lord, abide with me!

MORNING AND EVENING.

LANGRAN. 10s.

Sav-iour, a-gain to Thy dear Name we raise With one ac-cord our parting hymn of praise;
We stand to bless Thee ere our worship cease, Then, lowly bending, wait Thy word of peace.

41

SAVIOUR, again to Thy dear Name we raise
With one accord our parting hymn of praise;
We stand to bless Thee ere our worship cease,
Then, lowly bending, wait Thy word of peace.

Grant us Thy peace upon our homeward way;
With Thee began, with Thee shall end the day;
Guard Thou the lips from sin, the hearts from shame,
That in this house have called upon Thy Name.

Grant us Thy peace, Lord, thro' the coming night,
Turn Thou for us its darkness into light;
From harm and danger keep Thy children free,
For dark and light are both alike to Thee.

Grant us Thy peace throughout our earthly life,
Our balm in sorrow, and our stay in strife;
Then, when Thy voice shall bid our conflict cease,
Call us, O Lord, to Thine eternal peace.

To Father, Son, and Spirit ever blest,
Eternal praise and glory be addressed;
From age to age, ye saints, His Name adore,
And spread His fame, till time shall be no more.

MORNING AND EVENING.

HURSLEY. L. M.

42

SUN of my soul, Thou Saviour dear,
  It is not night if Thou be near;
O may no earth-born cloud arise
To hide Thee from Thy servants' eyes.

When the soft dews of kindly sleep
My weary eyelids gently steep,
Be my last thought, how sweet to rest
For ever on my Saviour's breast.

Abide with me from morn till eve,
For without Thee I cannot live;
Abide with me when night is nigh,
For without Thee I dare not die.

If some poor wandering child of Thine
Have spurn'd to-day the voice divine,
Now, Lord, the gracious work begin;
Let him no more lie down in sin.

Watch by the sick; enrich the poor
With blessings from Thy boundless store;
Be every mourner's sleep to-night,
Like infant slumbers, pure and light.

Come near and bless us when we wake,
Ere through the world our way we take,
Till in the ocean of Thy love
We lose ourselves in heaven above.

43

HOW sweet to leave the world awhile,
  And seek the presence of our Lord!
Dear Saviour! on Thy people smile,
  And come, according to Thy word.

From busy scenes we now retreat,
  That we may here converse with Thee:
Ah! Lord, behold us at Thy feet;—
  Let this the "gate of heaven" be.

"Chief of ten thousand!" now appear,
  That we by faith may see Thy face;
Oh! speak, that we Thy voice may hear,
  And let Thy presence fill this place.

HOLLEY. 7s.

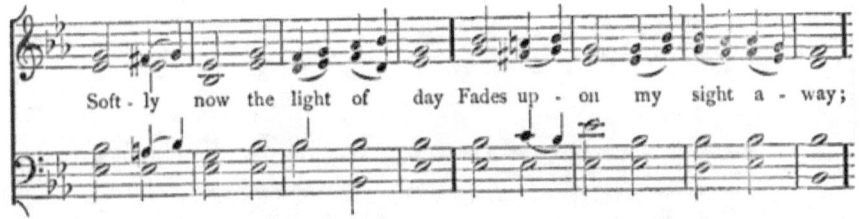

Soft-ly now the light of day Fades up-on my sight a-way;

Free from care, from la-bor free, Lord! I would commune with Thee.

44

SOFTLY now the light of day
  Fades upon my sight away;
Free from care, from labor free,
Lord! I would commune with Thee.

Thou whose all-pervading eye
  Naught escapes, without, within!
Pardon each infirmity,
  Open fault, and secret sin.

Soon, for me, the light of day
Shall for ever pass away;
Then, from sin and sorrow free,
Take me, Lord! to dwell with Thee.

45

FOR a season called to part,
  Let us then ourselves commend
To the gracious eye and heart
  Of our ever-present Friend.

Jesus! hear our humble prayer;
  Tender Shepherd of Thy sheep!
Let Thy mercy and Thy care
  All our souls in safety keep.

In Thy strength may we be strong;
  Sweeten every cross and pain;
Give us, if we live, ere long,
  Here to meet in peace again.

46

THOU from whom we never part,
  Thou whose love is everywhere,
Thou who seest every heart,
  Listen to our evening prayer.

Father, fill our hearts with love,
  Love unfailing, full and free;
Love that no alarm can move,
  Love that ever rests in Thee.

Heavenly Father, through the night
  Keep us safe from every ill;
Cheerful as the morning light,
  May we wake to do Thy will.

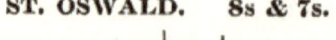

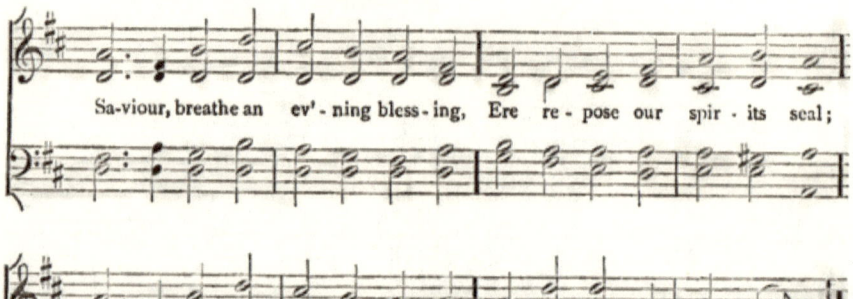

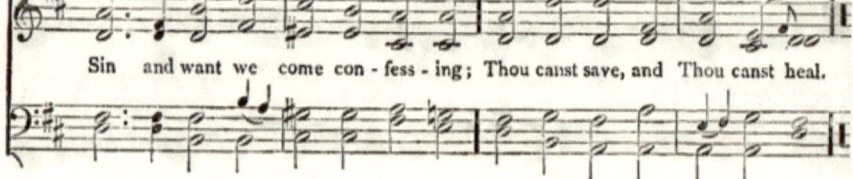

47

SAVIOUR, breathe an evening bless-
　Ere repose our spirits seal; [ing,
Sin and want we come confessing;
　Thou canst save, and Thou canst heal.

Though destruction walk around us,
　Though the arrow past us fly,
Angel-guards from Thee surround us;
　We are safe if Thou art nigh.

Though the night be dark and dreary,
　Darkness cannot hide from Thee;
Thou art He who, never weary,
　Watchest where Thy people be.

Should swift death this night o'ertake us,
　And our couch become our tomb,
May the heavenly morn awake us,
　Clad in bright and deathless bloom.

48

LO, the day of rest declineth,
　Gather fast the shades of night;
May the Sun which ever shineth
　Fill our souls with heavenly light!

While, Thine ear of love addressing,
　Thus our parting hymn we sing,
Father, grant Thine evening blessing,
　Fold us safe beneath Thy wing!

49

TARRY with me, O my Saviour!
　For the day is passing by;
See! the shades of evening gather,
　And the night is drawing nigh.

Deeper, deeper grow the shadows,
　Paler now the glowing west,
Swift the night of death advances;
　Shall it be the night of rest?

Feeble, trembling, fainting, dying,
　Lord, I cast myself on Thee;
Tarry with me through the darkness;
　While I sleep, still watch by me.

Tarry with me, O my Saviour!
　Lay my head upon Thy breast
Till the morning; then awake me,—
　Morning of eternal rest!

SICILIAN HYMN. 8s, 7s & 4.

50

LORD, dismiss us with Thy blessing;
  Fill our hearts with joy and peace;
Let us now, Thy love possessing,
  Triumph in redeeming grace:
    Oh refresh us,
  Travelling through this wilderness.

Thanks we give, and adoration,
  For Thy gospel's joyful sound;
May the fruits of Thy salvation
  In our hearts and lives abound;
    May Thy presence
  With us evermore be found.

51

IN Thy name, O Lord! assembling,
  We, Thy people, now draw near;
Teach us to rejoice with trembling;
  Speak, and let Thy servants hear,—
    Hear with meekness,—
  Hear Thy word with godly fear.

While our days on earth are lengthened,
  May we give them, Lord! to Thee;
Cheered by hope, and daily strengthened,
  May we run, nor weary be,
    Till Thy glory
  Without clouds in heaven we see.

Doxology.

MAY the grace of Christ our Saviour,
  And the Father's boundless love,
With the Holy Spirit's favor,
  Rest upon us from above!

Thus may we abide in union
  With each other and the Lord,
And possess, in sweet communion,
  Joys which earth can not afford.

EVENING WORSHIP.

VESPER CHANT.

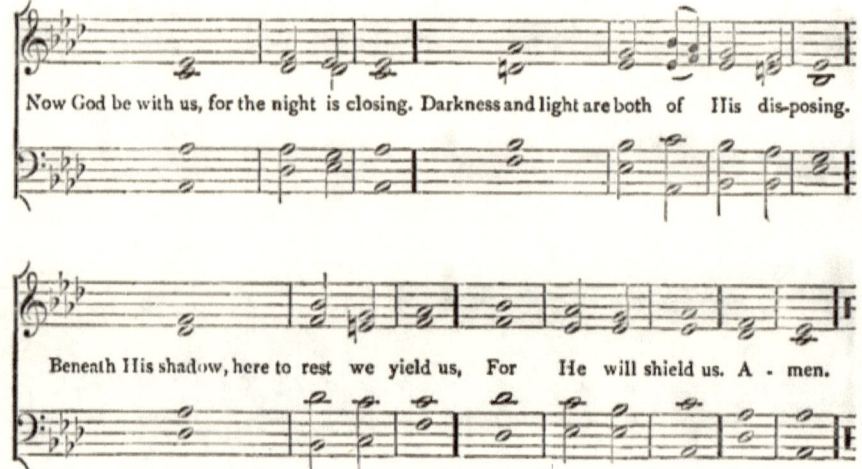

52

NOW God be with us, for the | night is | closing.
  Darkness and light are | both of | His dis- | posing.
Beneath His shadow, here to | rest we | yield us,
    For | He will | shield us.

Let evil thoughts and spirits | flee be- | fore us;
Till morning cometh, | watch, O | Master, | o'er us;
In soul and body Thou from | harm de- | fend us,
    Thine | angels | send us.

We have no refuge; none on | earth to | aid us,
Save Thee, O Father, | who Thine | own hast | made us:
But Thy dear presence will not | leave them | lonely
    Who | seek Thee | only.

Father, Thy Name be praised, Thy | Kingdom | given,
Thy will be done on | earth, as | 'tis in | Heaven;
Keep us in life, forgive our | sins, de- | liver
    Us | now and | ever.   Amen.

LYTE CHANT.

The day is gently sinking to a close, Fainter and yet more faint the sun-light glows;
O brightness of the Father's glo-ry, Thou Eternal light of light be with us now;
Where Thou art present, darkness can-not be, Midnight is glorious noon, O Lord, to Thee.

53

2.
Our changeful lives are ebbing | to an | end;
Onward to darkness | and to | death we | tend.
O Conqueror of the grave, be | Thou our | guide,
Be Thou our light in | death's dark | even- | tide;
Then in our mortal hour will | be no | gloom,
No sting in death, no | terror | in the | tomb.

3.
The weary world is mouldering | to de- | cay,
Its glories wane, its | pageants | fade a- | way;
In that last sunset when the | stars shall | fall,
May we arise, a- | waken'd | by Thy | call,
With Thee, O Lord, for ever | to a- | bide
In that blest day which | has no | even- | tide.

54

OH, praise ye the Lord, prepare your glad voice,
    His praise in the great assembly to sing;
In their great Creator let all men rejoice,
    And heirs of salvation be glad in their King.

Let them His great name devoutly adore,
    In loud-swelling strains His praises express,
Who graciously opens His bountiful store,
    Their wants to relieve, and His children to bless.

With glory adorned, His people shall sing
    To God, who defence and plenty supplies;
Their loud acclamations to Him, their great King,
    Through earth shall be sounded, and reach to the skies.

To Father, and Son, and Spirit, be given
    All glory on earth, all glory in Heaven:
We praise Thee, we bless Thee, we glorify Thee,
    Who wast, and who art, and who ever shalt be.

AUSTRIA. 8s & 7s.

55

Praise the Lord! ye heavens, adore
 Praise Him, angels in the height: [Him
Sun and moon, rejoice before Him,
 Praise Him, all ye stars and light:
Praise the Lord! for He hath spoken,
 Worlds his mighty voice obeyed;
Laws which never shall be broken,
 For their guidance He hath made.

Praise the Lord! for He is glorious;
 Never shall His promise fail;
God hath made His saints victorious,
 Sin and death shall not prevail.
Praise the God of our salvation;
 Hosts on high, His power proclaim:
Heaven and earth, and all creation,
 Laud and magnify His Name!

Worship, honor, glory, blessing,
 Lord, we offer to Thy Name;
Young and old, Thy praise expressing,
 Join their Saviour to proclaim.
As the saints in heaven adore Thee,
 We would bow before Thy throne;
As Thine angels serve before Thee,
 So on earth Thy will be done!

THE FATHER ALMIGHTY.

MISSIONARY CHANT. L. M.

O ho-ly, ho-ly, ho-ly Lord, Bright in Thy deeds and in Thy name.

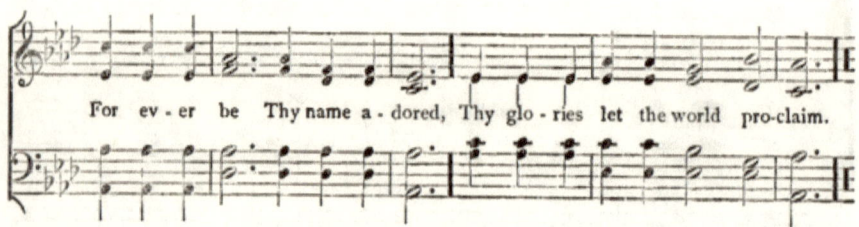

For ev-er be Thy name a-dored, Thy glo-ries let the world pro-claim.

56

O HOLY, holy, holy Lord, [Name,
  Bright in Thy deeds and in Thy
For ever be Thy name adored,
  Thy glories let the world proclaim.

O Jesus, Lamb oncé crucified
  To take our load of sins away,
Thine be the hymn that rolls its tide
  Along the realms of upper day.

O Holy Spirit from above,
  In streams of light and glory given,
Thou source of ecstacy and love,
  Thy praises ring through earth and
    heaven.

O God Triune, to Thee we owe
  Our every thought, our every song;
And ever may Thy praises flow
  From saint and seraph's burning
    tongue.

57

LORD God of hosts, by all adored,
  Thy name we praise with one accord;
The earth and heavens are full of Thee,
  Thy light, Thy love, Thy majesty.

To Thee aloud all angels cry,
The heavens and all the powers on high;
Thee, holy, holy, holy King,
Lord God of hosts, they ever sing.

The apostles join the glorious throng,
The prophets swell th' immortal song,
The martyrs' noble army raise
Eternal anthems to Thy praise.

The holy church in every place [grace;
Throughout the world, doth hymn Thy
Thy Name we worship and adore,
World without end, forevermore.

Vouchsafe, O Lord, we humbly pray,
To keep us safe from sin this day;
Have mercy, Lord, we trust in Thee!
Oh let us ne'er confounded be.

PARK ST. L. M.

58

O COME, loud anthems let us sing,
  Loud thanks to our almighty King,
And high our grateful voices raise,
As our Salvation's Rock we praise.

Into His presence let us haste
To thank Him for His favors past;
To Him address, in joyful songs,
The praise that to His Name belongs.

For God the Lord, enthroned in state,
Is with unrivall'd glory great;
The depths of earth are in His hand,
Her secret wealth at His command.

O let us to His courts repair,
And bow with adoration there;
Low on our knees with reverence fall,
And on the Lord our Maker call.

59

YE nations round the earth, rejoice
  Before the Lord your sovereign King;
Serve Him with cheerful heart and voice;
With all your tongues His glory sing.

The Lord is God; 'tis He alone
Doth life, and breath, and being give;
We are His work and not our own,
The sheep that on His pastures live.

Enter His gates with songs of joy,
With praises to His courts repair,
And make it your divine employ
To pay your thanks and honors there.

The Lord is good, the Lord is kind;
Great is His grace, His mercy sure;
And the whole race of man shall find
His truth from age to age endure.

THE FATHER ALMIGHTY.

JUDGMENT HYMN.   **8s & 7s.**

60

OUR Father-God, whose rule is just
    And wise, and changes never,
We praise, we worship Thee, and trust,
    And give Thee thanks forever.
Thy boundless power o'er all things reigns,
Whate'er Thy holy will ordains
    Is done in earth and heaven.

O Jesus Christ, our blessed Lord,
    Son of the heavenly Father,
O Thou who hast our peace restored,
    Who dost the lost sheep gather,
Thou Lamb of God, to Thee on high,
From out the depths of sin we cry,
    Have mercy on us, Jesus.

O Holy Spirit! precious gift!
    Thou Comforter unfailing!
O'er Satan's snares our souls uplift,
    And let Thy power prevailing
Avert our woes and calm our dread;
For us the Saviour's blood was shed,
    We trust in Thee to save us.

OLD HUNDREDTH. L. M.

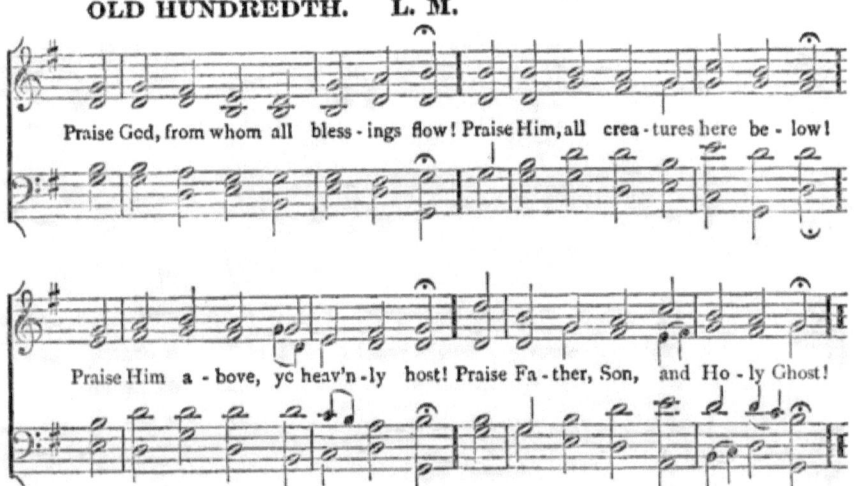

Praise God, from whom all blessings flow! Praise Him, all creatures here below!
Praise Him above, ye heav'nly host! Praise Father, Son, and Holy Ghost!

61

FROM all that dwell below the skies,
    Let the Creator's praise arise;
Let the Redeemer's name be sung,
Through every land, by every tongue.

Eternal are Thy mercies, Lord!
Eternal truth attends Thy word;
Thy praise shall sound from shore to shore,
Till suns shall rise and set no more.

62

NO change of time shall ever shock
    My firm affection, Lord, to Thee;
For Thou hast always been my Rock,
A fortress and defence to me.

Thou my Deliverer art, my God,
My trust is in Thy mighty power;
Thou art my shield from foes abroad,
At home, my safeguard and my tower.

To Thee will I address my prayer,
To whom all praise we justly owe;
So shall I, by Thy watchful care,
Be guarded safe from every foe.

63

WITH all my powers of heart and
    tongue,
I'll praise my Maker in my song;
Angels shall hear the notes I raise,
Approve the song, and join the praise.

To God I cried when troubles rose;
He heard me, and subdued my foes;
He did my rising fears control, [soul.
And strength diffused through all my

Amid a thousand snares, I stand
Upheld and guarded by Thy hand;
Thy words my fainting soul revive,
And keep my dying faith alive.

I'll sing Thy truth and mercy, Lord;
I'll sing the wonders of Thy word;
Not all Thy works and names below
So much Thy power and glory show.

WARD. L. M.

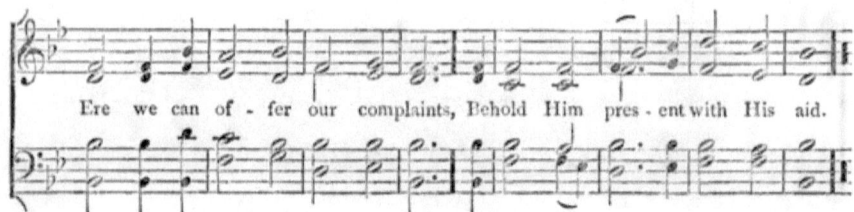

64

GOD is the Refuge of His saints,
  When storms of sharp distress invade;
Ere we can offer our complaints,
  Behold Him present with His aid.

Loud may the troubled ocean roar,—
  In sacred peace our souls abide,
While every nation, every shore,
  Trembles, and dreads the swelling tide.

There is a stream whose gentle flow
  Supplies the city of our God;
Life, love, and joy still gliding through,
  And watering our divine abode:—

That sacred stream,—Thy holy word,—
  That all our raging fear controls:
Sweet peace Thy promises afford,
  And give new strength to fainting souls.

Zion enjoys her Monarch's love,
  Secure against a threatening hour;
Nor can her firm foundations move,
  Built on His truth, and armed with power.

65

BEFORE Jehovah's awful throne,
  Ye nations, bow with sacred joy;
Know that the Lord is God alone;
  He can create, and He destroy.

His sovereign power, without our aid,
  Made us of clay, and form'd us men;
And when like wandering sheep we stray'd,
  He brought us to His fold again.

We are His people, we His care,
  Our souls, and all our mortal frame;
What lasting honors shall we rear,
  Almighty Maker, to Thy name?

We'll crowd Thy gates with thankful songs,
  High as the heaven our voices raise;
And earth, with her ten thousand tongues,
  Shall fill Thy courts with sounding praise.

Wide as the world is Thy command,
  Vast as eternity Thy love;
Firm as a rock Thy truth must stand,
  When rolling years shall cease to move.

RUSSIAN HYMN. L. M.

66

COME, O my soul! in sacred lays
  Attempt thy great Creator's praise :
But, oh, what tongue can speak His fame?
  What mortal verse can reach the theme?

Enthroned amid the radiant spheres,
  He glory like a garment wears;
To form a robe of light divine,
  Ten thousand suns around Him shine.

In all our Maker's grand designs,
  Almighty power with wisdom shines;
His works, thro' all this wondrous frame,
  Declare the glory of His Name.

Raised on devotion's lofty wing,
  Do thou, my soul, His glories sing;
And let His praise employ thy tongue,
  Till listening worlds shall join the song!

67

HIGH in the heavens, eternal God!
  Thy goodness in full glory shines;
Thy truth shall break through every cloud
  That vails and darkens Thy designs.

Forever firm Thy justice stands,
  As mountains their foundations keep:
Wise are the wonders of Thy hands;
  Thy judgments are a mighty deep.

My God, how excellent Thy grace!
  Whence all our hope and comfort springs;
The sons of Adam, in distress,
  Fly to the shadow of Thy wings.

Life, like a fountain rich and free,
  Springs from the presence of my Lord;
And in Thy light our souls shall see
  The glories promised in Thy word.

    Praise God, from whom all blessings flow!
    Praise Him, all creatures here below!
    Praise Him above, ye heavenly host!
    Praise Father, Son, and Holy Ghost!

ADORATION. 11s & 8s.

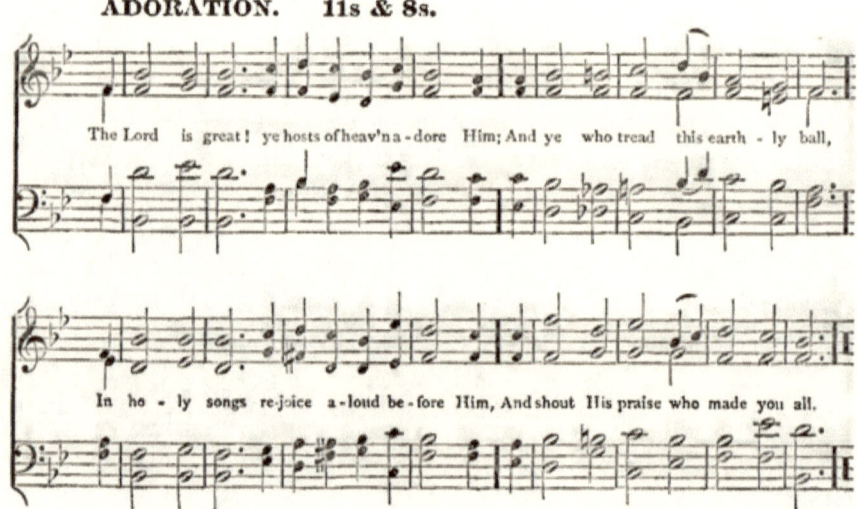

68

THE Lord is great! ye hosts of heaven adore Him;
   And ye who tread this earthly ball,
In holy songs rejoice aloud before Him,
   And shout His praise who made you all.

The Lord is great! His majesty how glorious!
   Resound His praise from shore to shore;
O'er sin, and death, and hell, now made victorious,
   He rules and reigns forevermore.

The Lord is great! His mercy how abounding!
   Ye angels, strike your golden chords!
Oh, praise our God, with voice and harp resounding,
   The King of kings, and Lord of lords.

To Father, Son, and Holy Ghost be given
   All glory now and evermore:
With saints on earth, and all the hosts of heaven,
   Thy Name we worship and adore.

WINDSOR. C. M.

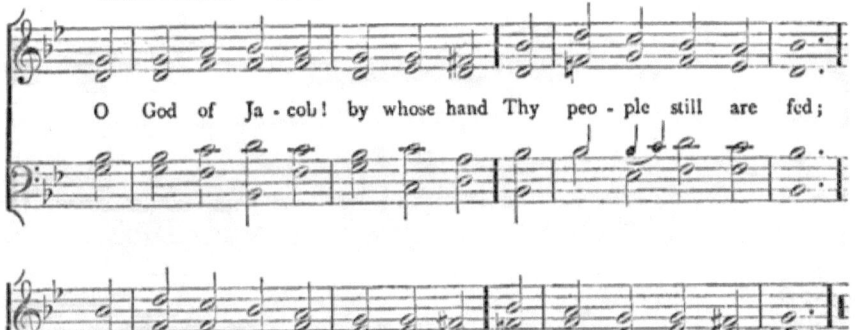

O God of Ja-cob! by whose hand Thy peo-ple still are fed;
Who through this wea-ry pil-grim-age Hast all our fa-thers led;

69

O GOD of Jacob! by whose hand
    Thy people still are fed ;
Who through this weary pilgrimage
    Hast all our fathers led ;

Our vows, our prayers, we now present
    Before Thy throne of grace ;
God of the fathers, be the God
    Of their succeeding race.

Through each perplexing path of life
    Our wandering footsteps guide ;
Give us each day our daily bread,
    And raiment fit provide.

Oh ! spread Thy covering wings around,
    Till all our wanderings cease,
And at our Father's loved abode
    Our souls arrive in peace.

70

JEHOVAH, God ! Thy gracious power
    On every hand we see ;
Oh, may the blessings of each hour
    Lead all our thoughts to Thee !

If, on the wings of morn, we speed
    To earth's remotest bound,
Thy hand will there our footsteps lead,
    Thy love our path surround.

Thy power is in the ocean deeps,
    And reaches to the skies ;
Thine eye of mercy never sleeps,
    Thy goodness never dies.

From morn till noon, till latest eve,
    Thy hand, O God, we see ;
And all the blessings we receive
    Proceed alone from Thee.

In all the varying scenes of time,
    On Thee our hopes depend ;
Through every age, in every clime,
    Our Father and our Friend.

THE FATHER ALMIGHTY.

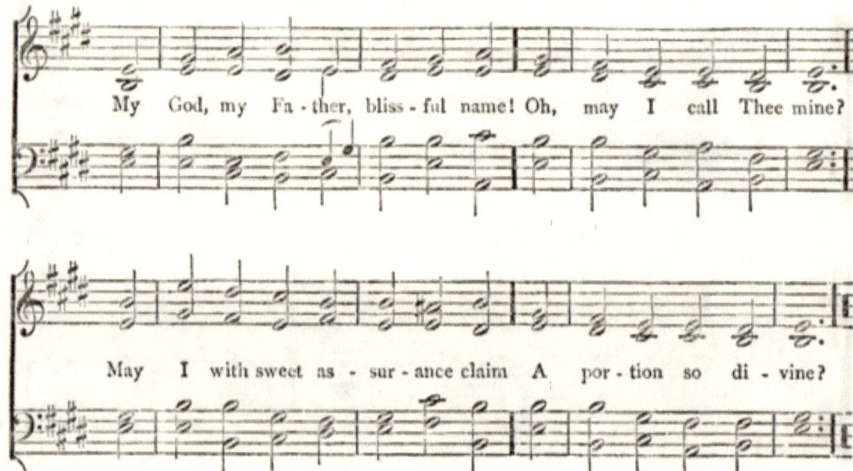

DUNDEE. C. M.

My God, my Father, blissful name! Oh, may I call Thee mine?
May I with sweet assurance claim A portion so divine?

71

My God, my Father, blissful name!
  Oh, may I call Thee mine?
May I with sweet assurance claim
  A portion so divine?

Whate'er Thy providence denies,
  I calmly would resign,
For Thou art good and just and wise,
  Oh, bend my will to Thine!

Whate'er Thy sacred will ordains,
  Oh, give me strength to bear!
And let me know my Father reigns,
  And trust His tender care.

Thy sovereign ways are all unknown
  To my weak, erring sight;
Yet let my soul adoring own
  That all Thy ways are right.

72

My God, how wonderful Thou art!
  Thy majesty how bright!
How glorious is Thy mercy seat,
  In depths of burning light!

Yet I may love Thee too, O Lord,
  Almighty as Thou art;
For Thou hast stooped to ask of me
  The love of my poor heart.

No earthly father loves like Thee,
  No mother half so mild
Bears and forbears, as Thou hast done
  With me, Thy sinful child.

My God, how wonderful Thou art,
  Thou everlasting Friend!
On Thee I stay my trusting heart,
  Till faith in vision end.

  To Father, Son, and Holy Ghost,
    The God whom we adore,
  Be glory as it was, is now,
    And shall be evermore.

SOUTHWELL. C. M.

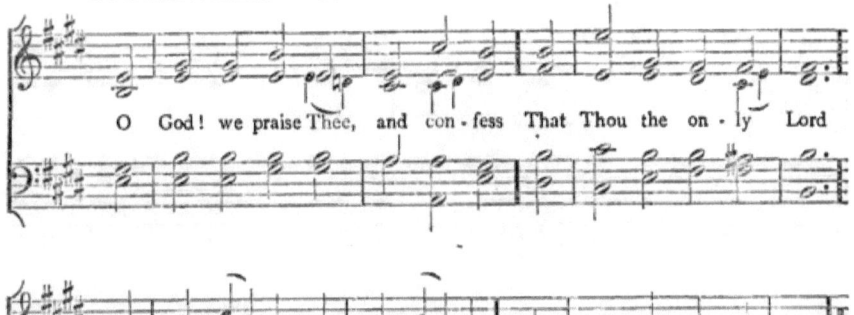
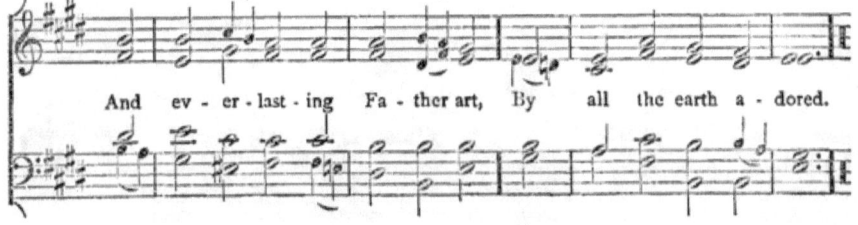

73

O GOD! we praise Thee, and confess
    That Thou the only Lord
And everlasting Father art,
    By all the earth adored.

To Thee, all angels cry aloud;
    To Thee, the powers on high,
Both cherubim and seraphim,
    Continually do cry:—

O holy, holy, holy Lord,
    Whom heavenly hosts obey,
The world is with the glory filled
    Of Thy majestic sway!

The apostles' glorious company,
    And prophets crowned with light,
With all the martyrs' noble host,
    Thy constant praise recite.

The holy church throughout the world,
    O Lord, confesses Thee,
That Thou th' eternal Father art,
    Of boundless majesty.

74

TO heaven I lift my waiting eyes:
    There all my hopes are laid;
The Lord that built the earth and skies
    Is my perpetual aid.

Their steadfast feet shall never fall
    Whom He designs to keep;
His ear attends the softest call,
    His eyes can never sleep.

Israel, rejoice, and rest secure;
    Thy keeper is the Lord:
His wakeful eyes employ His power
    For thine eternal guard.

He guards thy soul, He keeps thy breath,
    Where thickest dangers come;
Go and return, secure from death,
    Till God commands thee home.

THE FATHER ALMIGHTY.

AVON. C. M.

Great God! how in-fi-nite art Thou! What worth-less worms are we!

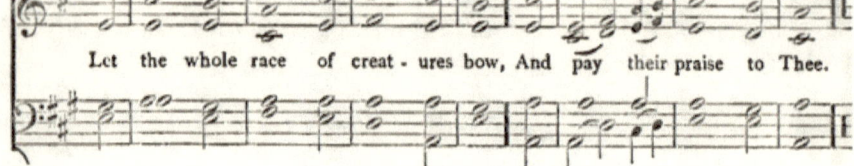

Let the whole race of creat-ures bow, And pay their praise to Thee.

75

GREAT God! how infinite art Thou!
  What worthless worms are we!
Let the whole race of creatures bow,
  And pay their praise to Thee.

Thy throne eternal ages stood,
  Ere seas or stars were made;
Thou art the ever-living God,
  Were all the nations dead.

Eternity, with all its years,
  Stands present in Thy view;
To Thee there's nothing old appears,
  Great God! there's nothing new.

Our lives through various scenes are drawn,
  And vexed with trifling cares;
While Thine eternal thoughts move on
  Thine undisturbed affairs.

Great God! how infinite art Thou!
  What worthless worms are we!
Let the whole race of creatures bow,
  And pay their praise to Thee.

76

GOD moves in a mysterious way,
  His wonders to perform;
He plants His footsteps in the sea,
  And rides upon the storm.

Ye fearful saints! fresh courage take;
  The clouds ye so much dread
Are big with mercy, and shall break
  In blessings on your head.

Judge not the Lord by feeble sense,
  But trust Him for His grace;
Behind a frowning providence,
  He hides a smiling face.

His purposes will ripen fast,
  Unfolding every hour;
The bud may have a bitter taste,
  But sweet will be the flower.

Blind unbelief is sure to err,
  And scan His work in vain;
God is His own interpreter,
  And He will make it plain.

DENFIELD. C. M.

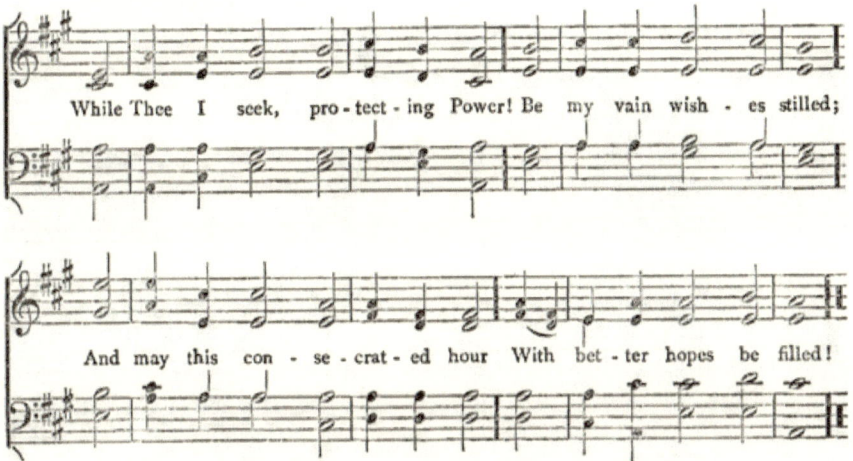

77

WHILE Thee I seek, protecting Power!
    Be my vain wishes stilled;
And may this consecrated hour
    With better hopes be filled!

Thy love the power of thought bestowed;
    To Thee my thoughts would soar;
Thy mercy o'er my life has flowed;
    That mercy I adore.

In each event of life, how clear
    Thy ruling hand I see!
Each blessing to my soul more dear,
    Because conferred by Thee.

In every joy that crowns my days,
    In every pain I bear,
My heart shall find delight in praise,
    Or seek relief in prayer.

When gladness wings my favored hour,
    Thy love my thoughts shall fill;
Resigned, when storms of sorrow lower,
    My soul shall meet Thy will.

My lifted eye, without a tear,
    The gathering storm shall see;
My steadfast heart shall know no fear;
    That heart will rest on Thee.

78

WHEN all Thy mercies, O my God,
    My rising soul surveys,
Transported with the view, I'm lost
    In wonder, love, and praise!

Ten thousand thousand precious gifts
    My daily thanks employ;
Nor is the least a cheerful heart,
    That tastes those gifts with joy.

Through every period of my life
    Thy goodness I'll pursue;
And, after death, in distant worlds,
    The glorious theme renew.

All glory to the Father be,
All glory to the Son:
All glory to the Holy Ghost,
While endless ages run.

THE FATHER ALMIGHTY.

ST. HELENA. S. M.

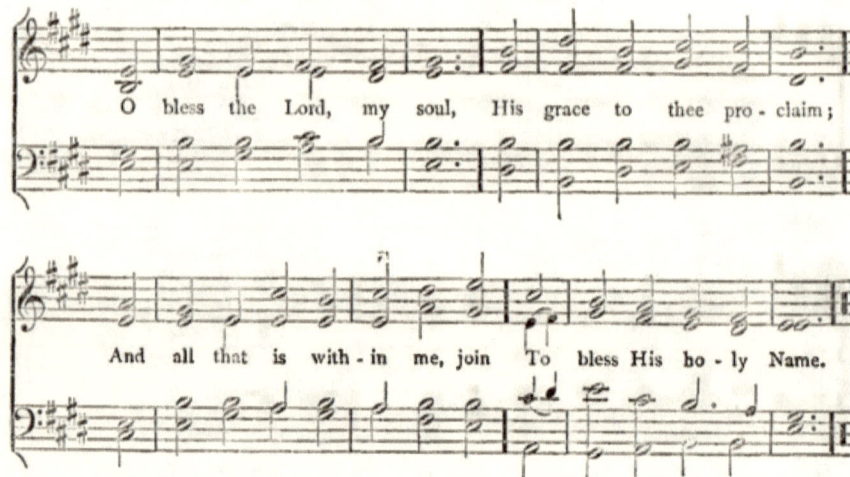

O bless the Lord, my soul, His grace to thee proclaim;
And all that is with-in me, join To bless His ho-ly Name.

79

O BLESS the Lord, my soul,
  His grace to thee proclaim;
And all that is within me, join
  To bless His holy Name.

O bless the Lord, my soul,
  His mercies bear in mind;
Forget not all His benefits,
  Who is to thee so kind.

He pardons all thy sins,
  Prolongs thy feeble breath;
He heals all thine infirmities,
  And ransoms thee from death.

He feeds thee with His love,
  Upholds thee with His truth;
And, like the eagle's, He renews
  The vigor of thy youth.

Then bless the Lord, my soul,
  His grace, His love proclaim;
Let all that is within me, join
  To bless His holy Name.

80

OUR Heavenly Father, hear
  The prayer we offer now:
Thy Name be hallowed far and near,
  To Thee all nations bow.

Thy kingdom come; Thy will
  On earth be done in love,
As saints and seraphim fulfill
  Thy perfect law above.

Our daily bread supply,
  While by Thy word we live;
The guilt of our iniquity
  Forgive, as we forgive.

From dark temptation's power
  Our feeble hearts defend;
Deliver in the evil hour,
  And guide us to the end.

Thine, then, forever be
  Glory and power divine;
The sceptre, throne, and majesty
  Of heaven and earth are Thine.

THE FATHER ALMIGHTY.

ST. MICHAEL'S.   S. M.

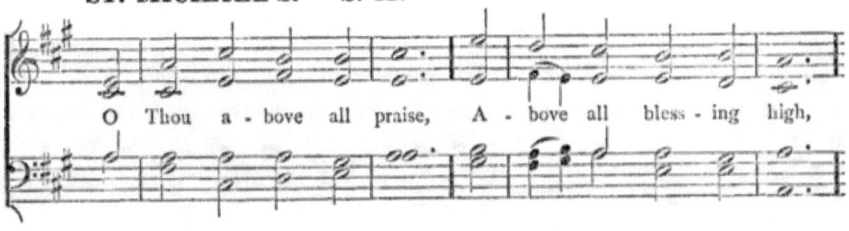

O Thou a-bove all praise, A-bove all bless-ing high,

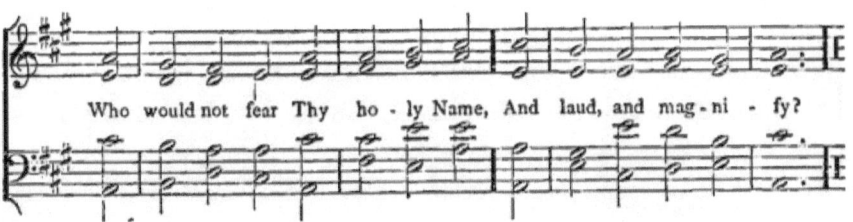

Who would not fear Thy ho-ly Name, And laud, and mag-ni-fy?

81

O THOU above all praise,
    Above all blessing high,
Who would not fear Thy holy Name,
    And laud, and magnify?

Oh for the living flame
    From Thine own altar brought,
To touch our lips, our souls inspire,
    And wing to heaven our thought.

God is our strength and song,
    And His salvation ours;
Then be His love in Christ proclaimed,
    With all our ransomed powers.

The Father and the Son,
    And Spirit we adore;
We praise, we bless, we worship Thee,
    Both now and evermore.

82

TO God, the only wise,
    Our Saviour and our King,
Let all the saints below the skies
    Their humble praises bring.

'Tis His almighty love,
    His counsel and His care,
Preserves us safe from sin and death,
    And every hurtful snare.

He will present our souls,
    Unblemished and complete,
Before the glory of His face,
    With joys divinely great.

Then all the chosen seed
    Shall meet around the throne,
Shall bless the conduct of His grace,
    And make His wonders known.

To our Redeemer, God,
    Wisdom and power belong,
Immortal crowns of majesty,
    And everlasting song.

THE FATHER ALMIGHTY.

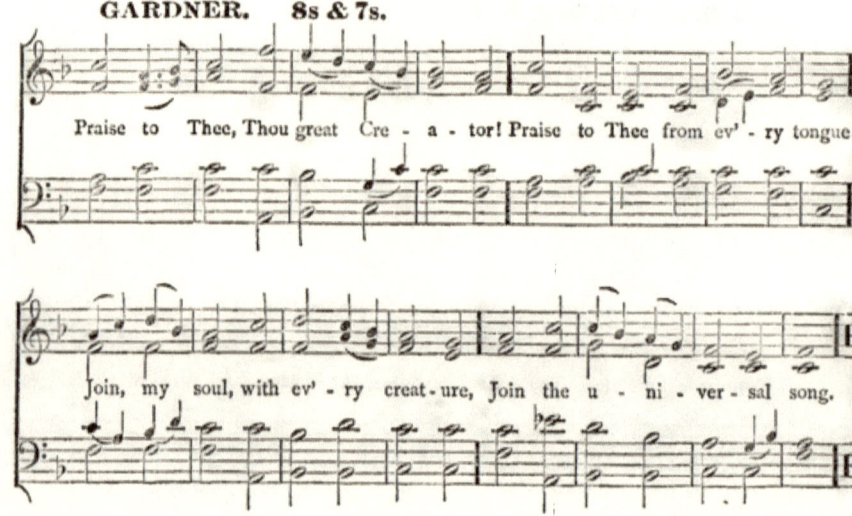

GARDNER. 8s & 7s.

Praise to Thee, Thou great Cre - a - tor! Praise to Thee from ev' - ry tongue:
Join, my soul, with ev' - ry creat-ure, Join the u - ni - ver - sal song.

83

PRAISE to Thee, Thou great Creator!
  Praise to Thee from every tongue:
Join, my soul, with every creature,
  Join the universal song.

Father, Source of all compassion,
  Pure, unbounded grace is Thine:
Hail the God of our salvation!
  Praise Him for His love divine.

For ten thousand blessings given,
  For the hope of future joy,
Sound His praise through earth and heaven,
  Sound Jehovah's praise on high.

Joyfully on earth adore Him,
  Till in heaven our song we raise;
There, enraptured, fall before Him,
  Lost in wonder, love, and praise.

84

GOD is love; His mercy brightens
  All the path in which we rove;
Bliss He wakes, and woe He lightens;
  God is mercy, God is love.

Chance and change are busy ever;
  Man decays, and ages move:
But His mercy waneth never;
  God is wisdom, God is love.

E'en the hour that darkest seemeth,
  Will His changeless goodness prove;
From the gloom His brightness streameth;
  God is wisdom, God is love.

He with earthly cares entwineth
  Hope and comfort from above:
Everywhere His glory shineth;
  God is wisdom, God is love.

Praise the Father, earth and heaven!
  Praise the Son, the Spirit praise;
As it was, and is, be given
  Glory, through eternal days.

85

PRAISE, my soul, the King of heaven;
  To His feet thy tribute bring;
Ransomed by Him, and forgiven,
  Who like me His praise should sing?
    Praise Him, praise Him,
    Praise the everlasting King.

Praise Him for His grace and favor
  To our fathers in distress;
Praise Him, still the same forever,
  Slow to chide and swift to bless.
    Praise Him, praise Him,
    Glorious in His faithfulness.

Father-like He tends and spares us;
  Well our feeble frame He knows;
In His hand He gently bears us;
  Rescues us from all our foes.
    Praise Him, praise Him,
    Widely as His mercy flows.

Frail as summer flowers we flourish,
  Blows the wind and they are gone;
But, while generations perish,
  God's unending years roll on.
    Praise Him, praise Him,
    Praise the everlasting One.

JESUS CHRIST OUR LORD.

ADVENT HYMN.

1. Come, quickly come, dread Judge of all; For, awful though Thine Advent be, All shadows from the truth will fall, And falsehood die, in sight of Thee: Come, quickly come: for doubt and fear Like clouds dissolve when Thou art near.

2
Come, quickly come, great King of all;
　Reign all around us, and within;
Let sin no more our souls enthrall,
　Let pain and sorrow die with sin:
Come, quickly come: for Thou alone
Canst make Thy scatter'd people one.

3.
Come, quickly come, true Life of all;
　The curse of death is on the ground;
On every home his shadows fall,
　On every heart his mark is found:
Come, quickly come: for grief and pain
Can never cloud Thy glorious reign.

4.
Come, quickly come, sure Light of all,
　For gloomy night broods o'er our way;
And fainting souls begin to fall
　With weary watching for the day:
Come, quickly come: for round Thy throne
No eye is blind, no night is known.

JESUS CHRIST OUR LORD.

ADESTE FIDELES. P. M.

1. O come all ye faithful, Joyful and triumphant, O come ye, O come ye to Bethlehem. Come and behold Him, Born the King of angels; O come let us adore Him, O come let us adore Him, O come let us adore Him, Christ the Lord.

87

2
Sing choirs of angels,
Sing in exultation,
Sing, all ye citizens of Heaven above.
Glory to Thee, Lord,
In the highest, glory!
O come let us adore Him,
O come let us adore Him,
O come let us adore Him, Christ the Lord.

3
Lord Jesus, we greet Thee
Son of the Father,
Born of the Virgin Mary, Word made flesh!
Glory and honor
Be to Thee, O Saviour.
O come let us adore Him,
O come let us adore Him,
O come let us adore Him, Christ the Lord.

JESUS CHRIST OUR LORD.

GREENVILLE. 8s, 7s.

88

LIGHT of those whose dreary dwelling
　Borders on the shades of death,
Rise on us, Thy love revealing—
　Dissipate the clouds beneath.
Thou, of heaven and earth Creator,
　In our deepest darkness rise,—
Scatt'ring all the night of nature,
　Pouring day upon our eyes.

Still we wait for Thine appearing;
　Life and joy Thy beams impart,
Chasing all our fears, and cheering
　Every poor benighted heart:
Come and manifest Thy favor
　To the ransomed, helpless race;
Come, Thou glorious God and Saviour!
　Come, and bring the gospel grace.

Save us, in Thy great compassion,
　O Thou mild, pacific Prince!
Give the knowledge of salvation,
　Give the pardon of our sins;
By Thine all-sufficient merit,
　Every burdened soul release;
Every weary, wandering spirit,
　Guide into Thy perfect peace.

89

COME, Thou long-expected Jesus,
　Born to set Thy people free;
From our fears and sins release us,
　Let us find our rest in Thee:
Israel's Strength and Consolation,
　Hope of all the saints Thou art;
Dear Desire of every nation,
　Joy of every longing heart.

Born, Thy people to deliver;
　Born a child, and yet a King;
Born to reign in us forever,
　Now Thy precious kingdom bring:
By Thine own eternal Spirit,
　Rule in all our hearts alone;
By Thine all-sufficient merit,
　Raise us to Thy glorious throne.

WILMOT. 8s & 7s.

Hark! what mean those ho-ly voic-es, Sweet-ly sound-ing through the skies? Lo, th' an-gel-ic host re-joic-es; Heav'n-ly hal-le-lu-jahs rise.

90

HARK! what mean those holy voices,
　　Sweetly sounding through the skies?
Lo, th' angelic host rejoices;
　　Heavenly hallelujahs rise.

Hear them tell the wondrous story,
　　Hear them chant in hymns of joy;
Glory in the highest, glory!
　　Glory be to God most high!

Peace on earth, good-will from heaven,
　　Reaching far as man is found;
Souls redeemed, and sins forgiven;
　　Loud our golden harps shall sound.

Christ is born, the Great Anointed;
　　Heaven and earth His praises sing;
Oh, receive whom God appointed;
　　For your Prophet, Priest, and King.

Haste, ye mortals, to adore Him;
　　Learn His Name, and taste His joy;
Till in heaven ye sing before Him,
　　"Glory be to God most high."

91

LET our songs of praise ascending,
　　Rise to Thee, O God most high;
While before Thee, humbly bending,
　　Glory to Thy Name we cry.

With the shepherds in the story,
　　Let our hearts to Bethlehem go,
Where the Lord of life and glory,
　　In a manger lieth low.

With the angels, filled with wonder,
　　Let us praise Him in the height!
With the blessed Virgin ponder
　　All love's mystery and might.

Age to age Thy glory beareth
　　On the stream of time abroad;
Race to race Thy Name declareth,
　　Son of Mary! Son of God!

Heaven exults and earth rejoices
　　In the work that Thou hast wrought;
Lord, attune our trembling voices,
　　Let us praise Thee as we ought.

JESUS CHRIST OUR LORD.

92

IT came upon the midnight clear,
  That glorious song of old,
From angels bending near the earth
  To touch their harps of gold:
Peace on the earth, good-will to men,
  From heaven's all-gracious King;
The world in solemn stillness lay,
  To hear the angels sing.

Still thro' the cloven skies they come,
  With peaceful wings unfurl'd;
And still their heavenly music floats
  O'er all the weary world:
Above its sad and lowly plains
  They bend on hovering wing,
And ever o'er its Babel sounds
  The blessed angels sing.

O ye beneath life's crushing load,
  Whose forms are bending low,
Who toil along the climbing way
  With painful steps and slow!
Look now, for glad and golden hours
  Come swiftly on the wing:
O rest beside the weary road,
  And hear the angels sing.

For lo, the days are hastening on,
  By prophets seen of old,
When with the ever-circling years
  Shall come the time foretold,
When the new heaven and earth shall own
  The Prince of Peace their King,
And the whole world send back the song
  Which now the angels sing.

JESUS CHRIST OUR LORD.

GLORIA. 7s.

1. Hark! the herald angels sing Glory to the new-born King,
Peace on earth, and mercy mild, God and sinners reconciled.
Joyful, all ye nations, rise, Join the triumph of the skies;
With th' angelic host proclaim, Christ is born in Bethlehem.

93

2.
Hail, the heaven-born Prince of peace,
Hail, the Sun of Righteousness!
Light and life to all He brings,
Risen with healing in His wings.
Mild He lays His glory by,
Born that man no more may die,
Born to raise the sons of earth,
Born to give them second birth.

94 Easter.

AT the Lamb's high feast we sing
Praise to our victorious King,
Who hath washed us in the tide
Flowing from His piercèd side;
Praise we Him, whose love divine
Gives His sacred blood for wine,
Gives His body for the feast,
Christ the Victim, Christ the Priest.

Mighty Victim from the sky!
Hell's fierce powers beneath Thee lie;
Thou hast conquer'd in the fight,
Thou hast brought us life and light:
Now no more can death appall,
Now no more the grave enthrall,
Thou hast opened Paradise,
And in Thee Thy saints shall rise.

JESUS CHRIST OUR LORD.

CHRISTMAS. C. M.

95

JOY to the world! the Lord is come!
　Let earth receive her King;
Let every heart prepare Him room,
　And heaven and nature sing.

Joy to the world! the Saviour reigns!
　Let men their songs employ; [plains
While fields and floods, rocks, hills, and
　Repeat the sounding joy.

No more let sin and sorrow grow,
　Nor thorns infest the ground;
He comes to make His blessings flow
　Far as the curse is found.

He rules the world with truth and grace,
　And makes the nations prove
The glories of His righteousness,
　And wonders of His love.

All glory to the Father be,
　All glory to the Son,
All glory to the Holy Ghost,
　While endless ages run.

96

HARK! the glad sound! the Saviour
　The Saviour promised long: [comes,
Let every heart prepare a throne,
　And every voice a song.

He comes the prisoners to release
　In Satan's bondage held;
The gates of brass before Him burst,
　The iron fetters yield.

He comes from thickest films of vice,
　To clear the mental ray,
And on the eyes oppress'd with night
　To pour celestial day.

He comes the broken heart to bind,
　The bleeding soul to cure:
And with the treasures of His grace
　To enrich the humble poor.

Our glad Hosannas, Prince of Peace,
　Thy welcome shall proclaim;
And heaven's eternal arches ring
　With Thy beloved Name.

CHRISTMAS HYMN.

With angel voices blending, Our joyful songs we raise To sing Messiah's praise, Before Him lowly bending. O Son of Mary! Son of God! We praise Thy Name with one accord; Thou art our true and only Lord, Our ever-blessed Lord.

97

WITH angel voices blending,
   Our joyful songs we raise
To sing Messiah's praise,
Before Him lowly bending.
O Son of Mary! Son of God!
We praise Thy Name with one accord;
Thou art our true and only Lord,
Our ever-blessed Lord.

The shepherds tell His story;
The sages see His star
And hail it from afar,
And haste to give Him glory.
Sweet incense, gold, and myrrh they bring,
And worship Mary's child as King!
Dear Lord, accept our offering—
Our humble offering.

    Now ends the night of sadness,
    Behold the Day-Star gleams!
    With healing in his beams
    Upsprings the Sun of gladness!
    O Sun of righteousness, we pray,
    Chase all the night of sin away,
    Pour forth the noontide light of day—
    The light of perfect day.

JESUS CHRIST OUR LORD.

MEAR. C. M.

What grace, O Lord, and beau-ty shone A-round Thy steps be-low;

What pa-tient love was seen in all Thy life and death of woe.

98

WHAT grace, O Lord, and beauty
  Around Thy steps below; [shone
What patient love was seen in all
  Thy life and death of woe.

For, ever on Thy burdened heart
  A weight of sorrow hung;
Yet no ungentle, murmuring word
  Escaped Thy silent tongue.

Thy foes might hate, despise, revile;
  Thy friends unfaithful prove;
Unwearied in forgiveness still,
  Thy heart could only love.

Oh, give us hearts to love like Thee!
  Like Thee, O Lord, to grieve
Far more for others' sins than all
  The wrongs that we receive.

One with Thyself, may every eye,
  In us, Thy brethren see
The gentleness and grace that spring
  From union, Lord! with Thee.

99

O THOU, who by a star didst guide
  The wise men on their way,
Until it came and stood beside
  The place where Jesus lay;

Although by stars Thou dost not lead
  Thy servants now below,
Thy Holy Spirit, when they need,
  Will show them how to go.

As yet we know Thee but in part
  But still we trust Thy word,
That blessed are the pure in heart,
  For they shall see the Lord.

O Saviour, give us then Thy grace,
  To make us pure in heart,
That we may see Thee face to face
  Hereafter, as Thou art.

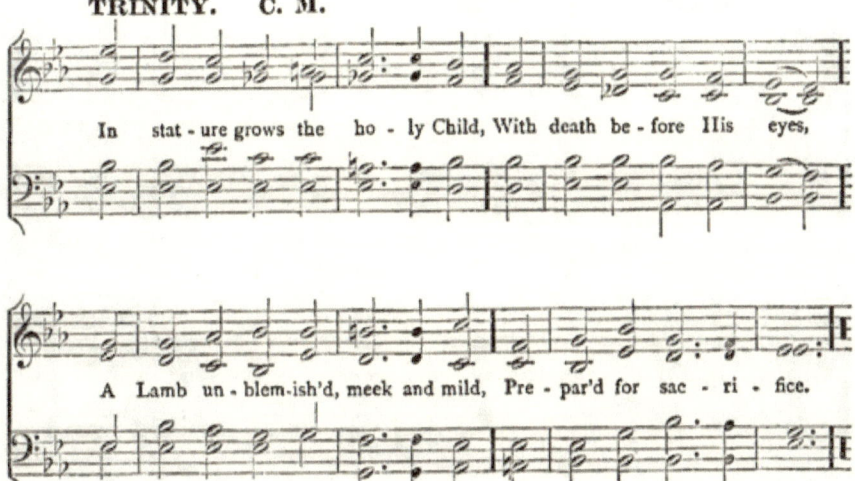

100

IN stature grows the holy Child,
  With death before His eyes,
A Lamb unblemished, meek and mild,
  Prepared for sacrifice.

The Son of God His glory hides,
  With parents meek and poor;
And He who made the heavens, abides
  In dwelling-place obscure.

Those mighty hands that rule the sky
  No earthly toil refuse;
And He who set the stars on high
  A lowly trade pursues.

He whom, as their Almighty Lord,
  The angel-hosts obey,
Now to an earthly parent's word
  Doth meek obedience pay.

O Jesus! by Thy grace incline
  Our hearts Thy steps to trace;
And by Thy lowliness Divine
  Our haughtiness abase.

101

THOU art the Way: to Thee alone
  From sin and death we flee;
And he who would the Father seek,
  Must seek Him, Lord, by Thee.

Thou art the Truth: Thy word alone
  True wisdom can impart;
Thou only canst inform the mind,
  And purify the heart.

Thou art the Life: the rending tomb
  Proclaims Thy conquering arm,
And those who put their trust in Thee
  Nor death, nor hell shall harm.

Thou art the Way, the Truth, the Life;
  Grant us that Way to know,
That Truth to keep, that Life to win,
  Whose joys eternal flow.

JESUS CHRIST OUR LORD.

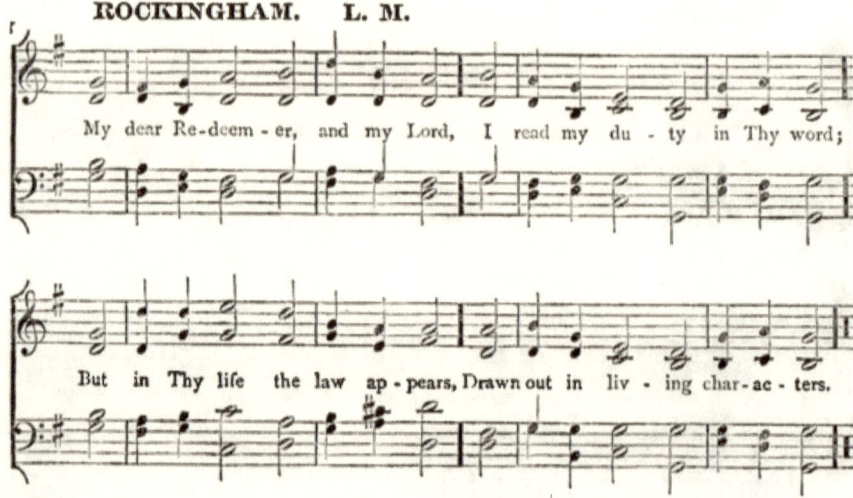

ROCKINGHAM. L. M.

My dear Re-deem-er, and my Lord, I read my du-ty in Thy word;
But in Thy life the law ap-pears, Drawn out in liv-ing char-ac-ters.

102

MY dear Redeemer, and my Lord,
   I read my duty in Thy word;
But in Thy life the law appears,
Drawn out in living characters.

Such was Thy truth, and such Thy zeal,
Such deference to Thy Father's will,
Such love, and meekness so divine,
I would transcribe and make them mine.

Cold mountains and the midnight air
Witnessed the fervor of Thy prayer;
The desert Thy temptations knew,
Thy conflict and Thy victory too.

Be Thou my pattern; make me bear
More of Thy gracious image here;
Then God, the Judge, shall own my name
Among the followers of the Lamb.

103

HOW sweetly flowed the gospel sound
   From lips of gentleness and grace,
When listening thousands gathered round,
And joy and gladness filled the place!

From heaven He came, of heaven He spoke,
To heaven He led His followers' way;
Dark clouds of gloomy night He broke,
Unvailing an immortal day.

"Come, wanderers, to my Father's home,
Come, all ye weary ones, and rest:"
Yes, sacred Teacher, we will come,
Obey Thee, love Thee, and be blest!

Decay then, tenements of dust;
Pillars of earthly pride, decay:
A nobler mansion waits the just,
And Jesus has prepared the way.

    Praise God, from whom all blessings flow!
    Praise Him, all creatures here below!
    Praise Him above, ye heavenly host!
    Praise Father, Son, and Holy Ghost!

FEDERAL STREET. L. M.

O Jesus, crucified for man, O Lamb, all glorious on Thy throne,
Teach Thou our won-d'ring souls to scan The mystery of Thy love unknown.

104

O JESUS, crucified for man,
  O Lamb, all glorious on Thy throne,
Teach Thou our wondering souls to scan
The mystery of Thy love unknown.

We pray Thee, grant us strength to take
Our daily Cross, whate'er it be,
And gladly for Thine own dear sake
In paths of pain to follow Thee.

As on our daily way we go,
Through light or shade, in calm or strife,
Oh, may we bear Thy marks below
In conquered sin and chastened life.

And week by week this day we ask
That holy memories of Thy Cross
May sanctify each common task,
And turn to gain each earthly loss.

Grant us, dear Lord, our Cross to bear
Till at Thy feet we lay it down, [there,
Win through Thy Blood our pardon
And through the Cross attain the Crown.

105

WHEN I survey the wondrous Cross
  On which the Prince of Glory died,
My richest gain I count but loss,
  And pour contempt on all my pride.

Forbid it, Lord, that I should boast,
  Save in the death of Christ my God:
All the vain things that charm me most,
  I sacrifice them to His Blood.

See, from His head, His hands, His feet,
  Sorrow and love flow mingled down!
Did e'er such love and sorrow meet?
  Or thorns compose so rich a crown?

Were the whole realm of nature mine,
  That were a tribute far too small;
Love so amazing, so divine,
  Demands my soul, my life, my all.

JESUS CHRIST OUR LORD.

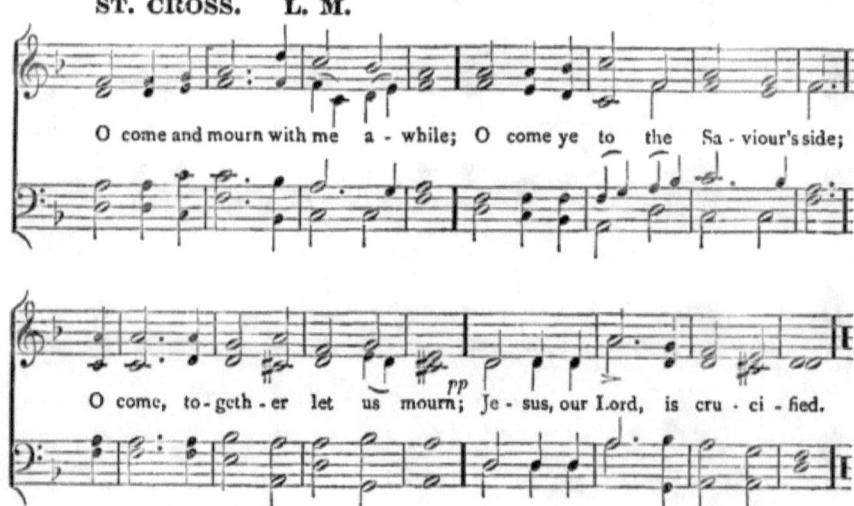

ST. CROSS. L. M.

O come and mourn with me a-while; O come ye to the Sa-viour's side;
O come, to-geth-er let us mourn; Je-sus, our Lord, is cru-ci-fied.

106

O COME and mourn with me awhile;
    O come ye to the Saviour's side;
O come, together let us mourn;
    Jesus, our Lord, is crucified.

Have we no tears to shed for Him,
    While soldiers scoff and Jews deride?
Ah! look how patiently He hangs;
    Jesus, our Lord, is crucified.

Seven times He spake, seven words of love;
    And all three hours His silence cried
For mercy on the souls of men;
    Jesus, our Lord, is crucified.

A broken heart, a fount of tears,
    Ask, and they will not be denied;
Lord Jesus, may we love and weep,
    Since Thou for us art crucified.

107

'TIS midnight,—and, on Olive's brow,
    The star is dimmed that lately shone;
'Tis midnight,—in the garden, now
    The suffering Saviour prays alone.

'Tis midnight,—and, from all removed,
    Immanuel wrestles, lone with fears;
E'en the disciple that He loved
    Heeds not his Master's grief and tears.

'Tis midnight,—and for others' guilt
    The Man of sorrows weeps in blood;
Yet He, who hath in anguish knelt,
    Is not forsaken by His God.

'Tis midnight,—and, from ether-plains,
    Is borne the song that angels know;
Unheard by mortals are the strains,
    That sweetly soothe the Saviour's woe.

LENOX. H. M.

108

ARISE, my soul, arise,
 Shake off thy guilty fears;
The bleeding Sacrifice
 In my behalf appears;
Before the throne my Surety stands:
My name is written on His hands.

He ever lives above,
 For me to intercede,
His all-redeeming love,
 His precious blood to plead;
His blood atoned for all our race,
And sprinkles now the throne of grace.

My God is reconciled;
 His pardoning voice I hear;
He owns me for His child—
 I can no longer fear;
His Spirit answers to the blood,
And tells me "Thou art born of God."

109

BLOW ye the trumpet, blow!
 The gladly solemn sound;
Let all the nations know,
 To earth's remotest bound,
The year of jubilee is come;
Return, ye ransomed sinners, home.

Exalt the Lamb of God,
 The sin-atoning Lamb!
Redemption by His blood,
 Through every land, proclaim:
The year of jubilee is come;
Return, ye ransomed sinners, home.

Jesus, our great High Priest,
 Has full atonement made;
Ye weary spirits, rest;
 Ye mourning souls, be glad;
The year of jubilee is come;
Return, ye ransomed sinners, home.

DAY-SPRING. S. M.

Not all the blood of beasts, On Jewish altars slain, Could give the guilty conscience peace, Or wash away the stain.

110

NOT all the blood of beasts,
  On Jewish altars slain,
Could give the guilty conscience peace,
  Or wash away the stain.

But Christ, the heavenly Lamb,
  Takes all our sins away—
A sacrifice of nobler name,
  And richer blood than they.

My faith would lay her hand
  On that dear head of Thine,
While like a penitent I stand,
  And there confess my sin.

My soul looks back to see
  The burdens Thou didst bear
When hanging on the cursed tree,
  And hopes her guilt was there.

Believing, we rejoice
  To see the curse remove;
We bless the Lamb with cheerful voice,
  And sing His bleeding love.

111

TO Christ, the Prince of peace,
  Our Saviour and our King,
The Father of the age to come,
  With holy joy we sing.

Deep in His heart for us
  The wound of love He bore;—
That love which still He kindles in
  The hearts which Him adore.

O Jesus, Victim blest!
  What else but love divine,
Could Thee constrain to open thus
  That sacred heart of Thine?

O Fount of endless life!
  O Spring of waters clear!
O Flame celestial, cleansing all
  Who unto Thee draw near!

Hide us in Thy dear heart,
  For thither do we fly;   [death,
There seek Thy grace thro' life, thro'
  Thine immortality.

CALVARY. 7, 6, 8, 7.

1. Je-sus, Name all names a-bove, Je-sus, best and dear-est,
Je-sus, Fount of per-fect love, Ho-liest, ten-d'rest, near-est;
Je-sus, Source of grace com-plet-est, Je-sus pur-est, Je-sus sweet-est,
Je-sus, Well of pow'r di-vine, Make me, seal me, keep me Thine.

112

2.
JESUS, open me the gate
   Which the sinner entered,
Who, in his last dying state,
   Wholly on Thee ventured;
Thou, whose wounds are ever pleading,
And Thy Passion interceding,
   From my misery let me rise
   To a home in Paradise.

3.
Jesus, crowned with thorns for me,
   Scourged for my transgression,
Witnessing, in agony,
   That Thy good confession;
Jesus, clad in purple raiment,
For my evil making payment,
   Let not all Thy woe and pain,
   Let not Calvary, be in vain.

OLMUTZ. S. M.

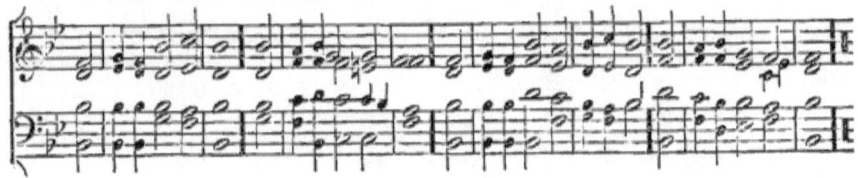

JESUS CHRIST OUR LORD.

O SACRED HEAD. 7s & 6s.

O sa-cred Head, now wound-ed, With grief and shame bow'd down, Now scorn-ful-ly sur-round-ed With thorns, Thine on-ly crown. O sa-cred Head, what glo-ry, What bliss till now was Thine! Yet, tho' de-spised and go-ry, I joy to call Thee mine.

113

O SACRED Head, now wounded,
   With grief and shame bowed down,
Now scornfully surrounded
   With thorns, Thine only crown.
O sacred Head, what glory,
   What bliss till now was Thine!
Yet, though despised and gory,
   I joy to call Thee mine.

What Thou, my Lord, hast suffered,
   Was all for sinners' gain:
Mine, mine was the transgression,
   But Thine the deadly pain.
Lo, here I fall, my Saviour:
   'Tis I deserve Thy place;
Look on me with Thy favor,
   Vouchsafe to me Thy grace.

What language shall I borrow
   To thank Thee, dearest Friend,
For this Thy dying sorrow,
   Thy pity without end?
O make me Thine for ever;
   And should I fainting be,
Lord, let me never, never
   Outlive my love for Thee.

Be near me when I'm dying,
   O show Thy Cross to me:
And to my succor flying,
   Come, Lord, and set me free.
These eyes, new faith receiving,
   From Jesus shall not move;
For he who dies believing,
   Dies safely through Thy love.

GERMANIA. 7s & 6s.

114

O JESUS, our Salvation,
  Low at Thy cross we lie;
Lord, in Thy great compassion,
  Hear our bewailing cry.
We come to Thee with mourning
  We come to Thee in woe;
With contrite hearts returning,
  And tears that overflow.

O gracious Intercessor,
  O Priest within the veil,
Plead, for each lost transgressor,
  The blood that cannot fail.
We spread our sins before Thee,
  We tell them one by one;
O for Thy Name's great glory,
  Forgive all we have done.

O by Thy cross and passion,
  Thy tears and agony,
And crown of cruel fashion,
  And death on Calvary;
By all that untold suffering
  Endured by Thee alone;
O Priest, O spotless offering,
  Plead for us, and atone.

And in these hearts now broken
  Re-enter Thou and reign;
And say, by that dear token,
  We are absolved again.
And build us up, and guide us,
  And guard us day by day;
And in Thy presence hide us,
  And take our sins away.

JESUS CHRIST OUR LORD.

BEHOLD THE LAMB. 6s, 4s & 8s.

Be-hold the Lamb of God! O Thou for sin-ners slain, Let it not be in vain That Thou hast died: Thee for my Sa-viour let me take, My on-ly ref-uge let me make Thy pierc-ed side.

115

BEHOLD the Lamb of God!
 O Thou for sinners slain,
Let it not be in vain
  That Thou hast died:
Thee for my Saviour let me take,
My only refuge let me make
  Thy pierced side.

Behold the Lamb of God!
Into the sacred flood
Of Thy most precious blood
  My soul I cast:
Wash me and make me clean within,
And keep me pure from every sin,
  Till life be past.

Behold the Lamb of God!
All hail, Incarnate Word,
Thou everlasting Lord,
  Saviour most blest;
Fill us with love that never faints,
Grant us with all Thy blessed saints
  Eternal rest.

Behold the Lamb of God!
Worthy is He alone,
That sitteth on the throne
  Of God above;
One with the Ancient of all days,
One with the Comforter in praise,
  All Light and Love.

ARDEN. C. M.

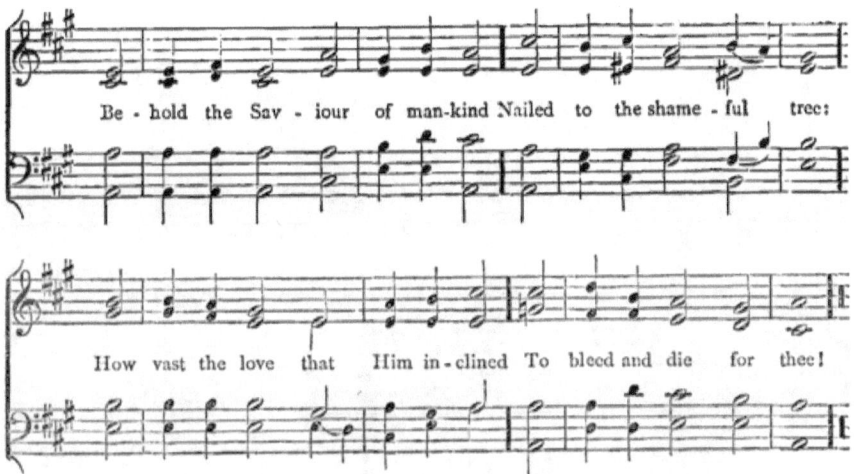

116

BEHOLD the Saviour of mankind
  Nailed to the shameful tree :
How vast the love that Him inclined
  To bleed and die for thee !

Though far unequal our low praise
  To Thy vast sufferings prove,
O Lamb of God, through all our days,
  Thus will we grieve and love.

'Tis done ; the precious ransom's paid ;
  "Receive my soul," He cries !
See where He bows His sacred head,
  He bows His head and dies !

But soon He'll break death's iron chain,
  And in full glory shine !
O Lamb of God, was ever pain,
  Was ever love like Thine ?

Thy loss our ruin did repair ;
  Death by Thy death is slain ;
Thou wilt at length exalt us where
  Thou dost in glory reign.

117

BEHOLD the glories of the Lamb
  Amid His Father's throne :
Prepare new honors for His Name,
  And songs before unknown.

Let elders worship at His feet,
  The Church adore around,
With vials full of odors sweet,
  And harps of sweeter sound.

Now to the Lamb that once was slain
  Be endless blessings paid ;
Salvation, glory, joy remain
  Forever on Thy head.

Thou hast redeemed our souls with blood,
  Hast set the prisoners free,
Hast made us kings and priests to God,
  And we shall reign with Thee.

All glory to the Father be,
  All glory to the Son,
All glory to the Holy Ghost,
  While endless ages run.

JESUS CHRIST OUR LORD.

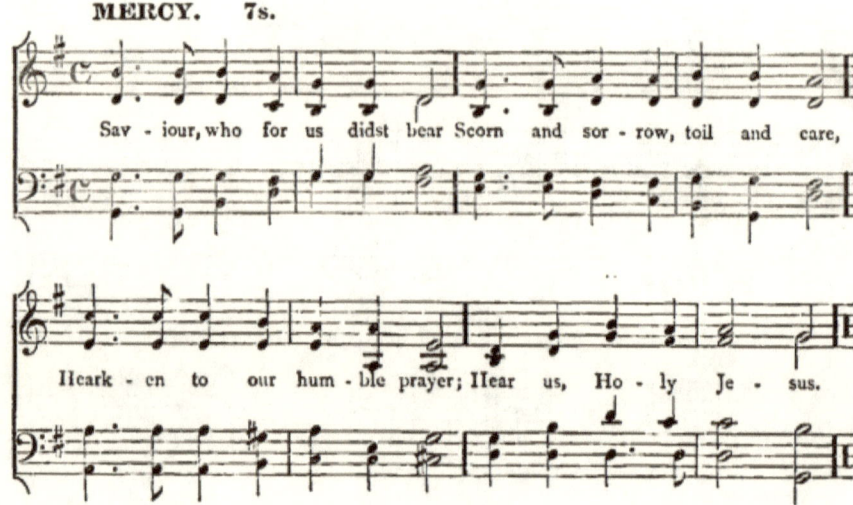

MERCY. 7s.

Sav-iour, who for us didst bear Scorn and sor-row, toil and care, Hark-en to our hum-ble prayer; Hear us, Ho-ly Je-sus.

118

SAVIOUR, who for us didst bear
   Scorn and sorrow, toil and care,
Hearken to our humble prayer;
   Hear us, Holy Jesus.

By Thy feeble childhood's tears,
By Thy growing manhood's fears,
By the grief of all Thy years;
   Hear us, Holy Jesus.

By Thy heart so calm and brave,
By Thy firm resolve to save,
By Thy triumph o'er the grave;
   Hear us, Holy Jesus.

By the scourging Thou hast borne,
By the purple robe of scorn,
By the reed and crown of thorn;
   Hear us, Holy Jesus.

Be Thou near us, Lord, we pray,
Turn our darkness into day,
Help us on the heavenward way;
   Hear us, Holy Jesus.

119

JESUS, Prince of life and light,
   Dwelling now in glory bright,
Ruling all things by Thy might;
   Hear us, Holy Jesus.

Jesus, evermore the same,
Who didst take our mortal frame,
Who didst die the death of shame;
   Hear us, Holy Jesus.

That unto Thy saints who pine,
Longing to be wholly Thine,
Thou wouldst send Thy power divine;
   Hear us, Holy Jesus.

That in mercy Thou wouldst come,
Seeking those who careless roam,
Bringing wanderers safely home;
   Hear us, Holy Jesus.

That when earthly toil is o'er,
We, in rest forevermore,
May enjoy Thee and adore;
   Hear us, Holy Jesus.

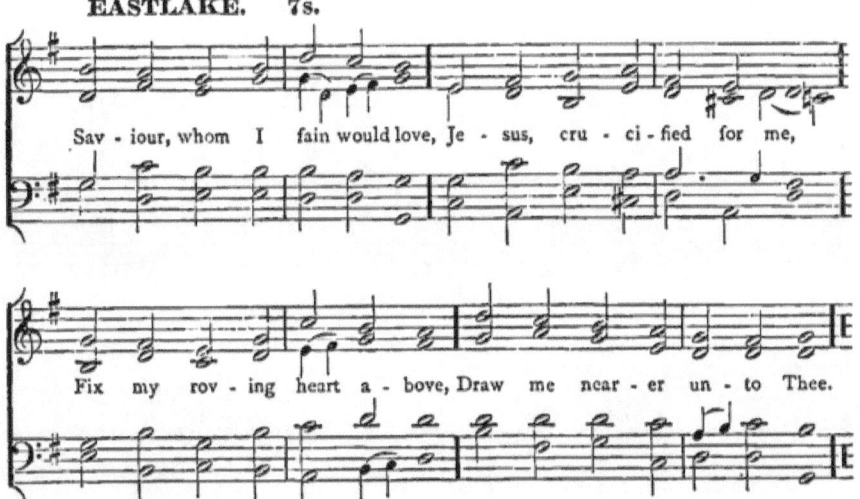

EASTLAKE. 7s.

Sav-iour, whom I fain would love, Je-sus, cru-ci-fied for me, Fix my rov-ing heart a-bove, Draw me near-er un-to Thee.

120

SAVIOUR, whom I fain would love,
Jesus, crucified for me,
Fix my roving heart above,
Draw me nearer unto Thee.

Thee to praise and Thee to know,
Make the joy of saints below:
Thee to see and Thee to love,
Make the bliss of saints above.

Lord, it is not life to live,
If Thy presence Thou deny:
Lord, if Thou Thy presence give,
'Tis no longer death to die.

Source and Giver of repose,
Only from Thy love it flows;
Peace and happiness are Thine,
Mine they are if Thou art mine.

121

THINE forever! God of love,
Hear us from Thy throne above:
Thine forever may we be
Here and in eternity.

Thine forever! Oh, how blest
They who find in Thee their rest!
Saviour, Guardian, heavenly Friend,
Oh, defend us to the end!

Thine forever! Saviour, keep
These Thy frail and trembling sheep;
Safe alone beneath Thy care,
Let us all Thy goodness share.

Thine forever! Thou our Guide,
All our wants by Thee supplied,
All our sins by Thee forgiven,
Lead us, Lord, from earth to heaven.

Holy Father! Holy Son!
Holy Spirit! Three in One!
Praise and glory be to Thee,
Now, and through eternity.

JESUS CHRIST OUR LORD.

REDHEAD. 7s. 6 lines.

Si-on's daughter, weep no more, Tho' thy troubled heart be sore;
He of whom the Psalmist sung, He who woke the Prophet's tongue,—
Christ, the Mediator blest, Brings thee everlasting rest.

122

SION'S daughter, weep no more,
  Though thy troubled heart be sore;
He of whom the Psalmist sung,
He who woke the Prophet's tongue,—
Christ, the Mediator blest,—
Brings thee everlasting rest.

In a garden man became
Heir of sin and death and shame;
Jesus in a garden wins
Life and pardon for our sins;
Through His hour of agony,
Praying in Gethsemane.

There for us He intercedes;
There with God the Father pleads;
Willing there for us to drain
To the dregs the cup of pain,
That, in everlasting day,
He may wipe our tears away.

Therefore to His Name be given
Glory, both in earth and heaven;
To the Father, and the Son,
And the Spirit, Three in One,
Honor, praise, and glory be,
Now, and through eternity.

123. LITANY OF THE SAVIOUR.

Ho-ly Sa-viour, from Thy throne, Hear us, we be-seech Thee.

Thou of God and man the Son, Hear us, we be-seech Thee.

Faster.

By Thy wondrous in-car-na-tion, By Thy birth for our sal-va-tion;
By Thy fast-ing and temp-ta-tion, By Thy life and sup-pli-ca-tion;
By Thy works of sweet compas-sion, By Thy cross and bit-ter pas-sion;
By Thy glorious res-ur-rec-tion, Ear-nest of our own per-fec-tion;

We be-seech Thee, O Je-sus, hear our prayer. From ev-'ry ill de-fend us;
Thy grace and mer-cy send us; Thy grace and mer-cy send us. A-men.

JESUS CHRIST OUR LORD.

GARDNER. 8s & 7s.

In the cross of Christ I glo-ry, Tow'r-ing o'er the wrecks of time;
All the light of sa-cred sto-ry Gath-ers round its head sub-lime.

124

IN the cross of Christ I glory,
　　Towering o'er the wrecks of time;
All the light of sacred story
　　Gathers round its head sublime.

When the woes of life o'ertake me,
　　Hopes deceive, and fears annoy,
Never shall the cross forsake me:
　　Lo! it glows with peace and joy.

When the sun of bliss is beaming
　　Light and love upon my way,
From the cross the radiance streaming,
　　Adds new lustre to the day.

Bane and blessing, pain and pleasure,
　　By the cross are sanctified;
Peace is there, that knows no measure,
　　Joys that through all time abide.

In the cross of Christ I glory,
　　Towering o'er the wrecks of time;
All the light of sacred story
　　Gathers round its head sublime.

125

CROWN His head with endless blessing,
　　Who, in God the Father's Name,
With compassions never ceasing,
　　Comes salvation to proclaim.

Lo! Jehovah, we adore Thee;
　　Thee, our Saviour; Thee, our God!
From His throne His beams of glory
　　Shine through all the world abroad.

Jesus, Thee our Saviour hailing,
　　Thee, our God, in praise we own;
Highest honors, never failing,
　　Rise eternal round Thy throne.

Now, ye saints, His power confessing,
　　In your grateful strains adore;
For His mercy, never ceasing,
　　Flows and flows forevermore.

Praise the Father, earth and heaven,
　　Praise the Son, the Spirit praise;
As it was, and is, be given
　　Glory through eternal days.

126

All ye that are weary, 'tis Jesus who calls you,
  O come to the Saviour, and rest in His love:
Though dark be the fortune on earth that befalls you,
  There's glory eternal with Jesus above.

Come humbly to Jesus, and tell Him your story
  Of suffering or sorrow, of guilt or of shame:
The pardon of sins is the crown of His glory,
  The joy of our Lord to be true to His Name.

Come trusting in Jesus, His arms are extended
  To fold you forever in fondest embrace;
O come, for your exile will shortly be ended,
  And Jesus will show you His beautiful face.

Then come to the Saviour; His mercy shines brighter
  The longer you look in the depth of His love;
Life's trials and burdens and cares shall grow lighter,
  While thinking of Jesus and glory above.

JESUS CHRIST OUR LORD.

DUKE ST. L. M.

Hail to the Prince of life and peace, Who holds the keys of death and hell,

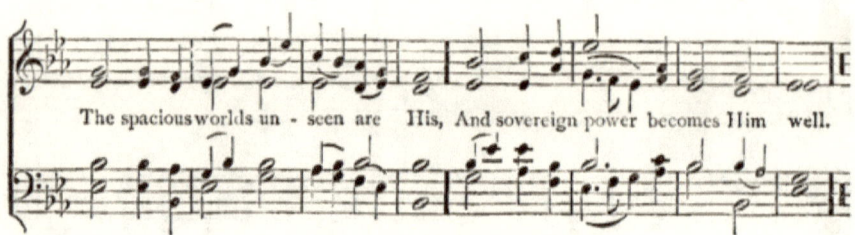

The spacious worlds unseen are His, And sovereign power becomes Him well.

127

Hail to the Prince of life and peace,
Who holds the keys of death and hell,
The spacious worlds unseen are His,
And sovereign power becomes Him well.

In shame and anguish once He died,
But now He lives forevermore:
Bow down, ye saints, around His seat,
And, all ye angel-bands, adore.

So live forever, glorious Lord,
To crush Thy foes and guard thy friends;
While all Thy chosen ones rejoice
That Thy dominion never ends.

Forever reign, victorious King!
Wide through the earth Thy Name be known;
Oh! call our longing souls to sing
Sublimer anthems round Thy throne.

128

Come, let us sing the song of songs—
The saints in heaven began the strain—
The homage which to Christ belongs:
"Worthy the Lamb, for He was slain!"

Slain to redeem us by His blood,
To cleanse from every sinful stain,
And make us kings and priests to God—
"Worthy the Lamb, for He was slain!"

To Him, enthroned by filial right,
All power in heaven and earth proclaim,
Honor, and majesty, and might:
"Worthy the Lamb, for He was slain!"

Long as we live, and when we die,
And while in heaven with Him we reign;
This song, our song of songs shall be:
"Worthy the Lamb, for He was slain!"

Glory to Thee, O God most high!
Father, we praise Thy majesty!
The Son, the Spirit, we adore,
One Godhead, blest forevermore!

RESURRECTION. 7s & 6s.

1. The day of Resurrection! Earth, tell it out abroad; The Passover of gladness, The Passover of God. From death to life eternal, From this world to the sky, Our Christ hath brought us o'er With hymns of victory.

129

2.
Our hearts be pure from evil,
 That we may see aright
The Lord in rays eternal
 Of resurrection-light;
And, listening to His accents,
 May hear, so calm and plain,
His own "All hail!" and, hearing,
 May raise the victor-strain.

3.
Now let the heavens be joyful!
 Let earth her song begin!
Let the round world keep triumph,
 And all there is therein!
Invisible and visible,
 Their notes let all things blend,
For Christ the Lord hath risen,
 Our Joy that hath no end.

130 L. M. Duke St.

OUR Lord is risen from the dead;
 Our Jesus is gone up on high;
The powers of hell are captive led,
 Dragged to the portals of the sky.

There His triumphal chariot waits,
 And angels chant the solemn lay:—
"Lift up your heads, ye heavenly gates,
 Ye everlasting doors, give way!"

Loose all your bars of massy light,
 And wide unfold th' ethereal scene;
He claims these mansions as His right;
 Receive the King of glory in.

Who is the King of glory, who?
 The Lord that all His foes o'ercame;
That sin and death and hell o'erthrew;
 And Jesus is the conqueror's name.

ABBEY. C. M.

131

THE golden gates are lifted up,
  The doors are opened wide,
The King of glory is gone in
  Unto His Father's side.

Thou art gone up before us, Lord,
  To make for us a place,
That we may be where now Thou art,
  And look upon God's face.

And ever on Thine earthly path
  A gleam of glory lies;
A light still breaks behind the cloud
  That veils Thee from our eyes.

Lift up our hearts, lift up our minds,
  Let Thy dear grace be given,
That while we tarry here below,
  Our treasure be in heaven!

That where Thou art, at God's right
  Our hope, our love may be, [hand,
Dwell Thou in us, that we may dwell
  For evermore in Thee!

132

O CHRIST, our Hope, our heart's De-
  Redemption's only Spring! [sire,
Creator of the world Thou art,
  Its Saviour and its King!

How vast the mercy and the love
  Which laid our sins on Thee,
And led Thee to a cruel death,
  To set Thy people free.

But now the bands of death are burst;
  The ransom has been paid,
And Thou art on the Father's throne,
  In glorious robes arrayed.

Oh, may Thy mighty love prevail,
  Our sinful souls to spare!
Oh, may we come before Thy throne
  And find acceptance there.

O Christ! be Thou our present Joy,
  Our future great Reward:
Our only glory may it be
  To glory in the Lord.

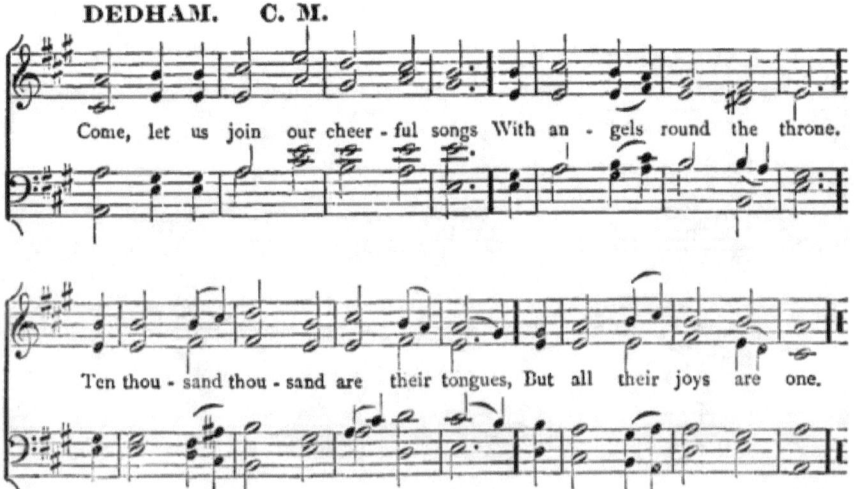

133

COME, let us join our cheerful songs
  With angels round the throne.
Ten thousand thousand are their tongues,
  But all their joys are one.

"Worthy the Lamb that died," they cry,
  "To be exalted thus:"
"Worthy the Lamb," our lips reply,
  For He was slain for us.

Jesus is worthy to receive
  Honor and power divine:
And blessings more than we can give,
  Be, Lord, forever Thine.

Let all that dwell above the sky,
  And air, and earth, and seas,
Conspire to lift Thy glories high,
  And speak Thine endless praise!

The whole creation join in one,
  To bless the sacred Name
Of Him that sits upon the throne,
  And to adore the Lamb.

134

THE head that once was crowned with
    thorns
  Is crowned with glory now;
A royal diadem adorns
  The mighty Victor's brow.

The highest place that heaven affords
  Is His by sovereign right;
The King of kings, and Lord of lords,
  He reigns in glory bright.

Jesus, the joy of all above!
  The joy of all below,
To whom He manifests His love,
  And grants His name to know.

To them the cross, with all its shame,
  With all its grace is given;
Their name—an everlasting name,
  Their joy—the joy of heaven.

To them the cross is life and health,
  Though shame and death to Him:
His people's hope, His people's wealth,
  Their everlasting theme.

LANCASTER. C. M.

Ye choirs of New Je-ru-sa-lem, Your sweet-est notes em-ploy,
The Pas-chal vic-to-ry to hymn In strains of ho-ly joy:

135

Ye choirs of New Jerusalem,
  Your sweetest notes employ,
The Paschal victory to hymn
  In strains of holy joy:

How Judah's Lion burst His chains,
  And bruised the serpent's head;
And cried aloud, thro' death's domains,
  To wake th' imprisoned dead.

Right gloriously He triumphs now;
  To Him all power is given;
To Him in one communion bow
  All saints in earth and heaven.

And we, as these His deeds we sing,
  His soldiers, Him implore,
Within His palace bright to bring
  And keep us evermore.

CORONATION. C. M.
FIRST TUNE.

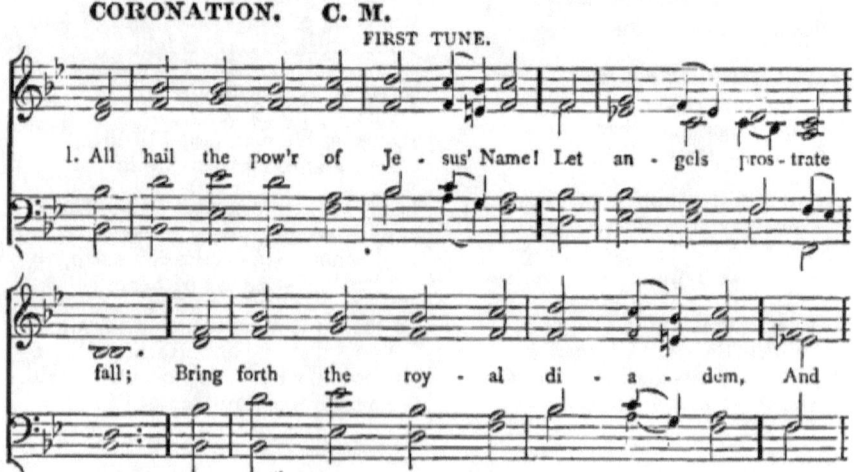

1. All hail the pow'r of Je-sus' Name! Let an-gels pros-trate fall; Bring forth the roy-al di-a-dem, And

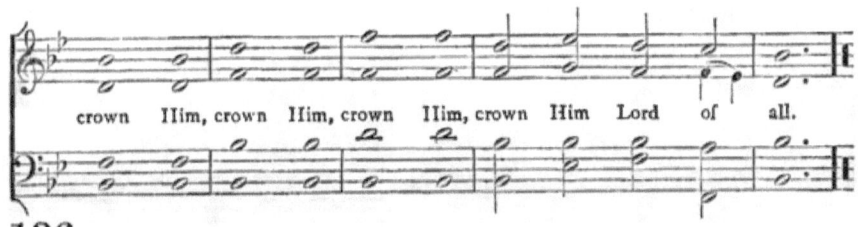

crown Him, crown Him, crown Him, crown Him Lord of all.

136

2.
Crown Him, ye martyrs of our God,
  Who from His altar call;
Extol the Stem of Jesse's rod,
  And crown Him Lord of all.

3.
Ye seed of Israel's chosen race,
  Ye ransomed of the fall,
Hail Him who saves you by His grace,
  And crown Him Lord of all.

4.
Sinners, whose love can ne'er forget
  The wormwood and the gall,
Go, spread your trophies at His feet,
  And crown Him Lord of all.

5.
Let every kindred, every tribe,
  On this terrestrial ball,
To Him all Majesty ascribe,
  And crown Him Lord of all.

CORONATION. C. M.

SECOND TUNE.

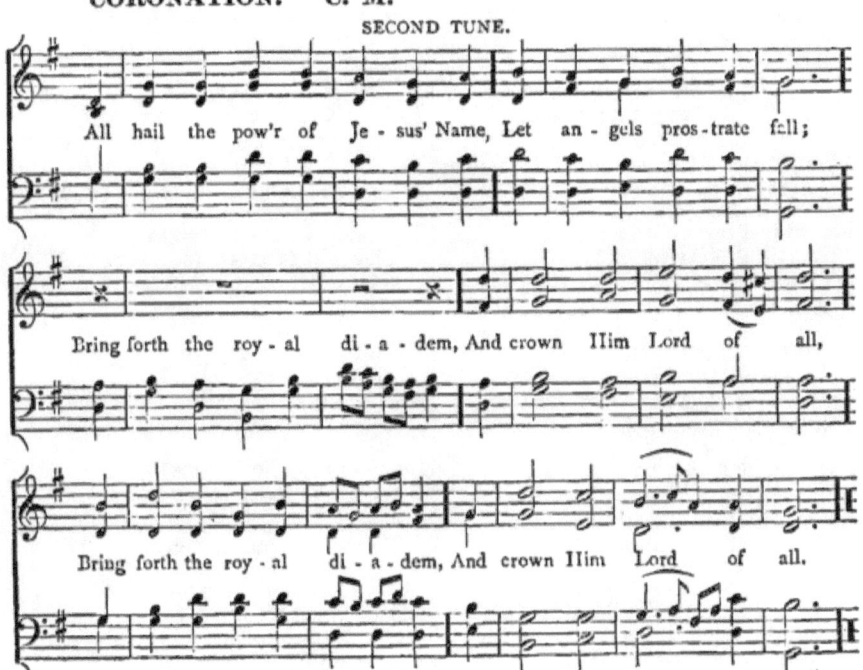

All hail the pow'r of Je-sus' Name, Let an-gels pros-trate fall; Bring forth the roy-al di-a-dem, And crown Him Lord of all, Bring forth the roy-al di-a-dem, And crown Him Lord of all.

JESUS CHRIST OUR LORD.

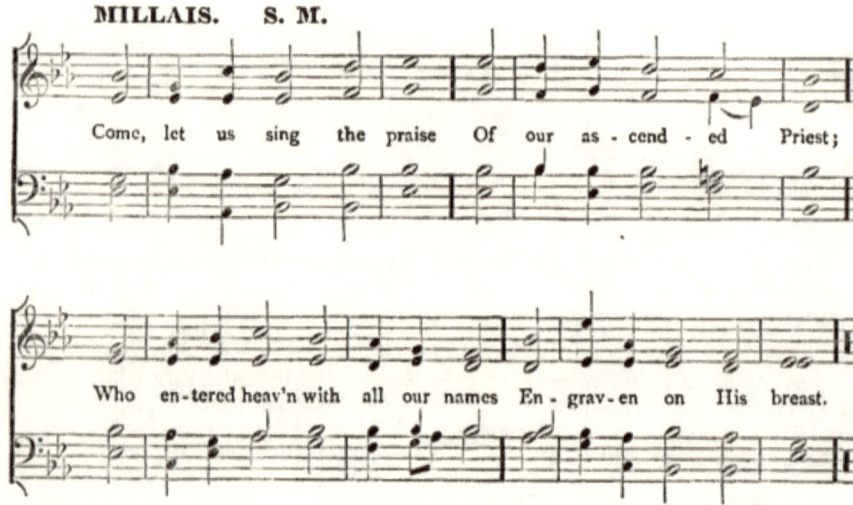

137

COME, let us sing the praise
   Of our ascended Priest;
Who entered heaven with all our names
   Engraven on His breast.

He washed our guilt away
   In His atoning blood;
And now He stands before the throne,
   And pleads our cause with God.

Clothed with our nature still,
   He knows our feeble frame;
And how to shield us from the foes
   Whom He, on earth, o'ercame.

Nor time nor distance quench
   The fervor of His love:
For us He died on Calvary,
   For us He lives above.

Jesus! we own Thy grace;
   We joy to bear Thy Name;
Our hearts shall ever hold Thy faith,
   Our lips Thy praise proclaim.

138

REJOICE! the Lord is King!
   Your Lord and King adore;
Ye ransomed saints, give thanks and sing,
   And triumph evermore.

The mighty Saviour reigns,
   The God of truth and love;
When He Himself had purged our stain,
   He took His seat above.

He sits at God's right hand,
   Till all His foes submit,
And humbly bow at His command,
   And fall beneath His feet.

Rejoice in glorious hope!
   Jesus, the Judge, shall come,
And take His waiting servants up
   To their eternal home.

The Father and the Son,
   And Spirit we adore;
We praise, we bless, we worship Thee,
   Both now and evermore.

MONKLAND. 7s.

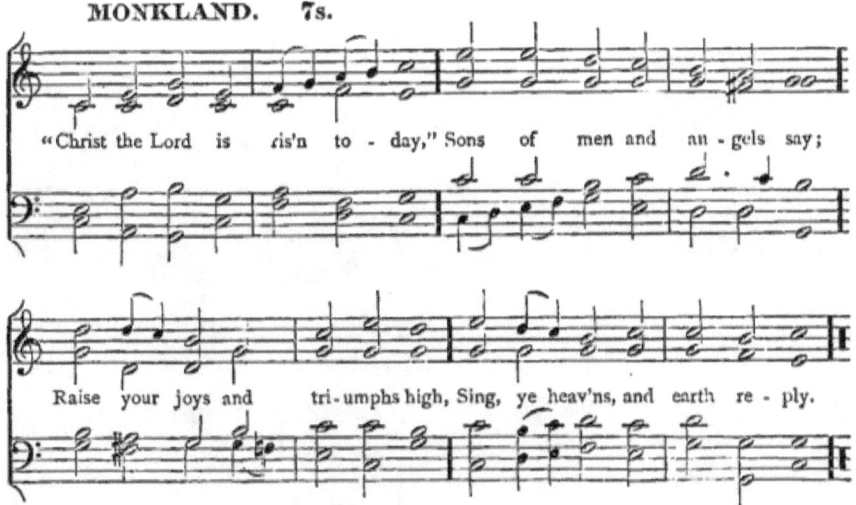

"Christ the Lord is ris'n to-day," Sons of men and an-gels say;
Raise your joys and tri-umphs high, Sing, ye heav'ns, and earth re-ply.

139

"CHRIST the Lord is risen to-day,"
  Sons of men and angels say;
Raise your joys and triumphs high,
Sing, ye heavens, and earth reply.

Love's redeeming work is done,
Fought the fight, the battle won;
Lo, the sun's eclipse is o'er;
Lo, he sets in blood no more.

Vain the stone, the watch, the seal;
Christ hath burst the gates of hell!
Death in vain forbids His rise;
Christ hath opened Paradise!

Lives again our glorious King;
"Where, O death, is now thy sting?"
Once He died, our souls to save;
"Where's thy victory, boasting grave?"

Hail, the Lord of earth and heaven!
Praise to Thee by both be given!
Thee we greet triumphant now;
Hail! the resurrection, Thou!

140

SONGS of praise the angels sang,
  Heaven with hallelujahs rang,
When Jehovah's work begun,
When He spake, and it was done.

Songs of praise awoke the morn
When the Prince of Peace was born;
Songs of praise arose, when He
Captive led captivity.

Heaven and earth must pass away,
Songs of praise shall crown that day;
God will make new heavens and earth,
Songs of praise shall hail their birth.

Saints below, with heart and voice,
Still in songs of praise rejoice;
Learning here, by faith and love,
Songs of praise to sing above.

Borne upon their latest breath,
Songs of praise shall conquer death;
Then, amid eternal joy,
Songs of praise their powers employ.

JESUS CHRIST OUR LORD.

EIN' FESTE BURG. P. M.

1. Lift up your heads, e-ter-nal gates; Ye ev-er-last-ing doors, give way;
The King, the King of glo-ry comes, As-cend-ing to His throne to-day!
Who is the King of glo-ry? Who is the King of glo-ry? It is the
Lord of might, The Vic-tor in the fight, Triumphant o'er the pow'rs of night!

141

2
Lift up your heads, eternal gates:
Ye gates of pearl, and streets of gold;
The King, the King of glory comes;
Before His chariot-wheels unfold!
   Who is the King of glory?
   Who is the King of glory?
     The Lord of Hosts is He,
     The God of Majesty,
He is the King eternally!

3
Now with the Father, God most high,
And with the Spirit, ever one,
The angels own the Christ, the King,
And bow before His shining throne.
   He is the King of glory!
   He is the King of glory!
     Him let all earth adore;
     To Him our praises pour,
Forever and forevermore!

EDOM. 8s & 7s.

142

WHO is this that comes from Edom
  All His raiment stained with blood,
To the captive speaking freedom,
  Bringing and bestowing good?
Glorious is the garb He wears,
Glorious is the spoil He bears.

'Tis the Saviour, now victorious,
  Travelling onward in His might;
'Tis the Saviour: Oh! how glorious
  To His people is the sight!
Satan conquered and the grave;
Jesus now is strong to save.

This the Saviour has effected
  By His mighty arm alone.
See the throne for Him erected;
  'Tis an everlasting throne.
'Tis the great reward He gains,
Glorious fruit of all His pains.

Mighty Victor! reign for ever;
  Wear the crown so dearly won:
Never shall Thy people, never,
  Cease to sing what Thou hast done.
Thou hast fought Thy people's foes,
Thou hast healed Thy people's woes.

HARWELL. 8s & 7s.

1. Hark! ten thousand harps and voices Sound the note of praise above;
Jesus reigns, and heav'n rejoices; Jesus reigns, the God of love:
See, He sits on yonder throne; Jesus rules the world alone.
Hallelujah! hallelujah! hallelujah! Amen.

143

2
King of glory! reign forever—
　Thine an everlasting crown;
Nothing, from Thy love, shall sever
　Those whom Thou hast made Thine own;—
Happy objects of Thy grace,
Destined to behold Thy face.

3
Saviour! hasten Thine appearing;
　Bring, oh, bring the glorious day,
When the awful summons hearing,
　Heaven and earth shall pass away;—
Then, with golden harps we'll sing,—
"Glory, glory to our King!"

144

HOLY Spirit! Lord of light!
From Thy clear celestial height,
Thy pure beaming radiance give.
Come, Thou Father of the poor!
Come, with treasures which endure!
Come, Thou Light of all that live!

Thou of all consolers best,
Visiting the troubled breast,
Dost refreshing peace bestow;
Thou in toil art comfort sweet,
Pleasant coolness in the heat,
Solace in the midst of woe.

Light immortal! Light divine!
Visit Thou these hearts of Thine,
And our inmost being fill:
If Thou take Thy grace away,
Nothing pure in man will stay;
All his good is turned to ill.

Thou, on those who evermore
Thee confess, and Thee adore,
In Thy sevenfold gifts, descend;
Give them comfort when they die;
Give them life with Thee on high;
Give them joys which never end.

THE HOLY GHOST.

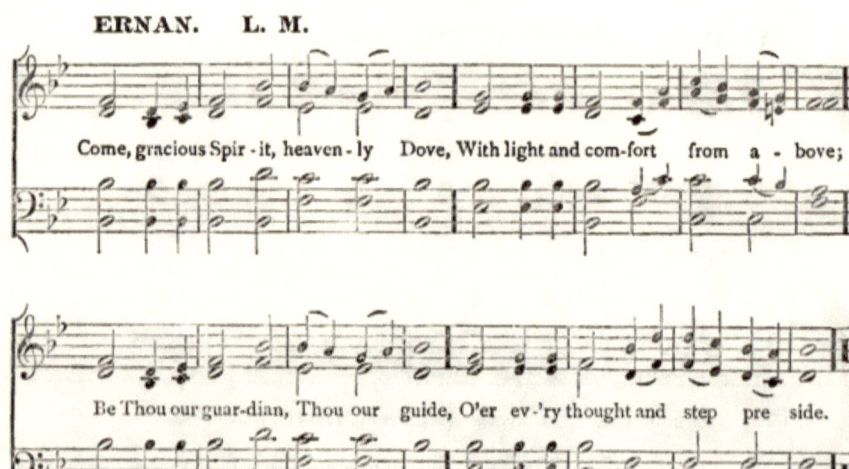

ERNAN. L. M.

Come, gracious Spirit, heavenly Dove, With light and comfort from above;
Be Thou our guardian, Thou our guide, O'er ev'ry thought and step preside.

145

COME, gracious Spirit, heavenly Dove,
With light and comfort from above;
Be Thou our guardian, Thou our guide,
O'er every thought and step preside.

The light of truth to us display,
And make us know and choose Thy way;
Plant holy fear in every heart,
That we from God may ne'er depart.

Lead us to holiness—the road
Which we must take to dwell with God;
Lead us to Christ, the living way,
Nor let us from His pastures stray.

Lead us to God, our final rest,
To be with Him forever blest;
Lead us to heaven, its bliss to share—
Fullness of joy forever there!

146

ETERNAL Spirit, we confess
And sing the wonders of Thy grace;
Thy power conveys our blessings down
From God the Father and the Son.

Enlightened by Thy heavenly ray,
Our shades and darkness turn to day,
Thine inward teachings make us know
Our danger, and our refuge, too.

Thy power and glory work within,
And break the chains of reigning sin;
All our imperious lusts subdue,
And form our wretched hearts anew.

The troubled conscience knows Thy voice
Thy cheering words awake our joys;
Thy words allay the stormy wind,
And calm the surges of the mind.

To God the Father, God the Son,
And God the Spirit, Three in One,
Be honor, praise, and glory given,
By all on earth, and all in heaven!

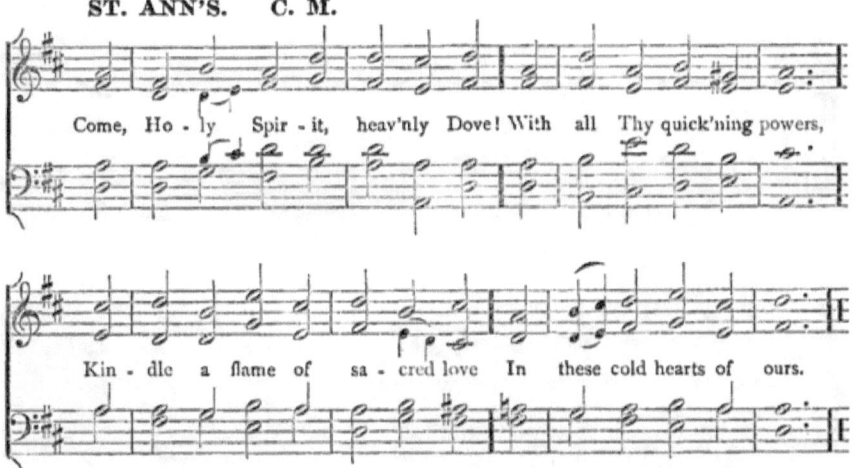

147

COME, Holy Spirit, heavenly Dove!
  With all Thy quickening powers,
Kindle a flame of sacred love
  In these cold hearts of ours.

Dear Lord, and shall we ever live
  At this poor, dying rate—
Our love so faint, so cold to Thee,
  And Thine to us so great?

Come, Holy Spirit, heavenly Dove!
  With all Thy quickening powers;
Come shed abroad a Saviour's love,
  And that shall kindle ours.

148

SPIRIT Divine! attend our prayer,
  And make our hearts Thy home;
Descend with all Thy gracious power;
  Come, Holy Spirit, come!

Come as the light; to us reveal
  Our sinfulness and woe;
And lead us in those paths of life
  Where all the righteous go.

Come as the fire, and purge our hearts,
  Like sacrificial flame:
Let our whole soul an offering be
  To our Redeemer's Name.

Come as the Dove; and spread Thy wings,
  The wings of peaceful love;
And let Thy church on earth become
  Blest as the church above.

149

THOU Holy Spirit, Lord of grace,
  Eternal fount of love,
Inflame, we pray, our inmost hearts
  With fire from heaven above.

As Thou in bond of love dost join
  The Father and the Son,
So fill us all with mutual love,
  And knit our hearts in one.

All glory to the Father be,
  All glory to the Son,
All glory to the Holy Ghost,
  While endless ages run.

THE HOLY GHOST.

INVOCATION. 6s & 4s.

Come, Ho-ly Ghost! in love, Shed on us, from above, Thine own bright ray: Divine-ly good Thou art; Thy sacred gifts impart, To gladden each sad heart; Oh, come to-day.

150

COME, Holy Ghost! in love,
  Shed on us, from above,
  Thine own bright ray:
Divinely good Thou art;
Thy sacred gifts impart,
To gladden each sad heart;
  Oh! come to-day!

Come, tenderest Friend, and best,
Our most delightful Guest!
  With soothing power;
Rest, which the weary know;
Shade, 'mid the noontide glow;
Peace, when deep griefs o'erflow;
  Cheer us, this hour!

Come, Light serene! and still
Our inmost bosoms fill;
  Dwell in each breast:
We know no dawn but Thine;
Send forth Thy beams divine,
On our dark souls to shine,
  And make us blest.

Exalt our low desires;
Extinguish passion's fires;
  Heal every wound;
Our stubborn spirits bend;
Our icy coldness end;
Our devious steps attend,
  While heavenward bound.

Come, all the faithful bless;
Let all who Christ confess,
  His praise employ:
Give virtue's rich reward;
Victorious death accord,
And, with our glorious Lord,
  Eternal joy!

AVON. C. M.

Oh for a clos-er walk with God, A calm and heav'n-ly frame, A light to shine up-on the road That leads me to the Lamb.

151

OH for a closer walk with God,
  A calm and heavenly frame,
A light to shine upon the road
  That leads me to the Lamb !

Return, O holy Dove, return,
  Sweet Messenger of rest ;
I hate the sins that made Thee mourn,
  And drove Thee from my breast.

The dearest idol I have known,
  Whate'er that idol be,
Help me to tear it from Thy throne,
  And worship only Thee.

So shall my walk be close with God,
  Calm and serene my frame ;
So purer light shall mark the road
  That leads me to the Lamb.

152

WHY should the children of a King
  Go mourning all their days ?
Great Comforter, descend, and bring
  Some token of Thy grace.

Dost Thou not dwell in all the saints,
  And seal the heirs of heaven ?
When wilt Thou banish my complaints,
  And show my sins forgiven ?

Assure my conscience of her part
  In the Redeemer's blood ;
And bear Thy witness with my heart
  That I am born of God.

Thou art the earnest of His love,
  The pledge of joys to come ;
And Thy soft wings, celestial Dove,
  Will safe convey me home.

Let God the Father, and the Son,
  And Spirit, be adored,
Where there are works to make Him known,
  Or saints to love the Lord !

THE HOLY GHOST.

ST. THOMAS. S. M.

Come, Ho-ly Spir-it, come! Let Thy bright beams a-rise: Dis-pel the sor-row from our minds, The dark-ness from our eyes.

153

COME, Holy Spirit, come!
  Let Thy bright beams arise:
Dispel the sorrow from our minds,
  The darkness from our eyes.

Convince us of our sin;
  Then lead to Jesus' blood,
And to our wondering view reveal
  The secret love of God.

Revive our drooping faith,
  Our doubts and fears remove,
And kindle in our breasts the flame
  Of never-dying love.

'Tis Thine to cleanse the heart,
  To sanctify the soul,
To pour fresh life in every part,
  And new-create the whole.

Dwell, Spirit, in our hearts;
  Our minds from bondage free;
Then shall we know, and praise, and love
  The Father, Son, and Thee.

154

BLEST Comforter Divine,
  Let rays of heavenly love
Amid our gloom and darkness shine,
  And guide our souls above.

Draw with Thy still small voice,
  From every sinful way,
And bid the mourning saint rejoice,
  Though earthly joys decay.

By Thine inspiring breath
  Make every cloud of care,
And e'en the gloomy vale of death,
  A smile of glory wear.

Oh fill Thou every heart,
  With love to all our race;
Great Comforter, to us impart
  These blessings of Thy grace.

The Father and the Son,
  And Spirit we adore;
We praise, we bless, we worship Thee,
  Both now and evermore!

THE HOLY GHOST.

ELYRIA. 7s.

Gracious Spirit, Love divine! Let Thy light within me shine;
All my guilty fears remove, Fill me with Thy heav'nly love.

155

GRACIOUS Spirit, Love divine!
Let Thy light within me shine;
All my guilty fears remove,
Fill me with Thy heavenly love.

Speak Thy pardoning grace to me,
Set the burdened sinner free;
Lead me to the Lamb of God,
Wash me in His precious blood.

Life and peace to me impart,
Seal salvation on my heart;
Breathe Thyself into my breast,—
Earnest of immortal rest.

Let me never from Thee stray,
Keep me in the narrow way;
Fill my soul with joy divine,
Keep me, Lord! forever Thine.

156

HEAVENLY Father, sovereign Lord,
Be Thy glorious Name adored!
Lord, Thy mercies never fail;
Hail, celestial goodness, hail!

Though unworthy, Lord, Thine ear,
Deign our humble songs to hear;
Purer praise we hope to bring,
When around Thy throne we sing.

While on earth ordained to stay,
Guide our footsteps in Thy way,
Till we come to dwell with Thee,
Till we all Thy glory see.

Then, with angel-harps again,
We will wake a nobler strain;
There, in joyful songs of praise,
Our triumphant voices raise.

Sing we to our God above,
Praise eternal as His love;
Praise Him, all ye heavenly host,—
Father, Son, and Holy Ghost.

THE HOLY GHOST.

ST. CUTHBERT.

157

OUR blest Redeemer, ere He breathed
  His tender, last farewell,
A Guide, a Comforter, bequeathed
  With us to dwell.

He came in semblance of a Dove
  With sheltering wings outspread,
The holy balm of peace and love
  On earth to shed.

He came sweet influence to impart,
  A gracious, willing Guest,
While He can find one humble heart
  Wherein to rest.

And His that gentle voice we hear,
  Soft as the breath of even,
That checks each thought, that calms each fear,
  And speaks of heaven.

And every virtue we possess,
  And every victory won,
And every thought of holiness
  Are His alone.

Spirit of purity and grace,
  Our weakness, pitying, see:
O make our hearts Thy dwelling-place,
  And meet for Thee.

TROYTE CHANT.

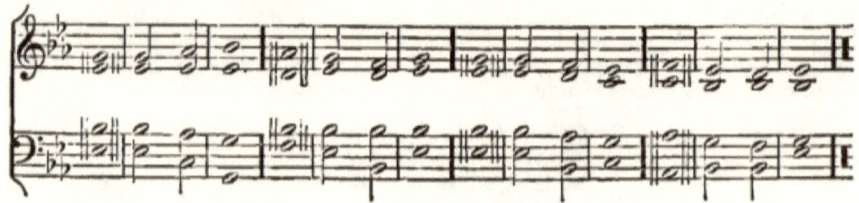

158

COME, Thou Almighty King!
 Help us Thy name to sing,
  Help us to praise.
Father all-glorious,
O'er all victorious,
Come, and reign over us,
  Ancient of days.

Come, Thou Incarnate Word!
Gird on Thy mighty sword,
  Our prayer attend.
Come, and Thy people bless,
And give Thy word success;
Spirit of holiness,
  On us descend.

Come, Holy Comforter!
Thy sacred witness bear,
  In this glad hour.
Thou, who almighty art,
Now rule in every heart,
And ne'er from us depart,
  Spirit of power.

To the great ONE in THREE
The highest praises be,
  Hence evermore!
His sovereign majesty
May we in glory see,
And to eternity,
  Love and adore!

THE CHRISTIAN LIFE.

159

WHAT shall I, a sinner, do?
   Whither shall I turn for aid?
Conscience waking, brings to view
   Sins that make me sore afraid:
This my confidence shall be,
Jesus, I will cling to Thee.

Though I have transgressed Thy will;
   Oft have grieved Thee by my sin;
Yet I know Thou lov'st me still,
   For I hear Thy voice within.
Then, though sin accuses me,
Jesus, I will cling to Thee.

If I die, I do but cease
   Sooner from all toil and care;
I shall rest in perfect peace
   In the grave, since Thou wert there:
There Thy light shall comfort me;
Jesus, I will cling to Thee.

Then, Lord Jesus, Thou art mine,
   Till Thou bring me to that place
Where I shall forever shine
   In Thy light, and see Thy face.
Blessed will that heaven be!
Jesus, I will cling to Thee.

ST. CLEMENT'S HYMN. 10s & 6.

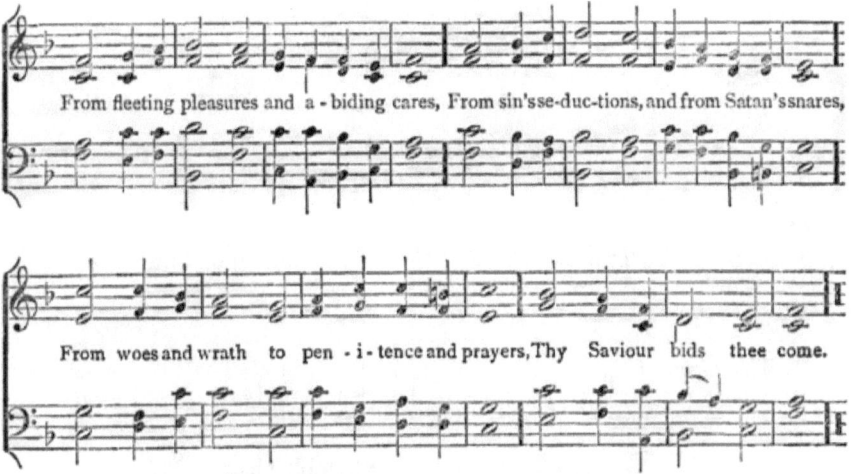

160

From fleeting pleasures and abiding cares,
  From sin's seductions, and from Satan's snares,
From woes and wrath to penitence and prayers,
  Thy Saviour bids thee come.

From this world's ways and being lost in them,
  From floods of evil which thou could'st not stem,
From tents of Kedar to Jerusalem,
  Thy Saviour bids thee come.

Blest be the loss that works thy heavenly gain,
  Blest be the blow that frees thee from thy chain,
Blest be the tears that wash thy spirit's stain;—
  Thy Saviour bids thee come.

Oh, dead and yet alive! oh, lost and found!
  Salvation's walls shall compass thee around:
Thy weary feet shall stand on holy ground;
  Thy Saviour bids thee come.

When death shall garner thee with all the blest,
  In God's own glory to be welcome guest
In light perpetual and eternal rest,
  Thy Saviour bids thee come.

THE CHRISTIAN LIFE.

ST. PHILIP. 7s.

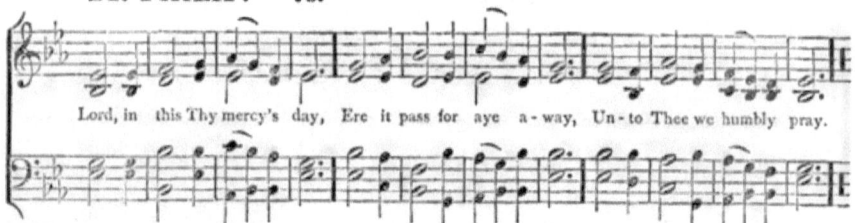

161

LORD, in this Thy mercy's day,
Ere it pass for aye away,
Unto Thee we humbly pray.

By Thy night of agony,
By Thy supplicating cry,
By Thy willingness to die:

By Thy tears of bitter woe
For Jerusalem below,
Let us not Thy love forego:

Lord, on us Thy Spirit pour,
Kneeling lowly at Thy door
Ere it close forevermore:

Grant us, Lord, some humble place
In the kingdom of Thy grace,
Where we may behold Thy face.

SULLIVAN. 7s.

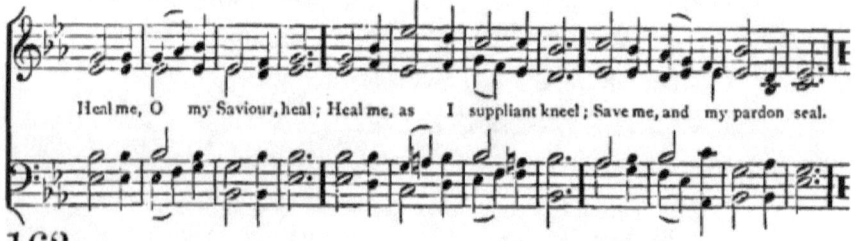

162

HEAL me, O my Saviour, heal;
Heal me, as I suppliant kneel;
Save me, and my pardon seal.

Thou the true Physician art,
Thou canst cure the wounded heart,
Thou canst life and health impart.

Other comforters are gone:
Thou who didst for sin atone,
Thou canst save, and Thou alone.

Lord, in mercy send Thine aid!
Hear the prayer I oft have prayed!
Heal the wounds that sin hath made!

Heal me, then, O Saviour, heal!
To Thy mercy I appeal;
Heal me, as I suppliant kneel.

CONFESSION. 7, 6, 8.

Dear Lord, I make con-fes-sion Of mul-ti-plied trans-gres-sion, My soul had lost Thy way: At last I see my er-rors, And trem-ble at Thy ter-rors; Have mer-cy on me, Lord, I pray.

163

DEAR Lord, I make confession
　Of multiplied transgression,
My soul had lost Thy way:
At last I see my errors,
And tremble at Thy terrors;
Have mercy on me, Lord, I pray.

Though conscience' voice appal me,
Thy child I dare not call me,
Yet will I seek Thy face.
Let not Thy love forsake me,
Let not Thy wrath o'ertake me,
O Lord, extend to me Thy grace.

Thy Son hath suffered for me,
Thy Spirit can restore me,
And cleanse my soul from sin ;
The love of Christ can vanquish
My guilty fears and anguish,
And quench the sinful fire within.

On Him I cast my burden,
Now let me feel Thy pardon,
Thy peace, O Lord, bestow :
Thy Spirit leave me never,
But dwell within forever,
And wash and make me white as snow.

THE CHRISTIAN LIFE.

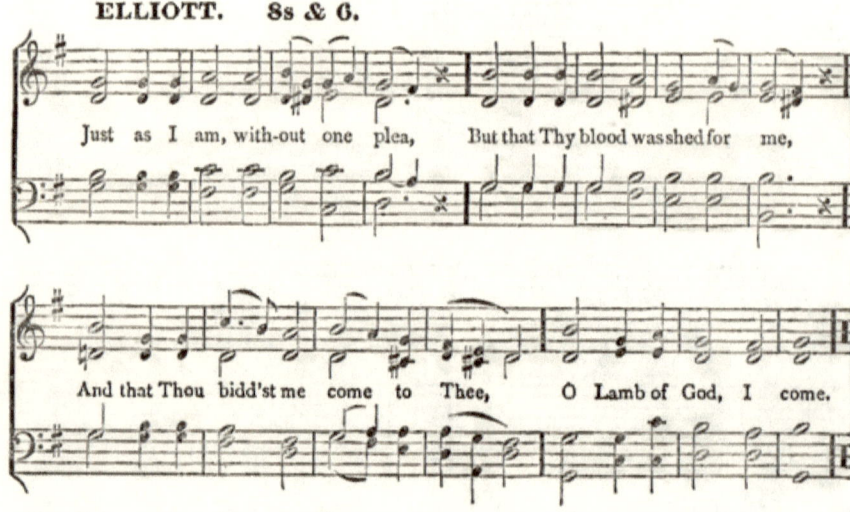

ELLIOTT. 8s & 6.

Just as I am, with-out one plea, But that Thy blood was shed for me, And that Thou bidd'st me come to Thee, O Lamb of God, I come.

164

JUST as I am,—without one plea,
   But that Thy blood was shed for me,
And that Thou bidd'st me come to Thee,
   O Lamb of God, I come.

Just as I am,—and waiting not
To rid my soul of one dark blot, [spot,
To Thee, whose blood can cleanse each
   O Lamb of God, I come.

Just as I am,—though toss'd about
With many a conflict, many a doubt,
Fightings and fears within, without,
   O Lamb of God, I come.

Just as I am,—Thou wilt receive,
Wilt welcome, pardon, cleanse, relieve;
Because Thy promise I believe,
   O Lamb of God, I come.

Just as I am,—Thy love unknown
Has broken every barrier down;
Now to be Thine, yea, Thine alone,
   O Lamb of God, I come.

165

BURDENED with guilt, wouldst thou
   be blest?
Trust not the world; it gives no rest:
I bring relief to hearts oppressed;
   O weary sinner, come!

Come, leave thy burden at the cross;
Count all thy gains but empty dross;
My grace repays all earthly loss:
   O needy sinner, come!

Come, hither bring thy boding fears,
Thy aching heart, thy bursting tears;
'Tis mercy's voice salutes thine ears;
   O trembling sinner, come!

The Spirit and the Bride say, Come!
Rejoicing saints re-echo, Come!
Who faints, who thirsts, who will, may
   come;
   Thy Saviour bids thee come.

HAMBURG. L. M.

With broken heart and con-trite sigh, A trembling sin-ner, Lord, I cry;

Thy pard'ning grace is rich and free: O God, be mer-ci-ful to me!

166

WITH broken heart and contrite sigh,
A trembling sinner, Lord, I cry;
Thy pardoning grace is rich and free:
O God, be merciful to me!

I smite upon my troubled breast,
With deep and conscious guilt oppressed,
Christ and His cross my only plea:
O God, be merciful to me!

Far off I stand with tearful eyes,
Nor dare uplift them to the skies;
But Thou dost all my anguish see:
O God, be merciful to me!

Nor alms, nor deeds that I have done,
Can for a single sin atone;
To Calvary alone I flee:
O God, be merciful to me!

167

COME, weary souls, with sin distressed,
Come, and accept the promised rest;
The Saviour's gracious call obey,
And cast your gloomy fears away.

Oppressed with guilt,—a painful load,—
Oh, come and bow before your God!
Divine compassion, mighty love
Will all the painful load remove.

Here mercy's boundless ocean flows,
To cleanse your guilt and heal your woes;
Pardon and life and endless peace,—
How rich the gift, how free the grace!

Dear Saviour! let Thy powerful love
Confirm our faith, our fears remove;
Oh, sweetly reign in every breast,
And guide us to eternal rest.

Praise God, from whom all blessings flow!
Praise Him, all creatures here below!
Praise Him above, ye heavenly host!
Praise Father, Son, and Holy Ghost!

THE CHRISTIAN LIFE.

LANGRAN. 10s.

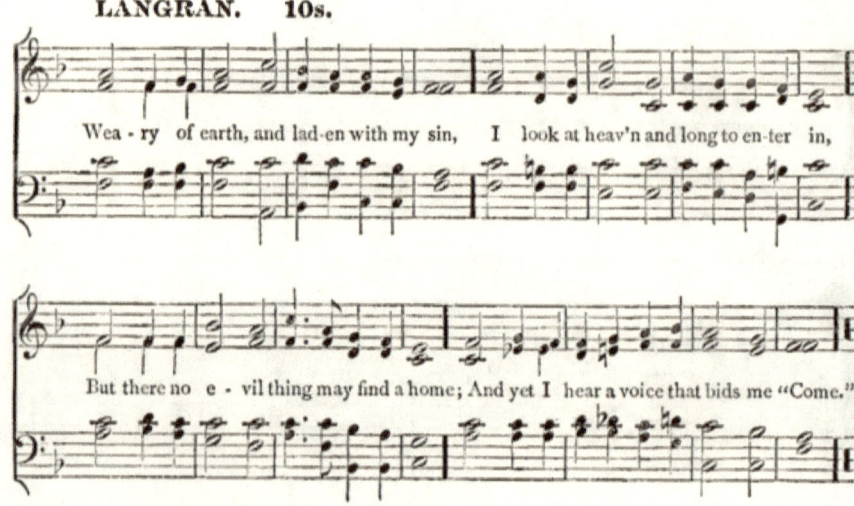

Wea-ry of earth, and lad-en with my sin, I look at heav'n and long to en-ter in,

But there no e-vil thing may find a home; And yet I hear a voice that bids me "Come."

168

WEARY of earth and laden with my sin,
    I look at heaven and long to enter in,
But there no evil thing may find a home;
And yet I hear a voice that bids me " Come."

So vile I am, how dare I hope to stand
In the pure glory of that holy land?
Before the whiteness of that Throne appear?
Yet there are hands stretched out to draw me near.

It is the voice of Jesus that I hear,
His are the hands stretched out to draw me near,
And His the blood that can for all atone,
And set me faultless there before the Throne.

'Twas He who found me on the deathly wild,
And made me heir of heaven, the Father's child,
And day by day, whereby my soul may live,
Gives me His grace of pardon, and will give.

Yea, Thou wilt answer for me, righteous Lord:
Thine all the merits, mine the great reward;
Thine the sharp thorns, and mine the golden crown,
Mine the life won, and Thine the life laid down.

PROCTOR. P. M.

The way is long and dreary, The path is bleak and bare, Our feet are worn and weary, But we will not despair. More heavy was Thy burden, More desolate Thy way: O Lamb of God, who takest the sins of the world away, Have mercy, have mercy, and give us Thy peace.

169

2.
The snows lie thick around us
  In the dark and gloomy night,
The tempest waves above us,
  And the stars have hid their light.
But blacker was the darkness
Round Calvary's cross that day:
  O Lamb of God, etc.

3.
Our hearts are faint with sorrow,
  Heavy and sad to bear;
For we dread the bitter morrow,
  But we will not despair.
Thou knowest all our anguish,
And Thou wilt bid it cease:
  O Lamb of God, etc.

DENFIELD. C. M.

How oft, a-las! this wretch-ed heart Has wan-dered from the Lord!

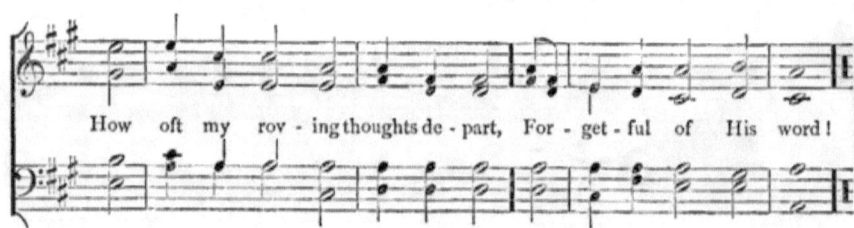

How oft my rov-ing thoughts de-part, For-get-ful of His word!

170

How oft, alas! this wretched heart
 Has wandered from the Lord!
How oft my roving thoughts depart,
 Forgetful of His word!

Yet sovereign mercy calls, "Return!"
 Dear Lord, and may I come?
My vile ingratitude I mourn:
 Oh, take the wanderer home!

Almighty grace, Thy healing power,
 How glorious, how divine!
That can to life and bliss restore
 A heart so vile as mine.

Thy pard'ning love, so free, so sweet,
 Dear Saviour, I adore;
Oh, keep me at Thy sacred feet,
 And let me rove no more!

171

Lord, when we bend before Thy throne
 And our confessions pour,
Teach us to feel the sins we own,
 And hate what we deplore.

Our broken spirits, pitying, see,
 And penitence impart;
And let a kindling glance from Thee
 Beam hope upon the heart.

When we disclose our wants in prayer,
 May we our wills resign;
And not a thought our bosom share
 Which is not wholly thine.

Let faith each weak petition fill,
 And waft it to the skies,
And teach our hearts 't is goodness still
 That grants it, or denies.

 To Father, Son, and Holy Ghost,
  One God whom we adore,
 Be glory as it was, is now,
  And shall be evermore.

NOTTINGHAM.   C. M.

172

WE sinners, Lord, with earnest heart,
  With sighs and prayers and tears,
To Thee our inmost cares impart,
  Our burdens and our fears.

Thy sovereign grace can give relief,
  Thou Source of peace and light!
Dispel the gloomy cloud of grief,
  And make our darkness bright.

Around Thy Father's throne on high,
  All heaven Thy glory sings;
And earth, for which Thou cam'st to die,
  Loud with Thy praises rings.

Dear Lord! to Thee our prayers ascend;
  Our eyes Thy face would see:
Oh! let our weary wanderings end,
  Our spirits rest in Thee!

173

JESUS! Thou art the sinner's Friend;
  As such I look to Thee;
Now, in the fullness of Thy love,
  O Lord! remember me.

Remember Thy pure word of grace,—
  Remember Calvary;
Remember all Thy dying groans,
  And, then, remember me.

Thou wondrous Advocate with God!
  I yield myself to Thee;
While Thou art sitting on Thy throne,
  Dear Lord! remember me.

And, when I close my eyes in death,
  When creature-helps all flee,
Then, O my dear Redeemer God!
  I pray, remember me.

To Father, Son, and Holy Ghost,
  One God whom we adore,
Be glory as it was, is now,
  And shall be evermore.

ARLINGTON. C. M.

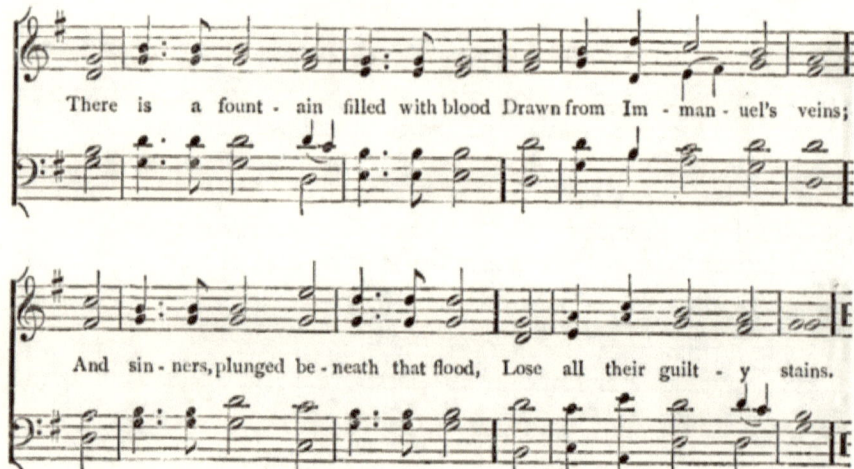

There is a fount-ain filled with blood Drawn from Im-man-uel's veins;
And sin-ners, plunged be-neath that flood, Lose all their guilt-y stains.

174

THERE is a fountain filled with blood
    Drawn from Immanuel's veins;
And sinners, plunged beneath that flood,
    Lose all their guilty stains.

The dying thief rejoiced to see
    That fountain in his day;
And there may I, though vile as he,
    Wash all my sins away.

Dear dying Lamb, Thy precious blood
    Shall never lose its power,
Till all the ransomed church of God
    Be saved, to sin no more.

E'er since, by faith, I saw the stream
    Thy flowing wounds supply,
Redeeming love has been my theme,
    And shall be till I die.

Then in a nobler, sweeter song,
    I'll sing Thy power to save, [tongue
When this poor lisping, stammering
    Lies silent in the grave.

175

WHEN I can read my title clear
    To mansions in the skies,
I bid farewell to every fear,
    And wipe my weeping eyes.

Should earth against my soul engage,
    And fiery darts be hurled,
Then I can smile at Satan's rage,
    And face a frowning world.

Let cares like a wild deluge come,
    And storms of sorrow fall;
May I but safely reach my home,
    My God, my heaven, my all!

There shall I bathe my weary soul
    In seas of heavenly rest;
And not a wave of trouble roll
    Across my peaceful breast.

All glory to the Father be,
    All glory to the Son,
All glory to the Holy Ghost,
    While endless ages run.

GERMANIA. 7s & 6.

O Lamb of God! still keep me Near to Thy wounded side; 'Tis only there in safety And peace I can abide! What foes and snares surround me! What doubts and fears within! The grace that sought and found me Alone can keep me clean.

176

O LAMB of God! still keep me
  Near to Thy wounded side;
'Tis only there in safety
  And peace I can abide!
What foes and snares surround me!
  What doubts and fears within!
The grace that sought and found me,
  Alone can keep me clean.

'Tis only in Thee hiding,
  I feel my life secure,—
Only in Thee abiding,
  The conflict can endure;
Thine arm the vict'ry gaineth
  O'er every hateful foe;
Thy love my heart sustaineth
  In all its care and woe.

Soon shall my eyes behold Thee,
  With rapture, face to face;
One half hath not been told me
  Of all Thy power and grace;
Thy beauty, Lord, and glory,
  The wonders of Thy love,
Shall be the endless story
  Of all Thy saints above.

THE CHRISTIAN LIFE.

ARDEN. C. M.

O Lord, our car-nal mind con-trol, And make us pure with-in;
Purge more and more our in-most soul From will-ful thoughts of sin.

177

O LORD, our carnal mind control
  And make us pure within;
Purge more and more our inmost soul
  From willful thoughts of sin.

Let not the world with spot or soil
  Our secret heart defile;
Nor Satan round our spirit coil
  His chain of fraud and guile.

Be ours the blessed lot of those
  Who every evil flee;
Whose holy converse clearly shows
  Communion full with Thee;—

That when Thou shalt in might appear,
  We may Thy grace declare,
And thence through heaven's eternal year
  Thy glorious kingdom share.

To Father, Son, and Holy Ghost,
  One God whom we adore,
Be glory as it was, is now,
  And shall be evermore.

178

I HEARD the voice of Jesus say,
  "Come unto Me and rest;
Lay down, thou weary one, lay down
  Thy head upon My breast."
I came to Jesus as I was,
  Weary and worn and sad;
I found in Him a resting-place,
  And He has made me glad.

I heard the voice of Jesus say,
  "Behold, I freely give
The living water! thirsty one,
  Stoop down, and drink, and live."
I came to Jesus, and I drank
  Of that life-giving stream;
My thirst was quenched, my soul revived,
  And now I live in Him.

I heard the voice of Jesus say,
  "I am this dark world's light:
Look unto Me; thy morn shall rise,
  And all the day be bright."
I looked to Jesus and I found
  In Him my Star, my Sun;
And in that light of life I'll walk
  Till all my journey's done.

ST. AGNES.   C. M.

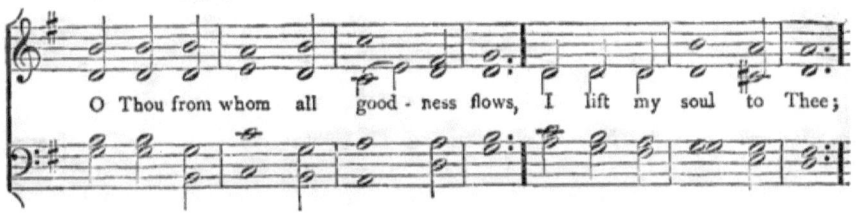

O Thou from whom all good-ness flows, I lift my soul to Thee;

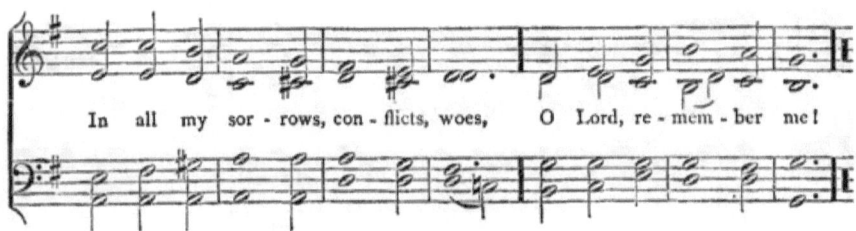

In all my sor-rows, con-flicts, woes, O Lord, re-mem-ber me!

179

O THOU from whom all goodness flows,
  I lift my soul to Thee;
In all my sorrows, conflicts, woes,
  O Lord, remember me!

When on my aching, burdened heart
  My sins lie heavily,
Thy pardon grant, new peace impart;
  Then, Lord, remember me!

When trials sore obstruct my way,
  And ills I cannot flee,
Oh, let my strength be as my day;
  Dear Lord, remember me!

When in the solemn hour of death
  I wait Thy just decree;
Be this the prayer of my last breath:
  Now, Lord, remember me!

And when before Thy throne I stand,
  And lift my soul to Thee,
Then with the saints at Thy right hand,
  O Lord, remember me!

180

APPROACH, my soul! the mercy-seat,
  Where Jesus answers prayer;
There humbly fall before His feet,
  For none can perish there.

Thy promise is my only plea,
  With this I venture nigh;
Thou callest burdened souls to Thee,
  And such, O Lord! am I.

Bowed down beneath a load of sin,
  By Satan sorely pressed;
By wars without, and fears within,
  I come to Thee for rest.

Oh! wondrous Love—to bleed and die,
  To bear the cross and shame,
That guilty sinners, such as I,
  Might plead Thy gracious Name!

All glory to the Father be,
  All glory to the Son,
All glory to the Holy Ghost,
  While endless ages run.

AVON. C. M.

O Lord! I would de-light in Thee, And on Thy care de-pend; To Thee in ev'-ry trou-ble flee, My best, my on-ly Friend.

181

O LORD! I would delight in Thee,
   And on Thy care depend;
To Thee in every trouble flee,
   My best, my only Friend.

When all created streams are dried,
   Thy fullness is the same;
May I with this be satisfied,
   And glory in Thy Name!

No good in creatures can be found,
   But may be found in Thee;
I must have all things, and abound,
   While God is God to me.

O Lord! I cast my care on Thee;
   I triumph and adore;
Henceforth my great concern shall be
   To love and please Thee more.

182

MY God, accept my heart this day,
   And make it always Thine,
That I from Thee no more may stray,
   No more from Thee decline.

Before the cross of Him who died,
   Behold, I prostrate fall;
Let every sin be crucified,
   And Christ be all in all.

Let every thought and work and word,
   To Thee be ever given;
Then life shall be Thy service, Lord,
   And death the gate of heaven!

183

RETURN, O wanderer, now return,
   And seek thy Father's face!
Those new desires, which in thee burn,
   Were kindled by His grace.

Return, O wanderer, now return;
   He hears thy humble sigh;
He sees thy softened spirit mourn,
   When no one else is nigh.

Return, O wanderer, now return;
   Thy Saviour bids thee live:
Go to His bleeding feet, and learn
   How freely He'll forgive.

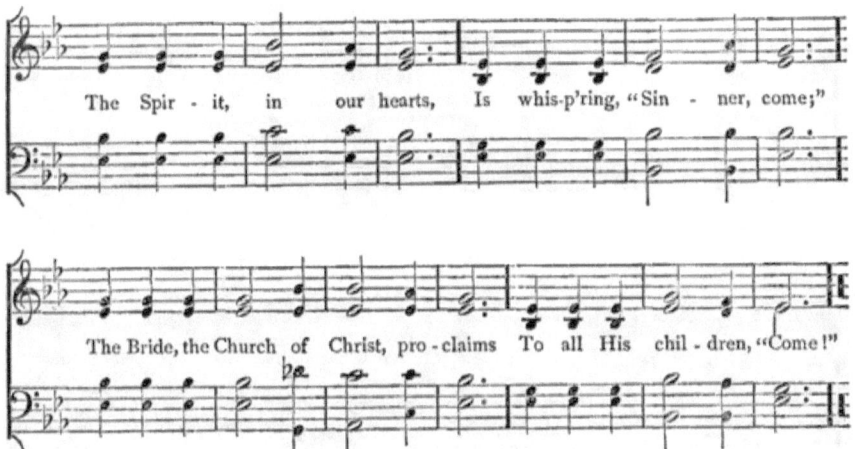

LANGTON. S. M.

184

THE Spirit, in our hearts,
   Is whispering, "Sinner, come;"
The Bride, the Church of Christ, pro-
   To all His children, "Come!" [claims

Let him that heareth say
   To all about him, "Come!"
Let him that thirsts for righteousness,
   To Christ, the fountain, come!

Yes, whosoever will,
   Oh, let him freely come,
And freely drink the stream of life;
   'Tis Jesus bids him come.

Lo! Jesus, who invites,
   Declares, "I quickly come:"
Lord, even so! we wait Thine hour;
   O blest Redeemer, come!

The Father and the Son,
   And Spirit we adore;
We praise, we bless, we worship Thee,
   Both now and evermore.

185

OH! where shall rest be found—
   Rest for the weary soul?
'Twere vain the ocean depths to sound,
   Or pierce to either pole.

The world can never give
   The bliss for which we sigh:
'Tis not the whole of life to live,
   Nor all of death to die.

Beyond this vale of tears
   There is a life above,
Unmeasured by the flight of years;
   And all that life is love.

There is a death whose pang
   Outlasts the fleeting breath:
Oh, what eternal horrors hang
   Around the second death!

Lord God of truth and grace!
   Teach us that death to shun;
Lest we be banished from Thy face,
   And evermore undone.

THE CHRISTIAN LIFE.

DAWN. S. M.

How gentle God's commands! How kind His precepts are!
Come, cast your burdens on the Lord, And trust His constant care.

186

HOW gentle God's commands!
  How kind His precepts are!
Come, cast your burdens on the Lord,
  And trust His constant care.

Beneath His watchful eye
  His saints securely dwell;
That hand which bears all nature up,
  Shall guard His children well.

Why should this anxious load
  Press down your weary mind?
Haste to your heavenly Father's throne,
  And sweet refreshment find.

His goodness stands approved,
  Unchanged from day to day:
I'll drop my burden at His feet,
  And bear a song away.

187

THE harvest dawn is near,
  The year delays not long;
And he who sows with many a tear
  Shall reap with many a song.

Sad to his toil he goes,
  His seed with weeping leaves;
But he shall come at twilight's close,
  And bring his golden sheaves.

188

OH, cease, my wandering soul,
  On restless wing to roam;
All this wide world, to either pole,
  Hath not for thee a home.

Behold the ark of God!
  Behold the open door!
Oh, haste to gain that dear abode,
  And rove, my soul, no more.

There safe thou shalt abide,
  There sweet shall be thy rest,
And every longing satisfied,
  With full salvation blest.

GRACE. S. M.

Sweet is Thy mer-cy, Lord; Be-fore Thy mer-cy seat, My soul, a-dor-ing, pleads Thy word, And owns Thy mer-cy sweet, And owns Thy mer-cy sweet.

189

SWEET is Thy mercy, Lord;
   Before Thy mercy-seat
My soul adoring pleads Thy word,
   And owns Thy mercy sweet.

Where'er Thy Name is blest,
   Where'er Thy people meet,
There I delight in Thee to rest,
   And find Thy mercy sweet.

My need and Thy desires,
   Are all in Christ complete;
Thou hast the justice truth requires,
   I have Thy mercy sweet.

Light Thou our weary way,
   Lead Thou our wandering feet,
That while we stay on earth we may
   Still find Thy mercy sweet.

Thus shall the heavenly host
   Hear all our songs repeat
To Father, Son, and Holy Ghost :—
   Our joy, Thy mercy sweet.

190

OUT of the deep I call
   To Thee, O Lord, to Thee;
Before Thy throne of grace I fall,
   Be merciful to me.

Out of the deep I cry,
   The woeful deep of sin,
Of evil done in days gone by,
   Of evil now within.

Out of the deep of fear,
   And dread of coming shame,
From morning watch till night is near
   I plead the precious Name.

Lord, there is mercy now,
   As ever was with Thee;
Before Thy throne of grace I bow,
   Be merciful to me.

The Father and the Son,
   And Spirit we adore;
We praise, we bless, we worship Thee,
   Both now and evermore!

HORTON. 7s.

Je-sus, take me for Thine own; To Thy will my Spir-it frame; Thou shalt reign, and Thou a-lone, O-ver all I have and am.

191

JESUS, take me for Thine own;
   To Thy will my spirit frame;
Thou shalt reign, and Thou alone,
   Over all I have and am.

Making thus the Lord my choice,
   I have nothing more to choose,
But to listen to Thy voice,
   And my will in Thine to lose.

Then, whatever may betide,
   I shall safe and happy be;
Still content and satisfied ;—
   Having all in having Thee.

192

'TIS my happiness below,
   Not to live without the cross;
But the Saviour's power to know,
   Sanctifying every loss.

Trials must and will befall;
   But with humble faith to see
Love inscribed upon them all—
   This is happiness to me.

Trials make the promise sweet;
   Trials give new life to prayer;
Bring me to my Saviour's feet,
   Lay me low and keep me there.

193

COME, said Jesus' sacred voice,
   Come, and make my paths your choice,
I will guide you to your home,
   Weary wanderer, hither come!

Hither come! for here is found
   Balm that flows for every wound,
Peace that ever shall endure,
   Rest eternal, sacred, sure.

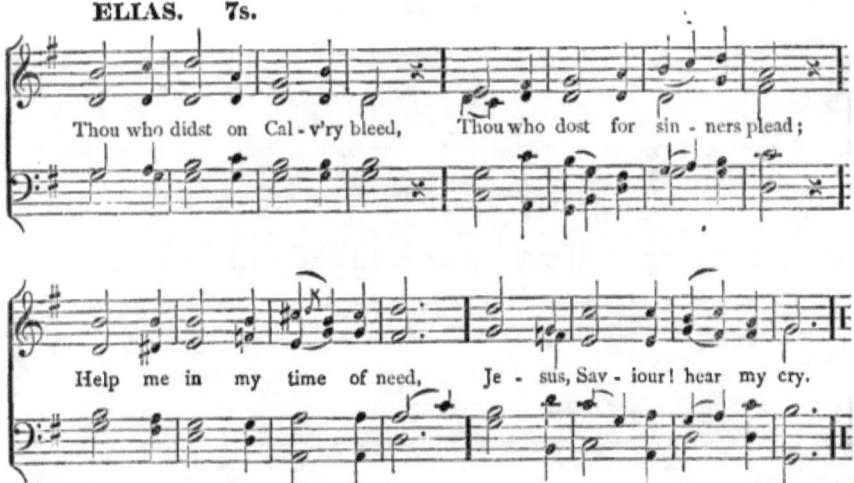

ELIAS. 7s.

Thou who didst on Cal-v'ry bleed, Thou who dost for sin-ners plead; Help me in my time of need, Je-sus, Sav-iour! hear my cry.

194

THOU who didst on Calvary bleed,
   Thou who dost for sinners plead;
Help me in my time of need,
   Jesus, Saviour! hear my cry.

In my darkness and my grief,
With my heart of unbelief,
I, who am of sinners chief,
   Jesus! lift to Thee mine eye.

Foes without and fears within,
With no plea Thy grace to win,
But that Thou canst save from sin,
   Jesus! to Thy cross I fly.

There on Thee I cast my care,
There to Thee I raise my prayer,
Jesus! save me from despair,
   Saviour, save me, or I die.

When the storms of trial lower,
When I feel temptation's power,
In the last and darkest hour,
   Jesus, Saviour! be Thou nigh.

195

DEPTH of mercy!—can there be
   Mercy still reserved for me?
Can my God His wrath forbear?
Me, the chief of sinners, spare?

I have scorned the Son of God,
Trampled on His precious blood,
Would not hearken to His calls,
Grieved Him by a thousand falls.

Lord, incline me to repent;
Let me now my fall lament—
Deeply my revolt deplore,
Weep, believe, and sin no more.

Still for me the Saviour stands, [hands:
Shows His wounds, and spreads His
God is love; I know, I feel;
Jesus weeps, and loves me still.

Sing we to our God above,
Praise eternal as His love;
Praise Him, all ye heavenly host,—
Father, Son, and Holy Ghost.

THE CHRISTIAN LIFE.

HEROLD. 8s & 7s.

Sweet the moments, rich in blessing, Which before the cross we spend;
Life, and health, and peace possessing, From the sinner's dying Friend.

196

SWEET the moments, rich in blessing,
  Which before the cross we spend;
Life, and health, and peace possessing,
  From the sinner's dying Friend.

Truly blessèd is this station,
  Low before His cross to lie,
While we see divine compassion,
  Beaming in His gracious eye.

Love and grief our hearts dividing,
  With our tears His feet we bathe;
Constant still, in faith abiding,
  Life deriving from His death.

For Thy sorrows we adore Thee,
  For the pains that wrought our peace;
Gracious Saviour, we implore Thee
  In our souls Thy love increase.

197

ONE there is, above all others,
  Well deserves the name of Friend;
His is love beyond a brother's,
  Costly, free, and knows no end.

Which of all our friends, to save us,
  Could or would have shed his blood?
But our Jesus died to have us
  Reconciled in Him to God.

When He lived on earth abased,
  Friend of sinners was His Name;
Now above all glory raised,
  He rejoices in the same.

Oh, for grace our hearts to soften,
  Teach us, Lord, at length to love;
We, alas! forget too often
  What a Friend we have above.

Worship, honor, glory, blessing,
  Lord, we offer to Thy Name;
Young and old their thanks expressing,
  Join Thy goodness to proclaim.

THE CHRISTIAN LIFE.

STOCKWELL. 8s & 7s.

Al-ways with us, al-ways with us,— Words of cheer and words of love;
Thus the ris-en Sav-iour whis-pers, From His dwell-ing-place a-bove.

198

ALWAYS with us, always with us,—
  Words of cheer and words of love;
Thus the risen Saviour whispers,
  From His dwelling-place above.

With us when we toil in sadness,
  Sowing much and reaping none;
Telling us that in the future
  Golden harvests shall be won.

With us when the storm is sweeping
  O'er our pathway dark and drear;
Waking hope within our bosoms,
  Stilling every anxious fear.

With us in the lonely valley,
  When we cross the chilling stream;
Lighting up the steps to glory
  With salvation's radiant beam.

199

GENTLY, Lord, oh, gently lead us
  Through this gloomy vale of tears;
Through the changes Thou'st decreed us,
  Till our last great change appears.

When temptation's darts assail us,
  When in devious paths we stray,
Let Thy goodness never fail us,
  Lead us in Thy perfect way.

In the hour of pain and anguish,
  In the hour when death draws near,
Suffer not our hearts to languish,
  Suffer not our souls to fear.

When this mortal life is ended,
  Bid us in Thine arms to rest,
Till by angel-bands attended,
  We awake among the blest.

Glory be to Thee, the Father,
  Glory be to Thee, the Son,
Glory to the Holy Spirit,
  While eternal ages run.

ROCK OF AGES. 7s. 6 lines.

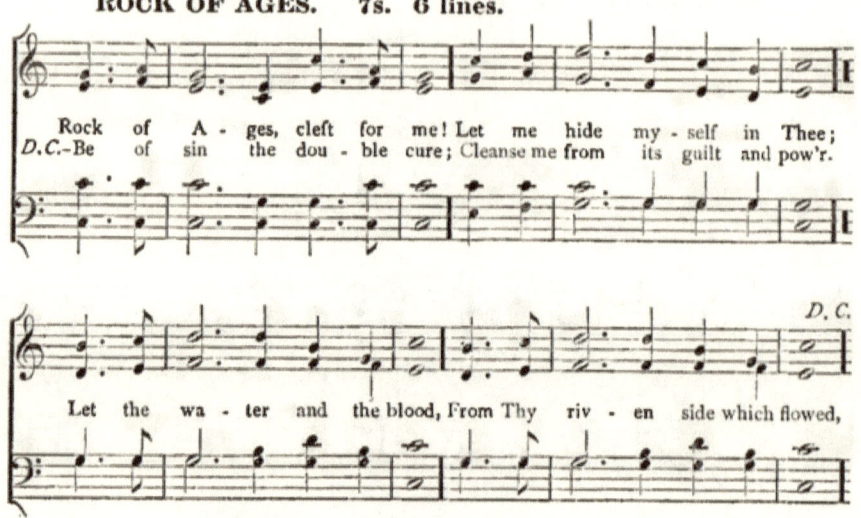

200

ROCK of Ages! cleft for me;
Let me hide myself in Thee!
Let the water and the blood,
From Thy riven side which flowed,
Be of sin the double cure,
Cleanse me from its guilt and power.

Could my zeal no respite know,
Could my tears forever flow,
All for sin could not atone,
Thou must save, and Thou alone!
Nothing in my hand I bring;
Simply to Thy cross I cling.

While I draw this fleeting breath,
When my eyelids close in death,
When I soar to worlds unknown,
See Thee on Thy judgment throne,
Rock of Ages! cleft for me,
Let me hide myself in Thee!

THE CHRISTIAN LIFE. 147

SOUTH CHURCH. 8s & 7s.

Take my heart, O Father, take it! Make and keep it all Thine own;
Let Thy Spir-it melt and break it— This proud heart of sin and stone.

201

TAKE my heart, O Father, take it!
  Make and keep it all Thine own;
Let Thy Spirit melt and break it—
  This proud heart of sin and stone.

Father, make it pure and lowly,
  Fond of peace, and far from strife;
Turning from the paths unholy
  Of this vain and sinful life.

Ever let Thy grace surround it,
  Strengthen it with power divine;
Till Thy cords of love have bound it,
  Make it to be wholly Thine.

May the blood of Jesus heal it,
  And its sins be all forgiven;
Holy Spirit, take and seal it,
  Guide it in the path to heaven.

202

LORD, I hear that showers of blessing
  Thou art scattering, full and free,—
Showers the thirsty land refreshing;
  Let thy blessing fall on me.

Long have I in sin been straying,
  Long been grieving, slighting Thee;
Slight me not as I stand praying;
  Oh, forgive and comfort me!

Pass me not, O gracious Saviour,
  Sinful though my heart may be;
Give me tokens of Thy favor,
  Speak some word of grace to me.

Love of God, so pure and changeless,
  Blood of Christ, so rich and free,
Grace of God, so strong and boundless,—
  Magnify it all to me!

    Glory be to Thee, the Father,
      Glory be to Thee, the Son,
    Glory to the Holy Spirit,
      While eternal ages run.

THE CHRISTIAN LIFE.

DORRNANCE.   8s & 7s.

Come, Thou Fount of ev'ry bless-ing, Tune my heart to sing Thy grace;
Streams of mer-cy, nev-er ceas-ing, Call for songs of loud-est praise.

203

COME, Thou Fount of every blessing,
  Tune my heart to sing Thy grace;
Streams of mercy, never ceasing,
  Call for songs of loudest praise.

Jesus sought me when a stranger,
  Wandering from the fold of God;
He, to save my soul from danger,
  Interposed His precious blood.

Oh! to grace how great a debtor
  Daily I'm constrained to be!
Let that grace, Lord, like a fetter,
  Bind my wandering heart to Thee.

Prone to wander, Lord, I feel it;
  Prone to leave the God I love;
Here's my heart—oh, take and seal it,—
  Seal it from Thy courts above.

204

HEAR what God, the Lord, hath
  O my people, faint and few, [spoken:
Comfortless, afflicted, broken,
  Fair abodes I build for you.

Scenes of heartfelt tribulation
  Shall no more perplex your ways;
You shall name your walls "Salvation,"
  And your gates shall all be "Praise."

Ye no more your suns descending,
  Waning moons no more shall see;
But your griefs forever ending,
  Find eternal noon in Me.

God shall rise, and, shining o'er you,
  Change to day the gloom of night;
He, the Lord, shall be your Glory,
  God, your everlasting Light.

Praise the Father, earth and heaven,
  Praise the Son, the Spirit praise;
As it was, and is, be given
  Glory through eternal days.

BLONDEL. 8s & 7s.

205

LOVE divine, all love excelling,
　Joy of heaven, to earth come down,
Fix in us Thy humble dwelling,
　All Thy faithful mercies crown:
Jesus, Thou art all compassion,
　Pure, unbounded love Thou art;
Visit us with Thy salvation,
　Enter every trembling heart.

Breathe, O breathe Thy loving Spirit
　Into every troubled breast;
Let us all in Thee inherit,
　Let us find Thy promised rest;

Come, Almighty to deliver,
　Let us all Thy grace receive;
Suddenly return, and never,
　Never more Thy temples leave.

Finish then Thy new creation,
　Pure and spotless let us be:
Let us see Thy great salvation
　Perfectly restored in Thee.
Changed from glory into glory,
　Till in heaven we take our place:
Till we cast our crowns before Thee,
　Lost in wonder, love, and praise.

THE CHRISTIAN LIFE.

BENEVENTO. 7s.

Jesus, Lover of my soul! Let me to Thy bosom fly,
While the nearer waters roll, While the tempest still is high;
D.S.—Safe into the haven guide; Oh! receive my soul at last.
Hide me, O my Saviour! hide, Till the storm of life is past;

206

JESUS, Lover of my soul!
  Let me to Thy bosom fly,
While the nearer waters roll,
  While the tempest still is high;
Hide me, O my Saviour! hide,
  Till the storm of life is past;
Safe into the haven guide;
  Oh! receive my soul at last.

Other refuge have I none,
  Hangs my helpless soul on Thee:
Leave, ah! leave me not alone,
  Still support and comfort me:
All my trust on Thee is stayed,
  All my help from Thee I bring;
Cover my defenceless head,
  With the shadow of Thy wing.

Thou, O Christ, art all I want;
  More than all in Thee I find:
Raise the fallen, cheer the faint,
  Heal the sick, and lead the blind!
Just and holy is Thy Name;
  I am all unrighteousness;
False and full of sin I am,
  Thou art full of truth and grace.

Plenteous grace with Thee is found,
  Grace to cover all my sin;
Let the healing streams abound;
  Make and keep me pure within!
Thou of life the fountain art,
  Freely let me take of Thee;
Spring Thou up within my heart!
  Rise to all eternity!

THE CHRISTIAN LIFE.

SOLEMN LITANY. 7s.

Saviour, when in dust to Thee, Low we bow th'adoring knee;
When, repentant, to the skies Scarce we lift our streaming eyes;
O, by all Thy pains and woe, Suffer'd once for man below;
Bending from Thy throne on high, Hear our solemn litany.

207

SAVIOUR, when in dust to Thee,
　Low we bow th' adoring knee;
When, repentant, to the skies
Scarce we lift our streaming eyes;
O, by all Thy pains and woe,
Suffered once for man below,
Bending from Thy throne on high,
Hear our solemn litany.

By Thy birth and early years,
By Thy human griefs and fears,
By Thy fasting and distress
In the lonely wilderness,
By Thy victory in the hour
Of the subtle tempter's power;
Jesus, look with pitying eye;
Hear our solemn litany.

By Thy conflict with despair,
By Thine agony of prayer,
By the purple robe of scorn,
By Thy wounds, Thy crown of thorn,
By Thy cross, Thy pangs, and cries,
By Thy perfect sacrifice;
Jesus, look with pitying eye;
Hear our solemn litany.

By Thy deep expiring groan,
By the sealed sepulchral stone,
By Thy triumph o'er the grave,
By Thy power from death to save;
Mighty God, ascended Lord,
To Thy throne in heaven restored,
Prince and Saviour, hear our cry,
Hear our solemn litany.

208

2.
In the midst of sin and strife,
　In the depths of mortal woe,
Teach us, Lord, to live a life
　Meet for sojourners below.
Though the road be often dark,
　Though our feet in weakness stray,
Lead us, Saviour, as the Ark
　Led Thy chosen on their way.

3.
Weak, and weary, and alone,
　When the vale of death we tread,
Then be all Thy mercy shown,
　Then be all Thy love displayed.
Guard us in that gloomy hour,
　Guide us to the land of rest,
Where, secure from Satan's power,
　We shall lean upon Thy breast.

THE CHRISTIAN LIFE.

209

MY faith looks up to Thee,
  Thou Lamb of Calvary,
    Saviour divine!
Now hear me while I pray;
Take all my guilt away;
O let me from this day
  Be wholly Thine.

May Thy rich grace impart
Strength to my fainting heart,
  My zeal inspire;
As Thou hast died for me,
O may my love to Thee
Pure, warm, and changeless be,
  A living fire.

While life's dark maze I tread,
And griefs around me spread,
  Be Thou my Guide:
Bid darkness turn to day;
Wipe sorrow's tears away;
Nor let me ever stray
  From Thee aside.

When ends life's transient dream,
When death's cold, sullen stream
  Shall o'er me roll:
Blest Saviour, then in love,
Fear and distrust remove;
O bear me safe above,
  A ransomed soul.

MORNING STAR. 8s & 6s.

210

O CHRIST, Thou bright and morn-
  ing Star,
  Now shed Thy light abroad;
Shine on us from Thy throne afar,
  In this dark place, O Lord,
  With Thy pure, holy Word.

O Jesus, comfort of the poor,
  I lift my heart to Thee;
I know Thy mercies still endure,
  And Thou wilt pity me:
  I trust alone to Thee.

For Thou didst suffer for my soul,
  Her burdens to remove;
Oh make me through Thy sorrow
  whole,
  Refresh me with Thy love,
  Lord, help me from above.

Then, Jesus, glory, honor, praise,
  I'll ever sing to Thee;
Increase my faith that Thou wilt raise
  Me once where I shall see
  Eternal joys with Thee.

THE CHRISTIAN LIFE.

SPANISH HYMN. 7s.

211

BLESSÈD are the sons of God,
 They are bought with Jesus' blood;
They are ransomed from the grave;
Life eternal they shall have:
With them numbered may we be,
Here, and in eternity.

They are justified by grace,
They enjoy the Saviour's peace;
All their sins are washed away;
They shall stand in God's great day:
With them numbered may we be,
Here, and in eternity.

They are lights upon the earth,
Children of a heavenly birth:
One with God, with Jesus one,
Glory is in them begun:
With them numbered may we be,
Here, and in eternity.

212

BLESSÈD Saviour! Thee I love,
 All my other joys above;
All my hopes in Thee abide;
Thou my hope, and naught beside:
Ever let my glory be
Blessèd Saviour! only Thee!

Once again beside the cross,
All my gain I count but loss;
Earthly pleasures fade away,
Clouds they are that hide my day:
Hence, vain shadows! let me see
Jesus crucified for me.

Blessèd Saviour! Thine am I,
Thine to live, and Thine to die;
Height or depth or earthly power
Ne'er shall hide my Saviour more:
Ever shall my glory be
Blessèd Saviour! only Thee!

Praise the name of God most high;
Praise Him all below the sky;
Praise Him, all ye heavenly host—
Father, Son, and Holy Ghost!
As through countless ages past,
Evermore His praise shall last.

THE CHRISTIAN LIFE.

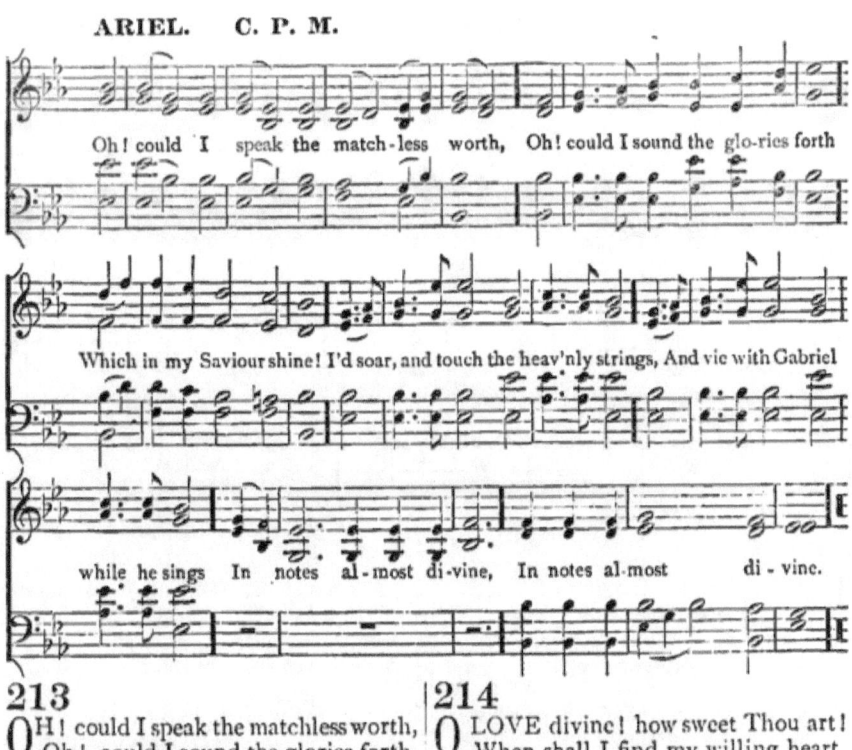

ARIEL. C. P. M.

Oh! could I speak the matchless worth, Oh! could I sound the glories forth Which in my Saviour shine! I'd soar, and touch the heav'nly strings, And vie with Gabriel while he sings In notes almost divine, In notes almost divine.

213

OH! could I speak the matchless worth,
  Oh! could I sound the glories forth
    Which in my Saviour shine!
I'd soar, and touch the heavenly strings,
And vie with Gabriel while he sings
    In notes almost divine.

I'd sing the precious blood He spilt,—
My ransom from the dreadful guilt
    Of sin and wrath divine:
I'd sing His glorious righteousness,
In which all-perfect, heavenly dress
    My soul shall ever shine.

I'd sing the characters He bears,
And all the forms of love He wears,
    Exalted on His throne:
In loftiest songs of sweetest praise,
I would, to everlasting days,
    Make all His glories known.

214

O LOVE divine! how sweet Thou art!
  When shall I find my willing heart
    All taken up by Thee?
I thirst, and faint, and die to prove
The greatness of redeeming love,
    The love of Christ to me.

God only knows the love of God;
Oh! that it now were shed abroad
    In this poor stony heart!
For love I sigh; for love I pine;
This only portion, Lord! be mine:—
    Be mine this better part!

Oh! that I could, with favored John,
Recline my weary head upon
    The dear Redeemer's breast;
From care and sin and sorrow free,
Give me! O Lord, to find in Thee
    My everlasting rest!

MESSENGERS. C. M.

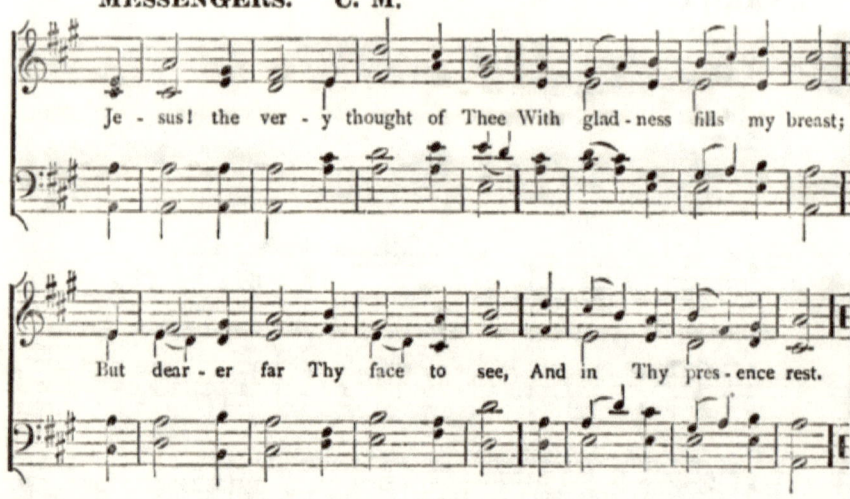

Je-sus! the ver-y thought of Thee With glad-ness fills my breast;
But dear-er far Thy face to see, And in Thy pres-ence rest.

215

JESUS! the very thought of Thee
  With gladness fills my breast;
But dearer far Thy face to see,
  And in Thy presence rest.

Nor voice can sing, nor heart can frame,
  Nor can the memory find
A sweeter sound than Thy blest Name,
  O Saviour of mankind!

O Hope of every contrite heart,
  O Joy of all the meek!
To those who fall, how kind Thou art,
  How good to those who seek!

And those who find Thee, find a bliss
  Nor tongue nor pen can show:
The love of Jesus—what it is,
  None but His loved ones know.

Jesus, our only joy be Thou.
  As Thou our prize wilt be;
Jesus, be Thou our glory now,
  And through eternity!

216

HOW sweet the Name of Jesus sounds
  In a believer's ear!
It soothes his sorrows, heals his wounds,
  And drives away his fear.

It makes the wounded spirit whole,
  And calms the troubled breast;
'Tis manna to the hungry soul,
  And to the weary rest.

Jesus! my Shepherd, Brother, Friend,
  My Prophet, Priest, and King,
My Lord, my Life, my Way, my End,
  Accept the praise I bring.

Weak is the effort of my heart,
  And cold my warmest thought;
But when I see Thee as Thou art,
  I'll praise Thee as I ought.

Till then I would Thy love proclaim
  With every fleeting breath;
And may the music of Thy Name
  Refresh my soul in death!

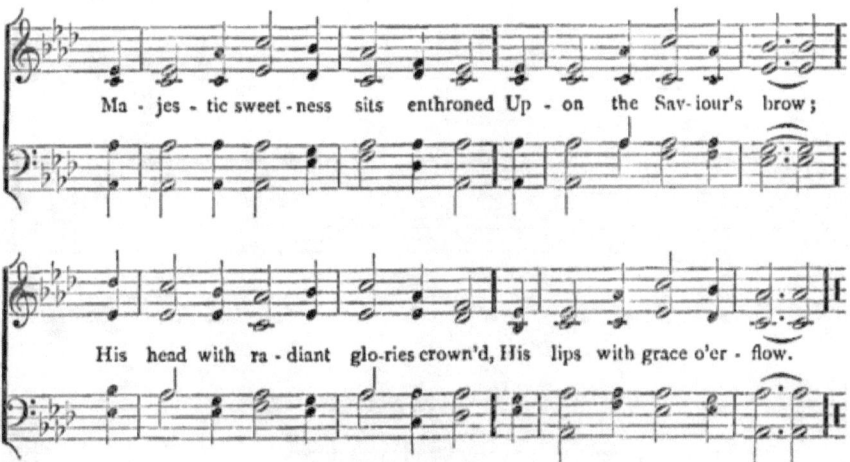

EVAN. C. M.

Majestic sweetness sits enthroned Upon the Saviour's brow;
His head with radiant glories crown'd, His lips with grace o'er-flow.

217

MAJESTIC sweetness sits enthroned
  Upon the Saviour's brow;
His head with radiant glories crowned,
  His lips with grace o'erflow.

No mortal can with Him compare,
  Among the sons of men;
Fairer is He than all the fair
  That fill the heavenly train.

He saw me plunged in deep distress,
  He flew to my relief;
For me He bore the shameful cross,
  And carried all my grief.

To Him I owe my life and breath,
  And all the joys I have;
He makes me triumph over death,
  He saves me from the grave.

To heaven, the place of His abode,
  He brings my weary feet;
Shows me the glories of my God,
  And makes my joy complete.

218

I'M not ashamed to own my Lord,
  Or to defend His cause;
Maintain the honor of His word,
  The glory of His cross.

Jesus, my God!—I know His Name;
  His Name is all my trust;
Nor will He put my soul to shame,
  Nor let my hope be lost.

Firm as His throne His promise stands,
  And He can well secure
What I've committed to His hands
  Till the decisive hour.

Then will He own my worthless name
  Before His Father's face,
And in the New Jerusalem
  Appoint my soul a place.

Let God the Father, and the Son,
  And Spirit, be adored, [known,
Where there are works to make Him
  Or saints to love the Lord!

THE CHRISTIAN LIFE.

ERNAN. L. M.

Je-sus! and shall it ev-er be, A mor-tal man a-shamed of Thee!
A-shamed of Thee whom an-gels praise, Whose glo-ries shine through end-less days.

219

JESUS! and shall it ever be,
  A mortal man ashamed of Thee!—
Ashamed of Thee whom angels praise,
  Whose glories shine through endless
    days.

Ashamed of Jesus! sooner far
  Let evening blush to own a star;
He sheds the beams of light divine
  O'er this benighted soul of mine.

Ashamed of Jesus! that dear Friend
  On whom my hopes of heaven depend!
No;—when I blush, be this my shame,
  That I no more revere His Name.

Ashamed of Jesus! yes, I may,
  When I've no guilt to wash away;
No tear to wipe, no good to crave,
  No fears to quell, no soul to save.

Till then—nor is my boasting vain—
  Till then I boast a Saviour slain!
And oh, may this my glory be,
  That Christ is not ashamed of me!

220

JESUS, Thou joy of loving hearts!
  Thou Fount of Life! Thou Light
    of men!
From the best bliss that earth imparts,
  We turn unfilled to Thee again.

Thy truth unchanged has ever stood;
  Thou savest those who on Thee call;
To them that seek Thee Thou art good,
  To them that find Thee, All in all!

We taste Thee, O Thou Living Bread,
  And long to feast upon Thee still;
We drink of Thee, the Fountain Head,
  And thirst our souls from Thee to fill.

Our restless spirits yearn for Thee,
  Where'er our changeful lot is cast;
Glad, when Thy gracious smile we see,
  Blest, when our faith can hold Thee
    fast.

O Jesus, ever with us stay,
  Make all our moments calm and bright;
Chase the dark night of sin away,—
  Shed o'er the world Thy holy light!

CHESTER. L. M.

Je-sus! the ver-y thought is sweet: In that dear Name all heart-joys meet:

But oh! than hon-ey sweet-er far The glimpses of His Pres-ence are.

221

JESUS! the very thought is sweet:
In that dear Name all heart-joys meet:
But oh! than honey sweeter far
The glimpses of His Presence are.

No word is sung more sweet than this,
No sound is heard more full of bliss,
No thought brings sweeter comfort nigh,
Than Jesus, Son of God most high.

Jesus, the hope of souls forlorn,
How good to them for sin that mourn!
To them that seek Thee, oh, how kind!
But what art Thou to them that find?

Abide with us, O Lord, to-day;
Fulfil us with Thy grace we pray;
And with Thine own true sweetness feed
Our souls, from sin and darkness freed.

222

O LOVE divine! that stooped to share
Our sharpest pang, our bitterest tear,
On Thee we cast each earth-born care,
We smile at pain while Thou art near.

Though long the weary way we tread,
And sorrow crown each lingering year,
No path we shun, no darkness dread,
Our hearts still whispering, Thou art near.

When drooping pleasure turns to grief,
And trembling faith is changed to fear,
The murmuring wind, the quivering leaf,
Shall softly tell us Thou art near.

On Thee we fling our burdening woe,
O Love divine, forever dear;
Content to suffer while we know,
Living or dying, Thou art near!

    Glory to Thee, O God, most high!
    Father, we praise Thy majesty!
    The Son, the Spirit, we adore,
    One Godhead, blest for evermore!

THE CHRISTIAN LIFE.

HYMN. C. M.

O Lord and Mas-ter of us all, Whate'er our name or sign;
We own Thy sway, we hear Thy call, We test our lives by Thine.

223

O LORD and Master of us all,
  Whate'er our name or sign;
We own Thy sway, we hear Thy call,
  We test our lives by Thine.

We faintly hear, we dimly see,
  In differing phrase we pray;
But, dim or clear, we own in Thee,
  The Light, the Truth, the Way!

Apart from Thee all gain is loss,
  And labor vainly done;
The solemn shadow of Thy cross
  Is better than the sun.

Alone, O Love ineffable!
  Thy saving Name is given;
To turn aside from Thee is hell,
  To walk with Thee is heaven.

Deep strike Thy roots, O heavenly Vine,
  Within our earthly sod;
Most human and yet most divine,
  The flower of man and God!

224

THOU dear Redeemer, dying Lamb,
  I love to hear of Thee;
No music's like Thy charming Name,
  Nor half so sweet can be.

Oh, may I ever hear Thy voice
  In mercy to me speak;
In Thee, my Priest, will I rejoice,
  And Thy salvation seek.

My Jesus shall be still my theme,
  While on this earth I stay;
I'll sing my Jesus' lovely Name,
  When all things else decay.

When I appear in yonder cloud,
  With all His favored throng,
Then will I sing more sweet, more loud,
  And Christ shall be my song.

To Father, Son, and Holy Ghost,
  One God whom we adore,
Be glory as it was, is now,
  And shall be evermore!

STANLEY.　C. M.

O for a heart to praise my God, A heart from sin set free!
A heart that al-ways feels the blood So free-ly shed for me.

225

O FOR a heart to praise my God,
　A heart from sin set free !
A heart that always feels the blood
　So freely shed for me.

A heart resigned, submissive, meek,
　My great Redeemer's throne ;
Where only Christ is heard to speak,
　Where Jesus reigns alone.

An humble, lowly, contrite heart,
　Believing, true, and clean ;
Which neither life nor death can part
　From Him that dwells within.

Thy nature, gracious Lord, impart ;
　Come quickly from above ;
Write Thy new Name upon my heart,
　Thy new, best Name of Love.

　　Let God the Father, and the Son,
　　　And Spirit, be adored,
　　Where there are works to make Him known,
　　　Or saints to love the Lord !

226

DEAR Father, to Thy mercy-seat
　My soul for shelter flies :
'Tis here I find a safe retreat
　When storms and tempests rise.

My cheerful hope can never die,
　If Thou my God, art near ;
Thy grace can raise my comforts high,
　And banish every fear.

My great Protector, and my Lord,
　Thy constant aid impart;
Oh, let Thy kind, Thy gracious word
　Sustain my trembling heart !

Oh, never let my soul remove
　From this divine retreat !
Still let me trust Thy power and love,
　And dwell beneath Thy feet.

THE CHRISTIAN LIFE.

GORTON.   S. M.

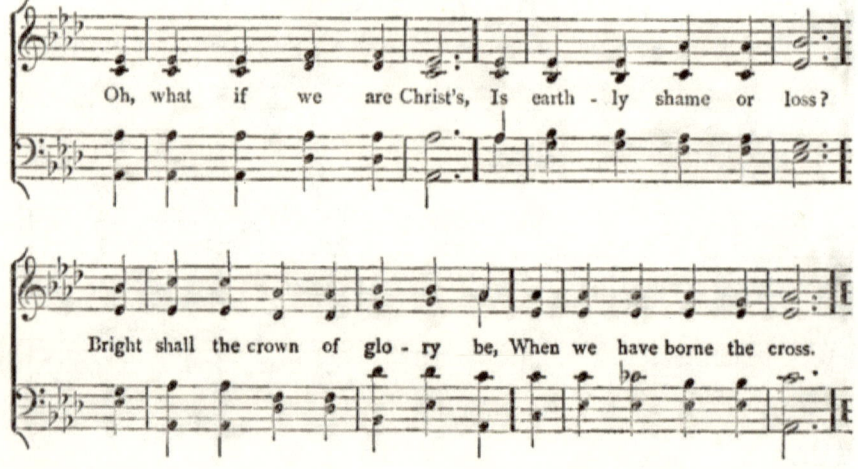

Oh, what if we are Christ's, Is earth-ly shame or loss?
Bright shall the crown of glo-ry be, When we have borne the cross.

227

OH, what if we are Christ's,
　Is earthly shame or loss?
Bright shall the crown of glory be,
　When we have borne the cross.

Keen was the trial once,
　Bitter the cup of woe,
When martyred saints, baptized in blood,
　Christ's sufferings shared below.

Bright is their glory now,
　Boundless their joy above,
Where, on the bosom of their God,
　They rest in perfect love.

Lord, may that grace be ours,
　Like them in faith to bear
All that of sorrow, grief, or pain
　May be our portion here.

228

O SAVIOUR! who didst come
　By water and by blood;
Confessed on earth, adored in heaven,
　Eternal Son of God!

Jesus, our Life and Hope,
　To endless years the same!
We plead Thy gracious promises,
　And rest upon Thy Name.

By faith in Thee we live,
　By faith in Thee we stand,
By Thee we vanquish sin and death,
　And gain the heavenly land.

O Lord! increase our faith;
　Our fearful spirits calm;
Sustain us through this mortal strife,
　Then give the victor's palm.

　　The Father and the Son,
　　　And Spirit we adore;
　　We praise, we bless, we worship Thee,
　　　Both now and evermore.

THE CHRISTIAN LIFE.

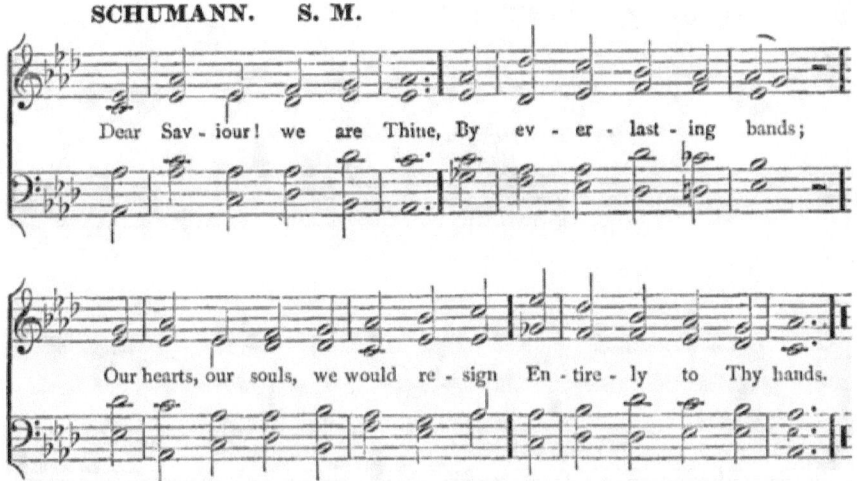

SCHUMANN. S. M.

Dear Saviour! we are Thine, By everlasting bands;
Our hearts, our souls, we would resign Entirely to Thy hands.

229

DEAR Saviour! we are Thine,
  By everlasting bands;
Our hearts, our souls, we would resign
  Entirely to Thy hands.

To Thee we still would cleave
  With ever-growing zeal;
If millions tempt us Christ to leave,
  Oh, let them ne'er prevail!

Thy Spirit shall unite
  Our souls to Thee, our Head;
Shall form us in Thine image bright,
  And teach Thy paths to tread.

Since Christ and we are one,
  Why should we doubt or fear?
If He in heaven has fixed His throne,
  He'll fix His members there.

The Father and the Son,
  And Spirit we adore;
We praise, we bless, we worship Thee,
  Both now and evermore!

230

BEHOLD, what wondrous grace
  The Father has bestowed
On sinners of a mortal race,
  To call them sons of God!

Nor doth it yet appear
  How great we must be made;
But when we see our Saviour here,
  We shall be like our Head.

A hope so much divine
  May trials well endure;
May purify our souls from sin,
  As Christ the Lord is pure.

If in my Father's love
  I share a filial part,
Send down Thy Spirit, like a dove,
  To rest upon my heart.

We would no longer lie
  Like slaves beneath the throne;
Our faith shall "Abba, Father," cry,
  And Thou the kindred own.

THE CHRISTIAN LIFE.

HOLLAND. L. M.

When sins and fears pre-vail-ing rise, And faint-ing hope al-most ex-pires,

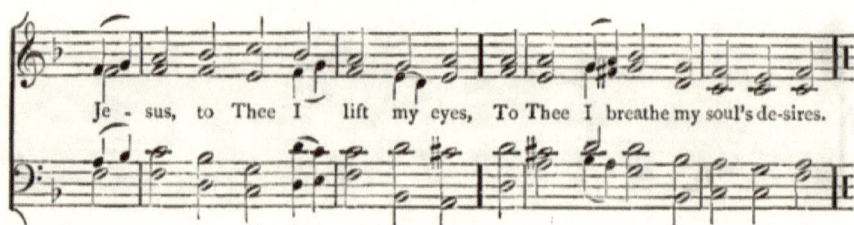
Je - sus, to Thee I lift my eyes, To Thee I breathe my soul's de-sires.

231

WHEN sins and fears prevailing rise,
    And fainting hope almost expires,
Jesus, to Thee I lift my eyes,
    To Thee I breathe my soul's desires.

If my immortal Saviour lives,
    Then my immortal life is sure;
His word a firm foundation gives;
    Here let me build and rest secure.

Here let my faith unshaken dwell;
    Immovable the promise stands;
Not all the powers of earth and hell
    Can e'er dissolve the sacred bands.

Here, O my soul! thy trust repose:
    If Jesus is forever mine,
Not death itself, that last of foes,
    Shall break a union so divine.

232

RETURN, my soul, and sweetly rest
    On Thy almighty Father's breast;
The bounties of His grace adore,
And count His wondrous mercies o'er.

Thy mercy, Lord, preserved my breath,
And snatch'd my fainting soul from death;
Removed my sorrows, dried my tears,
And saved me from surrounding snares.

What shall I render to the Lord?
Or how His wondrous grace record?
To Him my grateful voice I'll raise,
With just thanksgiving to His praise.

O Zion! in thy sacred courts,
Where glory dwells and joy resorts,
To notes divine I'll tune the song,
And praise shall flow from every tongue.

    Praise God, from whom all blessings flow!
    Praise Him, all creatures here below!
    Praise Him above, ye heavenly host!
    Praise Father, Son, and Holy Ghost!

THE CHRISTIAN LIFE.

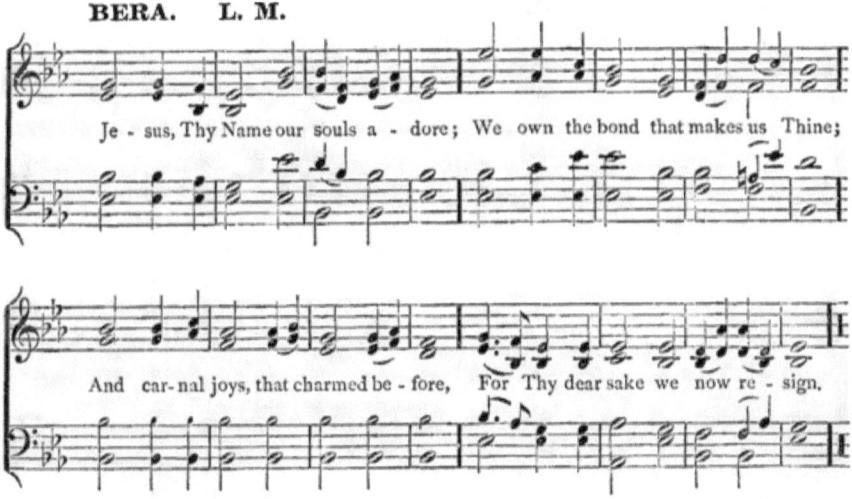

BERA. L. M.

Jesus, Thy Name our souls adore; We own the bond that makes us Thine; And carnal joys, that charmed before, For Thy dear sake we now resign.

233

JESUS, Thy Name our souls adore;
  We own the bond that makes us Thine;
And carnal joys, that charmed before,
  For Thy dear sake we now resign.

Our hearts, by dying love subdued,
  Accept Thine offered grace to-day;
Beneath the cross, with blood bedewed,
  We bow, and give ourselves away.

In Thee we trust,—on Thee rely;
  Tho' we are feeble, Thou art strong;
Oh, keep us till our spirits fly
  To join the bright, immortal throng!

234

LORD, in Thy great, Thy glorious Name,
  I place my hope, my only trust;
Save me from sorrow, guilt, and shame,
  Thou ever gracious, ever just.

Thou art my rock! Thy Name alone
  The fortress where my hopes retreat;
Oh, make Thy power and mercy known;
  To safety guide my wandering feet.

Blest be the Lord, forever blest,
  Whose mercy bids my fears remove;
The sacred walls which guard my rest
  Are His almighty power and love.

235

LIGHT of the soul! O Saviour blest!
  Soon as Thy presence fills the breast,
Darkness and guilt are put to flight,
And all is sweetness and delight.

Son of the Father! Lord most high!
How glad is He who feels Thee nigh!
Come in Thy hidden majesty;
Fill us with love, fill us with Thee.

THE CHRISTIAN LIFE.

ST. ANN'S. C. M.

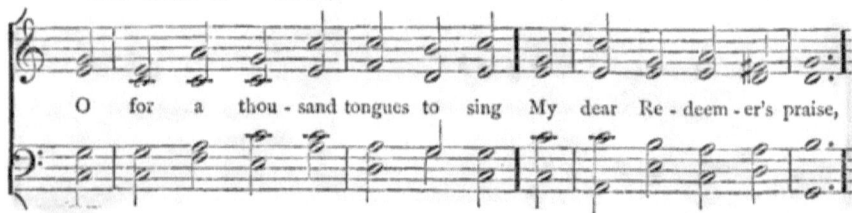

O for a thousand tongues to sing My dear Redeemer's praise, The glories of my God and King, The triumphs of His grace!

236

O FOR a thousand tongues to sing
    My dear Redeemer's praise,
The glories of my God and King,
    The triumphs of His grace!

Jesus—the Name that charms our fears,
    That bids our sorrows cease;
'Tis music in the sinner's ears;
    'Tis life, and health, and peace.

He breaks the power of reigning sin,
    And sets the prisoner free:
His blood can make the foulest clean;
    His blood availed for me.

He speaks; and, listening to His voice,
    New life the dead receive;
The mournful broken hearts rejoice;
    The humble poor believe.

237

LORD, as to Thy dear cross we flee,
    And pray to be forgiven,
So let Thy life our pattern be,
    And form our souls for heaven.

Help us, through good report and ill,
    Our daily cross to bear;
Like Thee, to do our Father's will,
    Our brother's griefs to share.

Let grace our selfishness expel,
    Our earthliness refine;
And kindness in our bosoms dwell
    As free and true as Thine.

Kept peaceful in the midst of strife,
    Forgiving and forgiven,
Oh, may we lead the pilgrim's life,
    And follow Thee to heaven!

To Father, Son, and Holy Ghost,
    One God whom we adore,
Be glory as it was, is now,
    And shall be evermore.

NEARER TO THEE.

238

NEARER, my God, to Thee,
   Nearer to Thee;
E'en though it be a cross
   That raiseth me,
Still all my song shall be,
Nearer, my God, to Thee,
   Nearer to Thee!

Though, like a wanderer,
   The sun gone down,
Darkness comes over me,
   My rest a stone,
Yet in my dreams I'd be
Nearer, my God, to Thee,
   Nearer to Thee!

There let my way appear
   Steps unto heaven:
All that Thou sendest me,
   In mercy given;
Angels to beckon me
Nearer, my God, to Thee,
   Nearer to Thee!

Then, with my waking thoughts
   Bright with Thy praise,
Out of my stony griefs
   Bethel I'll raise;
So by my woes to be
Nearer, my God, to Thee,
   Nearer to Thee!

BETHANY.

THE CHRISTIAN LIFE.

BARBY. C. M.

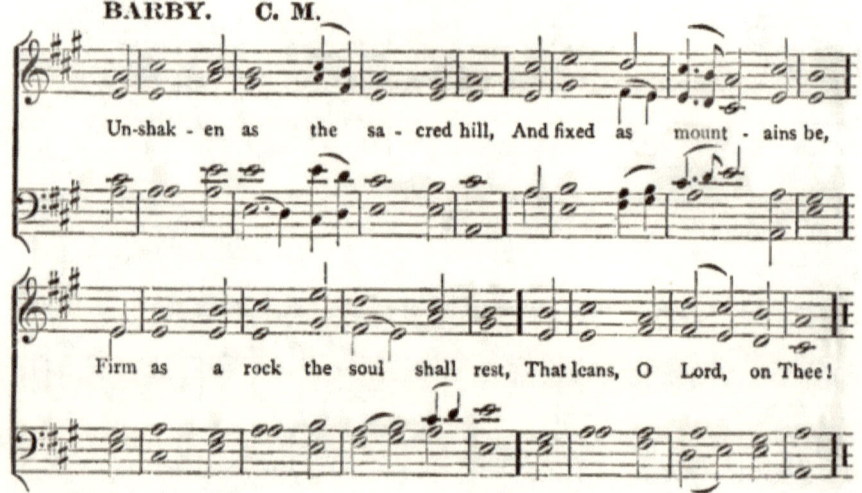

Un-shak-en as the sa-cred hill, And fixed as mount-ains be, Firm as a rock the soul shall rest, That leans, O Lord, on Thee!

239

UNSHAKEN as the sacred hill,
  And fixed as mountains be,
Firm as a rock the soul shall rest,
  That leans, O Lord, on Thee!

Not walls, nor hills, could guard so well
  Old Salem's happy ground,
As those eternal arms of love,
  That every saint surround.

Deal gently, Lord, with souls sincere,
  And lead them safely on
To the bright gates of paradise,
  Where Christ their Lord is gone.

240

LORD, I believe; Thy power I own,
  Thy word I would obey;
I wander comfortless and lone,
  When from Thy truth I stray.

Lord, I believe; but gloomy fears
  Sometimes bedim my sight;
I look to Thee with prayers and tears,
  And cry for strength and light.

Yes! I believe; and only Thou
  Canst give my soul relief:
Lord! to Thy truth my spirit bow;
  "Help Thou mine unbelief!"

NAOMI. C. M.

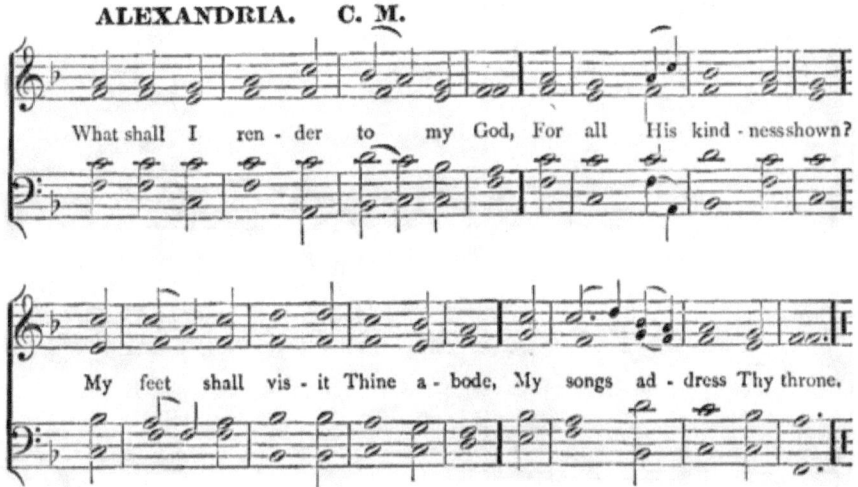

ALEXANDRIA. C. M.

241

WHAT shall I render to my God,
　For all His kindness shown?
My feet shall visit Thine abode,
　My songs address Thy throne.

Among the saints that fill Thy house,
　My offerings shall be paid;
There shall my zeal perform the vows
　My soul in anguish made.

Now I am Thine, for ever Thine,
　Nor shall my purpose move;
Thy hand hath loosed my bonds of pain,
　And bound me with Thy love.

Here in Thy courts I leave my vow,
　And Thy rich grace record;
Witness, ye saints! who hear me now,
　If I forsake the Lord.

242

FATHER, whate'er of earthly bliss
　Thy sovereign will denies,
Accepted at Thy throne of grace
　Let this petition rise.

Give me a calm and thankful heart,
　From every murmur free;
The blessings of Thy grace impart;
　And let me live to Thee.

Let the sweet hope that Thou art mine
　My life and death attend:
Thy presence through my journey shine,
　And crown my journey's end.

243

OH, could I find, from day to day,
　A nearness to my God!
Then would my hours glide sweet away,
　While leaning on His word.

Lord, I desire with Thee to live
　Anew from day to day,
In joys the world can never give,
　Nor ever take away.

Blest Jesus, come, and rule my heart,
　And make me wholly Thine,
That I may nevermore depart,
　Nor grieve Thy love divine.

THE CHRISTIAN LIFE.

ST. MICHAEL. S. M.

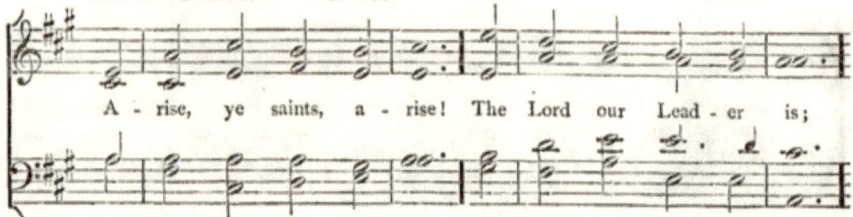

A-rise, ye saints, a-rise! The Lord our Lead-er is;

The foe be-fore His ban-ner flies, And vic-to-ry is His.

244

ARISE, ye saints, arise:
  The Lord our Leader is;
The foe before His banner flies,
  And victory is His.

We follow Thee, our Guide,
  Our Saviour, and our King!
We follow Thee, through grace supplied
  From heaven's eternal spring.

We soon shall see the day
  When all our toils shall cease;
When we shall cast our arms away,
  And dwell in endless peace.

This hope supports us here;
  It makes our burdens light,
'T will serve our drooping hearts to cheer,
  Till faith shall end in sight.

Till, of the prize possessed,
  We hear of war no more;
And ever with our Leader rest,
  On yonder peaceful shore.

245

COME, we that love the Lord,
  And let our joys be known;
Join in a song with sweet accord,
  And thus surround the throne.

Let those refuse to sing
  That never knew our God,
But children of the Heavenly King
  May speak their joys abroad.

Children of grace have found
  Glory begun below:
Celestial fruits on earthly ground
  From faith and hope may grow.

The hill of Sion yields
  A thousand sacred sweets,
Before we reach the heavenly fields,
  Or walk the golden streets.

Then let our songs abound,
  And every tear be dry;
We're marching through Immanuel's ground
  To fairer worlds on high.

THE CHRISTIAN LIFE.

ST. THOMAS.   S. M.

A-wake, and sing the song Of Mo-ses and the Lamb;
Wake, ev-'ry heart and ev-'ry tongue, To praise the Sav-iour's Name.

246

AWAKE, and sing the song
  Of Moses and the Lamb;
Wake, every heart and every tongue,
  To praise the Saviour's Name.

Sing of His dying love;
  Sing of His rising power;
Sing how He intercedes above
  For those whose sins He bore.

Sing on your heavenly way,
  Ye ransomed sinners, sing;
Sing on, rejoicing every day
  In Christ th' eternal King.

Soon shall ye hear Him say,
  "Ye blessèd children, come!"
Soon will He call you hence away,
  And take His wanderers home.

247

GRACE!—'t is a charming sound,
  Harmonious to the ear;
Heaven with the echo shall resound,
  And all the earth shall hear.

Grace first contrived a way
  To save rebellious man;
And all the steps that grace display,
  Which drew the wondrous plan.

Grace led my wandering feet
  To tread the heavenly road;
And new supplies each hour I meet,
  While pressing on to God.

Grace all the work shall crown,
  Through everlasting days;
It lays in heaven the topmost stone,
  And well deserves the praise.

The Father and the Son
  And Spirit we adore;
We praise, we bless, we worship Thee,
  Both now and evermore!

THE CHRISTIAN LIFE.

OLMUTZ. S. M.

Your harps, ye trembling saints, Down from the willows take;
Loud to the praise of love divine Bid ev'ry string awake.

248

YOUR harps, ye trembling saints,
   Down from the willows take;
Loud to the praise of love divine
   Bid every string awake.

Though in a foreign land,
   We are not far from home;
And nearer to our house above
   We every moment come.

His grace will to the end
   Stronger and brighter shine;
Nor present things, nor things to come,
   Shall quench the spark divine.

When we in darkness walk,
   Nor feel the heavenly flame,
Then is the time to trust our God,
   And rest upon His Name.

Soon shall our doubts and fears
   Subside at His control;
His loving-kindness shall break through
   The midnight of the soul.

249

OUR Heavenly Father calls,
   And Christ invites us near,
With both our friendship shall be sweet,
   And our communion dear.

God pities all our griefs;
   He pardons every day;
Almighty to protect our souls,
   And wise to guide our way.

Jesus, our Living Head,
   We bless Thy faithful care;
Our Advocate before the throne,
   And our Forerunner there.

Here fix, my roving heart!
   Here wait, my warmest love!
Till the communion be complete,
   In nobler scenes above.

The Father and the Son
   And Spirit we adore;
We praise, we bless, we worship Thee,
   Both now and evermore!

250

WHILE my Redeemer's near,
    My Shepherd and my Guide,
I bid farewell to anxious fear:
    My wants are all supplied.

To ever-fragrant meads,
    Where rich abundance grows,
His gracious hand indulgent leads,
    And guards my sweet repose.

Dear Shepherd, if I stray,
    My wand'ring feet restore;
And guard me with Thy watchful eye,
    And let me rove no more.

251

BLEST are the pure in heart,
    For they shall see their God;
The secret of the Lord is theirs,
    Their soul is Christ's abode.

He to the lowly soul
    Doth still Himself impart;
And for His dwelling and His throne,
    Chooseth the pure in heart.

Lord, we Thy presence seek:
    May ours this blessing be;
Oh, give the pure and lowly heart
    A temple meet for Thee!

252

THE Lord my Shepherd is;
    I shall be well supplied;
Since He is mine, and I am His,
    What can I want beside?

He leads me to the place
    Where heavenly pasture grows;
Where living waters gently pass,
    And full salvation flows.

If e'er I go astray,
    He doth my soul reclaim;
And guides me, in His own right way,
    For His most holy Name.

While He affords His aid,
    I cannot yield to fear;
Though I should walk through death's
        dark shade,
    My Shepherd's with me there.

The bounties of Thy love
    Shall crown my following days;
Nor from Thy house will I remove,
    Nor cease to speak Thy praise.

253

TEACH me, my God and King,
    In all things Thee to see;
And what I do in anything,
    To do it as for Thee!

To scorn the senses' sway,
    While still to Thee I tend;
In all I do, be Thou the way,
    In all, be Thou the end.

All may of Thee partake;
    Nothing so small can be
But draws, when acted for Thy sake,
    Greatness and worth from Thee.

If done beneath Thy laws,
    E'en servile labors shine;
Hallowed is toil, if this the cause;
    The meanest work, divine.

The Father and the Son
    And Spirit we adore;
We praise, we bless, we worship Thee,
    Both now and evermore!

THE CHRISTIAN LIFE.

HAMDEN. 8s, 7s & 4s.

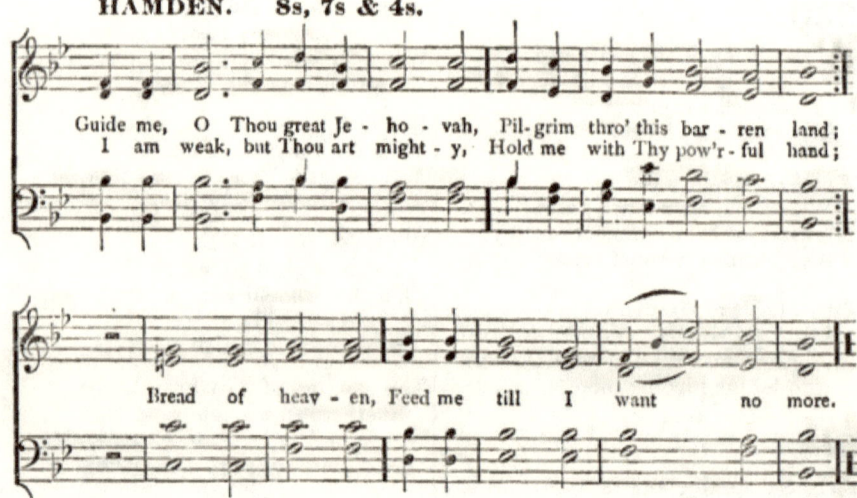

Guide me, O Thou great Jehovah, Pilgrim thro' this barren land;
I am weak, but Thou art mighty, Hold me with Thy pow'rful hand;
Bread of heaven, Feed me till I want no more.

254

GUIDE me, O Thou great Jehovah,
   Pilgrim through this barren land;
I am weak, but Thou art mighty,
   Hold me with Thy powerful hand;
     Bread of heaven,
   Feed me till I want no more.

Open Thou the crystal fountain
   Whence the healing streams do flow;
Let the fiery, cloudy pillar
   Lead me all my journey through;
     Strong Deliverer,
   Be Thou still my strength and shield.

When I tread the verge of Jordan,
   Bid my anxious fears subside;
Bear me through the swelling current,
   Land me safe on Canaan's side;
     Songs of praises
   I will ever give to Thee.

255

JESUS, Lord of life and glory,
   Bend from heaven Thy gracious ear;
While our waiting souls adore Thee,
   Friend of helpless sinners, hear:
     By Thy mercy,
   O deliver us, good Lord.

From the depths of nature's blindness,
   From the hardening power of sin,
From all malice and unkindness,
   From the pride that works within,
     By Thy mercy, etc.

When temptation sorely presses,
   In the day of Satan's power,
In our times of deep distresses,
   In each dark and trying hour,
     By Thy mercy, etc.

In the solemn hour of dying,
   In the awful judgment-day,
May our souls, on Thee relying,
   Find Thee still our hope and stay:
     By Thy mercy, etc.

THE CHRISTIAN LIFE.

NEWMAN. P. M.

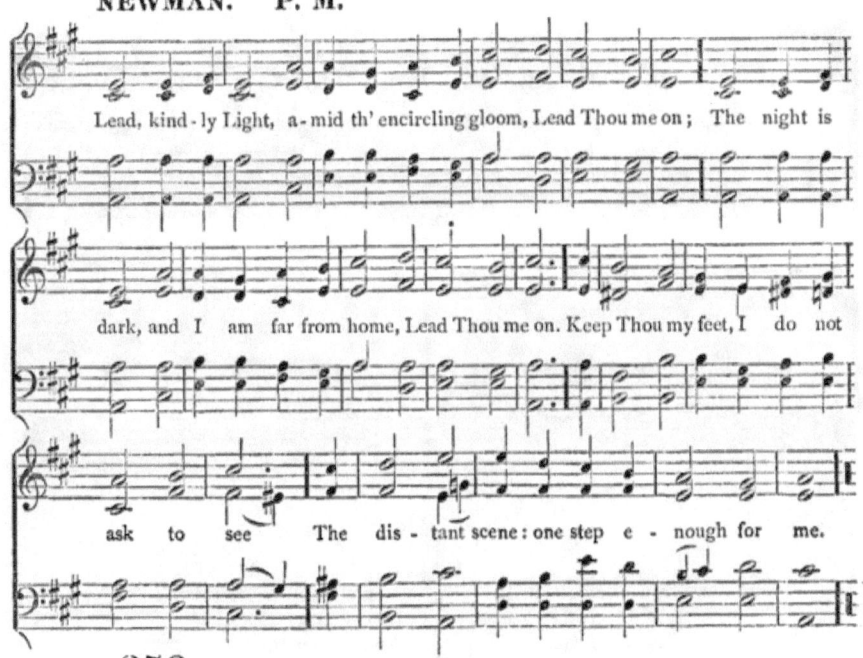

256

LEAD, kindly Light, amid th' encircling gloom,
　　Lead Thou me on ;
The night is dark, and I am far from home,
　　Lead Thou me on.
Keep Thou my feet, I do not ask to see
The distant scene : one step enough for me.

I was not ever thus, nor prayed that Thou
　　Shouldst lead me on ;
I loved to choose and see my path ; but now
　　Lead Thou me on.
I loved the garish day ; and, spite of fears,
Pride ruled my will : remember not past years.

So long Thy power has blest me, sure it still
　　Will lead me on
O'er moor and fen, o'er crag and torrent, till
　　The night is gone,
And with the morn those angel faces smile,
Which I have loved long since, and lost awhile.

M

MORNINGTON. S. M.

If through un-ruf-fled seas Toward heav'n we calm-ly sail,
With grate-ful hearts, O God, to Thee, We'll own the fos-t'ring gale.

257

IF through unruffled seas
  Toward heaven we calmly sail,
With grateful hearts, O God, to Thee,
  We'll own the fostering gale.

But should the surges rise,
  And rest delay to come,
Blest be the sorrow, kind the storm,
  Which drives us nearer home.

Soon shall our doubts and fears
  All yield to Thy control;
Thy tender mercies shall illume
  The midnight of the soul.

Teach us, in every state,
  To make Thy will our own;
And when the joys of sense depart,
  To live by faith alone.

258

FAR from my heavenly home,
  Far from my Father's breast,
Fainting, I cry,—"Blest Spirit! come,
  And speed me to my rest."

My spirit homeward turns,
  And fain would thither flee;
My heart, O Zion! droops and yearns,
  When I remember Thee.

To Thee, to Thee I press—
  A dark and toilsome road:
When shall I pass the wilderness,
  And reach the saints' abode?

God of my life! be near!
  On Thee my hopes are cast:
Oh! guide me through the desert here,
  And bring me home at last.

  The Father and the Son
   And Spirit we adore;
  We praise, we bless, we worship Thee,
   Both now and evermore.

ST. BRIDE. S. M.

259

"MY times are in Thy hand:"
  My God! I wish them there;
My life, my friends, my soul, I leave
  Entirely to Thy care.

"My times are in Thy hand,"
  Whatever they may be;
Pleasing or painful, dark or bright,
  As best may seem to Thee.

"My times are in Thy hand;"
  Why should I doubt or fear?
My Father's hand will never cause
  His child a needless tear.

"My times are in Thy hand,"—
  Jesus the Crucified!
The hand my cruel sins had pierced,
  Is now my guard and guide.

"My times are in Thy hand;"
  I'll always trust in Thee;
And, after death, at Thy right hand
  I shall forever be.

260

WHEN overwhelmed with grief,
  My heart within me dies;
Helpless, and far from all relief,
  To heaven I lift mine eyes.

Oh, lead me to the Rock
  That's high above my head,
And make the covert of Thy wings
  My shelter and my shade!

Within Thy presence, Lord,
  Forever I'll abide;
Thou art the tower of my defence,
  The refuge where I hide.

Thou givest me the lot
  Of those that fear Thy Name;
If endless life be their reward,
  I shall possess the same.

To God, the Father, Son,
  And Spirit, glory be,
As was, and is, and shall remain
  Through all eternity!

THE CHRISTIAN LIFE.

CALM. S. M.

My Spir-it on Thy care, Blest Sav-iour, I re-cline;

Thou wilt not leave me to des-pair, For Thou art love di-vine.

261

My spirit on Thy care,
　Blest Saviour, I recline;
Thou wilt not leave me to despair,
　For Thou art love divine.

In Thee I place my trust;
　On Thee I calmly rest:
I know Thee good, I know Thee just,
　And count Thy choice the best.

Whate'er events betide,
　Thy will they all perform;
Safe in Thy breast my head I hide,
　Nor fear the coming storm.

Let good or ill befall,
　It must be good for me,—
Secure of having Thee in all,
　Of having all in Thee.

262

For all Thy saints, O God,
　Who strove in Christ to live,
Who followed Him, obeyed, adored,
　Our grateful hymn receive.

For all Thy saints, O God,
　Accept our thankful cry,
Who counted Christ their great reward,
　And yearned for Him to die.

They all, in life and death,
　With Him, their Lord, in view,
Learned from Thy Holy Spirit's breath,
　To suffer and to do.

For this Thy Name we bless,
　And humbly pray that we
May follow them in holiness,
　And live and die in Thee.

To God, the Father, Son,
　And Spirit, glory be,
As was, and is, and shall remain
　Through all eternity!

263

FATHER of love, our Guide and
  Oh, lead us gently on,   [Friend,
Until life's trial-time shall end,
  And heavenly rest be won.

We know not what the path may be
  As yet by us untrod,
But we can trust our all to Thee,
  Our Father and our God.

And if some darker lot be good,
  Oh, teach us to endure
The sorrow, pain, or solitude,
  That makes the spirit pure.

264

O SON of Man, and Son of God,
  Thou very Light of Light!
Whose feet this world's dark valley trod
  That so it might be bright:—

Our hopes are weak, our fears are strong,
  Thick darkness blinds our eyes;
Cold is the night, and oh, we long
  For Thee, our Sun, to rise.

We wait in faith, and turn our face
  To where the daylight springs,
Till Thou shalt come our gloom to chase,
  With healing on Thy wings.

Oh, guide us till our goal is won,
  And we have reached the shore
Where Thou, the everlasting Sun,
  Art shining evermore.

265

WE bless Thee for Thy peace, O God!
  Deep as the soundless sea,
Which falls like sunshine on the road
  Of those who trust in Thee.

That peace which suffers and is strong,
  Trusts where it cannot see,
Deems not the trial-way too long,
  But leaves the end with Thee.

Such, Father, give our hearts such peace,
  Whate'er the outward be,
Till all life's discipline shall cease,
  And we go home to Thee.

THE CHRISTIAN LIFE.

FATHERLAND. 5s & 8s.

Je-sus, still lead on Till our rest be won: And, al-though the
D. S.—Guide us by Thy hand To our Fa-ther-land.
way be cheer-less, We will fol-low, calm and fear-less:

266

JESUS, still lead on
 Till our rest be won:
And, although the way be cheerless,
We will follow, calm and fearless:
 Guide us by Thy hand
 To our Fatherland!
If the way be drear,
If the foe be near,
Let not faithless fears o'ertake us,
Let not faith and hope forsake us;
 For, through many a foe,
 To our home we go!

When we seek relief
 From a long-felt grief;
When temptations come alluring,
Make us patient and enduring:
 Show us that bright shore
 Where we weep no more!
Jesus, still lead on,
 Till our rest be won;
Heavenly Leader, still direct us,
Still support, console, protect us,
 Till we safely stand
 In our Fatherland!

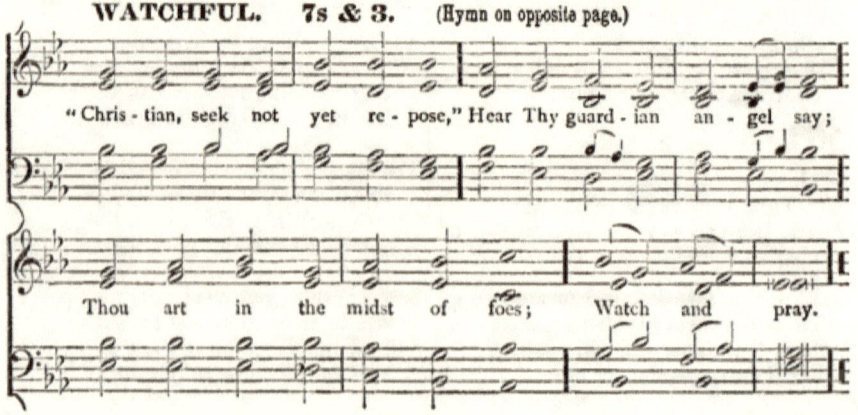

WATCHFUL. 7s & 3. (Hymn on opposite page.)

"Chris-tian, seek not yet re-pose," Hear Thy guard-ian an-gel say;
Thou art in the midst of foes; Watch and pray.

TROYTE. P. M.

1. My God, my Father, while I stray, Far from my home, on life's rough way, O teach me from my heart to say, "Thy will be done." A-men.

267

My God, my Father, while I stray
Far from my home, on life's rough way,
O teach me from my heart to say,
  "Thy will be done."

Though dark my path and sad my lot,
Let me be still and murmur not,
Or breathe the prayer divinely taught,
  "Thy will be done."

What though in lonely grief I sigh
For friends beloved no longer nigh,
Submissive still would I reply,
  "Thy will be done."

If Thou shouldst call me to resign
What most I prize—it ne'er was mine;
I only yield Thee what is Thine—
  "Thy will be done."

Let but my fainting heart be blest
With Thy sweet Spirit for its guest,
My God, to Thee I leave the rest;
  "Thy will be done."

Renew my will from day to day,
Blend it with Thine, and take away
All that now makes it hard to say,
  "Thy will be done."

WATCHFUL.   (Opposite page.)

268

"Christian, seek not yet repose,"
  Hear Thy guardian angel say;
Thou art in the midst of foes;
  Watch and pray!

Hear the victors who o'ercame;
Still they mark each warrior's way;
All with one sweet voice exclaim,
  Watch and pray!

Hear the warning of thy Lord,
Him thou lovest to obey;
Hide within thy heart His word,—
  Watch and pray!

Watch, as if on that alone
Hung the issue of the day;
Pray that help may be sent down:
  Watch and pray!

PORTUGUESE HYMN. 11s.

1. How firm a foun-da-tion, ye saints of the Lord! Is laid for your faith, in His ex-cellent Word! What more can He say, than to you He hath said, You, who un-to Je-sus for ref-uge have fled? You, who un-to Je-sus for ref-uge have fled?

269

2.
"Fear not, I am with thee; oh, be not dismayed,
For I am thy God, I will still give thee aid:
I'll strengthen thee, help thee, and cause thee to stand,
Upheld by My gracious, omnipotent hand.

3.
"When through the deep waters I call thee to go,
The rivers of sorrow shall not overflow;
For I will be with thee thy trials to bless,
And sanctify to thee thy deepest distress.

4.
"E'en down to old age all My people shall prove
My sovereign, eternal, unchangeable love;
And then, when gray hairs shall their temples adorn,
Like lambs they shall still in My bosom be borne.

5.
"The soul that on Jesus hath leaned for repose,
I will not—I will not desert to his foes;
That soul, though all hell should endeavor to shake,
I'll never—no, never—no, never forsake!"

THE CHRISTIAN LIFE.

270
FORSAKE me not, O Lord,
    Thou God of my salvation;
Give me Thy light to be
My sure illumination.
My soul to folly turns,
Seeking, it knows not what;
Oh, lead her to Thyself;
My God, forsake me not.

Forsake me not, O Lord!
Take not Thy Spirit from me,
And suffer not the might
Of sin to overcome me.

And when the sinful fire
Within my heart is hot,
Be not Thou far from me;
My God, forsake me not!

Forsake me not, O Lord!
I would be Thine forever:
Confirm me mightily
In every right endeavor.
And when my hour is come,
Cleansed from all sin and spot,
To rest receive my soul:
My God, forsake me not!

THE CHRISTIAN LIFE.

271

If thou but suffer God to guide thee,
  And hope in Him in all thy ways;
He'll give thee strength whate'er betide thee,
  And bear thee through all evil days.
Who trusts in God's unchanging love,
Builds on the rock that naught can move.

Only be still and wait His leisure,
  In cheerful hope, with heart content
To take whate'er thy Father's pleasure
  And all-deserving love hath sent:
Nor doubt our inmost wants are known
To Him who chose us for His own.

Sing, pray, and keep His ways unswerving,
  So do thine own part faithfully,
And trust His word, though undeserving,
  Thou yet shalt find it true for thee.
God never yet forsook at need
The soul that trusted Him indeed.

ROBINSON.   11s.

272

COME, Jesus, Redeemer, abide Thou with me;
Come, gladden my spirit that waiteth for Thee;
Thy smile every shadow shall chase from my heart,
And soothe every sorrow, though keen be the smart.

Thy love, oh, how faithful! so tender, so pure!
Thy promise, faith's anchor, how steadfast and sure!
That love, like sweet sunshine, my cold heart can warm,
That promise make steady my soul in the storm.

Breathe, breathe on my spirit, oft ruffled, Thy peace;
From restless, vain wishes, bid Thou my heart cease;
In Thee all its longings henceforward shall end,
Till glad, to Thy presence my soul shall ascend.

273

THOUGH faint, yet pursuing, we go on our way;
The Lord is our Leader, His Word is our stay;
Though suffering and sorrow and trial be near,
The Lord is our refuge, and whom can we fear?

He raiseth the fallen, He cheereth the faint;
The weak and oppressed—He will hear their complaint;
The way may be weary, and thorny the road,
But how can we falter? our help is in God!

Though clouds may surround us, our God is our light;
Though storms rage around us, our God is our might;
So faint, yet pursuing, still onward we come;
The Lord is our Leader, and heaven is our home!

SEYMOUR. 7s.

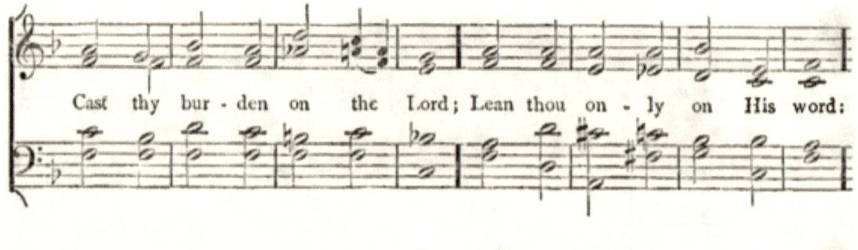

Cast thy bur-den on the Lord; Lean thou on-ly on His word:

Ev-er will He be thy stay, Though the heav'ns shall melt a-way.

274

Cast thy burden on the Lord;
  Lean thou only on His word:
Ever will He be thy stay,
Though the heavens shall melt away.

Ever in the raging storm,
Thou shalt see His cheering form,
Hear His pledge of coming aid:
"It is I, be not afraid."

Cast thy burden at His feet;
Linger near His mercy-seat:
He will lead thee by the hand
Gently to the better land.

He will gird thee by His power,
In thy weary, fainting hour;
Lean, then, loving, on His word;
Cast thy burden on the Lord.

275

Christ, of all my hopes the Ground,
  Christ, the Spring of all my joy!
Still in Thee may I be found,
  Still for Thee my powers employ:

Fountain of o'erflowing grace!
  Freely from Thy fullness give;
Till I close my earthly race,
  May I prove it "Christ to live!"

When I touch the blessèd shore,
  Back the closing waves shall roll;
Death's dark stream shall never more
  Part from Thee my ravished soul:

Thus,—Oh! thus, an entrance give
  To the land of cloudless sky;
Having known it, "Christ to live,"
  Let me know it, "gain to die."

Holy Father, Holy Son,
Holy Spirit, Three in One!
Glory, as of old, to Thee,
Now, and evermore shall be!

HATTON. 7s.

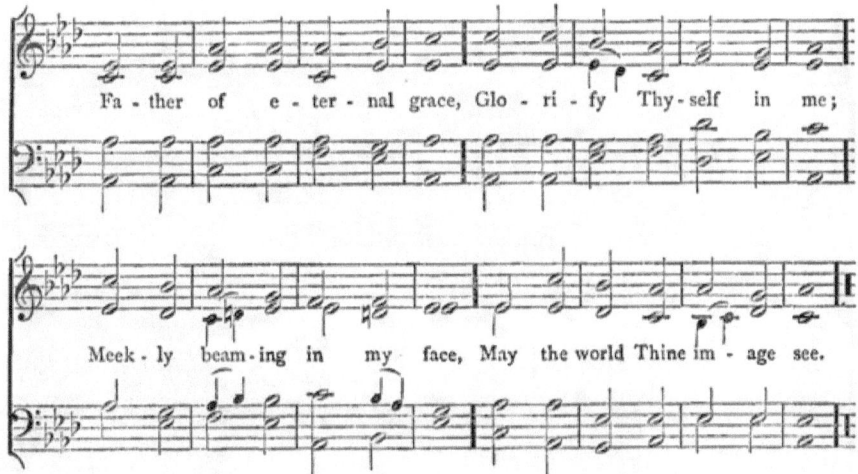

Father of eternal grace, Glorify Thyself in me;
Meekly beaming in my face, May the world Thine image see.

276

FATHER of eternal grace,
　Glorify Thyself in me;
Meekly beaming in my face,
　May the world Thine image see.

Happy only in Thy love,
　Poor, unfriended, or unknown,
Fix my thoughts on things above,
　Stay my heart on Thee alone.

Humble, holy, all resigned
　To Thy will—Thy will be done!
Give me, Lord, the perfect mind
　Of Thy well-beloved Son.

Counting gain and glory loss,
　May I tread the path He trod—
Die with Jesus on the cross,
　Rise with Him to Thee, my God.

277

PRINCE of peace! control my will;
　Bid this struggling heart be still;
Bid my fears and doubtings cease;
Hush my spirit into peace.

Thou hast bought me with Thy blood,
Opened wide the gate to God;
Peace I ask,—but peace must be,
Lord, in being one with Thee.

May Thy will, not mine, be done;
May Thy will and mine be one:
Chase these doubtings from my heart:
Now Thy perfect peace impart.

Saviour! at Thy feet I fall;
Thou my Life, my God, my All!
Let Thy happy servant be
One forevermore with Thee!

　　Sing we to our God above
　　Praise eternal as His love;
　　Praise Him, all ye heavenly host—
　　Father, Son, and Holy Ghost!

THE CHRISTIAN LIFE.

CECILIA. 8s & 7s.

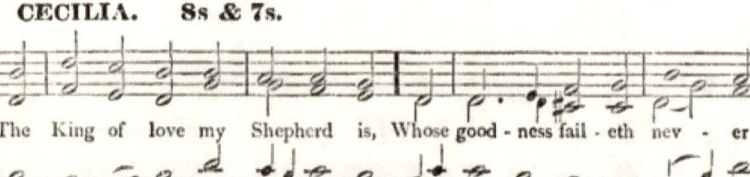
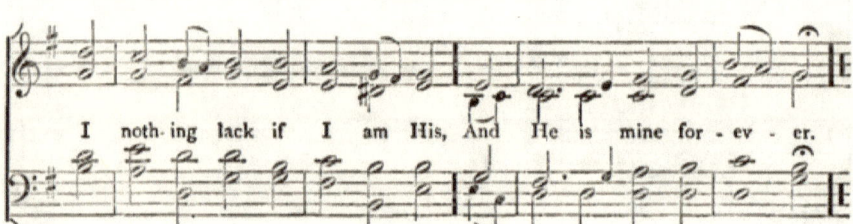

The King of love my Shepherd is, Whose goodness faileth never;
I nothing lack if I am His, And He is mine forever.

278

THE King of love my Shepherd is,
    Whose goodness faileth never;
I nothing lack if I am His,
    And He is mine forever.

Where streams of living water flow,
    My ransomed soul He leadeth,
And, where the verdant pastures grow,
    With food celestial feedeth.

Perverse and foolish oft I strayed,
    But yet in love He sought me,
And on His shoulder gently laid,
    And home, rejoicing, brought me.

In death's dark vale I fear no ill
    With Thee, dear Lord, beside me;
Thy rod and staff my comfort still,
    Thy Cross before to guide me.

And so through all the length of days,
    Thy goodness faileth never;
Good Shepherd, may I sing Thy praise
    Within Thy house forever.

279

WHO trusts in God, a strong abode
    In heaven and earth possesses;
Who looks in love to Christ above,
    No fear his heart oppresses.

In Thee alone, dear Lord, we own
    Sweet hope and consolation;
Our shield from foes, our balm for woes,
    Our great and sure salvation!

Thy rod and staff shall keep us safe,
    And guide our steps forever;
Nor shades of death, nor hell beneath,
    Our souls from Thee shall sever.

In all the strife of mortal life
    Our feet shall stand securely;
Temptation's hour shall lose its power
    For Thou shalt guard us surely.

O God, renew, with heavenly dew,
    Our body, soul, and spirit,
Until we stand at Thy right hand,
    Through Jesus' saving merit.

280

MY Jesus, as thou wilt!
  Oh, may Thy will be mine!
Into Thy hand of love
  I would my all resign.

Through sorrow or through joy,
  Conduct me as Thine own,
And help me still to say,
  My Lord, Thy will be done!

My Jesus, as Thou wilt!
  Though seen through many a tear,
Let not my star of hope
  Grow dim or disappear.

Thou, Lord, on earth along
  The thorny path hast gone;
Then lead me after Thee;—
  My Lord, Thy will be done!

My Jesus, as Thou wilt!
  When death itself draws nigh,
To Thy dear wounded side
  I would for refuge fly.

Leaning on Thee, to go
  Where Thou before hast gone;
The rest as Thou shalt please;—
  My Lord, Thy will be done!

281

THERE is a blessèd home
  Beyond this land of woe,
Where trials never come,
  Nor tears of sorrow flow;

Where faith is lost in sight,
  And patient hope is crowned,
And everlasting light
  Its glory throws around.

There is a land of peace;
  Good angels know it well;
Glad songs that never cease
  Within its portals swell.

Look up, ye saints of God!
  Nor fear to tread below
The path your Saviour trod
  Of daily toil and woe.

COMFORT. 11s & 10s.

282

COME unto Me, when shadows darkly gather,
When the sad heart is weary and distressed;
Seeking for comfort from your heavenly Father,
Come unto Me, and I will give you rest.

Large are the mansions in our Father's dwelling,
Glad are those homes that sorrows never dim;
Sweet are the harps in holy music swelling,
Soft are the tones that raise the heavenly hymn.

There, like an Eden blossoming in gladness,
Bloom the fair flowers by earth so rudely pressed;
"Come unto Me, all ye who droop in sadness,
Come unto Me, and I will give you rest."

283 (Tune on Opposite Page.)

O JESUS, my Saviour, Thine agony and woe,
Healeth all the sorrows that man can ever know.

O Jesus, my Saviour, the blood that Thou hast shed,
Cleanseth from transgression the living and the dead.

O Jesus, my Saviour, by Thy victorious power,
Sin is slain forever, and death appals no more.

O Jesus, my Saviour, now throned in majesty,
In Thy great compassion, have mercy upon me.

THE CHRISTIAN LIFE.

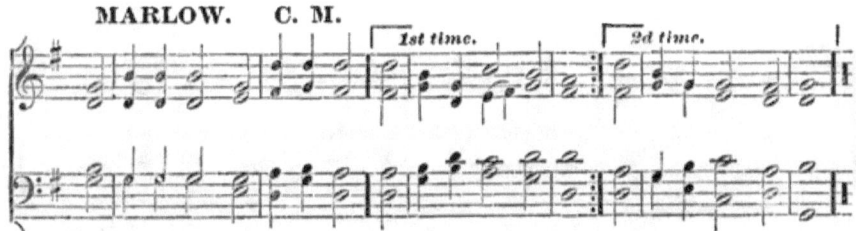

MARLOW. C. M.

284

HAPPY the souls to Jesus joined,
  And saved by grace alone;
Walking in all His ways, they find
  Their heaven on earth begun.

The church triumphant in Thy love,
  Their mighty joys we know:
They sing the Lamb in hymns above,
  And we in hymns below.

Thee in Thy glorious realm they praise,
  And bow before Thy throne;
We in the kingdom of Thy grace:
  The kingdoms are but one.

285

LET saints below in concert sing
  With those to glory gone;
For all the servants of our King
  In earth and heaven are one.

One family—we dwell in Him—
  One church above, beneath,
Though now divided by the stream,
  The narrow stream of death.

One army of the living God,
  To His command we bow;
Part of the host have crossed the flood,
  And part are crossing now.

Ev'n now, by faith, we join our hands
  With those that went before,
And greet the ransomed blessèd bands
  Upon th' eternal shore.

Lord Jesus! be our constant guide:
  And, when the word is given,
Bid death's cold flood its waves divide,
  And land us safe in heaven.

O JESUS, SAVIOUR. (Hymn on Opposite Page.)

THE CHRISTIAN LIFE.

HEBRON. L. M.

Thou Saviour, from Thy throne on high, Enrobed in light and girt with pow'r,
Dost note the thought, the prayer, the sigh, Of hearts that love the tranquil hour.

286

THOU Saviour, from Thy throne on high,
  Enrobed in light and girt with power,
Dost note the thought, the prayer, the sigh,
  Of hearts that love the tranquil hour.

Oft Thou Thyself didst steal away
  At eventide, from labor done,
In some still peaceful shade to pray
  Till morning watches were begun.

Thou hast not, dearest Lord, forgot
  Thy wrestlings on Judea's hills;
And still Thou lov'st the quiet spot
  Where praise the lowly spirit fills.

Now to our souls, withdrawn awhile
  From earth's rude noise, Thy face re-
And as we worship, kindly smile, [veal;
  And for Thine own our spirits seal.

To Thee we bring each grief and care,
  To Thee we fly while tempests lower;
Thou wilt the weary burdens bear
  Of hearts that love the tranquil hour.

287

FROM every stormy wind that blows,
  From every swelling tide of woes,
There is a calm, a sure retreat;
  'T is found beneath the mercy-seat.

There is a place where Jesus sheds
The oil of gladness on our heads:
A place than all beside more sweet;
It is the blood-bought mercy-seat.

There is a spot where spirits blend,
Where friend holds fellowship with friend;
Though sundered far, by faith they meet
Around one common mercy-seat.

There, there, on eagles' wings we soar,
And time and sense seem all no more;
And heaven comes down, our souls to greet,
And glory crowns the mercy-seat.

Praise God, from whom all blessings flow!
Praise Him, all creatures here below!
Praise Him above, ye heavenly host!
Praise Father, Son, and Holy Ghost!

BOYLSTON.   S. M.

Blest be the tie that binds Our hearts in Christian love:

The fellowship of kindred minds Is like to that above.

288

BLEST be the tie that binds
   Our hearts in Christian love:
The fellowship of kindred minds
   Is like to that above.

Before our Father's throne
   We pour united prayers;
Our fears, our hopes, our aims are one;
   Our comforts and our cares.

We share our mutual woes,
   Our mutual burdens bear;
And often for each other flows
   The sympathizing tear.

When we at death must part,
   Not like the world's, our pain;
But one in Christ, and one in heart,
   We part to meet again.

From sorrow, toil, and pain,
   And sin, we shall be free;
And perfect love and friendship reign
   Throughout eternity.

289

REVIVE Thy work, O Lord!
   Thy mighty arm make bare;
Speak, with the voice that wakes the dead,
   And make Thy people hear.

Revive Thy work, O Lord!
   Disturb this sleep of death;
Quicken the smouldering embers now,
   By Thine almighty breath.

Revive Thy work, O Lord!
   Exalt Thy precious Name;
And, by the Holy Ghost, our love
   For Thee and Thine inflame.

Revive Thy work, O Lord!
   And give refreshing showers;
The glory shall be all Thine own,
   The blessing, Lord! be ours.

To God, the Father, Son,
   And Spirit, glory be,
As was, and is, and shall remain
   Through all eternity!

THE CHRISTIAN LIFE.

STEPHENS. C. M.

Lord, lead the way the Sav-iour went, By lane and cell ob-scure,
And let our treas-ures still be spent, Like His, up-on the poor.

290

LORD, lead the way the Saviour went,
  By lane and cell obscure,
And let our treasures still be spent,
  Like His, upon the poor.

Like Him, through scenes of deep dis-[tress,
  Who bore the world's sad weight,
We, in their gloomy loneliness,
  Would seek the desolate.

For Thou hast placed us side by side
  In this wide world of ill;
And that Thy followers may be tried,
  The poor are with us still.

Small are the offerings we can make;
  Yet Thou hast taught us, Lord,
If given for the Saviour's sake,
  They lose not their reward.

291

AWAKE, my soul, stretch every nerve,
  And press with vigor on;
A heavenly race demands thy zeal,
  And an immortal crown.

A cloud of witnesses around
  Hold thee in full survey;
Forget the steps already trod,
  And onward urge thy way.

'Tis God's all-animating voice
  That calls thee from on high,
'Tis His own hand presents the prize
  To thine aspiring eye.

Then wake, my soul, stretch every nerve,
  And press with vigor on;
A heavenly race demands thy zeal,
  And an immortal crown.

To Father, Son, and Holy Ghost,
  One God whom we adore,
Be glory as it was, is now,
  And shall be evermore.

ST. PETER. C. M.

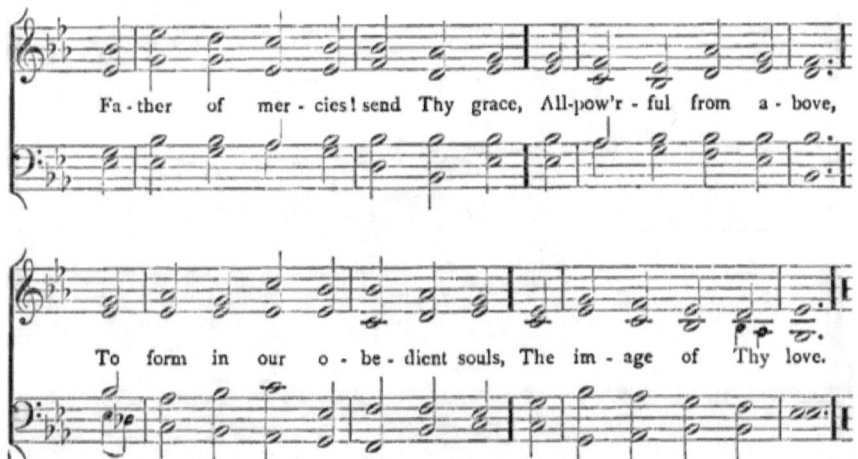

292

FATHER of mercies! send Thy grace,
　All-powerful from above,
To form in our obedient souls,
　The image of Thy love.

Oh! may our sympathizing breasts
　That generous pleasure know,
Kindly to share in others' joy,
　And weep for others' woe.

When the most helpless sons of grief
　In low distress are laid,
Soft be our hearts their pains to feel,
　And swift our hands to aid.

So Jesus looked on dying men,
　When throned above the skies;
And midst th' embraces of His God,
　He felt compassion rise.

On wings of love, the Saviour flew,
　To raise us from the ground;
And made the richest of His blood
　A balm for every wound.

293

O FOUNT of good, to own Thy love
　Our thankful hearts incline:
What can we render, Lord, to Thee,
　When all the worlds are Thine?

But Thou hast needy brethren here,
　Partakers of Thy grace,
Whose names Thou wilt Thyself confess
　Before the Father's face.

In each sad accent of distress
　Thy pleading voice is heard;
In them Thou may'st be clothed and fed,
　And visited, and cheered.

Help us then, Lord, Thy yoke to wear,
　To joy to do Thy will;
Each other's burdens gladly bear,
　And love's sweet law fulfil.

Do Thou, O Lord, our alms accept,
　And with Thy blessing speed;
Bless us in giving; greatly bless
　Our gifts to them that need.

SILVER STREET. S. M.

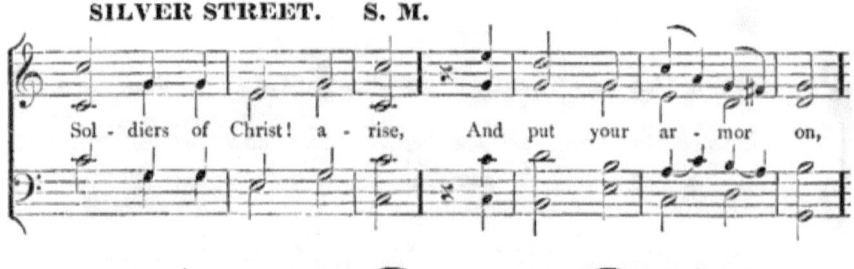

294

SOLDIERS of Christ! arise,
  And put your armor on, [plies
Strong in the strength which God sup-
  Through His eternal Son:

Strong in the Lord of Hosts,
  And in His mighty power:
Who in the strength of Jesus trusts
  Is more than conqueror!

Stand, then, in His great might,
  With all His strength endued;
And take, to arm you for the fight,
  The armor of your God.

From strength to strength go on,
  Wrestle, and fight, and pray,
Tread all the powers of darkness down,
  And win the well-fought day:

That, having all things done,
  And all your conflicts past,
Ye may o'ercome through Christ alone,
  And perfect stand at last.

295

MY soul, be on thy guard;
  Ten thousand foes arise;
And hosts of sin are pressing hard
  To draw thee from the skies.

O watch, and fight, and pray;
  The battle ne'er give o'er;
Renew it boldly every day,
  And help divine implore.

Ne'er think the victory won,
  Nor lay thine armor down:
Thy arduous work will not be done
  Till thou obtain thy crown.

Fight on, my soul, till death
  Shall bring thee to thy God;
He'll take thee at thy parting breath,
  Up to His blest abode.

The grace of Christ our Lord,
  God's love in boundless store,
The Holy Spirit's fellowship,
  Be with us evermore!

DOVER. S. M.

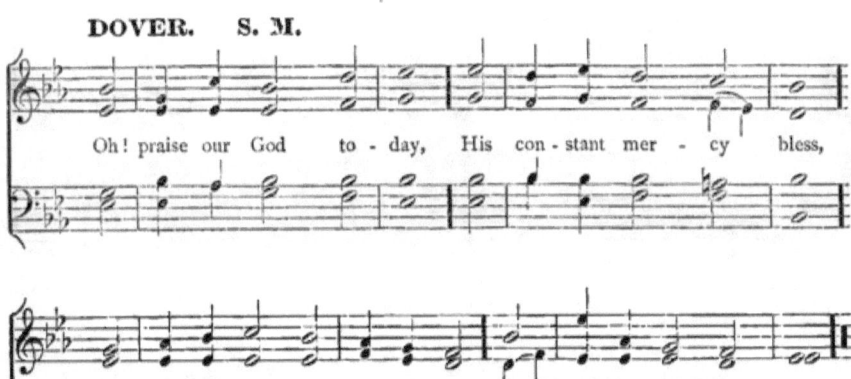

296

OH! praise our God to-day,
   His constant mercy bless,
Whose love hath helped us on our way,
   And granted us success.

His arm the strength imparts
   Our daily toil to bear;
His grace alone inspires our hearts,
   Each other's load to share.

Oh! happiest work below,
   Earnest of joy above,
To sweeten many a cup of woe,
   By deeds of holy love!

Lord! may it be our choice
   This blessèd rule to keep,
"Rejoice with them that do rejoice,
   And weep with them that weep."

God of the widow! hear;
   Our work of mercy bless;
God of the fatherless! be near,
   And grant us good success.

297

A CHARGE to keep I have,
   A God to glorify;
A never-dying soul to save,
   And fit it for the sky:—

To serve the present age,
   My calling to fulfil,—
Oh! may it all my powers engage—
   To do my Master's will.

Arm me with jealous care,
   As in Thy sight to live;
And, Oh! Thy servant, Lord! prepare
   A strict account to give.

Help me to watch and pray,
   And on Thyself rely;
Assured, if I my trust betray,
   I shall forever die.

The Father and the Son
   And Spirit we adore;
We praise, we bless, we worship Thee,
   Both now and evermore!

THE CHRISTIAN LIFE.

ALMSGIVING.   8s & 4s.

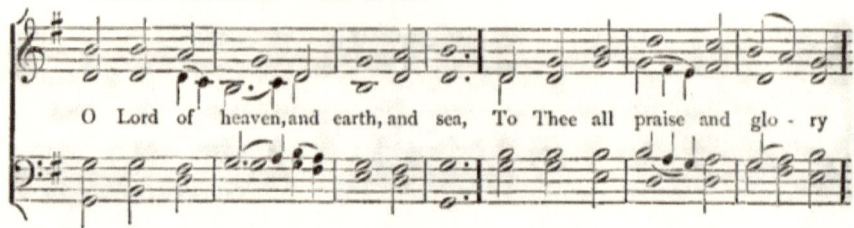

O Lord of heaven, and earth, and sea, To Thee all praise and glo-ry

be; How shall we show our love to Thee, Giv-er of all?

298

O LORD of heaven, and earth, and sea,
   To Thee all praise and glory be;
How shall we show our love to Thee,
    Giver of all?

For peaceful homes, and healthful days,
For all the blessings Earth displays,
We owe Thee thankfulness and praise,
    Giver of all!

For souls redeem'd, for sins forgiven,
For means of grace and hopes of heaven,
Father, what can to Thee be given,
    Who givest all?

We lose what on ourselves we spend,
We have as treasure without end
Whatever, Lord, to Thee we lend,
    Who givest all.

To Thee from whom we all derive
Our life, our gifts, our power to give:
O may we ever to Thee live,
    Giver of all!

299

HOLLEY. 7s. (Opposite page.)

FATHER, hear our humble claim;
  We are met in Thy great name;
In the midst do Thou appear,
Manifest Thy presence here.

Lord, our fellowship increase;
Knit us in the bond of peace;
Join our hearts, O Father! join
Each to each, and all to Thine.

Build us in one spirit up,
Called in one high calling's hope,
One the spirit, one the aim,
One the pure baptismal flame;—

One the faith, and one the Lord,
Whom by heaven and earth adored,
We our God and Father call;
O'er all, through all, with us all.

HOLLEY. 7s.

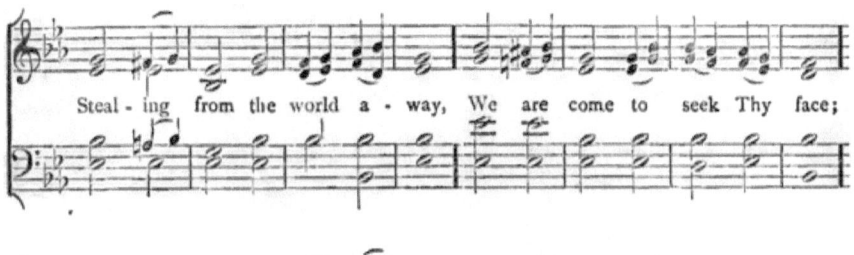

Steal-ing from the world a-way, We are come to seek Thy face;

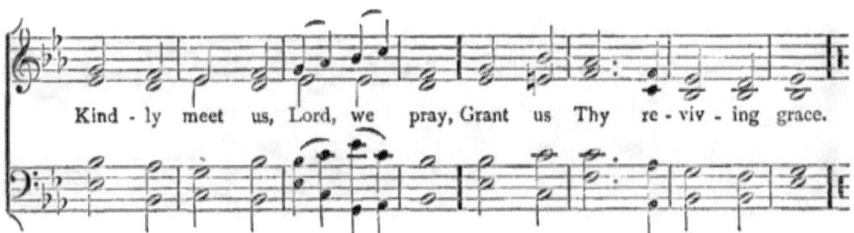

Kind-ly meet us, Lord, we pray, Grant us Thy re-viv-ing grace.

300

STEALING from the world away,
  We are come to seek Thy face;
Kindly meet us, Lord, we pray,
  Grant us Thy reviving grace.

Yonder stars that gild the sky
  Shine but with a borrowed light;
We, unless Thy light be nigh,
  Wander, wrapt in gloomy night.

Sun of Righteousness! dispel
  All our darkness, doubts, and fears;
May Thy light within us dwell,
  Till eternal day appears.

Warm our hearts in prayer and praise,
  Lift our every thought above;
Hear the grateful songs we raise,
  Fill us with Thy perfect love.

301

LORD! we come before Thee now;
  At Thy feet we humbly bow;
Oh! do not our suit disdain;—
Shall we seek Thee, Lord, in vain?

Lord! on Thee our souls depend,
In compassion, now descend;
Fill our hearts with Thy rich grace,
Tune our lips to sing Thy praise.

In Thine own appointed way,
Now we seek Thee, here we stay;
Lord! we know not how to go,
Till a blessing Thou bestow.

Send some message, from Thy word,
That may joy and peace afford;
Let Thy Spirit now impart
Full salvation to each heart.

    Holy Father, Holy Son,
    Holy Spirit, Three in One!
    Glory, as of old, to Thee,
    Now, and evermore shall be!

THE PRAYER MEETING.

GOLDEN HILL. S. M.

Je-sus, we look to Thee, Thy prom-ised pres-ence claim;

Thou in the midst of us shalt be, As-sem-bled in Thy Name.

302

JESUS, we look to Thee,
   Thy promised presence claim;
Thou in the midst of us shalt be,
   Assembled in Thy Name.

Not in the name of pride
   Or selfishness we meet;
From nature's paths we turn aside,
   And worldly thoughts forget.

We meet, the grace to take
   Which Thou hast freely given;
We meet on earth for Thy dear sake,
   That we may meet in heaven.

Oh, may Thy quickening voice
   The death of sin remove;
And bid our inmost souls rejoice
   In hope of perfect love.

303

BEHOLD the throne of grace!
   The promise calls me near;
There Jesus shows a smiling face,
   And waits to answer prayer.

My soul! ask what thou wilt;
   Thou canst not be too bold;
Since His own blood for thee He spilt,
   What else can He withhold?

Thine image, Lord! bestow,
   Thy presence and Thy love;
I ask to serve Thee here below,
   And reign with Thee above.

Teach me to live by faith;
   Conform my will to Thine;
Let me victorious be in death,
   And then in glory shine.

   The Father and the Son
      And Spirit we adore;
   We praise, we bless, we worship Thee,
      Both now and evermore!

DENNIS. S. M.

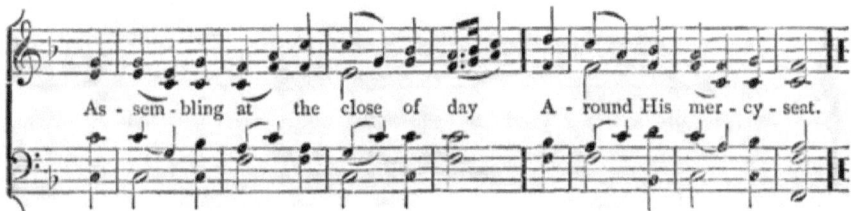

304

THE Lord be with us now,
   As here again we meet,
Assembling at the close of day
   Around His mercy-seat.

In Jesus' Name we come,
   To offer up our prayer,
And bowing low before the throne,
   We crave acceptance there.

Let worldly cares be gone;
   Bestow a heavenly mind;
May every heart and every tongue
   In sweet accord be joined.

If any meet us here
   Who ne'er Thy love have known,
Draw them, O Jesus, unto Thee,
   And seal them for Thine own.

Enfold us with Thy love,
   Thy special grace impart,
And let the perfect peace of God
   Abide in every heart.

305

WE come to sing Thy praise;
   We meet to offer prayer;
We come to learn of wisdom's ways;
   Blest Saviour! meet us here!

Thy Spirit, Lord, impart,
   That, while we raise the voice
In sacred melody, the heart
   In praises may rejoice.

And when the offered prayer
   Goes upward to Thy throne,
May we in each petition share,
   And make each want our own!

And as Thy holy word
   We study and are taught,
Let every truth and precept, Lord,
   Be with Thy blessing fraught.

To God the Father, Son,
   And Spirit, glory be,
As 'twas, and is, and shall be so
   To all eternity.

THE PRAYER MEETING.

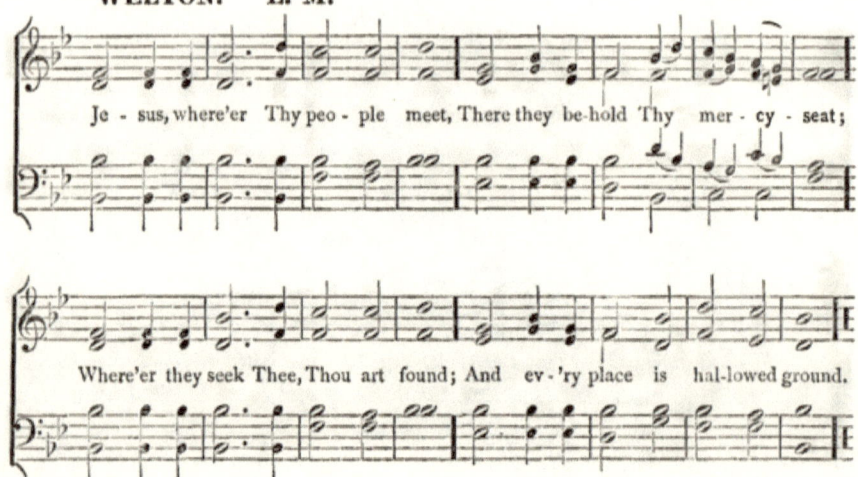

WELTON. L. M.

Je-sus, where'er Thy peo-ple meet, There they be-hold Thy mer-cy-seat;
Where'er they seek Thee, Thou art found; And ev-'ry place is hal-lowed ground.

306

JESUS, where'er Thy people meet,
  There they behold Thy mercy-seat;
Where'er they seek Thee, Thou art found;
And every place is hallowed ground.

For Thou, within no walls confined,
Inhabitest the humble mind;
Such ever bring Thee where they come,
And, going, take Thee to their home.

Dear Shepherd of Thy chosen few,
Thy former mercies here renew;
Here to our waiting hearts proclaim
The sweetness of Thy saving name.

307

MY God! is any hour so sweet,
  From blush of morn to evening star,
As that which calls me to Thy feet—
  The hour of prayer, the hour of prayer?

No words can tell what sweet relief,
  Here for my every want I find;
What strength for warfare, balm for grief,
  What peace of mind! what peace of mind!

Lord! till I reach yon blissful shore,
  No privilege so dear shall be,
As thus my inmost soul to pour
  In prayer to Thee, in prayer to Thee.

308

BEHOLD a Stranger at the door!
  He gently knocks, has knocked be-
Has waited long, is waiting still : [fore;
You treat no other friend so ill.

Rise, touched with gratitude divine,
Turn out His enemy and thine;
Turn out thy soul-enslaving sin,
And let the heavenly Stranger in.

Oh, welcome Him, the Prince of peace!
Now may His gentle reign increase!
Throw wide the door, each willing mind,
And be His empire all mankind.

ARLINGTON.   C. M.

When cold our hearts, and far from Thee Our wand'ring spirits stray, And thoughts and lips move heav-i-ly; Lord, teach us how to pray.

309

WHEN cold our hearts, and far from
   Our wandering spirits stray, [Thee
And thoughts and lips move heavily;
   Lord, teach us how to pray.

Too vile to venture near Thy Throne,
   Too poor to turn away;
Our only voice Thy Spirit's groan;
   Lord, teach us how to pray.

We know not how to seek Thy face,
   Unless Thou lead the way;
We have no words, unless Thy grace,
   Lord, teach us how to pray.

Here every thought and fond desire
   We on Thy altar lay;   [fire,
And when our souls have caught Thy
   Lord, teach us how to pray.

THE SAVIOUR'S CALL.   6s & 4s.

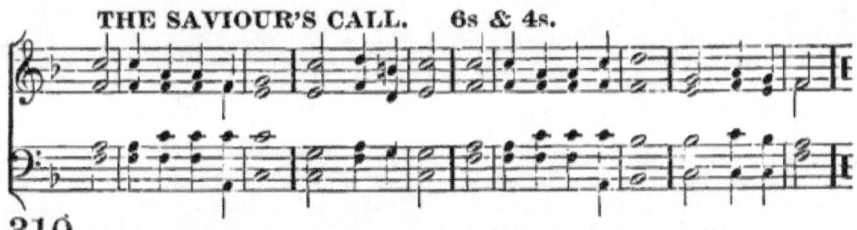

310

TO-DAY the Saviour calls:
   Ye wanderers, come;
O ye benighted souls,
   Why longer roam?

To-day the Saviour calls;
   O hear Him now;
Within these sacred walls
   To Jesus bow.

To-day the Saviour calls;
   For refuge fly;
The storm of justice falls,
   And death is nigh.

The Spirit calls to-day;
   Yield to His power;
O, grieve Him not away:
   'Tis mercy's hour.

THE PRAYER MEETING.

ROSEFIELD. 8s & 7s, or 7s.

Come to Cal-v'ry's ho-ly mountain, Sin-ners, ru-ined by the fall!
Here a pure and heal-ing fountain Flows to you, to me, to all,—
In a full per-pet-ual tide, O-pen'd when our Sav-iour died.

311

COME to Calv'ry's holy mountain,
  Sinners ruined by the fall!
Here a pure and healing fountain
  Flows to you, to me, to all,—
In a full perpetual tide,
Opened when our Saviour died.

Come, in sorrow and contrition,
  Wounded, impotent, and blind;
Here the guilty, free remission,
  Here the troubled, peace may find;
Health this fountain will restore;
He that drinks shall thirst no more:

He that drinks shall live forever,
  'Tis a soul-renewing flood:
God is faithful;— God will never
  Break His covenant in blood,
Signed, when our Redeemer died,
Sealed, when He was glorified.

312

CHRIST, whose glory fills the skies,
  Christ, the true, the only light,
Sun of righteousness! arise,
  Triumph o'er the shades of night:
Day-spring from on high, be near;
Day-star, in my heart appear!

Dark and cheerless is the morn,
  If Thy light is hid from me;
Joyless is the day's return,
  Till Thy mercy's beams I see,—
Till they inward light impart,
Glad my eyes, and warm my heart.

Visit, then, this soul of mine;
  Pierce the gloom of sin and grief;
Fill me, radiant Sun divine!
  Scatter all my unbelief:
More and more Thyself display,
Shining to the perfect day.

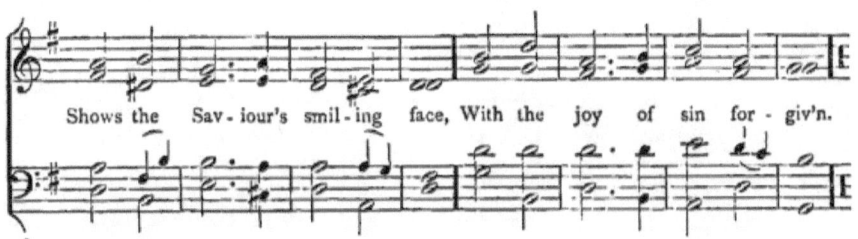

313

SOFT and holy is the place, [heav'n
Where the light that beams from
Shows the Saviour's smiling face,
With the joy of sin forgiven.

There, with one accord we meet,
All the words of life to hear;
Bending low at Jesus' feet,
Worshipping with godly fear.

Let the world and all its cares
Now retire from every breast;
Let the tempter and his snares
Cease to hinder or molest.

314

BLESSED fountain, full of grace!
Grace for sinners, grace for me;
To this source alone I trace
What I am and hope to be.

What I am, as one redeemed,
Saved and rescued by the Lord;
Hating what I once esteemed,
Loving what I once abhorred.

What I hope to be ere long,
When I take my place above,
When I join the heavenly throng,
When I see the God of love.

315

CHILDREN of the heavenly King,
As ye journey, sweetly sing;
Sing your Saviour's worthy praise,
Glorious in His works and ways.

Ye are traveling home to God
In the way the fathers trod;
They are happy now, and ye
Soon their happiness shall see.

Shout, ye little flock, and blest!
You on Jesus' throne shall rest;
There your seat is now prepared;
There your kingdom and reward.

THE PRAYER MEETING.

ST. THOMAS. S. M.

O Lord, Thy work re-vive, In Zi-on's gloom-y hour;
And make her dy-ing grac-es live, By Thy re-stor-ing pow'r.

316

O LORD, Thy work revive,
    In Zion's gloomy hour;
And make her dying graces live
    By Thy restoring power.

Awake Thy chosen few
    To fervent, earnest prayer;
Again their sacred vows renew,
    Thy blessèd presence share.

Thy Spirit then will speak
    Through lips of feeble clay,
And hearts of adamant will break,
    And rebels will obey.

Lord! lend Thy gracious ear;
    Oh, listen to our cry!
Oh, come and bring salvation here!
    Our hopes on Thee rely.

317

BLEST Jesus! come Thou down,
    And fill this hallowed place;
Oh! make Thy glorious goings known,
    Diffuse around Thy grace.

Shine, Lord! from realms of day
    Disperse the gloom of night;
Chase all our clouds and doubts away,
    And turn the shades to light.

Revive, O God, Thy saints,
    Who languish, droop, and sigh;
Refresh the soul that tires and faints,
    Fill mourning hearts with joy.

Make known Thy power, O King!
    Subdue each stubborn will;
Then sovereign grace we'll join to sing
    On Zion's sacred hill.

The Father and the Son
    And Spirit we adore;
We praise, we bless, we worship Thee,
    Both now and evermore.

GERMANIA. 7s & 6s.

1. In humble supplication We come, O Lord, to Thee; Thy grace alone can save us; To Thee alone we flee. We come for this our parish Thy mercy to implore; On church, and homes, and people, O Lord, Thy mercy pour.

318

Blot out our sins, O Father!
  Forgive the guilty past;
Loose from their bonds the captives
  Whom Satan holdeth fast.
Wake Thou the slumbering conscience,
  To listen to Thy call;
The weak and wavering strengthen,
  And raise up them that fall.

3.
Lord, banish strife and variance,
  Knit sundered hearts in one,
And bind us all together
  In love to Thy dear Son.
O Father, bless our parish,
  That all may grow in grace,
And daily love Thee better,
  Until we see Thy face.

319

HOW long, O Lord, our Saviour,
  Wilt Thou remain away?
Our hearts are growing weary
  Of Thy so long delay.
Oh, when shall come the moment
  When, brighter far than morn,
The sunshine of Thy glory
  Shall on Thy people dawn.

Oh, wake Thy slumbering virgins,
  Send forth the solemn cry,
Let all the saints repeat it—
  "The Bridegroom draweth nigh!"
May all our lamps be burning,
  Our loins well girded be,
Each longing heart preparing
  With joy Thy Face to see.

THE PRAYER MEETING.

BALERMA. C. M.

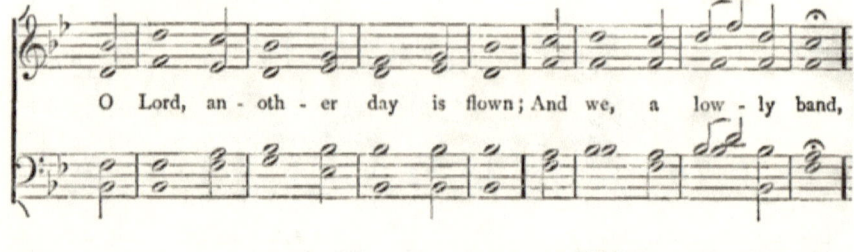

O Lord, an-oth-er day is flown; And we, a low-ly band,
Are met once more be-fore Thy throne, To bless Thy fos-t'ring hand.

320

O LORD, another day is flown;
  And we, a lowly band,
Are met once more before Thy throne,
  To bless Thy fostering hand.

Thy heavenly grace to each impart;
  All evil far remove;
And shed abroad in every heart
  Thy everlasting love.

Thus chastened, cleansed, entirely Thine,
  A flock by Jesus led,
The Sun of holiness shall shine
  In glory on our head.

And Thou wilt turn our wandering feet,
  And Thou wilt bless our way; [greet
Till worlds shall fade, and faith shall
  The dawn of lasting day.

321

GREAT Shepherd of Thy people, hear!
  Thy presence now display:
As Thou hast given a place for prayer,
  So give us hearts to pray.

Within these walls let holy peace,
  And love and concord dwell:
Here give the troubled conscience ease,
  The wounded spirit heal.

May we in faith receive Thy word,
  In faith present our prayers;
And in the presence of our Lord
  Unbosom all our cares.

The hearing ear, the seeing eye,
  The contrite heart bestow;
And shine upon us from on high,
  That we in grace may grow.

  The grace of Jesus Christ our Lord,
    God's love in boundless store,
  The Holy Spirit's fellowship,
    Be with us evermore!

ART THOU WEARY.

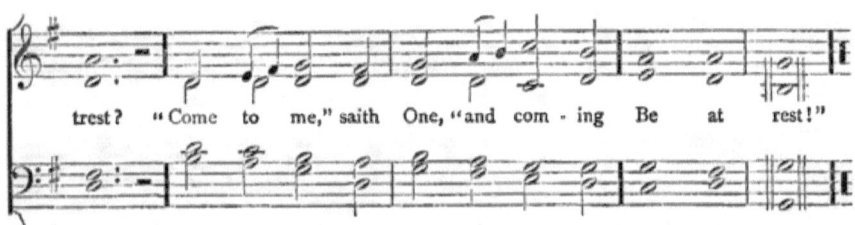

322

ART thou weary, art thou languid,
  Art thou sore distrest?
"Come to me," saith One, "and coming
          Be at rest!"

Hath He marks to lead me to Him,
  If He be my guide?   [prints,
"In His feet and hands are wound-
          And His side."

If I find Him, if I follow,
  What His guerdon here?
"Many a sorrow, many a labor,
          Many a tear."

If I still hold closely to Him,
  What hath He at last?
"Sorrow vanquished, labor ended,
          Jordan past."

If I ask Him to receive me,
  Will He say me nay?
"Not till earth, and not till heaven
          Pass away."

323 BALERMA. C. M.

ALAS! and did my Saviour bleed?
  And did my Sovereign die?
Would He devote that sacred head
  For such a worm as I?

Was it for crimes that I had done
  He groaned upon the tree?
Amazing pity! grace unknown!
  And love beyond degree!

Well might I hide my blushing face,
  While His dear cross appears;
Dissolve my heart in thankfulness,
  And melt mine eyes to tears.

But drops of grief can ne'er repay
  The debt of love I owe:
Here, Lord, I give myself away;
  'Tis all that I can do.

THE PRAYER MEETING.

ASPIRATION. S. M.

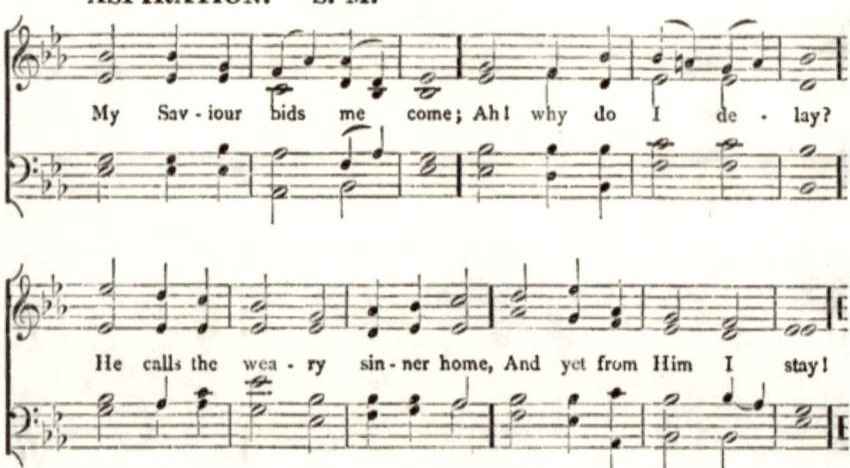

My Sav-iour bids me come; Ah! why do I de-lay?
He calls the wea-ry sin-ner home, And yet from Him I stay!

324

MY Saviour bids me come;
  Ah! why do I delay?
He calls the weary sinner home,
  And yet from Him I stay!

What worldly tie must break?
  What idol yet depart,
Which will not let the Saviour take
  Possession of my heart?

Jesus, the hind'rance show
  Which I have feared to see;
And let me now consent to know
  What keeps me back from Thee.

Oh! break the fatal chain,
  And all my bonds remove;
Nor let one bosom-sin remain,
  To keep me from Thy love.

325

NOW is th' accepted time,
  Now is the day of grace;
O sinners! come, without delay,
  And seek the Saviour's face.

Now is th' accepted time,
  The Saviour calls to-day;
To-morrow it may be too late;—
  Then why should you delay?

Now is th' accepted time,
  The gospel bids you come;
And every promise in His word
  Declares there yet is room.

Lord, draw reluctant souls,
  And feast them with Thy love;
Then will the angels spread their wings,
  And bear the news above.

  The Father and the Son
    And Spirit we adore;
  We praise, we bless, we worship Thee,
    Both now and evermore!

SAVIOUR AND LORD.

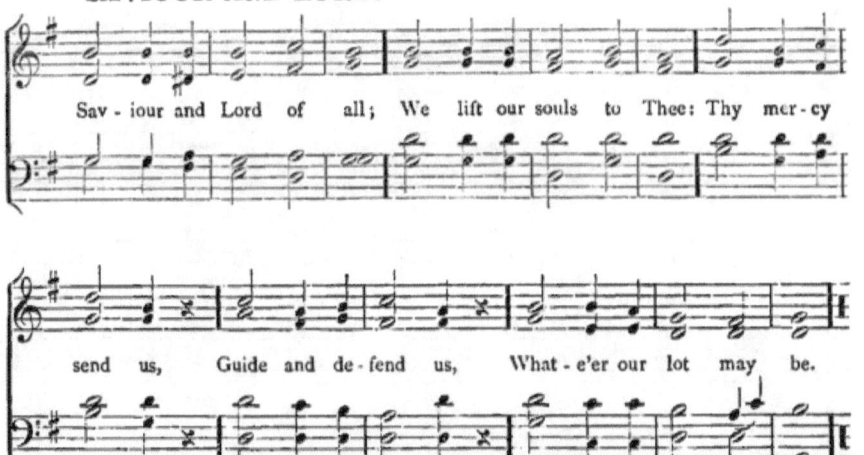

326

SAVIOUR and Lord of all;
  We lift our souls to Thee:
    Thy mercy send us,
    Guide and defend us,
  Whate'er our lot may be.

Our sins forgive, we pray;
Our faith and love increase;
    Lord, we adore Thee!
    Lord, we implore Thee
  Grant us Thy holy peace!

When darkness clouds our way,
Oh, Jesus, then be near:
    With Thee abiding,
    In Thee confiding,
  Let us not faint nor fear.

Brighten our darkest hours
Till the last hour shall come;
    Then o'er us bending,
    All sorrow ending,
  Lord, take Thy children home.

THE HOLY CHURCH.

AUSTRIA. 8s & 7s.

Glorious things of thee are spoken, Zion, city of our God!
He, whose word cannot be broken, Form'd thee for His own abode:
On the Rock of Ages founded, What can shake thy sure repose?
With salvation's walls surrounded, Thou shalt smile at all thy foes.

327

GLORIOUS things of thee are spoken,
  Zion, city of our God:
He, whose word cannot be broken,
  Formed thee for His own abode;
On the Rock of Ages founded,
  What can shake thy sure repose?
With salvation's walls surrounded,
  Thou shalt smile at all thy foes.

See, the streams of living waters,
  Springing from eternal love,
Well supply thy sons and daughters,
  And all fear of want remove;

Who can faint, while such a river
  Ever flows their thirst t' assuage?
Grace, which like the Lord, the Giver,
  Never fails from age to age.

Round each habitation hovering,
  See the cloud and fire appear,
For a glory and a covering,
  Showing that the Lord is near.
Blest inhabitants of Zion,
  Wash'd in the Redeemer's blood!
Jesus, whom their souls rely on,
  Makes them kings and priests to God.

328

CHRIST is made the sure foundation,
　Christ the Head and Corner-stone,
Chosen of the Lord, and precious,
　Binding all the Church in one;
Holy Sion's help for ever,
　And her confidence alone.

All that dedicated city,
　Dearly loved of God on high,
In exultant jubilation
　Pours perpetual melody;
God the One in Three adoring
　In glad hymns eternally.

To this temple where we call Thee,
　Come, O Lord of hosts, to-day:
With Thy wonted loving-kindness
　Hear Thy servants as they pray,
And Thy fullest benediction
　Shed within its walls alway.

Here vouchsafe to all Thy servants
　What they ask of Thee to gain,
What they gain from Thee forever
　With the blessèd to retain,
And hereafter in Thy glory
　Evermore with Thee to reign.

Praise and honor to the Father,
　Praise and honor to the Son,
Praise and honor to the Spirit,
　Ever Three, and ever One,
One in might, and One in glory,
　While eternal ages run.

THE HOLY CHURCH.

PLAYFORD. L. M.

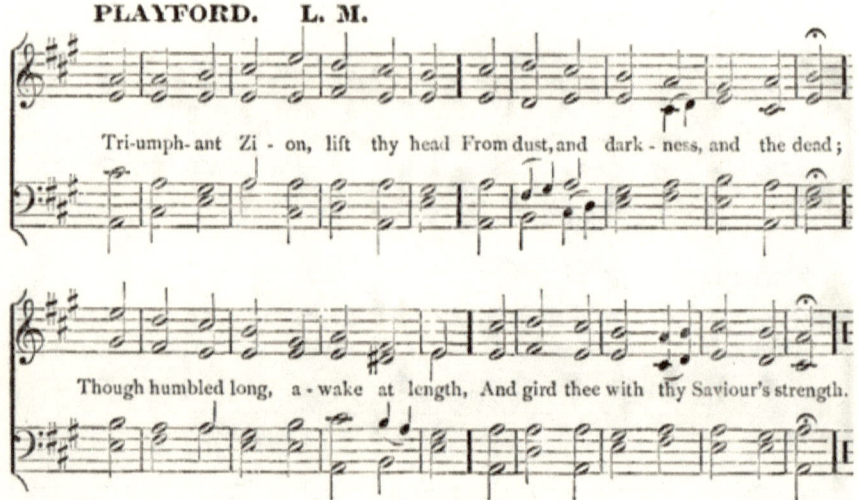

Triumphant Zion, lift thy head From dust, and darkness, and the dead;
Though humbled long, a-wake at length, And gird thee with thy Saviour's strength.

329

TRIUMPHANT Zion, lift thy head
From dust, and darkness, and the dead;
Though humbled long, awake at length,
And gird thee with thy Saviour's strength.

Put all thy beauteous garments on,
And let thy various charms be known:
The world thy glories shall confess,
Decked in the robes of righteousness.

No more shall foes unclean invade,
And fill thy hallowed walls with dread;
No more shall hell's insulting host
Their victory and thy sorrows boast.

God, from on high, thy groans will hear;
His hand thy ruins shall repair;
Nor will thy watchful monarch cease
To guard thee in eternal peace.

330

THE heavens declare Thy glory, Lord!
In every star Thy wisdom shines;
But when our eyes behold Thy Word,
We read Thy Name in fairer lines.

The rolling sun, the changing light,
And nights and days Thy power confess,
But the blest volume Thou hast writ,
Reveals Thy justice and Thy grace.

Sun, moon, and stars, convey Thy praise
Round the whole earth, and never stand:
So, when Thy truth began its race,
It touched and glanced on every land.

Nor shall Thy spreading gospel rest,
Till through the world Thy truth has run;
Till Christ has all the nations blessed
That see the light, or feel the sun.

To God the Father, God the Son,
And God the Spirit, Three in One,
Be honor, praise, and glory given,
By all on earth, and all in heaven!

WAREHAM. L. M.

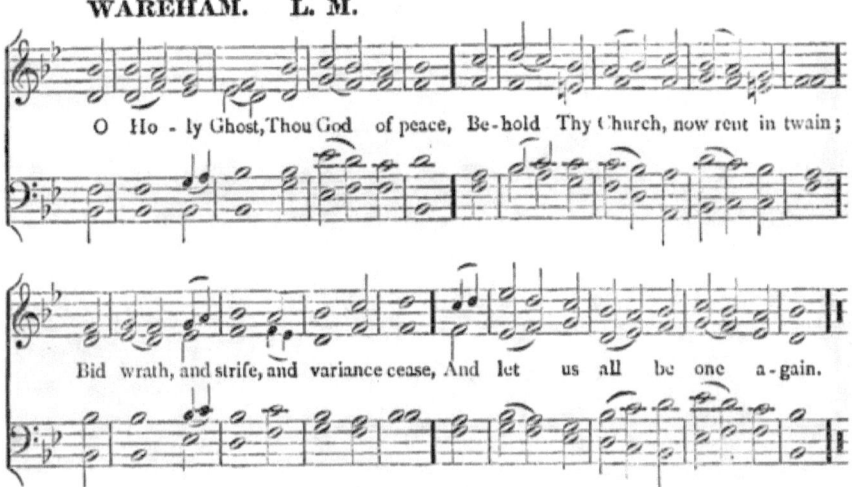

O Ho-ly Ghost, Thou God of peace, Be-hold Thy Church, now rent in twain;
Bid wrath, and strife, and variance cease, And let us all be one a-gain.

331

O HOLY Ghost, Thou God of peace,
  Behold Thy Church, now rent in twain;
Bid wrath, and strife, and variance cease,
  And let us all be one again.

One with our brethren here in love,
  And one with saints who are at rest,
And one with angel hosts above,
  And one with God forever blest.

For one the Lord on whom we call,
  The Spirit one which He hath given,
One God and Father of us all, [heav'n.
  One Faith on earth, one Hope of

332

MY only Saviour! when I feel
  O'erwhelmed in spirit, faint, oppressed,
'Tis sweet to tell Thee, while I kneel
  Low at Thy feet, Thou art my rest.

I'm weary of the strife within; [test;
  Strong powers against my soul con-
Oh, let me turn from self and sin
  To Thy dear cross, for there is rest!

Oh, sweet will be the welcome day,
  When from her toils and woes released,
My parting soul in death shall say,
  "Now, Lord, I come to Thee for rest."

333

GREAT Shepherd of Thine Israel,
  Who didst between the cherubs dwell,
And lead the tribes, Thy chosen sheep,
  Safe through the desert and the deep:

Thy Church is in the desert now:
  Shine from on high and guide us thro';
Turn us to Thee, Thy love restore;
  We shall be saved, and sigh no more.

Return, Almighty God, return!
  Nor let Thy bleeding vineyard mourn:
Turn us to Thee, Thy love restore;
  We shall be saved, and sigh no more.

THE HOLY CHURCH.

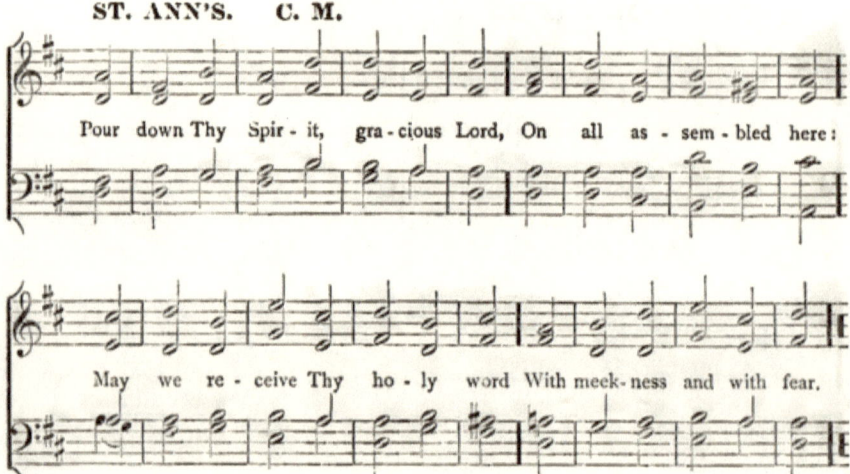

ST. ANN'S.   C. M.

Pour down Thy Spir-it, gra-cious Lord, On all as-sem-bled here: May we re-ceive Thy ho-ly word With meek-ness and with fear.

334

POUR down Thy Spirit, gracious Lord,
　On all assembled here:
May we receive Thy holy word
　With meekness and with fear.

Through faith in Thee the soul receives
　New life, though dead before;
And he who in Thy Name believes
　Shall live to die no more.

Preserve the power of faith alive
　In those who fear Thy Name;
For sin and Satan daily strive
　To quench the sacred flame.

To Thee we look; to Thee we bow;
　On Thee for help we call;
Our life and resurrection Thou,
　Our hope, our joy, our all.

335

OH, where are kings and empires now
　Of old that went and came?
But, Lord, Thy church is praying yet,
　A thousand years the same.

We mark her goodly battlements,
　And her foundations strong;
We hear within the solemn voice
　Of her unending song.

For not like kingdoms of the world
　Thy holy church, O God! [ing her,
Though earthquake shocks are threaten-
　And tempests are abroad;—

Unshaken as eternal hills,
　Immovable she stands,
A mountain that shall fill the earth,
　A house not made by hands.

　　All glory to the Father be,
　　　All glory to the Son,
　　All glory to the Holy Ghost,
　　　While endless ages run.

OLMUTZ. S. M.

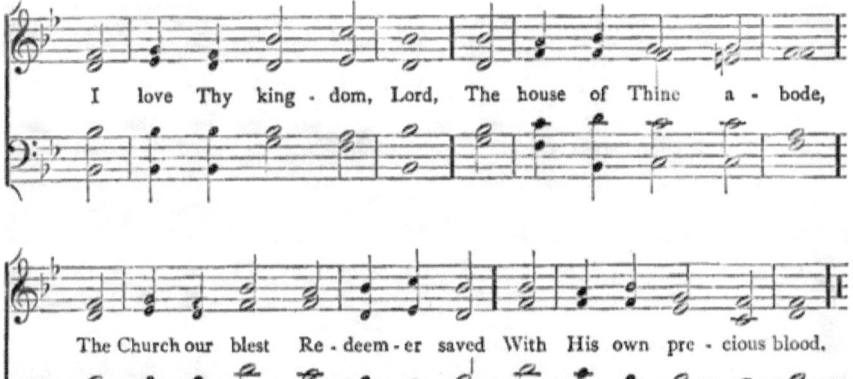

I love Thy king-dom, Lord, The house of Thine a-bode,
The Church our blest Re-deem-er saved With His own pre-cious blood.

336

I LOVE Thy kingdom, Lord,—
  The house of Thine abode,
The Church our blest Redeemer saved
  With His own precious blood.

I love Thy Church, O God!
  Her walls before Thee stand,
Dear as the apple of Thine eye,
  And graven on Thy hand.

For her my tears shall fall,
  For her my prayers ascend;
To her my cares and toils be given,
  Till toils and cares shall end.

Beyond my highest joy
  I prize her heavenly ways,
Her sweet communion, solemn vows,
  Her hymns of love and praise.

Sure as thy truth shall last,
  To Zion shall be given
The brightest glories earth can yield,
  And brighter bliss of heaven.

337

HOW long, O Lord, our God,
  Holy, and true, and good,
Wilt Thou not judge Thy suffering
    Church,
  Her sighs, her tears, and blood?

We long to hear Thy voice,
  To see Thee face to face,
To share Thy crown and glory there
  As here we share Thy grace.

Should not the loving Bride
  The absent Bridegroom mourn;
Should she not wear the weeds of grief
  Until her Lord return?

The whole creation groans,
  And waits to hear that voice,
That shall restore her comeliness,
  And make her wastes rejoice.

Come, Lord, and wipe away
  The curse, the sin, the stain,
And make this blighted world of ours
  Thine own fair world again.

ALEXANDRIA. C. M.

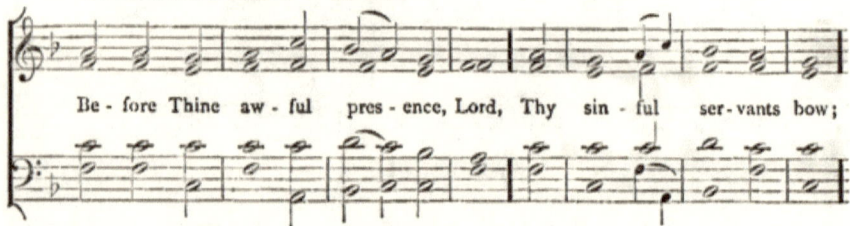
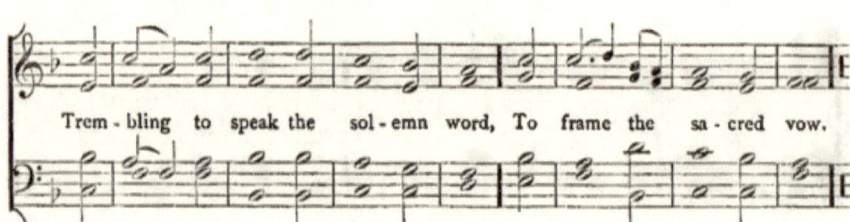

Before Thine aw-ful pres-ence, Lord, Thy sin-ful ser-vants bow;
Trem-bling to speak the sol-emn word, To frame the sa-cred vow.

338

BEFORE Thine awful presence, Lord,
   Thy sinful servants bow;
Trembling to speak the solemn word,
   To frame the sacred vow.

The sins in hours of weakness wrought,
   The vain things loved before,
The wanton deed, and word, and thought,
   Lord, we renounce once more.

Once more we vow the holy Faith
   To keep unstained and true;
Once more we promise unto death
   Thy holy will to do.

O Father, pardon all the past;
   Give back Thy wasted grace;
And strengthen us, while life shall last,
   To run the heavenward race.

Still let Thy blessèd Spirit's aid
   Our strength and comfort be;
Then, though we sometime be afraid,
   We still will trust in Thee.

339

MY God! the covenant of Thy love
   Abides forever sure;
And in its matchless grace I feel
   My happiness secure.

Since Thou, the everlasting God,
   My Father art become,
Jesus, my Guardian and my Friend,
   And heaven my final home,—

I welcome all Thy sovereign will,
   For all that will is love;
And when I know not what Thou dost,
   I wait the light above.

Thy covenant in the darkest gloom
   Shall heavenly rays impart,
And when my eyelids close in death,
   Sustain my fainting heart.

To Father, Son, and Holy Ghost,
   One God whom we adore,
Be glory as it was, is now,
   And shall be evermore!

PRAYER FOR PEACE. 11s & 5.

1. Lord of our life, and God of our salvation, Star of our night, and Hope of ev'ry nation, Hear and receive Thy Church's supplication, Lord God Almighty.

340

2
Lord, Thou canst help when earthly armor faileth,
Lord, Thou canst save when deadly sin assaileth,
Lord, o'er Thy Rock nor death nor hell prevaileth:
  Grant us Thy peace, Lord:

3
Peace in our hearts, our evil thoughts assuaging,
Peace in Thy Church, where brothers are engaging,
Peace, when the world its busy war is waging;
  Calm Thy foes raging.

4
Grant us Thy help till backward they are driven,
Grant them Thy truth, that they may be forgiven,
Grant peace on earth, and after we have striven,
  Peace in Thy heaven.

341 MARLOW. C. M.

OUR children, Lord, in faith and prayer,
  We now devote to Thee;
Let them Thy covenant mercies share,
  And Thy salvation see.

In early days their hearts secure
  From worldly snares, we pray;
And make them to the end endure
  In every righteous way.

Help us before them, Lord, to live
  In holy faith and fear;
And then to heaven our souls receive,
  And bring our children there.

COVENANT AND COMMUNION.

ROCKINGHAM. L. M.

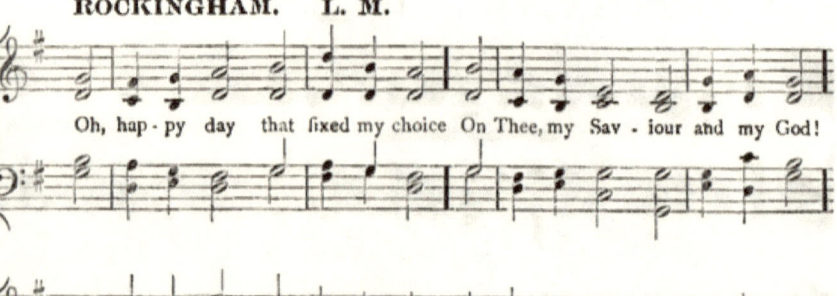

Oh, hap-py day that fixed my choice On Thee, my Sav-iour and my God!

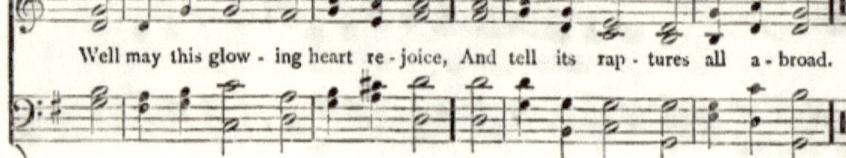

Well may this glow-ing heart re-joice, And tell its rap-tures all a-broad.

342

OH, happy day that fixed my choice
 On Thee, my Saviour and my God!
Well may this glowing heart rejoice,
 And tell its raptures all abroad.

Oh, happy bond that seals my vows
 To Him who merits all my love!
Let cheerful anthems fill His house,
 While to that sacred shrine I move.

Now rest, my long-divided heart!
 Fixed on this blissful centre, rest;
Here have I found a nobler part,
 Here heavenly pleasures fill my breast.

High heaven, that hears the solemn vow,
 That vow renewed shall daily hear;
Till, in life's latest hour, I bow,
 And bless in death a bond so dear.

343

OH! the sweet wonders of that cross
 Where my Redeemer loved and died!
Her noblest life my spirit draws   [side.
 From His dear wounds, and bleeding

I would forever speak His Name
 In sounds to mortal ears unknown;
With angels join to praise the Lamb,
 And worship at His Father's throne.

344

FATHER of love, Thy grace bestow
 On those who at Thine altar bow;
Their vows accept, Thy blessing give,
And to Thy glory make them live.

We bring our little ones to Thee,
O loving Saviour, Thine to be;
Defend them through this earthly strife,
And lead them in the path of life.

O God! we speak, but Thine's the pow'r!
Baptise us all this very hour
With faith, and hope, and joyful love,
Thou Sun of all below, above.

COMMUNION. L. M.

My God, and is Thy ta-ble spread, And doth Thy cup with love o'er-flow? Thith-er be all Thy chil-dren led, And let them all Thy sweetness know.

345

MY God, and is Thy table spread,
  And doth Thy cup with love o'er-
Thither be all Thy children led, [flow?
And let them all Thy sweetness know.

Hail, sacred feast, which Jesus makes,
  Rich banquet of His flesh and blood!
Thrice happy he who here partakes
That sacred stream, that heavenly food.

Why are its dainties all in vain
Before unwilling hearts displayed?
Was not for them the Victim slain?
Are they forbid the children's bread?

Oh, let Thy table honored be,
And furnished well with joyful guests,
And may each soul salvation see,
That here its sacred pledges tastes!

346

COME in, thou blessèd of the Lord!
  Enter in Jesus' precious Name;
We welcome thee, with one accord,
  And trust the Saviour does the same.

Those joys which earth cannot afford,
  We'll seek in fellowship to prove,
Joined in one spirit to our Lord,
  Together bound by mutual love.

And, while we pass this vale of tears,
  We'll make our joys and sorrows known;
We'll share each other's hopes and fears,
  And count a brother's case our own.

Once more our welcome we repeat;
  Receive assurance of our love;
Oh! may we all together meet,
  Around the throne of God above.

All glory to the Father be,
  All glory to the blessed Son,
All glory to the Holy Ghost
  While everlasting ages run.

THE HOLY CHURCH

INTERCESSION. 7s.

Je-sus, with Thy Church a-bide, Be her Sav-iour, Lord, and Guide, While on earth her faith is tried: We be-seech Thee, hear us.

347

JESUS, with Thy Church abide,
  Be her Saviour, Lord, and Guide,
While on earth her faith is tried:
    We beseech Thee, hear us.

Be Thou with her all the days,
May she, safe from error's ways,
Toil for Thine eternal praise:
    We beseech Thee, hear us.

All her ruined works repair,
Build again Thy temple fair,
Manifest Thy presence there:
    We beseech Thee, hear us.

May she guide the poor and blind,
Seek the lost until she find,
And the broken-hearted bind:
    We beseech Thee, hear us.

All her evil purge away,
All her doubts and fears allay,
Hasten, Lord, her triumph-day:
    We beseech Thee, hear us.

348

JESUS, to Thy table led,
  Now let every heart be fed
With the true and living bread:
    We beseech Thee, hear us.

While on Thy dear cross we gaze,
Mourning o'er our sinful ways,
Turn our sadness into praise:
    We beseech Thee, hear us.

While we taste the bread and wine,
Of Thy sacrifice the sign,
Fill our hearts with love divine:
    We beseech Thee, hear us.

From the bonds of sin release,
Cold and wavering faith increase;
Lamb of God! grant us Thy peace!
    We beseech Thee, hear us.

Lead us by Thy piercèd hand
Till around Thy throne we stand,
In the bright and better land!
    We beseech Thee, hear us.

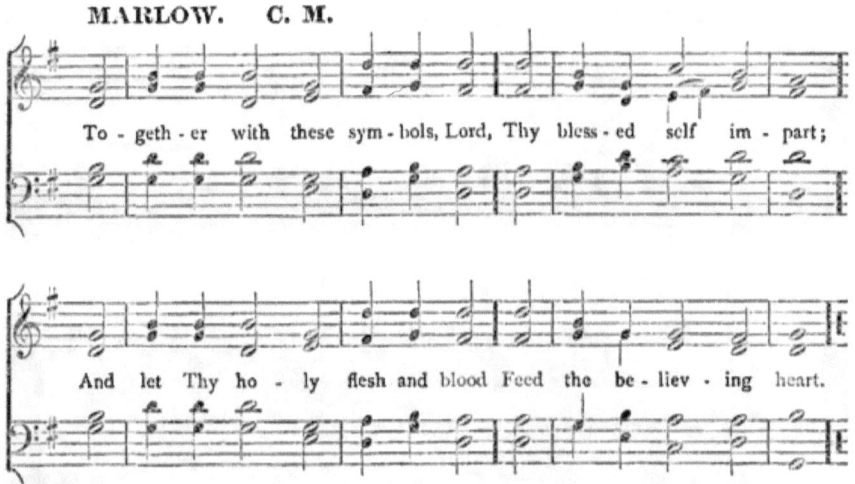

MARLOW. C. M.

Together with these symbols, Lord, Thy blessed self impart;
And let Thy holy flesh and blood Feed the believing heart.

349

TOGETHER with these symbols, Lord,
Thy blessed self impart;
And let Thy holy flesh and blood
Feed the believing heart.

Let us from all our sins be washed
In Thy atoning blood;
And let Thy Spirit be the seal
That we are born of God.

Come, Holy Ghost, with Jesus' love,
Prepare us for this feast;
Oh! let us banquet with our Lord,
And lean upon His breast.

350

O GOD, unseen yet ever near,
Thy presence may we feel;
And, thus inspired with holy fear,
Before Thine altar kneel!
P

Here may Thy faithful people know
The blessings of Thy love;
The streams that through the desert flow,
The manna from above.

We come, obedient to Thy word,
To feast on heavenly food;
Our meat, the body of the Lord,
Our drink, His precious blood.

Thus may we all Thy words obey,
For we, O God, are Thine;
And go rejoicing on our way,
Renewed with strength divine.

351

PREPARE us, Lord, to view Thy cross,
Who all our griefs hast borne;
To look on Thee whom we have pierced,
To look on Thee, and mourn.

While thus we mourn, we would rejoice,
And, as Thy cross we see,
Let each exclaim, in faith and hope,—
"The Saviour died for me!"

THE LORD'S SUPPER.

CŒNA DOMINI. 8, 8, 7.

352

COME, O Jesus, to Thy table,
　Come, for else we are not able
　　True refreshment to receive:
But, if Thou vouchsafe to feed us,
To this feast of blessing lead us,
　There to taste Thee and believe.

In the Bread which here is broken,
In the Wine, no empty token
　Of an absent Lord we see.

Flesh and Blood indeed are given,
When by faith, O Bread of Heaven,
　Not by sense, we feed on Thee.

Sweet it is, O Christ, to meet Thee,
In Thy Sacrament to greet Thee,
　Thee, our God, as Host and Friend.
By Thy presence here prepare us
For the day when Thou shalt bear us
　To the feast that knows no end.

EVENTIDE. 10s.

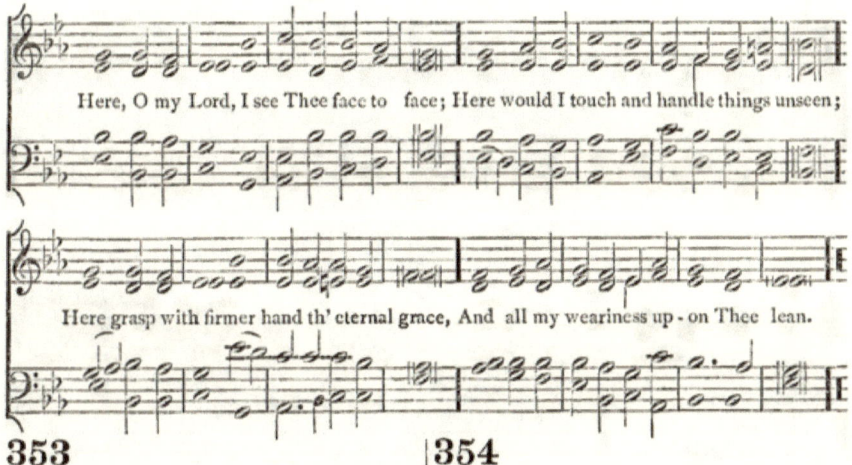

Here, O my Lord, I see Thee face to face; Here would I touch and handle things unseen;

Here grasp with firmer hand th' eternal grace, And all my weariness up-on Thee lean.

353

Here, O my Lord, I see Thee face
  to face;
Here would I touch and handle things
  unseen;
Here grasp with firmer hand th' eternal
  grace,
And all my weariness upon Thee lean.

Here would I feed upon the bread of God;
Here drink with Thee the royal wine of
  heaven;
Here would I lay aside each earthly load,
Here taste afresh the calm of sin forgiven.

Too soon we rise; the symbols disappear;
The feast, though not the love, is passed
  and gone;
The bread and wine remove, but Thou art
  here,
Nearer than ever, still my Shield and Sun.

Feast after feast thus comes and passes by;
Yet, passing, points to the glad feast
  above,—
Giving sweet foretaste of the festal joy,
The Lamb's great bridal feast of bliss
  and love.

354

Thee we adore, O unseen Saviour!
  Thee,
Who in Thy feast art pleased with us to
  be.
Both flesh and spirit at Thy presence fail,
Yet here Thy presence we devoutly hail.

Oh, blest memorial of our dying Lord,
Who living bread to men doth here afford!
Oh, may our souls forever feed on Thee,
And Thou, O Christ, forever precious be!

Fountain of goodness! Jesus, Lord and
  God!
Cleanse us, unclean, with Thy most
  cleansing Blood;
Increase our faith and love, that we may
  know
The hope and peace which from Thy
  presence flow.

O Christ! whom now beneath a veil we see,
May what we thirst for soon our portion
  be;
To gaze on Thee unveiled, and see Thy
  face,
The vision of Thy glory and Thy grace.

HYMNS OF COVENANT LOVE.

BOWDOIN SQUARE. C. M.

A mother may forgetful be, For human love is frail;
But Thy Creator's love to thee, O Zion, cannot fail.

355

A MOTHER may forgetful be,
　For human love is frail;
But thy Creator's love to thee,
　O Zion, cannot fail.

No, thy dear name engraven stands,
　In characters of love,
On thy almighty Father's hands,
　And never shall remove.

Before His ever-watchful eye
　Thy mournful state appears,
And every groan, and every sigh,
　Divine compassion hears.

O Zion, learn to doubt no more,
　Be every fear suppressed;
Unchanging truth, and love, and power,
　Dwell in thy Saviour's breast.

356 MISS. CHANT. (Opposite page.)

DEAR Saviour, if these lambs should stray
　From Thy secure enclosure's bound,
And, lured by worldly joys away, [found;
　Among the thoughtless crowd be

Remember still that they are Thine,
　That Thy dear sacred Name they bear;
Think that the seal of love divine,
　The sign of cov'nant grace they wear.

In all their erring, sinful years,
　Oh, let them ne'er forgotten be!
Remember all the prayers and tears
　Which made them consecrate to Thee.

And when these lips no more can pray,
　These eyes can weep for them no more,
Turn Thou their feet from folly's way;
　The wanderers to Thy fold restore.

To Father, Son, and Holy Ghost,
　One God whom we adore,
Be glory as it was, is now,
　And shall be evermore.

THY KINGDOM COME.

MISSIONARY CHANT. L. M.

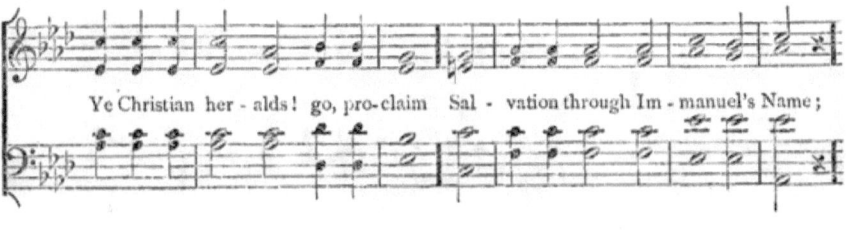

Ye Christian her-alds! go, pro-claim Sal-vation through Im-manuel's Name; To dis-tant climes the ti-dings bear, And plant the Rose of Sha-ron there.

357

YE Christian heralds! go, proclaim
Salvation through Immanuel's Name;
To distant climes the tidings bear,
And plant the Rose of Sharon there.

He'll shield you with a wall of fire,
With flaming zeal your breast inspire,
Bid raging winds their fury cease,
And hush the tempest into peace.

And when our labors all are o'er,
Then we shall meet to part no more,—
Meet with the blood-bought throng, to
And crown our Jesus—Lord of all! [fall,

358

O Sun of righteousness, arise,
With gentle beams on Zion shine;
Dispel the darkness from our eyes,
And souls awake to life divine.

On all around let grace descend,
Like heavenly dew, or copious showers;
That we may call our God our Friend;
That we may hail salvation ours.

359

O SPIRIT of the living God,
In all Thy plenitude of grace,
Where'er the foot of man hath trod,
Descend on our apostate race.

Give tongues of fire and hearts of love,
To preach the reconciling word;
Give power and unction from above,
Where'er the joyful sound is heard.

Be darkness, at Thy coming, light;
Confusion—order, in Thy path;
Souls without strength inspire with
might;
Bid mercy triumph over wrath.

Baptize the nations far and nigh;
The triumphs of the cross record;
The name of Jesus glorify,
Till every kindred call him Lord.

THY KINGDOM COME.

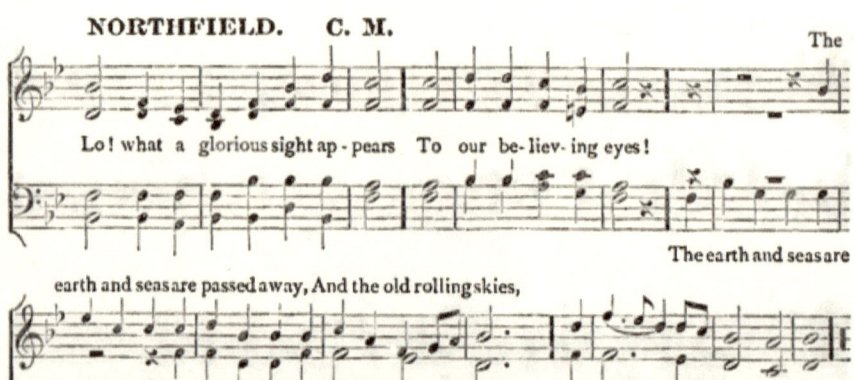

NORTHFIELD. C. M.

360

LO! what a glorious sight appears
   To our believing eyes!
The earth and seas are passed away,
   And the old rolling skies.

From the third heaven where God resides,
   That holy, happy place,
The new Jerusalem comes down,
   Adorned with shining grace.

Attending angels shout for joy,
   And the bright armies sing,
"Mortals! behold the sacred seat
   Of your descending King.

His own soft hand shall wipe the tears
   From every weeping eye,   [fears,
And pains, and groans, and griefs, and
   And death itself shall die."

How long, dear Saviour! Oh! how long
   Shall this bright hour delay?
Fly swifter round, ye wheels of time!
   And bring the welcome day.

361

SHINE, mighty God, on Zion shine
   With beams of heavenly grace;
Reveal Thy power through all our coasts,
   And show Thy smiling face.

When shall Thy Name, from shore to
   shore,
   Sound all the earth abroad,
And distant nations know and love
   Their Saviour and their God?

Sing to the Lord, ye distant lands!
   Sing loud with solemn voice;
Let every tongue exalt His praise,
   And every heart rejoice.

All glory to the Father be,
   All glory to the Son,
All glory to the Holy Ghost
   While endless ages run.

ST. MARTIN.   C. M.

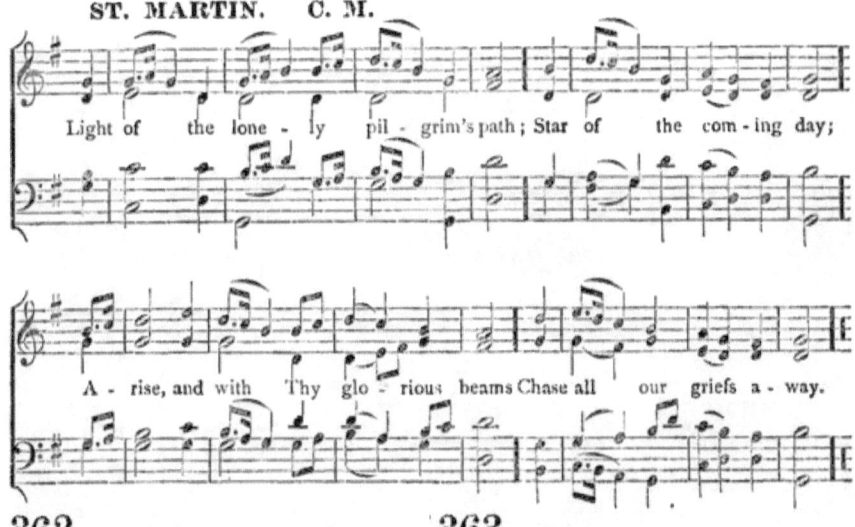

Light of the lone - ly pil - grim's path; Star of the com - ing day;
A - rise, and with Thy glo - rious beams Chase all our griefs a - way.

362

LIGHT of the lonely pilgrim's path;
  Star of the coming day;
Arise, and with Thy glorious beams
  Chase all our griefs away.

Jesus, Thy fair creation groans;
  The air, the earth, the sea,
In unison with all our hearts,
  Cries out aloud for Thee.

Come, blessèd Lord! let every shore
  And answering island sing
The praises of Thy Royal Name,
  And hail Thee as their King.

Bid the whole earth, responsive now
  To the bright world above,
Break forth in sweetest strains of joy,
  In memory of Thy love.

363

O GOD! our God! Thou shinest here,
  Thine own this latter day;
To us Thy radiant steps appear;
  Here beams Thy glorious way!

The fathers had not all of Thee!
  New births are in Thy grace;
All open to our souls shall be
  Thy glory's hiding-place.

On us Thy Spirit hast Thou poured,
  To us Thy word has come;
We feel, we bless Thee, quickening Lord,
  Thou shalt not find us dumb.

Thou comest near; Thou standest by;
  Our work begins to shine;
Thou dwellest with us mightily;
  On speed the years divine!

  All Glory to the Father be,
    All glory to the Son,
  All glory to the Holy Ghost,
    While endless ages run.

THY KINGDOM COME.

ST. MICHAEL.   S. M.

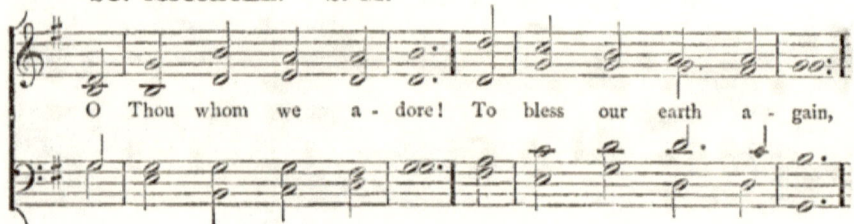

O Thou whom we a-dore! To bless our earth a-gain,

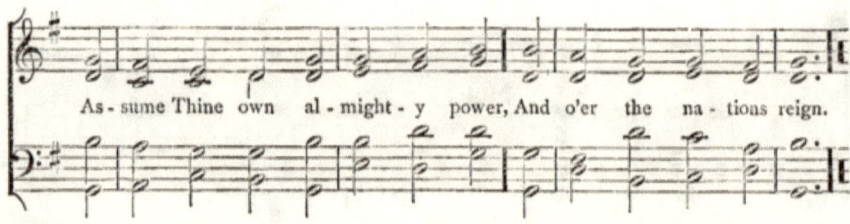

As-sume Thine own al-might-y power, And o'er the na-tions reign.

364

O THOU whom we adore!
  To bless our earth again,
Assume Thine own almighty power,
  And o'er the nations reign.

The world's Desire and Hope,
  All power to Thee is given;
Now set the last great empire up,
  Eternal Lord of heaven.

According to Thy word,
  Now be Thy grace revealed;
And with the knowledge of the Lord,
  Let all the earth be filled.

365

COME, kingdom of our God,
  Sweet reign of light and love!
Shed peace, and hope, and joy abroad,
  And wisdom from above.

Over our spirits first
  Extend Thy healing reign;
There raise and quench the sacred thirst
  That never pains again.

Come, kingdom of our God!
  And make the broad earth Thine;
Stretch o'er her lands and isles the rod
  That flowers with grace divine.

Soon may all tribes be blest
  With fruit from life's glad tree;
And in its shade like brothers rest,
  Sons of one family.

366

COME, Lord, and tarry not;
  Bring the long-looked-for day;
Oh! why these years of waiting here,
  These ages of delay?

Come, for Thy Saints still wait;
  Daily ascends their sigh;
The Spirit and the Bride say, Come:
  Dost Thou not hear the cry?

Come, and begin Thy reign
  Of everlasting peace:
Come, take the kingdom to Thyself,
  Great King of Righteousness!

THY KINGDOM COME.

UXBRIDGE. L. M.

Arm of the Lord, a-wake, a-wake, Put on Thy strength, the na-tions shake; And let the world a-dor-ing see Triumphs of mer-cy wrought by Thee.

367

ARM of the Lord, awake, awake,
Put on Thy strength, the nations
And let the world adoring see [shake;
Triumphs of mercy wrought by Thee.

Say to the heathen from Thy Throne,
I am Jehovah, God alone:
Thy voice their idols shall confound,
And cast their altars to the ground.

Let Zion's time of favor come;
O bring the tribes of Israel home:
And let our wondering eyes behold
Gentiles and Jews in Jesus' fold.

Almighty God, Thy grace proclaim
In every clime, of every name;
Let adverse powers before Thee fall,
And crown the Saviour Lord of all.

368

JESUS shall reign where'er the sun
Does his successive journeys run;
His kingdom stretch from shore to shore,
Till moons shall wax and wane no more.

People and realms of every tongue
Dwell on His love with sweetest song;
And infant voices shall proclaim
Their early blessings on His Name.

Blessings abound where'er He reigns;
The prisoner leaps to loose his chains;
The weary find eternal rest,
And all the sons of want are blest.

Let every creature rise and bring
Peculiar honors to our King;
Angels descend with songs again,
And earth repeat the loud Amen!

Praise God, from whom all blessings flow!
Praise Him, all creatures here below!
Praise Him above, ye heavenly host!
Praise Father, Son, and Holy Ghost!

THY KINGDOM COME.

MISSIONARY HYMN. 7s & 6s.

From Greenland's icy mountains, From India's coral strand,
Where Afric's sunny fountains Roll down their golden sand;
From many an ancient river, From many a palmy plain,
They call us to deliver Their land from error's chain.

369

2.
What though the spicy breezes
　Blow soft o'er Ceylon's isle;
Though every prospect pleases,
　And only man is vile:
In vain with lavish kindness
　The gifts of God are strewn;
The heathen in his blindness
　Bows down to wood and stone.

3.
Shall we, whose souls are lighted
　With wisdom from on high;
Shall we to men benighted
　The lamp of life deny?
Salvation, O salvation,
　The joyful sound proclaim,
Till each remotest nation
　Has learnt Messiah's name.

4.
Waft, waft, ye winds, His story,
　And you, ye waters, roll,
Till, like a sea of glory,
　It spreads from pole to pole:
'Till o'er our ransom'd nature
　The Lamb for sinners slain,
Redeemer, King, Creator,
　In bliss returns to reign.

THY KINGDOM COME.

WEBB. 7s & 6s.

370

THE morning light is breaking;
  The darkness disappears;
The sons of earth are waking
  To penitential tears;
Each breeze that sweeps the ocean
  Brings tidings from afar,
Of nations in commotion,
  Prepared for Zion's war.

See heathen nations bending
  Before the God we love,
And thousand hearts ascending
  In gratitude above;
While sinners, now confessing,
  The gospel call obey,
And seek the Saviour's blessing—
  A nation in a day.

Blest river of salvation!
  Pursue thine onward way;
Flow thou to every nation,
  Nor in thy richness stay:
Stay not till all the lowly
  Triumphant reach their home:
Stay not till all the holy
  Proclaim—"The Lord is come!"

371

HAIL to the Lord's Anointed,
  Great David's greater Son!
Hail, in the time appointed,
  His reign on earth begun!
He comes to break oppression,
  To set the captive free;
To take away transgression,
  And rule in equity.

He comes with succour speedy
  To those who suffer wrong;
To help the poor and needy,
  And bid the weak be strong;
To give them songs for sighing,
  Their darkness turn to light,
Whose souls, condemned and dying,
  Were precious in His sight.

Kings shall fall down before Him,
  And gold and incense bring;
All nations shall adore Him,
  His praise all people sing;
O'er every foe victorious,
  He on His throne shall rest;
From age to age more glorious,
  All-blessing and all-blessed.

THY KINGDOM COME.

ZION. 8s, 7s & 4s.

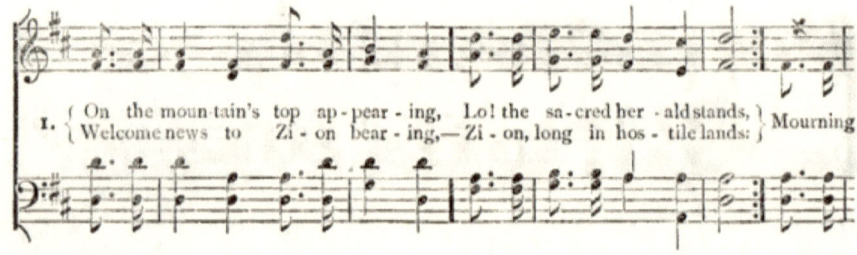

372

ON the mountain's top appearing,
  Lo! the sacred herald stands,
Welcome news to Zion bearing—
  Zion, long in hostile lands:
    Mourning captive!
  God Himself shall loose thy bands.

God, thy God, will now restore thee;
  He Himself appears thy Friend;
All thy foes shall flee before thee;
  Here their boasts and triumphs end:
    Great deliverance
  Zion's King will surely send.

Peace and joy shall now attend thee;
  All thy warfare now is past;
God thy Saviour will defend thee;
  Victory is thine at last:
    All thy conflicts
  End in everlasting rest.

373

ZION stands with hills surrounded—
  Zion, kept by power divine;
All her foes shall be confounded,
  Though the world in arms combine;
    Happy Zion,
  What a favored lot is thine!

Every human tie may perish;
  Friend to friend unfaithful prove;
Mothers cease their own to cherish;
  Heaven and earth at last remove:
    But no changes
  Can attend Jehovah's love.

In the furnace God may prove thee,
  Thence to bring thee forth more bright,
But can never cease to love thee;
  Thou art precious in His sight;
    God is with thee—
  God, thine everlasting Light.

NUREMBURG. 7s.

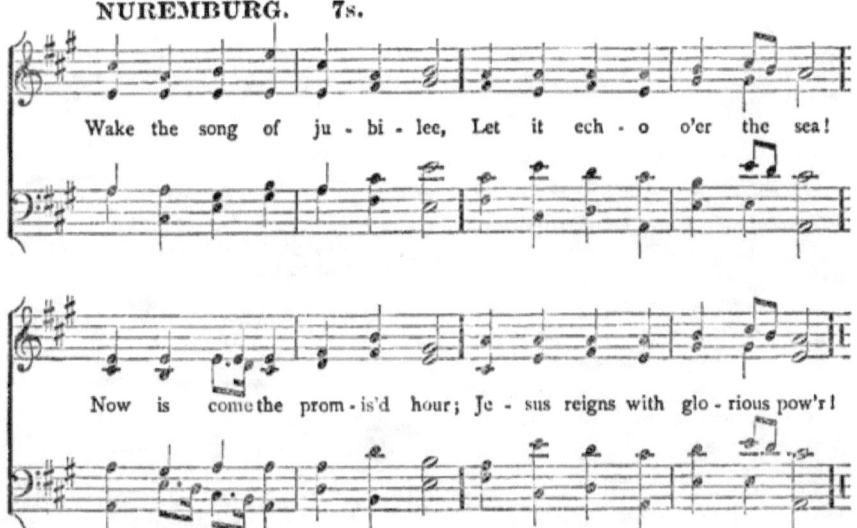

Wake the song of ju-bi-lee, Let it ech-o o'er the sea!
Now is come the prom-is'd hour; Je-sus reigns with glo-rious pow'r!

374

WAKE the song of jubilee,
  Let it echo o'er the sea !
Now is come the promised hour ;
Jesus reigns with glorious power !

All ye nations, join and sing,
Praise your Saviour, praise your King ;
Let it sound from shore to shore,
" Jesus reigns for evermore !"

Hark ! the desert lands rejoice,
And the islands join their voice ;
Joy ! the whole creation sings,
" Jesus is the King of kings !"

Sing we to our God above,
Praise eternal as His love ;
Praise Him, all ye heavenly host,—
Father, Son, and Holy Ghost.

375

HASTEN, Lord, the glorious time,
  When, beneath Messiah's sway,
Every nation, every clime,
  Shall the gospel call obey.

Mightiest kings His power shall own ;
  Heathen tribes His Name adore ;
Satan and his host o'erthrown,
  Bound in chains, shall hurt no more.

Then shall wars and tumults cease,
  Then be banished grief and pain ;
Righteousness, and joy, and peace,
  Undisturbed, shall ever reign.

Bless we then our gracious Lord ;
  Ever praise His glorious Name ;
All His mighty acts record ;
  All His wondrous love proclaim.

376 C. M.

A GLORY gilds the sacred page,
  Majestic, like the sun;
It gives a life to every age;
  It gives, but borrows none.

The hand that gave it still supplies
  The gracious light and heat;
Its truths upon the nations rise,—
  They rise, but never set.

Let everlasting thanks be Thine,
  For such a bright display
As makes a world of darkness shine
  With beams of heavenly day.

My soul rejoices to pursue
  The steps of Him I love,
Till glory breaks upon my view,
  In brighter worlds above.

377 C. M.

HOW precious is the book divine,
  By inspiration given!
Bright as a lamp its doctrines shine,
  To guide our souls to heaven.

Its light, descending from above,
  Our gloomy world to cheer,
Displays a Saviour's boundless love,
  And brings His glories near.

It sweetly cheers our drooping hearts,
  In this dark vale of tears;
Life, light, and joy, it still imparts,
  And quells our rising fears.

This lamp, through all the tedious night
  Of life, shall guide our way,
Till we behold the clearer light
  Of an eternal day.

378 C. M.

HOW shall the young secure their hearts,
  And guard their lives from sin?
Thy word the choicest rules imparts
  To keep the conscience clean.

When once it enters to the mind,
  It spreads such light abroad,
The meanest souls instruction find,
  And raise their thoughts to God.

'Tis like the sun, a heavenly light,
  That guides us all the day;
And, through the dangers of the night,
  A lamp to lead our way.

Thy precepts make me truly wise;
  I hate the sinner's road;
I hate my own vain thoughts that rise,
  But love Thy law, my God!

Thy word is everlasting truth;
  How pure is every page!
That holy book shall guide our youth,
  And well support our age.

379 C. M.

FATHER of mercies! in Thy word,
  What endless glory shines!
Forever be Thy Name adored,
  For these celestial lines.

Here, the fair tree of knowledge grows,
  And yields a free repast;
Sublimer sweets than nature knows
  Invite the longing taste.

Here, the Redeemer's welcome voice
  Spreads heavenly peace around;
And life, and everlasting joys
  Attend the blissful sound.

Oh! may these heavenly pages be
  My ever dear delight;
And still new beauties may I see,
  And still increasing light.

Divine Instructor, gracious Lord!
  Be Thou forever near;
Teach me to love Thy sacred word,
  And view my Saviour there.

380 L. M.

OH, bow Thine ear, Eternal One!
  On Thee our heart adoring calls;
To Thee the followers of Thy Son
  Have raised, and now devote these walls.

Here let Thy holy days be kept;
  And be this place to worship given,
Like that bright spot where Jacob slept,
  The house of God, the gate of heaven.

Here may Thine honor dwell; and here,
  As incense, let Thy children's prayer,
From contrite hearts and lips sincere,
  Rise on the still and holy air.

Here be Thy praise devoutly sung;
  Here let Thy truth beam forth to save,
As when, of old, Thy Spirit hung
  On wings of light, o'er Jordan's wave.

And when the lips, that with Thy Name
  Are vocal now, to dust shall turn,
On others may devotion's flame
  Be kindled here, and purely burn.

381 C. M.

O THOU, whose own vast temple
  Built over earth and sea, [stands,
Accept the walls that human hands
  Have raised to worship Thee!

Lord, from Thine inmost glory send,
  Within these courts to bide,
The peace that dwelleth without end
  Serenely by Thy side!

May erring minds that worship here
  Be taught the better way;
And they who mourn, and they who fear,
  Be strengthened as they pray.

May faith grow firm, and love grow warm,
  And pure devotion rise,
While round these hallowed walls the storm
  Of earth-born passion dies.

382 L. M.

HERE, Lord of life and light, to Thee,
  Our pilgrim fathers bowed the knee;
Thou heard'st their prayer, and in this place
They reared the temple of Thy grace.

Here Thy own servants preached Thy word,
  Safe from the prison and the sword;
Nor preached in vain, each rolling year
Gave witness that the Lord was here.

Here still Thy word is preached, and still,
As once on Zion's sacred hill,
Thy grace descends like timely showers,
For still our fathers' God is ours.

Amid our fathers' graves to-day,
To Thee, our fathers' God, we pray:
Here on Thy Church, till time shall end,
Let showers of heavenly grace descend.

To God the Father, and the Son,
And Holy Spirit, Three in One,
Be honor, praise, and glory given,
By all on earth, by all in heaven!

383 C. M.

FATHER of mercies! condescend
  To hear our fervent prayer,
While this our brother we commend
  To Thy paternal care.

Before him set an open door;
  His various efforts bless;
On him Thy Holy Spirit pour,
  And crown him with success.

In every tempting, trying hour,
  Uphold him by Thy grace;
And guard him by Thy mighty power
  Till he shall end his race.

To Father, Son, and Holy Ghost,
  One God whom we adore,
Be glory as it was, is now,
  And shall be evermore.

384   ITALIAN HYMN.

O HOLY Lord our God,
  By heavenly hosts adored,
    Hear us, we pray:
To Thee the cherubim,
Angels and seraphim,
Unceasing praises bring—
    Their homage pay.

Here give Thy word success;
And this Thy servant bless;
    His labors own;
And while the sinner's Friend
His life and words commend,
Thy Holy Spirit send,
    And make Him known.

May every passing year
More happy still appear
    Than this glad day;
With numbers fill the place,
Adorn Thy saints with grace;
Thy truth may all embrace,
    O Lord, we pray.

385   L. M.

SOON may the last glad song arise
  From all the millions of the skies—
That song of triumph which records
That all the earth is now the Lord's!

Let thrones, and powers, and kingdoms be
Obedient, mighty God, to Thee!
And, over land, and stream, and main,
Wave Thou the sceptre of Thy reign!

Oh, let that glorious anthem swell,
Let host to host the triumph tell,
That not one rebel heart remains,
But over all the Saviour reigns!

386   L. M.

SOVEREIGN of worlds! display Thy power;
Be this Thy Zion's favored hour:
Oh! bid the morning star arise;
Oh! point the heathen to the skies.

Set up Thy throne where Satan reigns,
In western wilds and eastern plains;
Far let the gospel's sound be known;
Make Thou the universe Thine own.

Speak, and the world shall hear Thy voice:
Speak, and the desert shall rejoice:
Dispel the gloom of heathen night;
Bid every nation hail the light.

To God the Father, God the Son,
And God the Spirit, Three in One,
Be honor, praise, and glory given,
By all on earth, and all in heaven!

387   L. M.

AROUND a Table, not a Tomb,
  He willed our gathering-place to be;
When going to prepare our home,
Our Saviour said, "Remember Me."

We kneel around no sculptured stone,
Marking the place where Jesus lay;—
Empty the tomb, the angels gone,
The stone forever rolled away!

Nay! sculptured stones are for the dead!
Thy three dark days of death are o'er;
Thou art the Life, our living Head,
Our living Light for evermore!

Of no fond relics, sadly dear,
O Master! are Thine own possest;
The crown of thorns, the cross, the spear,
The purple robe, the seamless vest.

Nay! relics are for those who mourn
The memory of an absent friend;
Not absent Thou, nor we forlorn!
Art Thou not with us to the end?

Thus round Thy Table, not Thy Tomb,
We keep Thy sacred feast with Thee;
Until within the Father's Home
Our endless gathering-place shall be.

BENEVENTO. 7s.

1. While, with cease-less course, the sun Hast-ed through the for-mer year,
Ma-ny souls their race have run, Nev-er-more to meet us here:
Fixed in an e--ter-nal state, They have done with all be-low;
We a lit-tle long-er wait; But how lit-tle none can know.

388

2
As the wingèd arrow flies
  Speedily the mark to find,
As the lightning from the skies
  Darts, and leaves no trace behind,—
Swiftly thus our fleeting days
  Bear us down life's rapid stream;
Upward, Lord, our spirits raise,
  All below is but a dream.
    Q

3.
Thanks for mercies past receive;
  Pardon of our sins renew;
Teach us henceforth how to live
  With eternity in view:
Bless Thy word to old and young;
  Fill us with a Saviour's love;
When our life's short race is run,
  May we dwell with thee above.

THE NEW YEAR.

DUKE ST. L. M.

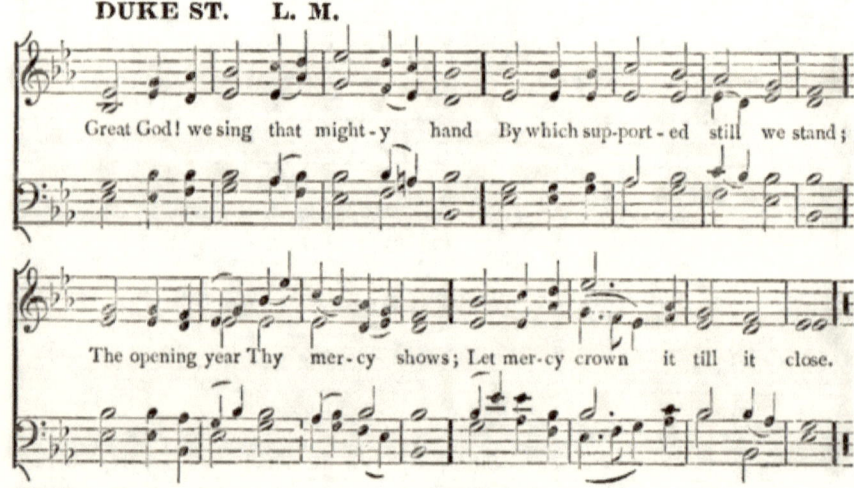

Great God! we sing that mighty hand By which sup-port-ed still we stand; The opening year Thy mer-cy shows; Let mer-cy crown it till it close.

389

GREAT God! we sing that mighty hand
By which supported still we stand;
The opening year Thy mercy shows;
Let mercy crown it till it close.

By day, by night, at home, abroad,
Still we are guarded by our God;
By His incessant bounty fed,
By His unerring counsel led.

With grateful hearts the past we own;
The future, all to us unknown,
We to Thy guardian care commit,
And peaceful leave before Thy feet.

In scenes exalted or depressed,
Be Thou our joy, and Thou our rest;
Thy goodness all our hopes shall raise,
Adored through all our changing days.

When death shall interrupt our songs,
And seal in silence mortal tongues,
Our Helper, God, in whom we trust,
In better worlds our souls shall boast.

390

OUR Helper, God! we bless Thy Name,
The same Thy power, Thy grace the [same;
The tokens of Thy loving care
Open, and crown, and close the year.

Amid ten thousand snares we stand,
Supported by Thy guardian hand;
And see, when we survey our ways,
Ten thousand monuments of praise.

Thus far Thine arm hath led us on;
Thus far we make Thy mercy known;
And while we tread this desert land,
New mercies shall new songs demand.

Our grateful souls on Jordan's shore
Shall raise one sacred pillar more;
Then bear, in Thy bright courts above,
Inscriptions of immortal love.

Praise God, from whom all blessings flow!
Praise Him, all creatures here below!
Praise Him above, ye heavenly host!
Praise Father, Son, and Holy Ghost!

OUR COUNTRY.—THE NEW YEAR.

BEDFORD. C. M.

Lord! while for all man-kind we pray, Of ev-'ry clime and coast,
Oh, hear us for our na-tive land,—The land we love the most.

391

LORD! while for all mankind we pray,
  Of every clime and coast,
Oh, hear us for our native land,—
  The land we love the most.

Our fathers' sepulchres are here,
  And here our kindred dwell;
Our children, too; how should we love
  Another land so well?

Oh, guard our shores from every foe,
  With peace our borders bless;
With prosperous times our cities crown,
  Our fields with plenteousness.

Unite us in the sacred love
  Of knowledge, truth, and Thee;
And let our hills and valleys shout
  The songs of liberty.

Lord of the nations! thus to Thee
  Our country we commend;
Be Thou her Refuge and her Trust,
  Her everlasting Friend!

392

OUR Father! through the coming year
  We know not what shall be;
But we would leave without a fear,
  Its ordering all to Thee.

It may be we shall toil in vain
  For what the world holds fair;
And all the good we thought to gain,
  Deceive, and prove but care.

It may be it shall darkly blend
  Our love with anxious fears,
And snatch away the valued friend,
  The tried of many years.

It may be it shall bring us days
  And nights of lingering pain;
And bid us take a farewell gaze
  Of these loved haunts of men.

But calmly, Lord, on Thee we rest;
  No fears our trust shall move;
Thou knowest what for each is best,
  And Thou art Perfect Love.

DENTON. S. M.

We give Thee but Thine own, What-e'er the gift may be:

All that we have is Thine a-lone, A trust, O Lord, from Thee.

393

WE give Thee but Thine own,
    Whate'er the gift may be:
All that we have is Thine alone,
    A trust, O Lord, from Thee.

May we Thy bounties thus
    As stewards true receive,
And gladly, as Thou blessest us,
    To Thee our first-fruits give.

To comfort and to bless,
    To find a balm for woe,
To tend the lone and fatherless,
    Is Angels' work below.

The captive to release,
    To God the lost to bring,
To teach the way of life and peace,—
    It is a Christ-like thing.

And we believe Thy word,
    Though dim our faith may be,—
Whate'er for Thine we do, O Lord,
    We do it unto Thee.

394

HOW blest, from bonds of care
    And earthly fetters free,
In singleness of heart and aim,
    Thy servants, Lord, to be.

With eager hearts and hands
    To watch before Thy gate,
Ready to run each weary race,
    To bear each heavy weight.

Thus would we serve Thee, Lord,
    Thus ever Thine alone;
Our souls and bodies given to Thee,
    The purchase Thou hast won.

How happily the days
    Spent in Thy service fly!
How rapidly the closing hour,
    The time of rest, draws nigh!

Through good or ill report
    Still keep us near Thy side,
In joy or grief, in life or death,
    Let Christ be magnified.

FAST-DAY.

DUNDEE. C. M.

Al-might-y Lord, be-fore Thy Throne Thy mourn-ing peo-ple bend:

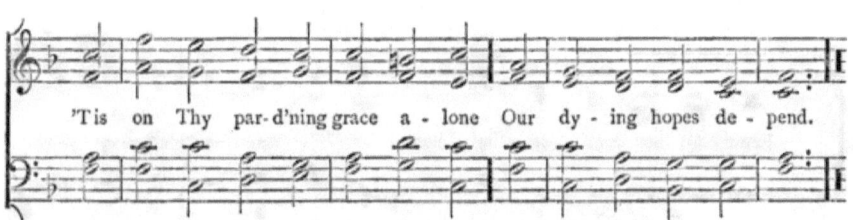

'Tis on Thy par-d'ning grace a-lone Our dy-ing hopes de-pend.

395

ALMIGHTY Lord, before Thy Throne
  Thy mourning people bend;
'Tis on Thy pardoning grace alone
  Our dying hopes depend.

Dark judgments, from Thy heavy hand,
  Thy dreadful power display;
Yet mercy spares our guilty land,
  And still we live to pray.

How changed, alas! are truths divine
  For error, guilt, and shame!
What impious numbers, bold in sin,
  Disgrace the Christian name!

O turn us, turn us, mighty Lord!
  Convert us by Thy grace;
Then shall our hearts obey Thy word,
  And see again Thy face.

Then, should oppressing foes invade,
  We will not yield to fear,
Secure of all-sufficient aid,
  When Thou, O God, art near.

396

ONCE more the solemn season calls,
  A holy fast to keep;
And now, within the temple walls,
  Let priest and people weep.

Yet all in vain the sound of woe,
  To reach the Father's ear,
If from the heart it does not flow,
  To prove our grief sincere.

Vain, vain, in ashes though we mourn,
  Our garments rent in twain,
Unless the smitten heart is torn
  With penitential pain.

Then let us cry to God betimes,
  Nor let His anger flow;
Lest, mindful of our numerous crimes,
  It deal the threatened blow.

O Father, righteous Judge, and God!
  Thy wrath be slow to burn;
Thou givest time to mark the rod,—
  Give also hearts to turn.

THANKSGIVING.

NUREMBURG. 7s.

Praise to God, immortal praise, For the love that crowns our days!
Bounteous Source of ev'ry joy, Let Thy praise our tongues employ!

397

Praise to God, immortal praise,
  For the love that crowns our days!
Bounteous Source of every joy,
Let Thy praise our tongues employ!

For the blessings of the field,
For the stores the gardens yield,
For the joy which harvests bring,
Grateful praises now we sing.

Clouds that drop refreshing dews;
Suns that genial heat diffuse;
Flocks that whiten all the plain;
Yellow sheaves of ripened grain;

All that Spring, with bounteous hand,
Scatters o'er the smiling land;
All that liberal Autumn pours
From her overflowing stores;

These, great God, to Thee we owe,
Source whence all our blessings flow;
And, for these, our souls shall raise
Grateful vows and solemn praise.

398

Praise, O praise our God and King!
  Hymns of adoration sing;
For His mercies still endure,
Ever faithful, ever sure.

Praise Him for our harvest-store,
He hath fill'd the garner-floor;
  For His mercies still endure,
  Ever faithful, ever sure.

And for richer food than this,
Pledge of everlasting bliss;
  For His mercies still endure,
  Ever faithful, ever sure.

Glory to our bounteous King!
Glory let creation sing!
  Glory to the Father, Son,
  And blest Spirit, Three in One.

CRUGER. P. M.

1. Lord God, we worship Thee! In loud and happy chorus;
We praise Thy love and power, Whose goodness reigneth o'er us.
To heaven our song shall soar, Forever shall it be
Resounding o'er and o'er, Lord God, we worship Thee!

399

2.
Lord God, we worship Thee!
  For Thou our land defendest;
Thou pourest down Thy grace,
  And strife and war Thou endest.
Since golden peace, O Lord,
  Thou grantest us to see,
Our land, with one accord,
  Lord God, gives thanks to Thee!

3.
Lord God, we worship Thee!
  Thou didst indeed chastise us,
Yet still Thy anger spares,
  And still Thy mercy tries us:
Once more our Father's hand
  Doth bid our sorrows flee,
And peace rejoice our land;
  Lord God, we worship Thee!

400

NOW thank we all our God,
  With heart, and hands, and voices,
Who wondrous things hath done,
  In whom His world rejoices;
Who, from our mother's arms,
  Hath bless'd us on our way
With countless gifts of love,
  And still is ours to-day.

O may this bounteous God
  Through all our life be near us,
With ever-joyful hearts
  And blessèd peace to cheer us;
And keep us in His grace,
  And guide us when perplexed,
And free us from all ills
  In this world and the next.

HARVEST-HOME. 7s.

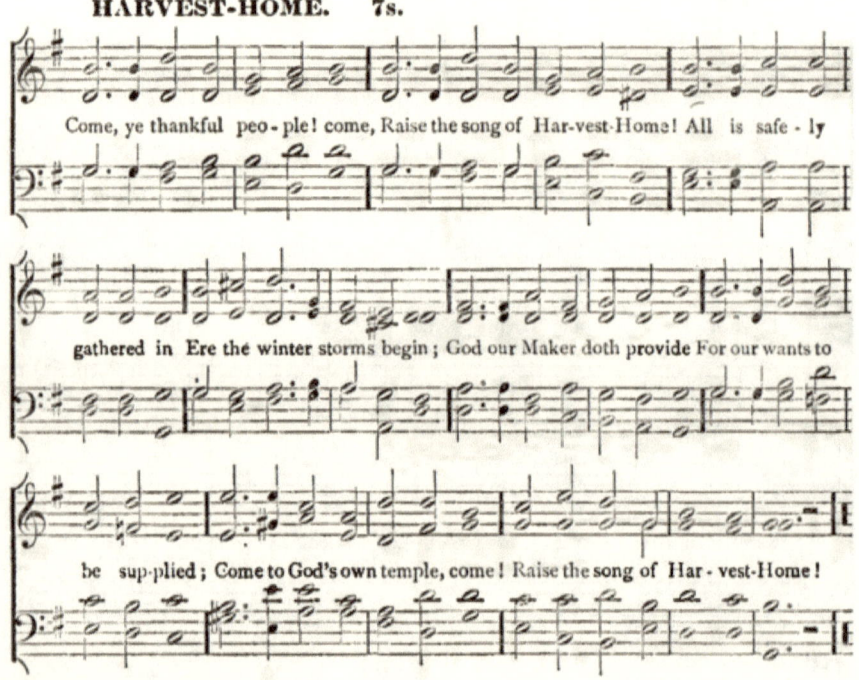

Come, ye thankful peo-ple! come, Raise the song of Har-vest-Home! All is safe-ly gathered in Ere the winter storms begin; God our Maker doth provide For our wants to be sup-plied; Come to God's own temple, come! Raise the song of Har-vest-Home!

401

COME, ye thankful people! come,
   Raise the song of Harvest-Home!
All is safely gathered in
Ere the winter storms begin;
God our Maker doth provide
For our wants to be supplied;
Come to God's own temple, come!
Raise the song of Harvest-Home!

We ourselves are God's own field,
Fruit unto His praise we yield;
Wheat and tares together sown,
Unto joy or sorrow grown;
First the blade and then the ear,
Then the full corn shall appear:
Grant, O Harvest-Lord, that we
Wholesome grain and pure may be.

For the Lord our God shall come
And shall take His harvest home;
From His field shall, in that day,
All offences purge away;
Give His angels charge, at last,
In the fire the tares to cast;
But the fruitful ears to store
In His garner evermore.

Then, thou church triumphant! come,
Raise the song of Harvest-Home!
All are safely gathered in,
Free from sorrow, free from sin,
There forever, purified,
In God's garner to abide:
Come, ten thousand angels, come!
Raise the glorious Harvest-Home!

MISSIONARY CHANT. L. M.

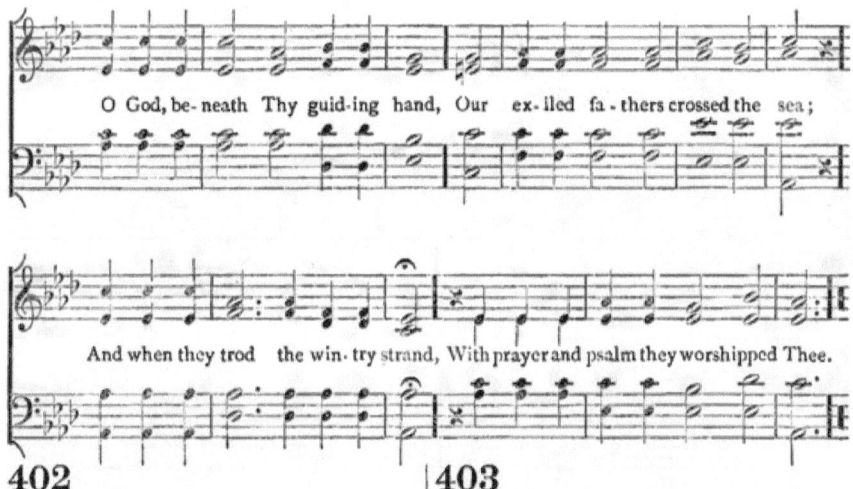

O God, beneath Thy guiding hand, Our exiled fathers crossed the sea;
And when they trod the wintry strand, With prayer and psalm they worshipped Thee.

402

O GOD, beneath Thy guiding hand,
  Our exiled fathers crossed the sea;
And when they trod the wintry strand,
  With prayer and psalm they worshipped Thee.

Thou heard'st, well-pleased, the song,
  the prayer,—
Thy blessing came; and still its power
Shall onward, through all ages, bear
  The memory of that holy hour.

Laws, freedom, truth, and faith in God,
  Came with those exiles o'er the waves,
And where their pilgrim feet have trod,
  The God they trusted guards their graves.

And here Thy Name, O God of love,
  Their children's children shall adore,
Till these eternal hills remove,
  And spring adorns the earth no more.

403

GREAT God of nations! now to Thee
  Our hymn of gratitude we raise;
With humble heart and bending knee,
  We offer Thee our song of praise.

Thy Name we bless, Almighty God!
  For all the kindness Thou hast shown
To this fair land the pilgrims trod,—
  This land we fondly call our own.

Here Freedom spreads her banner wide,
  And casts her soft and hallowed ray:
Here Thou our fathers' steps didst guide
  In safety, through their dangerous way.

We praise Thee, that the gospel's light
  Through all our land its radiance sheds,
Dispels the shades of error's night,
  And heavenly blessings round us spreads.

    All glory to the Father be,
    All glory be to Christ, His Son,
    All glory to the Holy Ghost,
      While everlasting ages run.

BETHESDA. H. M.

To Thee, our God, we fly For mer-cy and for grace; Oh! hear our low-ly cry, And hide not Thou Thy face. O Lord, stretch forth Thy might-y hand, And guard and bless our Fa-ther-land.

404

TO Thee, our God, we fly
    For mercy and for grace;
Oh! hear our lowly cry,
    And hide not Thou Thy face.
O Lord, stretch forth Thy mighty hand,
And guard and bless our Fatherland.

    Arise, O Lord of Hosts!
    Be jealous for Thy Name,
    And drive from out our coasts
    The sins that put to shame.
O Lord, stretch forth Thy mighty hand,
And guard and bless our Fatherland.

    Thy best gifts from on high
    In rich abundance pour,
    That we may magnify
    And praise Thee more and more.
O Lord, stretch forth Thy mighty hand,
And guard and bless our Fatherland.

    The powers ordained by Thee
    With heavenly wisdom bless,
    May they Thy servants be,
    And rule in righteousness.
O Lord, stretch forth Thy mighty hand,
And guard and bless our Fatherland.

    The Church of Thy dear Son
    Inflame with love's pure fire,
    Bind her once more in one,
    And life and truth inspire.
O Lord, stretch forth Thy mighty hand,
And guard and bless our Fatherland.

NATIONAL HYMN, (English.)

405

GOD bless our native land!
  Firm may she ever stand,
    Through storm and night;
When the wild tempests rave,
Ruler of winds and wave,
Do Thou our country save
    By Thy great might.

For her our prayer shall rise
To God, above the skies;
  On Him we wait;
Thou who art ever nigh,
Guarding with watchful eye,
To Thee aloud we cry,
  God save the state!

Almighty God, to Thee
Our humble praise shall be
  Forever given;
Crown Him in every song,
To whom all hearts belong,
Let all His praise prolong,
  In earth and heaven.

406

MY country! 'tis of thee,
  Sweet land of liberty,
    Of thee I sing;
Land where my fathers died!
Land of the pilgrims' pride!
From every mountain side,
  Let freedom ring!

My native country, thee,—
Land of the noble free,—
  Thy name I love;
I love thy rocks and rills,
Thy woods and templed hills:
My heart with rapture thrills
  Like that above.

Let music swell the breeze,
And ring from all the trees,
  Sweet freedom's song:
Let mortal tongues awake;
Let all that breathe partake;
Let rocks their silence break,—
  The sound prolong.

MORTALITY AND IMMORTALITY.

AMSTERDAM. 7s & 6s.

1. Rise, my soul, and stretch thy wings, Thy better portion trace;
   Rise from transitory things Towards heaven, thy native place:
   Sun, and moon, and stars decay; Time shall soon this earth remove;
   Rise, my soul, and haste away To seats prepared above.

407

2.
Rivers to the ocean run,
　Nor stay in all their course;
Fire, ascending, seeks the sun;
　Both speed them to their source:
So a soul that's born of God,
　Pants to view His glorious face,
Upward tends to His abode,
　To rest in His embrace.

3.
Cease, ye pilgrims, cease to mourn,
　Press onward to the prize;
Soon our Saviour will return
　Triumphant in the skies:
Yet a season, and you know
　Happy entrance will be given,
All our sorrows left below,
　And earth exchanged for heaven.

408

TIME is winging us away
　To our eternal home:
Life is but a winter's day—
　A journey to the tomb:
Youth and vigor soon will flee,
　Blooming beauty lose its charms;
All that's mortal soon shall be
　Enclosed in death's cold arms.

Time is winging us away
　To our eternal home;
Life is but a winter's day—
　A journey to the tomb:
But the Christian shall enjoy
　Health and beauty soon above,
Far beyond the world's alloy,
　Secure in Jesus' love.

MORTALITY AND IMMORTALITY.

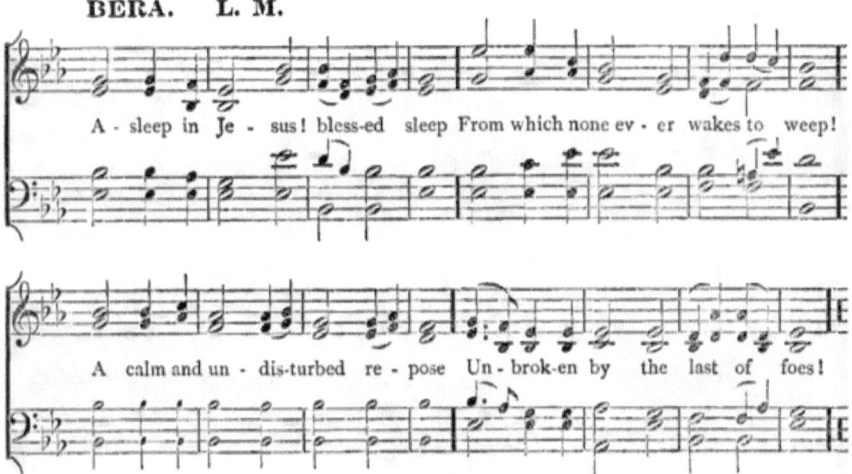

BERA. L. M.

A-sleep in Jesus! bless-ed sleep From which none ev-er wakes to weep!
A calm and un-disturbed re-pose Un-brok-en by the last of foes!

409

ASLEEP in Jesus! blessèd sleep
From which none ever wakes to weep!
A calm and undisturbed repose
Unbroken by the last of foes!

Asleep in Jesus! oh, how sweet
To be for such a slumber meet!
With holy confidence to sing
That death has lost his venomed sting!

Asleep in Jesus! peaceful rest
Whose waking is supremely blest!
No fear, no woe, shall dim that hour
That manifests the Saviour's power.

Asleep in Jesus! oh, for me
May such a blissful refuge be:
Securely shall my ashes lie,
And wait the summons from on high.

410

UNVEIL thy bosom, faithful tomb!
   Take this new treasure to thy trust;
And give these sacred relics room
   To slumber in the silent dust.

Nor pain, nor grief, nor anxious fear,
   Invade thy bounds; no mortal woes
Can reach the peaceful sleeper here,
   While angels watch the soft repose.

So Jesus slept; God's dying Son
   Passed thro' the grave and blessed the
     bed:
Rest here, blest saint, till from His throne
   The morning break, and pierce the
     shade.

Break from His throne, illustrious morn!
   Attend, O earth, His sovereign word!
Restore thy trust: a glorious form
   Shall then ascend to meet the Lord!

    Praise God, from whom all blessings flow!
    Praise Him, all creatures here below!
    Praise Him above, ye heavenly host!
    Praise Father, Son, and Holy Ghost!

MORTALITY AND IMMORTALITY.

GERMANY. L. M.

Almight-y Mak-er of my frame! Teach me the meas-ure of my days;

Teach me to know how frail I am, And spend the rem-nant to Thy praise.

411

ALMIGHTY Maker of my frame!
　Teach me the measure of my days;
Teach me to know how frail I am,
　And spend the remnant to Thy praise.

My days are shorter than a span,
　A little point my life appears;
How frail at best is dying man!
　How vain are all his hopes and fears!

Oh! be a nobler portion mine!
　My God! I bow before Thy throne;
Earth's fleeting treasures I resign,
　And fix my hopes on Thee alone.

Oh! spare me, and my strength restore,
　Ere my few hasty minutes flee;
And, when my days on earth are o'er,
　Let me forever dwell with Thee.

412

LET me be with Thee where Thou art,
　My Saviour, my eternal Rest;
Then only will this longing heart
　Be fully and forever blest.

Let me be with Thee where Thou art,
　Thine unveiled glory to behold;
Then only will this wandering heart
　Cease to be false to Thee and cold.

Let me be with Thee where Thou art,
　Where spotless saints Thy Name adore;
Then only will this sinful heart
　Be evil and defiled no more.

Let me be with Thee where Thou art,
　Where none can die, where none remove;
There neither death nor life will part
　Me from Thy presence and Thy love.

　　　To God the Father, God the Son,
　　　And God the Spirit, Three in One,
　　　Be honor, praise, and glory given,
　　　By all on earth, and all in heaven!

MORTALITY AND IMMORTALITY.

HURSLEY. L. M.

Lord, when I quit this earth-ly stage, Where shall I fly but to Thy breast? For I have sought no oth-er home, For I have found no oth-er rest.

413

LORD, when I quit this earthly stage,
　Where shall I fly but to Thy breast?
For I have sought no other home,
　For I have found no other rest.

I cannot live contented here,
　Without some glimpses of Thy face;
And heaven, without Thy presence there,
　Would be a dark and tiresome place.

My God, and can a humble child
　That loves Thee with a flame so high,
Be ever from Thy face exiled,
　Without the pity of Thine eye?

It cannot be: for Thine own hands
　Have tied my heart so fast to Thee;
And in Thy word Thy promise stands,
　That where Thou art, Thy friends
　　shall be.

414

HOW vain is all beneath the skies!
　How transient every earthly bliss!
How slender all the fondest ties,
　That bind us to a world like this!

The evening cloud, the morning dew,
　The withering grass, the fading flower,
Of earthly hopes are emblems true,—
　The glory of a passing hour.

But, though earth's fairest blossoms die,
　And all beneath the skies is vain,
There is a land, whose confines lie
　Beyond the reach of care and pain.

Then let the hope of joys to come
　Dispel our cares, and chase our fears:
If God be ours, we're traveling home,
　Though passing through a vale of

MORTALITY AND IMMORTALITY.

STANLEY. C. M.

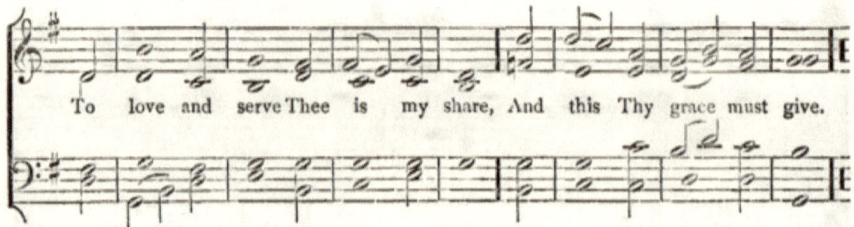

Lord, it be-longs not to my care Wheth-er I die or live;
To love and serve Thee is my share, And this Thy grace must give.

415

LORD, it belongs not to my care
  Whether I die or live;
To love and serve Thee is my share,
  And this Thy grace must give.

If life be long, I will be glad
  That I may long obey;
If short, yet why should I be sad
  To soar to endless day?

Christ leads me through no darker rooms
  Than He went through before;
No one into His kingdom comes,
  But through His opened door.

Come, Lord, when grace has made me
  Thy blessèd face to see;   [meet,
For if Thy work on earth be sweet,
  What will Thy glory be!

Then shall I end my sad complaints,
  And weary, sinful days,
And join with all triumphant saints
  Who sing Jehovah's praise.

416

O God, our help in ages past,
  Our hope for years to come,
Our shelter from the stormy blast,
  And our eternal home!

Before the hills in order stood,
  Or earth received her frame,
From everlasting Thou art God,
  To endless years the same.

A thousand ages in Thy sight
  Are like an evening gone;
Short as the watch that ends the night
  Before the rising sun.

Time, like an ever-rolling stream,
  Bears all its sons away;
They fly, forgotten, as a dream
  Dies at the opening day.

O God, our help in ages past,
  Our hope for years to come,
Be Thou our guard while troubles last,
  And our eternal home!

GORTON. S. M.

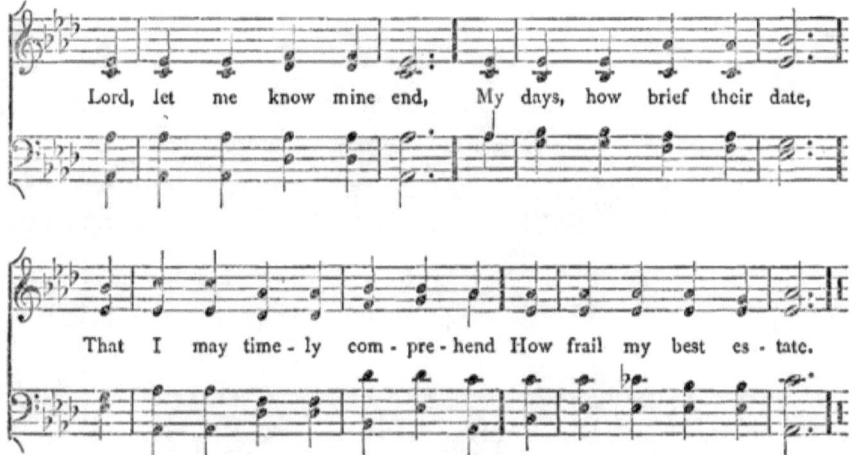

Lord, let me know mine end, My days, how brief their date, That I may time-ly com-pre-hend How frail my best es-tate.

417

LORD, let me know mine end,
  My days, how brief their date,
That I may timely comprehend
  How frail my best estate.

Dumb at Thy feet I lie,
  For Thou hast brought me low;
Remove Thy judgments lest I die;
  I faint beneath Thy blow.

At Thy rebuke the bloom
  Of man's vain beauty flies;
And grief shall like a moth consume
  All that delights our eyes.

Have pity on my fears,
  Hearken to my request,
Turn not in silence from my tears,
  But give the mourner rest.

Oh spare me yet, I pray,
  Awhile my strength restore,
Ere I am summoned hence away,
  And seen on earth no more.
    R

418

OH for the death of those
  Who slumber in the Lord !
Oh, be like theirs my last repose,
  Like theirs my last reward !

Their bodies in the ground,
  In silent hope may lie,
Till the last trumpet's joyful sound
  Shall call them to the sky.

Their ransomed spirits soar
  On wings of faith and love,
To meet the Saviour they adore,
  And reign with Him above.

With us their names shall live
  Through long, succeeding years,
Embalmed with all our hearts can give,
  Our praises and our tears.

Oh for the death of those
  Who slumber in the Lord !
Oh, be like theirs my last repose,
  Like theirs my last reward !

DAWN. S. M.

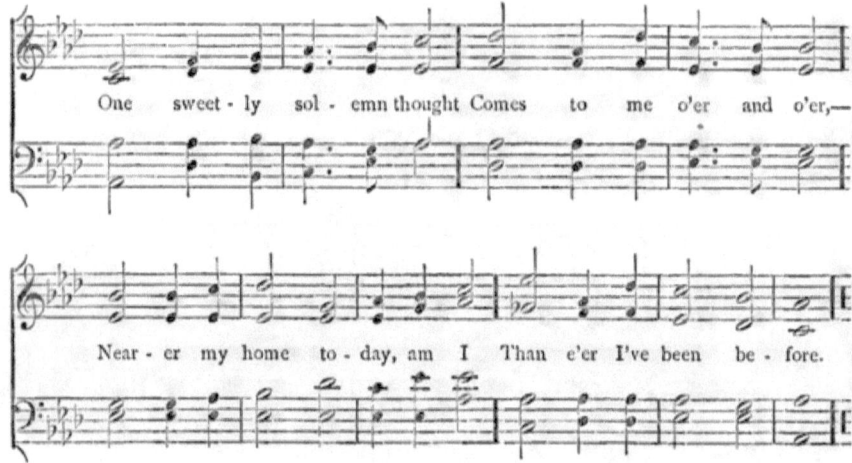

One sweet-ly sol-emn thought Comes to me o'er and o'er,—
Near-er my home to-day, am I Than e'er I've been be-fore.

419

ONE sweetly solemn thought
    Comes to me o'er and o'er,—
Nearer my home, to-day, am I
    Than e'er I've been before;

Nearer my Father's house,
    Where many mansions be;
Nearer my Saviour's glorious throne;
    Nearer the crystal sea;

Nearer the bound of life,
    Where burdens are laid down;
Nearer to leave the heavy cross;
    Nearer to gain the crown.

[But, lying dark between,
    Winding down through the night,
There rolls the deep and unknown stream
    That leads at last to light.

E'en now, perchance, my feet
    Are slipping on the brink,
And I, to-day, am nearer home,—
    Nearer than now I think.]

Father, perfect my trust!
    Strengthen my power of faith!
Nor let me stand, at last, alone
    Upon the shore of death.

420

"FOREVER with the Lord!"
    Amen! so let it be;
Life from the dead is in that word;
    'Tis immortality.

Here, in the body pent,
    Absent from Him I roam,
Yet nightly pitch my moving tent
    A day's march nearer home.

"Forever with the Lord!"
    Father! if 'tis Thy will,
The promise of that faithful word
    Ev'n here to me fulfill.

So, when my latest breath
    Shall rend the veil in twain,
By death, I shall escape from death,
    And life eternal gain.

MORTALITY AND IMMORTALITY.

SCHUMANN. S. M.

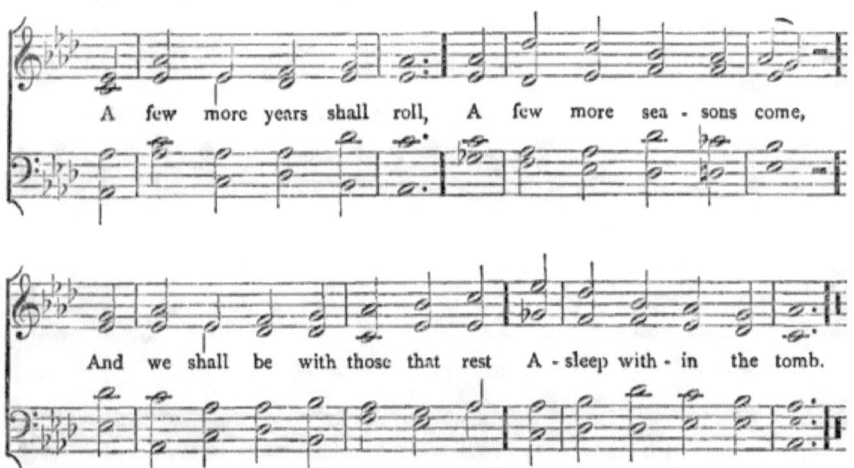

A few more years shall roll, A few more sea-sons come,
And we shall be with those that rest A-sleep with-in the tomb.

421

A FEW more years shall roll,
   A few more seasons come,
And we shall be with those that rest
   Asleep within the tomb.

A few more storms shall beat
   On this wild, rocky shore,
And we shall be where tempests cease,
   And surges swell no more.

A few more struggles here,
   A few more partings o'er,
A few more toils, a few more tears,
   And we shall weep no more.

'Tis but a little while
   And He shall come again,
Who died that we might live, who lives
   That we with Him may reign.

Then, O my Lord! prepare
   My soul for that great day;
Oh! wash me in Thy precious blood,
   And take my sins away.

422

HOW swift the torrent rolls,
   That bears us to the sea!
The tide which hurries thoughtless souls
   To vast eternity!

Our fathers, where are they,
   With all they called their own?
Their joys, and griefs, and hopes, and
   And wealth, and honor, gone! [cares,

God of our fathers, hear,
   Thou everlasting Friend!
While we, as on life's utmost verge,
   Our souls to Thee commend.

Of all the pious dead,
   May we the footsteps trace,
Till with them in the land of light,
   We dwell before Thy face!

The Father and the Son
   And Spirit we adore;
We praise, we bless, we worship Thee,
   Both now and evermore!

MORTALITY AND IMMORTALITY.

HATTON. 7s.

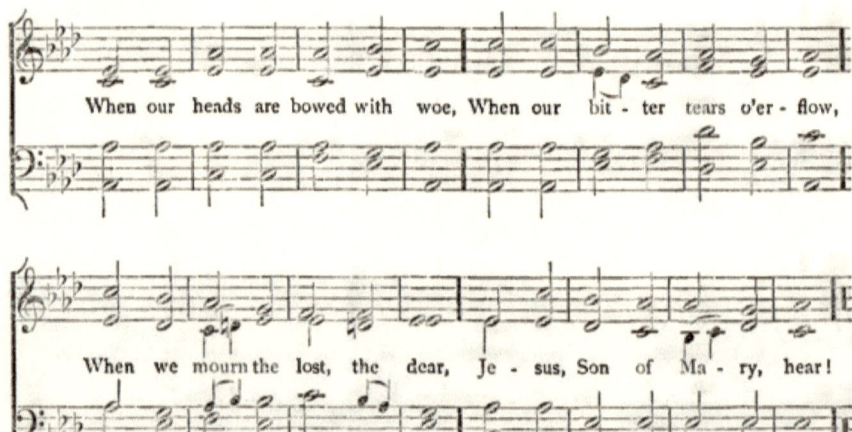

When our heads are bowed with woe, When our bitter tears o'er-flow, When we mourn the lost, the dear, Jesus, Son of Mary, hear!

423

WHEN our heads are bowed with woe,
　　When our bitter tears o'erflow,
When we mourn the lost, the dear,
Jesus, Son of Mary, hear!

Thou our throbbing flesh hast worn,
Thou our mortal griefs hast borne,
Thou hast shed the human tear,
Jesus, Son of Mary, hear!

When the heart is sad within
With the thought of all its sin,
When the spirit shrinks with fear,
Jesus, Son of Mary, hear!

Thou the shame, the grief, hast known,
Though the sins were not Thine own,
Thou hast deigned their load to bear,
Jesus, Son of Mary, hear!

When the solemn death-bell tolls
For our own departing souls,
When the final doom is near,
Jesus, Son of Mary, hear!

Thou hast bowed the dying head,
Thou the blood of life hast shed,
Thou hast filled a mortal bier:
Jesus, Son of Mary, hear!

424

HARK! a voice divides the sky!
　　Happy are the faithful dead
In the Lord who sweetly die!
　　They from all their toils are freed.

Ready for their glorious crown,
　　Sorrows past and sins forgiven,—
Here they lay their burden down,
　　Hallowed and made meet for heaven.

Yes! the Christian's course is run!
　　Ended is the glorious strife;
Fought the fight, the work is done;
　　Death is swallowed up in life!

SUPPLICATION. 7, 7, 7, 6.

We are dy-ing day by day, Soon from earth we pass a-way;

Lord of life, to Thee we pray: Hear us, Ho-ly Je-sus.

425

WE are dying day by day,
    Soon from earth we pass away;
Lord of life, to Thee we pray:
    Hear us, Holy Jesus.

Ere we hear the Angel's call,
And the shadows round us fall,
Be our Saviour, be our All:
    Hear us, Holy Jesus.

Wean our thoughts from things below,
Make us all Thy love to know:
Guard us from our ghostly foe:
    Hear us, Holy Jesus.

Shelter us with angel's wing,
To our souls Thy pardon bring;
So shall death have lost its sting:
    Hear us, Holy Jesus.

In the gloom Thy light provide,
Safely through the valley guide;
Thee we trust, for Thou hast died!
    Hear us, Holy Jesus.

426

WHERE Thy saints in glory reign,
    Free from sorrow, free from pain,
Pure from every guilty stain:
    Bring us, Holy Jesus.

Where the captives find release,
Where all foes from troubling cease,
Where the weary rest in peace:
    Bring us, Holy Jesus.

Where the pleasures never cloy,
Where in angels' holy joy,
God-like men their powers employ:
    Bring us, Holy Jesus.

Where in wondrous light are shown
All Thy dealings with Thine own,
Who shall know as they are known:
    Bring us, Holy Jesus.

Where, with loved ones gone before,
We may love Thee, and adore
In Thy presence evermore:
    Bring us, Holy Jesus.

427

I WOULD not live alway: I ask not to stay
Where storm after storm rises dark o'er the way;
The few lurid mornings that dawn on us here,
Are enough for life's woes, full enough for its cheer.

I would not live alway; no, welcome the tomb;
Since Jesus hath lain there, I dread not its gloom;
There sweet be my rest, till He bid me arise
To hail Him in triumph descending the skies.

Who, who would live alway, away from his God,
Away from yon heaven, that blissful abode,
Where the rivers of pleasure flow o'er the bright plains,
And the noontide of glory eternally reigns:

Where the saints of all ages in harmony meet,
Their Saviour and brethren transported to greet;
While the anthems of rapture unceasingly roll,
And the smile of the Lord is the feast of the soul?

CHESTER. P. M.

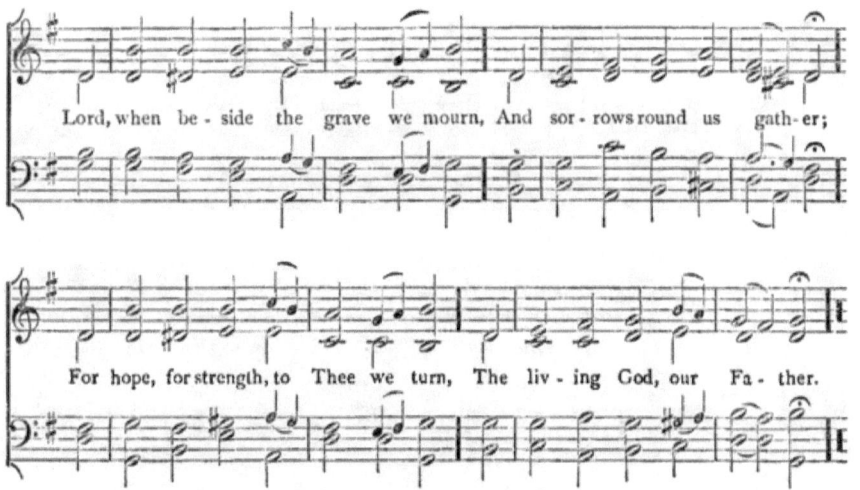

428

Lord, when beside the grave we mourn,
  And sorrows round us gather;
For hope, for strength, to Thee we turn,
  The living God, our Father.

Thy children blest, in Christ that die,
  What power from Thee can sever?
All peaceful in Thine arms they lie;
  To Thee they live forever.

Thy saving might, Eternal Son,
  The grave's dark fears hath banished;
Through Thy dear cross, Thy victory won,
  The sting from death hath vanished.

O Jesus, by those tears of Thine
  For human sorrow flowing,
Uphold us with Thine arm divine,
  Thy comfort still bestowing.

Lift up, O Lord, each mourner's heart,
  Our feeble faith sustaining;
For Thou our risen Saviour art,
  In heaven forever reigning.

THE JUDGMENT.

JUDGMENT HYMN.

429

WHEN my last hour is close at hand,
  My last sad journey taken,
Do Thou, Lord Jesus! by me stand;
  Let me not be forsaken:
O Lord! my spirit I resign
Into Thy loving hands divine:
  'Tis safe within Thy keeping.

Countless as sands upon the shore
  My sins may then appall me;
Yet, though my conscience vex me sore,
  Despair shall not enthrall me;
For as I draw my latest breath,
I'll think, Lord Christ! upon Thy death,
  And there find consolation.

I shall not in the grave remain, [ered;
  Since Thou death's bonds hast sev-
By hope with Thee to rise again
  From fear of death delivered,
I'll come to Thee, where'er Thou art,
Live with Thee, from Thee never part;
  Therefore I die in rapture.

And so to Jesus Christ I'll go,
  My longing arms extending;
So fall asleep in slumber deep,—
  Slumber that knows no waking,
Till Jesus Christ, God's only Son,
Opens the gates of bliss, leads on
  To heaven, to life eternal.

THE JUDGMENT.

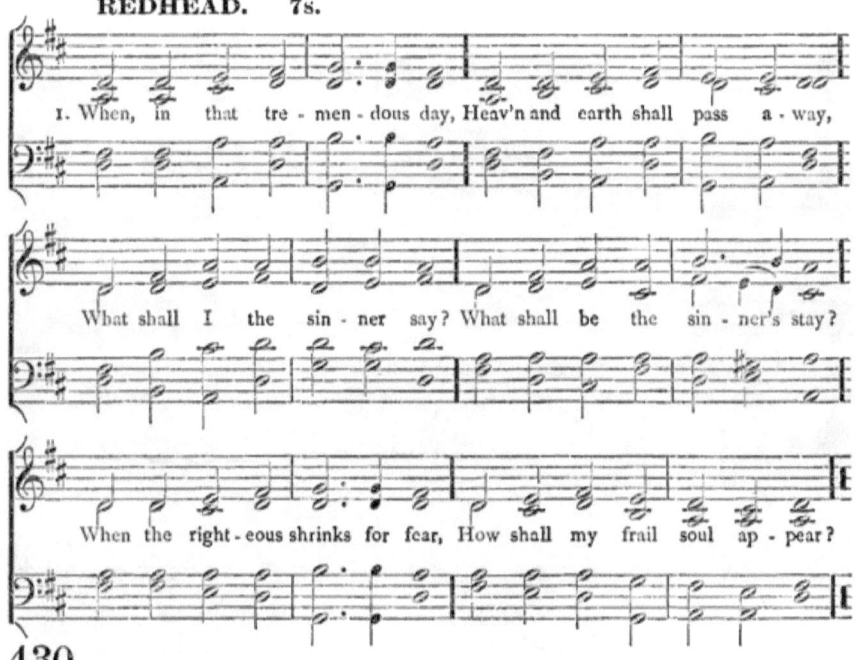

REDHEAD. 7s.

1. When, in that tremendous day, Heav'n and earth shall pass away,
What shall I the sinner say? What shall be the sinner's stay?
When the righteous shrinks for fear, How shall my frail soul appear?

430

WHEN, in that tremendous day,
Heaven and earth shall pass away,
What shall I the sinner say?
What shall be the sinner's stay?
When the righteous shrinks for fear
How shall my frail soul appear?

King of kings, enthroned on high,
In Thine awful Majesty,
Thou who of Thy mercy free
Savest those who saved shall be:
In Thy boundless charity,
Fount of pity, save Thou me.

Thou who bad'st the sinner cease
From her tears, and go in peace;
Thou who to the dying thief
Spakest pardon and relief;
Thou, O Lord, to me hast given,
E'en to me, the hope of heaven!

Thou in search of me didst sit
Weary with the noonday heat;
Thou to save my soul hast borne
Cross and grief, and hate and scorn;
O may all that toil and pain
Not be wholly spent in vain!

O remember, Saviour dear,
What the cause that brought Thee here;
All Thy long and toilsome way
Was for me who went astray:
When that day at last is come,
Call, O call the wanderer home.

Full of tears, and full of dread,
Is the day that wakes the dead,
Calling all, with solemn blast,
From the ashes of the past;
Lord of Mercy, Jesus Blest,
Grant us Thine eternal rest.

THE JUDGMENT.

MERIBAH. C. P. M.

When Thou, my righteous Judge, shalt come To take Thy ransom'd people home, Shall I among them stand? Shall such a worthless worm as I, Who sometimes am afraid to die, Be found at Thy right hand?

431

WHEN Thou, my righteous Judge,
   shalt come
To take Thy ransomed people home,
   Shall I among them stand?
Shall such a worthless worm as I,
Who sometimes am afraid to die,
   Be found at Thy right hand?

I love to meet Thy people now,
Before Thy feet with them to bow,
   Though vilest of them all;
But, can I bear the piercing thought,
What if my name should be left out,
   When Thou for them shalt call?

O Lord, prevent it by Thy grace,
Be Thou my only hiding-place,
   In this th' accepted day;
Thy pardoning voice, oh, let me hear,
To still my unbelieving fear,
   Nor let me fall, I pray.

Among Thy saints let me be found,
Whene'er the archangel's trump shall
   sound,
   To see Thy smiling face;
Then loudest of the throng, I'll sing,
While heaven's resounding mansions
   ring
   With shouts of sovereign grace.

PARK STREET. L. M.

432

HARK! how the choral song of heaven
  Swells full of peace and joy above;
Hark! how they strike their golden harps,
  And raise the tuneful notes of love.

No anxious care nor thrilling grief,
  No deep despair, nor gloomy woe
They feel, when high their lofty strains
  In noblest, sweetest concord flow.

When shall we join the heavenly host,
  Who sing Immanuel's praise on high,
And leave behind our doubts and fears,
  To swell the chorus of the sky?

Oh, come, thou rapture-bringing morn!
  And usher in the joyful day;
We long to see thy rising sun
  Drive all these clouds of grief away.

433

SHALL man, O God of light and life!
  Forever moulder in the grave?
Canst Thou forget Thy glorious work,
  Thy promise, and Thy power to save?

Cease, cease, ye vain desponding fears!
  When Christ our Lord from darkness sprang,
Death, the last foe, was captive led,
  And heaven with praise and wonder rang.

Faith sees the bright eternal doors
  Unfold, to make His children way;
They shall be clothed with endless life,
  And shine in everlasting day.

The trump shall sound; the dust awake;
  From the cold tomb the slumberers spring;   [rise,
Through heaven, with joy, the myriads
  And hail their Saviour and their King.

  To God the Father, and the Son,
  And Holy Spirit, Three in One,
  Be honor, praise, and glory given,
  By all on earth, by all in heaven.

HEAVENLY GLORY.

JERUSALEM. C. M.

1. Jerusalem, my happy home, When shall I come to thee?
When shall my sorrows have an end? Thy joys when shall I see?
O happy harbor of God's saints! O sweet and pleasant soil!
In thee no sorrow may be found, No grief, no care, no toil.

434

2
There lust and lucre cannot dwell,
  There envy bears no sway;
There is no hunger, heat, nor cold,
  But pleasure every way.
Thy walls are made of precious stones,
  Thy bulwarks diamond square;
Thy gates are of right orient pearl,
  Exceeding rich and rare.

3.
Our sweet is mixed with bitter gall,
  Our pleasure is but pain,
Our joys scarce last the looking on,
  Our sorrows still remain.
Ah, my sweet home, Jerusalem,
  Would God I were in Thee!
Would God my woes were at an end,
  Thy joys that I might see!

435

THERE is a land of pure delight,
  Where saints immortal reign,
Infinite day excludes the night,
  And pleasures banish pain.
There everlasting spring abides,
  And never-withering flowers;
Death, like a narrow sea divides
  This heavenly land from ours.

Oh, could we make our doubts remove
  These gloomy doubts that rise,
And see the Canaan that we love,
  With unbeclouded eyes:—
Could we but climb where Moses stood,
  And view the landscape o'er, [flood,
Not Jordan's stream, nor death's cold
  Should fright us from the shore.

PETERBOROUGH. C. M.

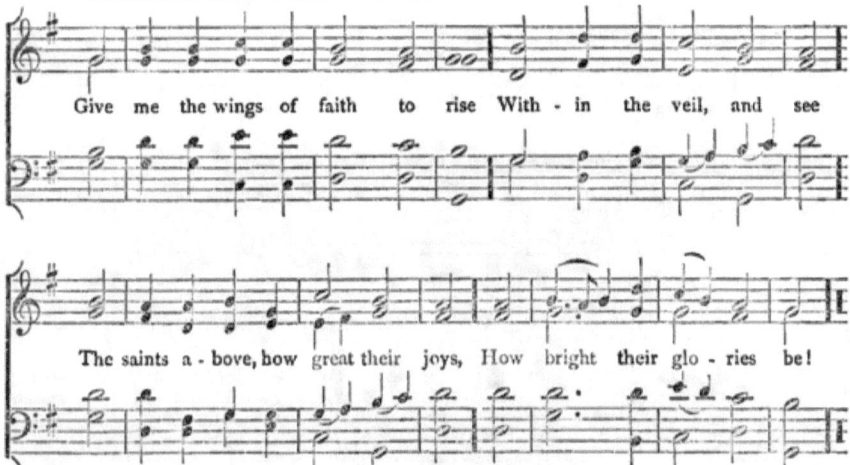

436

Give me the wings of faith to rise
  Within the veil, and see
The saints above, how great their joys,
  How bright their glories be!

Once they were mourning here below,
  And wet their couch with tears;
They wrestled hard, as we do now,
  With sins, and doubts, and fears.

I ask them whence their victory came:
  They, with united breath,
Ascribe their conquest to the Lamb,
  Their triumph to His death.

They marked the footsteps that He trod;
  His zeal inspired their breast;
And, following their incarnate God,
  Possess the promised rest.

Our glorious Leader claims our praise
  For His own pattern given,
While the long cloud of witnesses
  Show the same path to heaven.

437

Nor eye hath seen, nor ear hath heard,
  Nor sense nor reason known,
What joys the Father has prepared
  For those that love His Son!

But the good Spirit of the Lord
  Reveals a heaven to come;
The beams of glory in His word
  Allure and guide us home.

Pure are the joys above the sky,
  And all the region peace;
No wanton lips nor envious eye
  Can see or taste the bliss.

Those holy gates forever bar
  Pollution, sin, and shame;
None shall obtain admittance there,
  But followers of the Lamb.

To Father, Son, and Holy Ghost,
  One God whom we adore,
Be glory as it was, is now,
  And shall be evermore.

HEAVENLY GLORY.

BARTHOLOMEW. C. M.

1. How bright these glorious spirits shine! Whence all their white array?
How came they to the blissful seats Of everlasting day?
Lo! these are they from suff'rings great, Who came to realms of light:
And in the blood of Christ have wash'd Their robes which shine so bright.

438

2
Now with triumphal palms they stand
  Before the throne on high,
And serve the God they love amidst
  The glories of the sky.
His presence fills each heart with joy,
  Tunes every mouth to sing;
By day, by night, the sacred courts
  With glad hosannas ring.

3.
The Lamb which reigns upon the throne
  Shall o'er them still preside;
Feed them with nourishment divine,
  And all their footsteps guide. [flock,
'Mong pastures green He'll lead His
  Where living streams appear;
And God the Lord from every eye
  Shall wipe off every tear.

BEULAH. 7s.

1. What are these in bright array, This innumerable throng, Round the altar, night and day, Hymning one triumphant song? "Worthy is the Lamb, once slain, Blessing, honor, glory, power, Wisdom, riches, to obtain, New dominion ev'ry hour."

439

2.
These through fiery trials trod,
 These from great affliction came;
Now, before the throne of God,
 Sealed with His Almighty Name,
Clad in raiment pure and white,
 Victor-palms in every hand,
Through their dear Redeemer's might,
 More than conquerors they stand.

3.
Hunger, thirst, disease unknown,
 On immortal fruits they feed;
Them the Lamb amidst the throne,
 Shall to living fountains lead:
Joy and gladness banish sighs;
 Perfect love dispels all fear;
And forever from their eyes
 God shall wipe away the tear.

HEAVENLY GLORY.

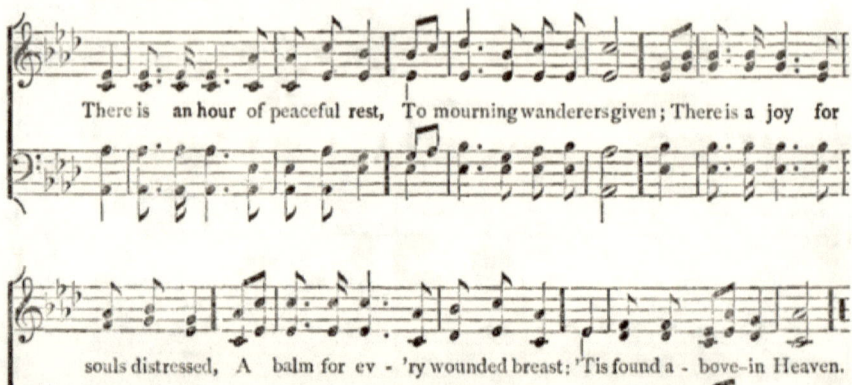

NAUMANN. C. M.

There is an hour of peaceful rest, To mourning wanderers given; There is a joy for souls distressed, A balm for ev-'ry wounded breast; 'Tis found a-bove—in Heaven.

440

THERE is an hour of peaceful rest,
  To mourning wanderers given;
There is a joy for souls distressed,
A balm for every wounded breast:
  'Tis found above—in Heaven.

There is a home for weary souls,
  By sin and sorrow driven,—
When tossed on life's tempestuous shoals,
Where storms arise and ocean rolls,
  And all is drear—but Heaven.

There faith lifts up her cheerful eye,
  To brighter prospects given;
And views the tempest passing by,
The evening shadows quickly fly,
  And all serene—in Heaven.

There fragrant flowers immortal bloom,
  And joys supreme are given;
There rays divine disperse the gloom;
Beyond the confines of the tomb
  Appears the dawn of Heaven.

441

HEAR what the voice from heaven proclaims
  For all the pious dead;—
Sweet is the savor of their names,
Sweet is the savor of their names,
  And soft their sleeping bed.

They die in Jesus and are blessed;
  How kind their slumbers are!
From sufferings and from sins released,
From sufferings and from sins released,
  And freed from every snare.

Far from this world of toil and strife,
  They're present with the Lord;
The labors of their mortal life,
The labors of their mortal life
  End in a large reward.

HEAVENLY HOME.

HOMELAND. 7s & 6s.

1. The Home-land! O the Home-land! the land of the free-born!
No gloom-y night is known there, but aye the fade-less morn;
I'm sigh-ing for that coun-try, my heart is ach-ing here;
There is no pain in the Home-land to which I'm draw-ing near.

442

2.
My Lord is in the Homeland, with angels bright and fair;
No sinful thing nor evil can ever enter there;
The music of the ransomed is ringing in my ears,
And when I think of the Homeland, my eyes are wet with tears.

3.
For loved ones in the Homeland are waiting me to come
Where neither death nor sorrow invade their holy home:
O dear, dear Native Country! O rest and peace above!
Christ bring us all to the Homeland of His eternal love.

HEAVENLY HOME.

EWING. 7s & 6s.

1. Je-ru-sa-lem the gold-en! With milk and hon-ey blest;
Be-neath thy con-tem-pla-tion Sink heart and voice op-prest.
We know not, oh! we know not What joys a-wait us there!
What ra-dian-cy of glo-ry! What bliss be-yond com-pare!

443

2.
They stand, those halls of Sion,
　All jubilant with song,
And bright with many an angel,
　And all the martyr throng:
The King is ever in them;
　The daylight is serene;
The pastures of the blessèd
　Are decked in glorious sheen.

3.
There is the throne of David;
　And there from care released,
The shout of them that triumph,
　The song of them that feast.
And they, who with their Leader,
　Have conquered in the fight,
Forever and forever
　Are clad in robes of white.

ANSELM. 7s & 6s.

444

BRIEF life is here our portion,
  Brief sorrow, short-lived care;
The life that knows no ending,
  The tearless life is there.
O happy retribution!
  Short toil, eternal rest;
For mortals and for sinners
  A mansion with the blest.

And now we fight the battle,
  But then shall wear the crown
Of full and everlasting
  And passionless renown.
But He whom now we trust in,
  Shall then be seen and known;
And they that know and see Him
  Shall have Him for their own.

The morning shall awaken,
  The shadows shall decay,
And each true-hearted servant
  Shall shine as doth the day.
There God, our King and Portion,
  In fullness of His grace,
Shall we behold forever,
  And worship face to face.

O sweet and blessèd country,
  The home of God's elect!
O sweet and blessèd country,
  That eager hearts expect!
Jesus, in mercy bring us
  To that dear land of rest;
Who art, with God the Father,
  And Spirit, ever blest.

HEAVENLY HOME.

ANGELS OF JESUS.

HEAVENLY HOME.

445

2
Onward we go, for still we hear them singing,
  "Come, weary souls, for Jesus bids you come;"
And, through the dark, its echoes sweetly ringing,
  The music of the Gospel leads us home.—*Chorus.*

3
Far, far away, like bells at evening pealing,
  The voice of Jesus sounds o'er land and sea,
And laden souls by thousands meekly stealing,
  Kind Shepherd, turn their weary steps to Thee.—*Chorus.*

4.
Angels, sing on! your faithful watches keeping;
  Sing us sweet fragments of the songs above;
Till morning's joy shall end the night of weeping,
  And life's long shadows break in cloudless love.—*Chorus.*

THE LAST SLEEP.

1. Sleep thy last sleep! Free from care and sorrow; Rest, where none weep, Till th' eternal morrow: Though dark waves roll, O'er the silent river, Thy fainting soul, Jesus can deliver.

446

2.
Life's dream is past;
  All its sin, and sadness;
Brightly, at last,
  Dawns the day of gladness.
Under thy sod,
  Earth, receive our treasure,
To rest in God!
  Waiting all His pleasure.

3.
Though we may mourn
  Those in life the dearest,
They shall return,
  Christ, when Thou appearest!
Soon shall Thy voice
  Comfort those now weeping,
Bidding rejoice
  All in Jesus sleeping.

FOR A CHILD.

447

LET no bitter tears be shed;
  Holy is this narrow bed;
Death eternal life bestows,
Open heaven's portal throws.

Not salvation hardly won,
Not the meed of race well run;
But the goodness of the Lord
Gives this child a full reward.

God, who loveth innocence,
Called this stainless spirit hence;
Christ, who took them to His breast,
Gives the little children rest.

Christ, when this sad life is done,
Join us to Thy little one!
And, in Thine own tender love,
Bring us all to rest above.

PARADISE. P. M.

1. O Paradise, O Paradise, Who doth not crave for rest?
Who would not seek the happy land Where they that loved are blest?

Chorus.
Where loyal hearts and true Stand ever in the light,
All rapture through and through, In God's most holy sight.

448

2.
O Paradise, O Paradise,
 The world is growing old;
Who would not be at rest and free
 Where love is never cold?—*Chorus.*

3.
O Paradise, O Paradise,
 I want to sin no more,
I want to be as pure on earth
 As on thy spotless shore.—*Chorus.*

4.
Lord Jesus, King of Paradise,
 O keep me in Thy love,
And guide me to that happy land
 Of perfect rest above.—*Chorus.*

HEAVENLY HOME.

PILGRIMAGE. P. M.

From Egypt's bondage come, Where death and darkness reign,
We seek our new and better home, Where we our rest shall gain.
Al-le-lu-ia, Al-le-lu-ia, We are trav-'ling home to Heaven.

449

FROM Egypt's bondage come,
　Where death and darkness reign,
We seek our new, our better home,
　Where we our rest shall gain.
　　Alleluia!
We are travelling home to Heaven!

To Canaan's sacred bound
　We haste with songs of joy,
Where peace and liberty are found,
　And sweets that never cloy.
　　Alleluia!
We are travelling home to Heaven!

There sin and sorrow cease,
　And all the strife is o'er;
There we shall dwell in endless peace,
　And never hunger more.
　　Alleluia!
We are travelling home to Heaven!

There in celestial strains
　The ransomed captives sing:
There love in every bosom reigns,
　For God Himself is King;
　　Alleluia!
We are travelling home to Heaven!

ONWARD, CHRISTIAN SOLDIERS.

1. Onward, Christian soldiers, Marching as to war, With the cross of Jesus Going on before. Christ, our Royal Master, Leads against the foe; Forward into battle, See His banners go.

450

2.
Like a mighty army,
  Moves the Church of God.
Brothers, we are treading
  Where the saints have trod.
We are not divided,
  All one body we,
One in hope, in doctrine,
  One in charity.
      Onward, Christian soldiers, etc.

3.
Crowns and thrones may perish,
  Kingdoms rise and wane,
But the Church of Jesus
  Constant will remain:
Gates of hell can never
  'Gainst that Church prevail;
We have Christ's own promise,
  And that cannot fail.
      Onward, Christian soldiers, etc.

4.
Onward then, ye people,
  Join our happy throng,
Blend with ours your voices
  In the triumph song;
Glory, praise, and honor,
  Unto Christ the King;
This through countless ages
  Men and angels sing.
      Onward, Christian soldiers, etc.

VESPER HYMN.

451

SAVIOUR, like a shepherd lead us;
  Much we need Thy tender care;
In Thy pleasant pastures feed us;
  For our use Thy folds prepare.
Blessèd Jesus! Blessèd Jesus!
  Thou hast bought us, Thine we are.

Thou hast promised to receive us,
  Poor and sinful though we be;
Thou hast mercy to relieve us;
  Grace to cleanse, and power to free:
Blessèd Jesus! Blessèd Jesus!
  Let us early turn to Thee.

Early let us seek Thy favor;
  Early let us learn Thy will;
Do Thou, Lord, our only Saviour,
  With Thy love our bosoms fill:
Blessèd Jesus! Blessèd Jesus!
  Thou hast loved us,—love us still.

452

GRACIOUS Saviour, gentle Shepherd,
  Little ones are dear to Thee;
Gathered with Thine arms, and carried
  In Thy bosom may we be;
Sweetly, fondly, safely tended,
  From all want and danger free.

Tender Shepherd, never leave us
  From Thy fold to go astray;
By Thy look of love directed
  May we walk the narrow way;
Thus direct us, and protect us,
  Lest we fall an easy prey.

Cleanse our hearts from sinful folly
  In the stream Thy love supplied,
Mingled stream of blood and water,
  Flowing from Thy wounded Side;
And to heavenly pastures lead us
  Where Thine own still waters glide.

SUPPLICATION.

Heav'n-ly Father, from Thy throne, Look in love and pi-ty down;
Thou canst save, and Thou a-lone; Lord, in mer-cy hear us.

453

HEAVENLY Father, from Thy throne,
  Look in love and pity down;
Thou canst save, and Thou alone;
  Lord, in mercy hear us.

By the great and tender love
Thou didst once for sinners prove,
Love which brought Thee from above,
  Jesus, Saviour, hear us.

Blessèd Spirit, gentle Dove,
From Thy home in heaven above,
Come, and fill our hearts with love;
  Holy Spirit, hear us.

When our feet are led to stray
From Thy pure and perfect way,
Then withhold us, Lord, we pray;
  Jesus, Saviour, hear us.

From all deeds of sinful stain,
From all wicked words and vain,
From all evil thoughts restrain;
  Jesus, Saviour, hear us.

454

JESUS, Saviour, ever mild,
  Born for us a little child
Of the Virgin undefiled;
  Hear us, Holy Jesus.

Jesus, at whose infant feet
Shepherds, coming Thee to greet,
Knelt to pay their worship meet;
  Hear us, Holy Jesus.

By Thy birth and childhood's years,
By Thy conflicts and Thy fears,
By Thy sorrows and Thy tears;
  Save us, Holy Jesus.

By Thy pattern, bright and pure,
By the pains Thou didst endure
Our salvation to procure;
  Save us, Holy Jesus.

Saviour, Prince of life and light,
Dwelling now in glory bright,
Ruling all things by Thy might;
  Save us, Holy Jesus.

THE STORY OF LOVE.

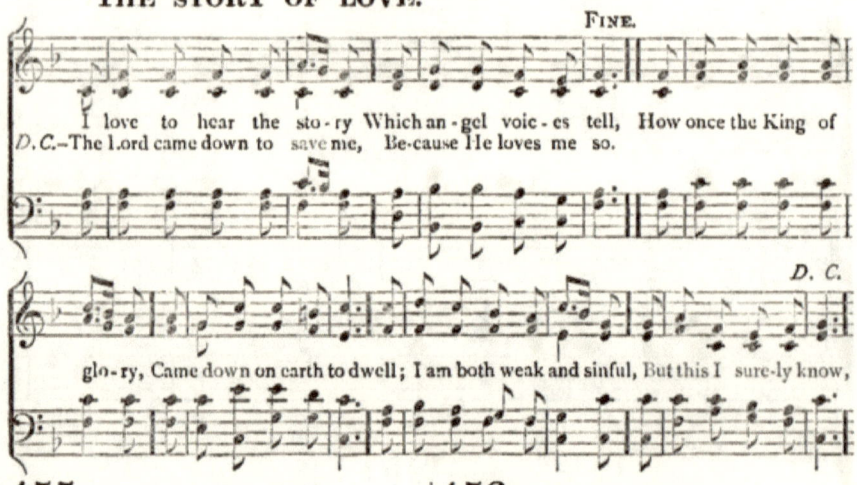

455

I LOVE to hear the story
   Which angel voices tell,
How once the King of glory,
   Came down on earth to dwell;
I am both weak and sinful,
   But this I surely know,
The Lord came down to save me,
   Because He loves me so.

I'm glad my blessèd Saviour
   Was once a child like me,
To show how pure and holy
   His little ones should be.
And if I try to follow
   His footsteps here below,
He never will forget me,
   Because He loves me so.

To sing His love and mercy,
   My sweetest songs I'll raise;
And though I cannot see Him,
   I know He hears my praise:
And He has kindly promised
   That I shall surely go
To sing among His angels,
   Because He loves me so.

456

I NEED Thee, precious Jesus,
   For I am very poor;
A stranger and a pilgrim,
   I have no earthly store.
I need the love of Jesus
   To cheer me on my way,
To guide my doubting footsteps,
   To be my strength and stay.

I need Thee, precious Jesus,
   I need a friend like Thee,
A friend to soothe and pity,
   A friend to care for me.
I need the heart of Jesus
   To feel each anxious care,
To tell my every trial,
   And all my sorrows share.

I need Thee, precious Jesus,
   And hope to see Thee soon
Encircled with the rainbow,
   And seated on Thy throne.
There, with Thy blood-bought children,
   My joy shall ever be
To sing Thy praises, Jesus,
   To gaze, my Lord, on Thee.

OVER YONDER.

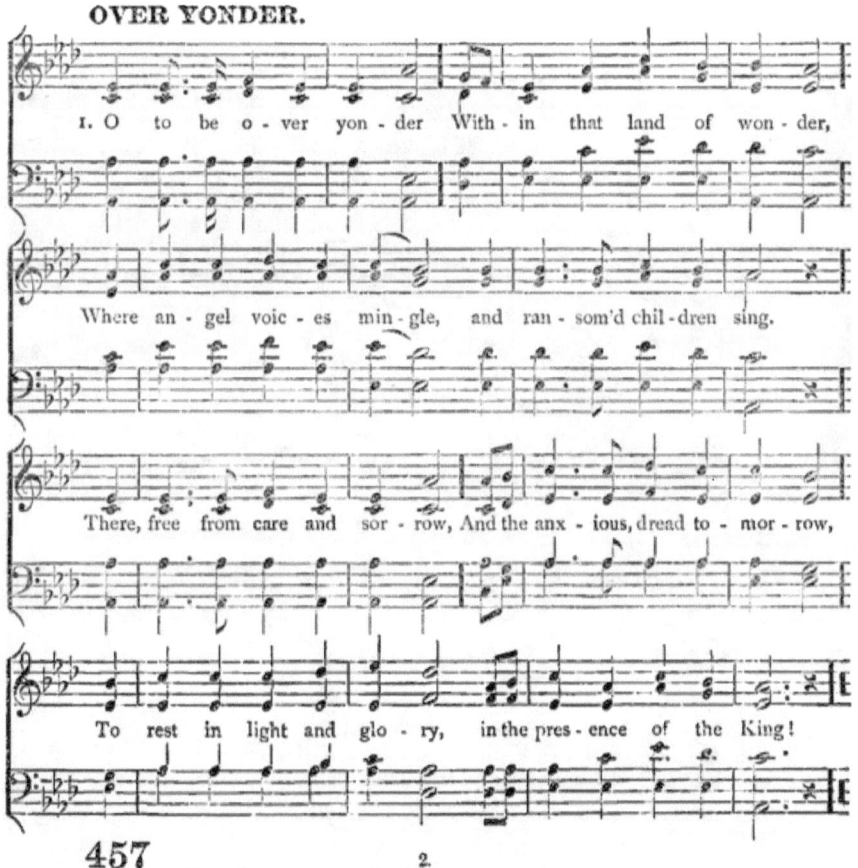

1. O to be over yonder
Within that land of wonder,
Where angel voices mingle, and ransom'd children sing.
There, free from care and sorrow, And the anxious, dread to-morrow,
To rest in light and glory, in the presence of the King!

2.
O to be over yonder!
My weary heart grows fonder
Of looking to the East, to see the Day-Star bring
  Some tidings of the waking,
  The cloudless, pure day-breaking:
My heart is longing, yearning, for the coming of the King.

3.
O when shall I be yonder?
  The longing groweth stronger
To join in all the praises the ransomed ones do sing,
  Within those holy places,
  Where angels veil their faces
In awe and adoration, in the presence of the King.

GENERAL HYMNS.

BANNER.

1. Brightly gleams our banner, Pointing to the sky, Waving wanderers onward, To their home on high. Journeying o'er the desert, Gladly thus we pray, And, with hearts united, Take our heavenward way. *Chorus.* Brightly gleams our banner, Pointing to the sky, Waving wanderers onward, To their home on high.

458

2.
Jesus, Lord and Master,
  At Thy sacred Feet,
Here with hearts rejoicing
  See Thy children meet;
Often have we left Thee,
  Often gone astray,
Keep us, mighty Saviour,
  In the narrow way.—*Chorus.*

3.
All our days direct us
  In the way we go,
Lead us on victorious
  Over every foe:

Bid Thine angels shield us
  When the storm-clouds lour,
Pardon Thou and save us
  In the last dread hour.—*Chorus.*

4.
Then with saints and angels
  May we join above,
Offering prayers and praises
  At Thy throne of love;
When the toil is over,
  Then comes rest and peace,
Jesus in His beauty,
  Songs that never cease.—*Chorus.*

MARCH ONWARD.

1. March, march on-ward, sol-diers true! Take through clouds and mist your way,
Yon-der flows the fount of life, Yon-der dwells e-ter-nal day.
March, though my-riad foes are nigh, For-ward till ye reach the shore,
Then when all the strife is done, Rest in peace for-ev-er-more.

459

2.
Hark, hark, loud the trumpet sounds!
  Wake, ye children of the light;
Time is past for sloth and sleep,
  Wake, and arm you for the fight.
Spear and sword each warrior needs,
  Foes are 'round you, friends are few;
Faint not, though the way be long,
  Fainting, still your way pursue.

3.
See, see, yonder shines your home!
  Gates of pearl and walls of gold;
Joy that heart hath never known,
  Bliss that tongue hath never told!
Praise your Leader, ye who fight;
  Praise Him, ye who bear the palm;
As the sound of mighty seas,
  Pour your everlasting psalm.

GENERAL HYMNS.

PSALM OF PRAISE.

460

FOR the beauty of the earth,
　For the glory of the skies,
For the love which from our birth,
　Over and around us lies;
Lord of all, to Thee we raise
　This our grateful psalm of praise.

For the wonder of each hour
　Of the day and of the night;
Hill and vale, and tree and flower,
　Sun and moon, and stars of light,
Lord of all, to Thee we raise
　This our grateful psalm of praise.

For the joy of human love,
　Brother, sister, parent, child;
Friends on earth, and friends above,
　Pleasures pure and undefiled;
Lord of all, to Thee we raise
　This our grateful psalm of praise.

For Thy church that evermore
　Lifts her holy hands above,
Offering up on every shore
　Her pure sacrifice of love;
Lord of all, to Thee we raise
　This our grateful psalm of praise.

461

WE come to Thee, dear Saviour,
    Just because we need Thee so;
None need Thee more than we do;
Bless us, Saviour, ere we go.
      We come, we come, etc.

We come to Thee, dear Saviour;
It is love that makes us come;
We are certain of our welcome,
Of our Father's welcome home.
      We come, we come, etc.

We come to Thee, dear Saviour,—
For to whom, Lord, can we go?
The words of life eternal
From Thy lips forever flow.
      We come, we come, etc.

We come to Thee, dear Saviour,
And Thou wilt not ask us why;
We cannot live without Thee,
And still less without Thee die.
      We come, we come, etc.

DAILY WORK.

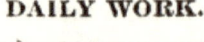

In the vine-yard of our Fa-ther, Dai-ly work we find to do;
Scat-ter'd glean-ings we may gath-er, Tho' we are but young and few.
Lit-tle clus-ters, lit-tle clus-ters, Help to fill the gar-ners too.

462

IN the vineyard of our Father,
  Daily work we find to do;
Scattered gleanings we may gather,
  Though we are but young and few.
    :||: Little clusters,:||:
  Help to fill the garners too.

Toiling early in the morning;
  Catching moments through the day;
Nothing small or lowly scorning
  While we work, and watch, and pray;
    :||: Gathering gladly :||:
  Free-will offerings by the way.

Not for selfish praise or glory;
  Not for objects nothing worth;
But to send the blessèd story
  Of the Gospel o'er the earth,
    :||: Telling mortals :||:
  Of our Lord and Saviour's birth.

Steadfast, then, in our endeavor,
  Heavenly Father, may we be;
And forever and forever
  We will give the praise to Thee:
    :||: Hallelujah :||:
  Singing, all eternity.

HOSANNA TO JESUS.

1. When, His salvation bringing, To Zion Jesus came, The children all stood singing, Hosanna to His Name: Nor did their zeal offend Him, But as He rode along, He let them still attend Him, And smiled to hear their song;—Hosanna! Hosanna to Jesus they sang.

463

2.
The loving Lord retaineth
  His love to children still,
Though now as King He reigneth
  On Zion's heavenly hill;
We'll flock around His banner,
  Who sits upon the throne,
And cry aloud, Hosanna
  To David's royal Son:
    Hosanna to Jesus we'll sing.

3.
For should we fail proclaiming
  Our great Redeemer's praise,
The stones, our silence shaming,
  Would their hosannas raise.
But shall we only render
  The tribute of our words?
No; while our hearts are tender,
  They too shall be the Lord's..
    Hosanna to Jesus our King.

GENERAL HYMNS.

STAND UP FOR JESUS.

1. Stand up!—stand up for Jesus! Ye soldiers of the cross;
Lift high His royal banner, It must not suffer loss:
From vict'ry unto vict'ry His army shall He lead,
Till ev'ry foe is vanquish'd, And Christ is Lord indeed.

464

2
Stand up!—stand up for Jesus!
  The trumpet call obey;
Forth to the mighty conflict,
  In this His glorious day:
"Ye that are men, now serve Him,"
  Against unnumbered foes;
Your courage rise with danger,
  And strength to strength oppose.

3
Stand up!—stand up for Jesus!
  Stand in His strength alone;
The arm of flesh will fail you—
  Ye dare not trust your own:
Put on the gospel armor,
  And, watching unto prayer,
Where duty calls, or danger,
  Be never wanting there.

465

GO forward, Christian soldier,
  Beneath His banner true;
The Lord Himself, Thy Leader,
  Shall all thy foes subdue.
His love foretells thy trials;
  He knows thy hourly need;
He can, with bread of heaven,
  Thy fainting spirit feed.

Go forward, Christian soldier,
  Fear not the gathering night;
The Lord will be thy shelter,
  The Lord will be thy Light!
When morn His face revealeth,
  Thy dangers shall be past;
Oh, pray that faith and courage
  May keep thee to the last!

KREUZNACH.

1. O Jesus, I have promised To serve Thee to the end;
Be Thou forever near me, My Master and my Friend.
I shall not fear the battle, If Thou art by my side,
Nor wander from the pathway, If Thou wilt be my Guide.

466

2.
Oh, let me feel Thee near me,—
　The world is ever near;
I see the sights that dazzle,
　The tempting sounds I hear.
My foes are ever near me,
　Around me and within;
Blest Jesus, draw Thou nearer,
　And shield my soul from sin.

3.
O Jesus, Thou hast promised
　To all who follow Thee,
That where Thou art in glory,
　There shall Thy servants be:
And Jesus, I have promised
　To serve Thee to the end:
O give me grace to follow
　My Master and my Friend!

467

COME, Christian children, come, and
  Your voice with one accord; [raise
Come, sing in joyful songs of praise
  The glories of your Lord.
Sing of the wonders of His love,
  And loudest praises give
To Him who left His throne above,
  And died that you might live.

Sing of the wonders of His truth,
  And read in every page
The promise made to earliest youth
  Fulfilled to latest age.
Sing of the wonders of His power,
  Who with His own right arm
Upholds and keeps you hour by hour,
  And shields from every harm.

DAILY PRAISE.

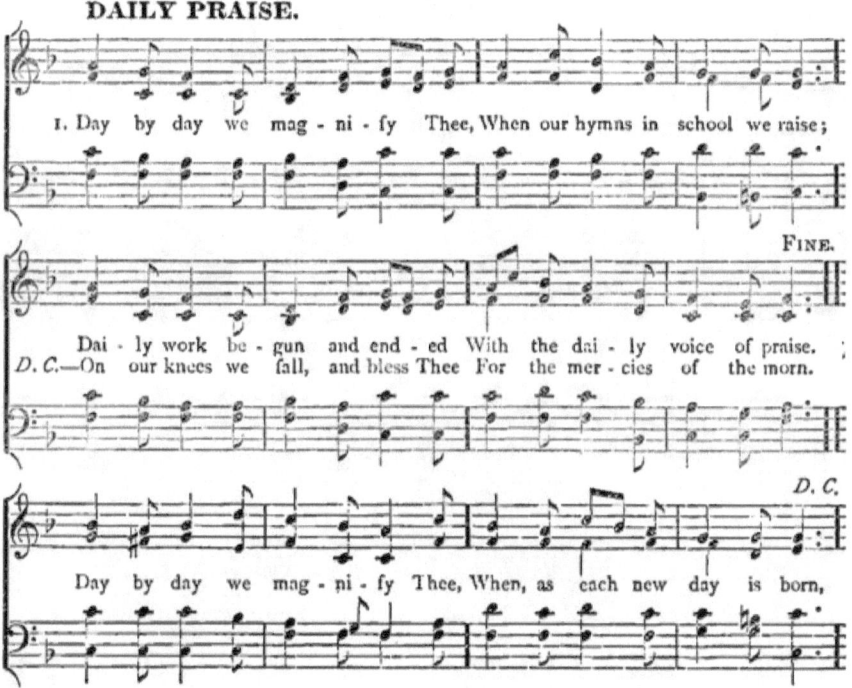

1. Day by day we magnify Thee, When our hymns in school we raise;
Dai-ly work be-gun and end-ed With the dai-ly voice of praise.
D.C.—On our knees we fall, and bless Thee For the mer-cies of the morn.
Day by day we magnify Thee, When, as each new day is born,

468

2.
Day by day we magnify Thee,
In our hymns before we sleep,
Angels hear them, watching o'er us,
Christ's dear lambs all night to keep.
Day by day we magnify Thee,
Not in words of praise alone;
Truthful lips and faithful conduct
Show Thy glory in Thine own.

3.
Day by day we magnify Thee,
When for Jesus' sake we try
Every ill to bear with patience,
Every sin to mortify:
Day by day we magnify Thee,
Till our days on earth shall cease,
Till we rest from all our labors,
Till we enter rest and peace.

469

HOLY Father, send Thy blessing
  On Thy children gathered here;
Let them all, Thy Name confessing,
  Be to Thee forever dear.
Holy Saviour, who in meekness
  Didst vouchsafe a child to be;
Guide their steps and help their weakness,
  Bless, and make them like to Thee.

Bear the lambs, when they are weary,
  In Thine arms and at Thy breast;
Through life's desert dark and dreary
  Bring them to Thy heavenly rest.
Spread Thy wings of blessing o'er them,
  Holy Spirit, from above;
Guide, and lead, and go before them,
  Give them peace, and joy, and love.

GENERAL HYMNS.

AGNUS.

1. I think when I read that sweet story of old, When Jesus was here among men, How He call'd little children as lambs to His fold, I should like to have been with them then.

470

2
I wish that His hands had been placed on my head,
  That His arm had been thrown around me,
And that I might have seen His kind look when He said,
  Let the little ones come unto me.

3.
Yet still to His footstool in prayer I may go,
  And ask for a share in His love;
And if I thus earnestly seek Him below,
  I shall see Him and hear Him above.

4.
In that beautiful place He has gone to prepare
  For all who are washed and forgiven;
And many dear children shall be with Him there,
  For of such is the kingdom of heaven.

5.
But thousands and thousands who wander and fall,
  Never heard of that heavenly home;
I wish they could know there is room for them all,
  And that Jesus had bid them to come.

SAVIOUR, BLESSED SAVIOUR.

1. Saviour, blessèd Saviour, Listen while we sing, Hearts and voices raising, Praises to our King. All we have to offer, All we hope to be, Body, soul, and spirit, All we yield to Thee.

471

2.
Nearer, ever nearer,
  Christ, we come to Thee;
Deep in adoration,
  Bending low the knee.
Thou for our redemption,
  Cam'st on earth to die;
Thou, that we may follow,
  Hast gone up on high.

3.
Clearer still, and clearer,
  Dawns the light from heaven;
In our sadness bringing
  News of sin forgiven:
Time will soon be over,
  Toil and sorrow past;
May we, Blessèd Saviour,
  Rest with Thee at last.

4.
Onward, ever onward,
  Journeying o'er the road
Worn by saints before us,
  Journeying on to God:
Leaving all behind us,
  May we hasten on,
Backward never looking
  Till the prize be won.

5.
Unto Thee, O Father,
  Joyful songs we sing;
Unto Thee, O Saviour,
  Thankful hearts we bring;
Unto Thee, blest Spirit,
  Bow we and adore,
On our way rejoicing,
  Now and evermore.

JESUS, PRAY FOR ME.

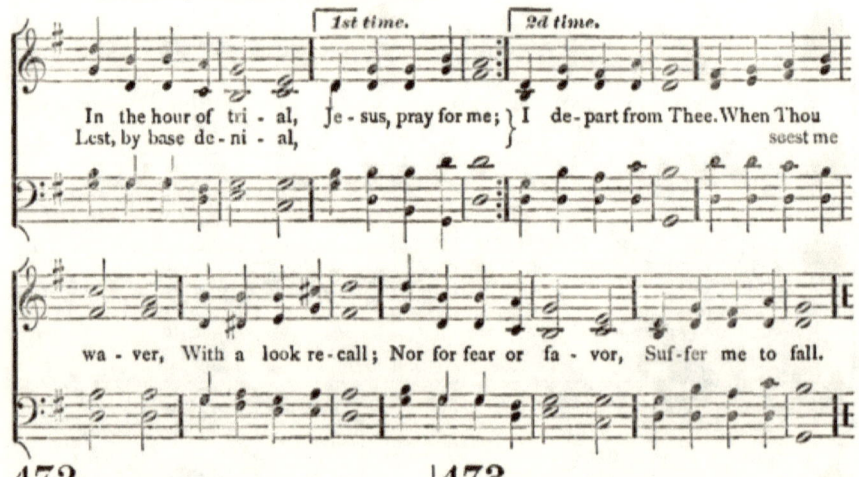

472

IN the hour of trial,
  Jesus pray for me;
Lest, by base denial,
  I depart from Thee.
When Thou seest me waver,
  With a look recall;
Nor for fear or favor,
  Suffer me to fall.

If with sore affliction
  Thou in love chastise,
Pour Thy benediction
  On the sacrifice.
Freely on Thine altar
  I will lay my will,
And though flesh may falter,
  Bless and praise Thee still.

When my lamp low burning,
  Sinks in mortal pain;
Earth to earth returning,
  Dust to dust again;
On Thy truth relying,
  In that hour of strife,
Jesus, take me, dying,
  To eternal life.

473

LO! the voice of Jesus
  Fondly speaks to all;
He it is who frees us
  From sin's bitter thrall.
He it is whose nature,
  Human as our own,
Pleads for every creature
  At the Father's throne.

Lo! the voice of Jesus
  Heard within the breast,
Tells us He will ease us
  Howsoe'er distrest;
Tells us that our sorrow
  For the night may last,
But a glad to-morrow,
  Breaks upon us fast.

Lo! the voice of Jesus
  Bids us still endure;
Seek not what will please us,
  But things just and pure:
Strive through self-denial
  Upwards to the Light,
Where faith's year of trial
  Shall be lost in sight.

GENERAL HYMNS. 299

INTO A DESOLATE LAND. 474.

1. In-to a des-o-late land, White with the drift-ed snow:
2. O-ver the path-less wild Do we not see Him come?

In-to a wea-ry land, Our tru-ant footsteps go. Yet doth Thy care, O Father,
Him, who shall bear us back, Him, who shall lead us home? Listen! between the storm gusts,

Ever Thy wanderers keep; Still doth Thy love, O Shepherd, Follow and guide Thy sheep.
Un-to the straining ear Comes not the cheering whisper, "Courage! for I am near"?

EVENING PRAYER. 475.

1. Je - sus, ten - der Shep - herd, hear me; Bless Thy lit - tle lamb to - night:
2. All this day Thy hand hath led me, And I thank Thee for Thy care;
3. Let my sins be all for - giv - en; Bless the friends I love so well;

Through the dark - ness be Thou near me, Watch my sleep till morn - ing light.
Thou hast kept, and clothed, and fed me,— Lis - ten to my hum - ble prayer.
Take me, when I die, to hea - ven, Hap - py there with Thee to dwell.

GENERAL HYMNS.

CHRISTMAS CAROL.

1. Wake, O, wake, ye weary! once more th' angelic strain, Floating down from Heaven o'er all the earth again, Sheds its benediction on human want and pain; For Christ the Lord is born. Glory in the highest! Glory in the highest, For Christ the Lord is born.

476

2
Fear not, O ye sinful, who shed the contrite tear;
Fear not, ye who sorrow for those who were most dear;
Fear not, O ye trembling, the grave that seems so drear;
    For Christ the Lord is born!

3.
Fear not, O ye troubled, whose pathway clouds surround;
Fear not, O ye faithful, though foes may rage around;
Fear not, O ye peoples in bitter bondage bound;
    For Christ the Lord is born!

4.
Wake, and sing, ye weary! for yours is all the light,—
All the heavenly music of angels in the height;—
All the joy and glory of that first Christmas night
    When Christ the Lord was born.

EASTER-SONG.

1. Christ hath ris-en! Christ hath ris-en! He hath burst His bonds in twain! Christ is ris-en! Christ is ris-en! Earth and Heav'n pro-long the strain. He who suf-fer'd pain and loss, In His love for us, Dy-ing on the bit-ter cross, Lives vic-to-ri-ous!

477

2.
Lo, the chains of death are broken!
 Earth below, and Heaven above
Joy anew in every token
 Of Thy triumph, Lord of love!
He o'er earth and heaven shall reign
 At His Father's side,
Till He cometh once again,
 Bridegroom, to His Bride.
   Cho.—Christ hath risen, etc.

3.
Angel legions, downward thronging,
 Hail the Lord of earth and skies!
Ye who watched with holy longing
 Till your Sun again should rise:—
He is risen! Earth, rejoice!
 Sing, ye starry train!
All things living find a voice!
 Jesus lives again!
   Cho.—Christ hath risen, etc.

TOPICAL INDEX.

ABBA FATHER, 71, 230.
ABSENCE FROM GOD, 151, 172, 243, 337.
ACCEPTED TIME, 183, 308, 310, 325.
ACTIVITY, 27, 253, 291.
ADOPTION, 71, 211, 230.
ADORATION:—
  Of God, 3, 15, 23, 27, 29, 38, 54, 55, 56, 57, 58, 59, 61, 63, 65, 67, 68, 72, 73, 80, 82, 83, 85, 156, 158, 398, 399.
  Of Christ, 5, 19, 56, 61, 66, 82, 83, 85, 87, 111, 117, 125, 127, 128, 133, 137, 213, 217, 233, 236, 246, 304, 374.
  Of Holy Spirit, 144, 146, 158.
  Of Trinity. 23, 158.
ADVENT HYMNS, 86, 89, 96, 99, 319, 366.
AFFLICTIONS, 169, 179, 190, 192, 193, 198, 206, 222, 257, 259, 261, 267, 269, 274, 281, 423.
ALMSGIVING, 293, 393.
ANGELS, 90, 93, 133, 140, 445.
ASCENSION OF CHRIST, 127, 130, 131, 141.
ASHAMED OF CHRIST, 134, 218, 219.
ASLEEP IN JESUS, 409, 446.
ASPIRATION, 16, 20, 36, 62, 64, 74, 151, 152, 175, 218, 231, 238, 239, 240, 248, 258, 260, 261, 260, 291, 407, 412, 442, 443.
ATONING SACRIFICE, 104, 105, 106, 108, 109, 110, 111, 113, 115, 116, 122, 168, 174, 194, 196, 200, 203, 213, 217, 224, 283, 323.
BAPTISM, 341.
BENEVOLENCE OF GOD, 78, 79, 282, 241, 252, 278, 339, 397, 398.
BREVITY OF LIFE, 49, 388, 408, 411, 414, 417, 419, 421, 425.
BROTHERLY LOVE, 237, 284, 285, 288, 290, 394.
BURDENS, 169, 186, 198, 222, 250, 260, 261, 274.
BURIAL OF DEAD.—See *Funeral Hymns.*
CARE, 13, 160, 172, 186, 198, 199, 257, 259, 260, 261, 277, 415.
CHILDREN, 341, 452, 454, 455, 456, 461, 463, 467, 470, 475.
CHRIST JESUS:—
  His birth, 87, 90, 91, 92, 93, 95, 96.
  His life, 98, 100, 102, 237, 290.
  His passion, 104, 106, 107, 113, 116, 200, 209.—*Sufferings.*
  His resurrection, 14, 94, 127, 129, 130, 139, 477.
  His ascension, 127, 131, 141.
  His glorification, 117, 125, 127, 134, 143.
  His intercession, 122.
CHRIST AS
  Bread of Life, 220, 254.
  Captain, 127, 244, 450, 459, 464.
  Conqueror, 94, 136, 142, 143, 477.
CHRIST AS
  Corner-stone, 328.
  Day-star, 210, 275.
  Desire of all, 89.
  Fountain, 174, 220, 293, 314.
  Friend, 173, 196, 197, 213, 217.
  High-Priest, 90, 137, 213, 216.
  King, 90, 93, 94, 368.
  Lamb, 94, 117, 128, 176, 209, 224, 246.
  Light of World, 88, 235, 256, 362.
  Man of Sorrows, 107, 207.
  Messiah, 97, 369, 375.
  Physician, 162.
  Prince of Glory, 105.
  Prince of Life, 119, 127.
  Prince of Peace, 111, 127, 277.
  Refuge, 115, 168, 200, 206, 226.
  Shepherd, 216, 278, 306, 321, 333, 452.
  Son of Mary, 91, 100, 264, 423.
  Son of God, 176, 264.
  Sun of righteousness, 9, 358.
  Way, truth, and life, 101, 223.
CHRISTMAS, 87, 90—97, 476.
CHURCH, 184, 204, 327, 329, 335, 336, 340, 347, 374.
CLOSE OF WORSHIP, 16, 30, 32, 39, 41, 45, 46, 50, 61. See *Evening Hymns,* and *Lord's Day.*
COMMUNION OF SAINTS, 262, 285, 286, 287, 288, 300, 346.—See *Saints.*

TOPICAL INDEX.   303

CONFESSION, 162—168, 180, 190, 195, 200, 208, 323, 395, 471.—See *Penitence.*
CONFLICT, 227, 244, 257, 277, 294, 332, 464.
CONSCIENCE, 110, 146, 151, 165, 180, 251, 378.
CONSECRATION, 121, 164, 182, 191, 201, 212, 229, 233, 241, 333, 342, 466.
CONTENTMENT, 242, 257, 261, 280, 415.
CONVICTION, 163, 165, 166, 183, 195.—See *Confession* and *Penitence.*
CORNER-STONE, 328.
CORONATION, 117, 125, 136, 143.
COURAGE, 108, 169, 244, 273, 291.
COVENANT LOVE, 33, 269, 339, 355.—See *Faithfulness.*
COVENANT VOWS, 338, 342.
CROSS, 105, 106, 110, 111, 116, 124, 196, 200, 208, 212, 311, 323, 341, 351, 722.
DAILY DUTIES, 27, 462, 468.
DEATH, 49, 409, 417, 418, 419, 429, 441, 446.—See *Funeral* and *Mortality.*
DEDICATION, 380, 381.
DEPENDENCE ON GOD, 27, 31, 62, 63, 69, 72, 76, 77, 181, 186, 231, 232, 239, 248, 260, 278, 279, 296, 320, 416.
DOUBT, 240, 324.
EASTER, 90, 93, 94, 127, 129, 130, 139, 477.
ETERNITY, 75, 185, 211, 416, 420, 422.
EXAMPLE OF CHRIST, 98, 100, 102, 223, 237, 290.
EXHORTATIONS, 126, 165, 183, 244, 246, 268, 274, 294, 308, 310, 311, 325, 422, 459, 464, 465.
FAITH IN CHRIST, 108, 110, 112, 164, 168, 173, 174, 206, 208, 209, 220, 229, 240, 255, 275, 436.
FAITHFULNESS OF GOD, 26, 62, 64, 72, 181, 204, 239, 269, 271, 327, 339, 355.

FAST-DAY, 395, 396.—See *Confession.*
FATHER:—
  God our, 71, 231, 232, 242, 249, 263, 267, 276, 299, 344, 383.
FELLOWSHIP.—See *Saints* and *Communion.*
FORBEARANCE, 79, 98, 237.
FORGIVENESS, 110, 126, 153, 161, 166, 167, 170, 174, 180, 195, 200, 202, 208, 430.
FREEDOM, 89, 145, 153, 225.
FRIEND, 72, 173, 181, 196, 197, 213, 216, 217, 219, 273, 308, 339.
FUNERAL HYMNS, 403, 409, 410, 415, 417, 418, 423, 424, 428, 441, 446, 447.
FUTURE PUNISHMENT, 185, 430, 431.
GENTLENESS, 103, 186.
GOD:—
  His being and attributes, 34, 62—79, 84, 138, 181—189, 252, 274, 350, 355, 416.
GOODNESS OF GOD, 67, 70, 186, 232, 252, 278, 293.
GRACE OF GOD, 230, 247, 303.
GUIDANCE, 69, 199, 254, 256, 263, 271, 290, 451.
HAPPINESS, 181, 192, 245. See *Joy.*
HARVEST, 187, 401.
HEART, 151, 166, 170, 201, 225, 242, 251.
HEAVEN, 281, 414, 432—443.
HOLY SCRIPTURE, 376—379.
HOLY SPIRIT, 145—157, 331, 453.
HOPE, 74, 110, 187, 226, 248, 413.
HUMILITY, 207, 417, 471.
IMITATION OF CHRIST, 7, 98, 102, 205, 237, 290.
INDEBTEDNESS TO CHRIST, 118, 122, 169, 196, 207, 213, 219, 232, 264, 275, 343.
INDWELLING OF CHRIST, 88, 153, 176, 184, 189, 191, 198, 205, 215, 220, 235, 238, 243, 251, 270, 276, 277.

INVITATIONS, 126, 160, 165, 167, 168, 178, 184, 193, 249, 282, 295, 308, 310, 311, 322, 473.
JERUSALEM, 434, 443.
JOINING CHURCH, 338, 342, 346.—See *Consecration.*
JOY, 62, 108, 138, 175, 181, 189, 196, 213—221, 235.
JUDGMENT, 430, 431.
KINGDOM OF CHRIST, 138, 336, 358—368, 385.
LAMB OF GOD, 94, 110, 117, 128, 133, 176, 209, 224, 246.
LIKENESS TO CHRIST, 7, 98, 102, 205, 230, 237, 264, 290.
LONGING FOR CHRIST, 36, 132, 151, 215, 221, 272, 412.
LONGING FOR HEAVEN, 258, 427, 442, 448, 457.
LORD'S DAY AND HOUSE, 1—22, 35.—See *Morning* and *Evening.*
LORD'S SUPPER, 345, 348, 349, 351, 352, 353, 354, 387. See *Atonement.*
LOVE:—
  Of God, 26, 78, 82, 84, 121, 183, 186, 195, 226, 230, 263, 293, 339, 355, 397, 413.
  Of Christ, 19, 105, 116, 126, 133, 197, 198, 203—206, 214, 222, 261, 272, 455, 461.
  To God, 36, 71, 72, 85, 182, 189, 238, 245, 293, 307.
  To Christ, 41, 120, 212, 214, 215, 221, 224, 243, 461.
  To Brethren, 237, 288, 290, 293, 298, 393.
MAJESTY OF GOD, 56, 57, 65, 68, 72, 73.
MEEKNESS, 51, 98, 102, 237, 276.
MERCY AND GRACE OF GOD, 61, 70, 78, 79, 84, 85, 156, 170, 180—189, 205, 214, 222, 226, 232, 247, 248, 252, 278, 279, 287, 306, 339, 413.

MERCY SEAT, 180, 226, 287, 303, 306.
MINISTRY, 334, 380—384, 464.
MISSIONS, 327, 333, 354, 357, 361, 369, 370—375.
MORNING HYMNS, 1, 2, 3, 4, 7, 9, 10, 14, 15, 18, 21, 23, 24, 27, 28, 36, 56, 58, 80, 81, 210, 245.
MORTALITY, 44, 49, 408, 409, 411, 414, 417, 419, 421, 425, 444.—See *Brevity of Life.*
NATIONAL HYMNS, 382, 391, 399, 403—406.
NATURE, 55, 186, 330, 460.
NEARNESS TO CHRIST, 151, 225, 229, 238, 243.
NEW YEAR, 388, 392, 407, 408.
OBEDIENCE, 103, 167, 253, 292, 394, 436.
OPENING OF WORSHIP.—See *Morning Hymns* and *Lord's Day.*
PARDON, 110, 126, 153, 161, 166, 167, 168, 170, 174, 180, 195, 202, 208, 249, 430.—See *Forgiveness.*
PEACE, 30, 41, 110, 146, 169, 265, 272, 282, 394.
PENITENCE, 159, 160—172, 180, 190, 195, 207, 208. See *Confession.*
PERSEVERANCE, 169, 244, 268, 273, 291, 294.
PILGRIM FATHERS, 382, 402.
PILGRIMAGE, 245, 254, 266, 315, 449, 458.
PRAISE.—See *Adoration.*
PRAYER, 33, 148, 180, 303, 307.
  For Church, 321, 333, 337, 340, 347, 361.
  For Comfort, 45, 88, 179, 199, 200, 206, 256, 270, 277.
  For Guidance, 254, 266, 270, 452.
  For Holy Spirit, 144, 145, 147, 150, 153, 154, 155, 157, 334, 453.
  For Nation, 391, 395, 402, 403, 405.
  For Pardon, 112, 121, 150, 155, 162, 200—202, 208, 209, 430.—See *Pardon.*

PRAYER:—
  For Penitence, 161, 162, 170, 195, 201, 208, 255, 324.
  For presence of Christ, 40, 86, 132, 225, 243, 255, 272, 275, 317.
  For Renewal, 147, 150, 155, 161, 177, 201, 242.
  For spread of Gospel, 210, 354, 365, 367, 375, 385.
  In view of Death, 40, 113, 199, 412, 413, 419, 421, 422, 429.
PRAYER MEETINGS, 29, 31, 34, 37, 42, 47, 49, 72, 110, 126, 153, 154, 155, 161, 162, 164, 170, 178, 180, 182, 184, 186, 191, 197—206, 211, 216—222, 229, 230, 242—249, 261—265, 281, 289, 297, 299, 300—316, 322, 324, 325, 347, 466.
PRECIOUSNESS OF CHRIST, 112, 132, 136, 197, 198, 213—220, 452, 456.
PRIESTHOOD OF CHRIST, 90, 137, 213, 216.
PROCRASTINATION, 183, 184, 324, 325.
PROMISES, 269, 302, 303, 466.
PROVIDENCE, 70—77, 181, 252, 278.
PURITY, 157, 177, 225, 251.
REFUGE, 115, 168, 200, 206, 226.
REGENERATION, 147, 150, 153, 155, 177, 201, 225, 242, 292.
REPENTANCE.—See *Penitence.*
RESIGNATION, 77, 242, 259—261, 267, 277, 280.
REST, 8, 34, 167, 178, 185, 188, 193, 282, 322, 332, 409, 440, 448.
RESURRECTION, 129, 433.
REVIVALS, 202, 228, 289, 300, 516.
SAINTS:—
  Communion of, 262, 284—288, 346.
  Death of, 409, 418, 424, 441.
  In glory, 227, 426, 432—439, 457.

SHEPHERD, 252, 278, 321, 333, 451, 452.
SERVICE OF CHRIST, 187, 253, 293, 394, 436, 462, 466.
SIN.—See *Confession,* &c.
SUBMISSION, 77, 259, 261, 267, 277, 280.
SUFFERINGS OF CHRIST, 104—108, 113, 116, 118, 194, 283, 323.
TEMPTATION, 170, 198, 199, 255.
THANKSGIVING DAY, 241, 381, 390, 401.
THIRSTING FOR GOD, 10, 20, 71, 151, 155, 200, 214, 225, 238, 242, 243, 270, 276, 307, 420.
THRONE OF GRACE, 180, 303.
TRIALS, 169, 179, 190, 192, 204, 206, 222, 227, 231, 260, 266, 281, 332, 472.
TRINITY, 23, 56, 158, 331.
TRUST IN GOD, 33, 62, 74, 186, 226, 231, 234, 248, 256—271, 279, 413, 415.
TRUST IN CHRIST, 95, 206, 209, 227, 229, 261, 413. See *Faith in Christ.*
UNION:—
  Of Christians with Christ, 218, 220, 229, 249, 272, 284, 312, 420.
  Of Christians with each other, 223, 249, 284, 287, 331.
VICTORY, 175, 187, 360, 436, 438, 439, 443.
WANDERING, 170, 182, 183, 188.
WARFARE, 294, 450, 459, 464, 465.
WATCHFULNESS, 268, 295, 297.
WISDOM OF GOD, 67, 76, 82, 249.
WITNESS OF SPIRIT, 145, 150, 152, 154, 157.
WORSHIP.—See *Lord's Day, Morning* and *Evening, Opening* and *Closing* Hymns.
ZION, 22, 122, 327, 329, 361, 372, 373, 443.

INDEX OF FIRST LINES.

First Line	Author	No. of Hymns
Abide with me, fast falls the	H. F. Lyte.	40
A charge to keep I have	C. Wesley.	297
A few more years shall roll	H. Bonar.	421
Again our earthly cares we	J. Newton.	13
A glory gilds the sacred page	Wm. Cowper.	376
Alas, and did my Saviour bleed	I. Watts.	323
All hail the power of Jesus'	E. Perronet.	136
All ye that are weary, 'tis	Hymnal Noted.	126
Almighty God, before Thy	Anne Steele.	395
Almighty Maker of my frame	Anne Steele.	411
Always with us, always with	E. H. Nevin.	198
A mother may forgetful be	Anne Steele.	355
And now the wants are told	Sullivan's Coll.	34
Another six days' work is	J. Stennett.	6
Approach, my soul, the mercy	J. Newton.	180
Arise, my soul, arise	C. Wesley.	108
Arise, O King of grace, arise	I. Watts.	4
Arise, ye Saints, arise	T. Kelly.	244
Arm of the Lord, awake	W. Shrubsole.	367
Around a table, not a tomb		387
Art thou weary, art thou	Ancient Greek.	322
Asleep in Jesus, blessed	Mrs. Mackay.	409
At the Lamb's high feast	Tr. by Campbell.	94
Awake, and sing the song	W. Hammond.	246
Awake, my soul, and with the sun	T. Ken.	27
Awake, my soul, stretch	P. Doddridge.	291
Before Jehovah's awful throne	I. Watts.	65
Before thine awful presence, Lord		338
Behold a stranger at the door	J. Grigg.	308
Behold the glories of the Lamb	I. Watts.	117
Behold the Lamb of God	M. Bridges.	115
Behold the Saviour of mankind	S. Wesley.	116
Behold the throne of grace	J. Newton.	303
Behold, what wondrous grace	I. Watts.	230
Blessed are the sons of God	J. Humphreys.	211
Blessed Fountain, full of grace	P. Kelly.	314
Blessed Saviour, Thee I love	S. Duffield.	212
Blest are the pure in heart		251
Blest be the tie that binds	J. Fawcett.	288
Blest Comforter divine	Mrs. Sigourney.	154
Blest Jesus, come Thou down	Luth. Coll.	317
Blow ye the trumpet, blow	C. Wesley.	109
Brief life is here our portion	Tr. by Neale.	444
Brightly gleams our banner	J. T. Potter.	458
Burdened with guilt, would'st	R. S. Cook.	165
Cast thy burden on the Lord	R. Hill.	274
Children of the Heavenly King	J. Cennick.	315
Christian, seek not yet repose		268
Christ is made the sure	Tr. by Neale.	328
Christ is risen, Christ is	Sullivan's Coll.	477
Christ of all my hopes the	R. Wardlaw.	275
Christ the Lord is risen to-day	C. Wesley.	139
Christ, whose glory fills the	C. Wesley.	312
Come, Christian children	Church Hymns.	467
Come, gracious Spirit	S. Browne.	145
Come, Holy Ghost, in love	Tr. by Palmer.	150
Come, Holy Spirit, come	J. Hart.	153
Come, Holy Spirit, Heavenly	I. Watts.	147
Come in, thou blessed of the	T. Kelly.	346
Come, Jesus, Redeemer, abide	R. Palmer.	272
Come, Kingdom of our God	Johns.	365
Come, let us join our cheerful	I. Watts.	133
Come, let us sing the praise	Epis. Coll.	137
Come, let us sing the song of	Montgomery.	128
Come, Lord, and tarry not	H. Bonar.	366
Come, O Jesus, to Thy table	Sullivan's Coll.	352
Come, O my soul, in sacred	T. Blacklock.	66
Come, quickly come, dread Judge	Tuttiett.	86
Come, said Jesus' sacred	Mrs. Barbauld.	193
Come, Thou Almighty King	C. Wesley.	158
Come, Thou desire of all Thy	Miss Steele.	12
Come, Thou fount of every	R. Robinson.	203

INDEX OF FIRST LINES.

First Line	Author	Page
Come, Thou long-expected	C. Wesley	89
Come to Calvary's holy	J. Montgomery	311
Come unto me, when shadows		282
Come, weary souls with sin	Miss Steele	167
Come, we that love the Lord	I. Watts	245
Come, ye thankful people, come	H. Alford	401
Crown His head with endless	W. Goode	125
Day by day we magnify	Church Hymns	468
Dear Father, to Thy mercy-seat	Miss Steele	226
Dear Lord, I make confession	German	163
Dear Saviour, if these lambs should stray		356
Dear Saviour, we are Thine	P. Doddridge	229
Depth of mercy, can there be	C. Wesley	195
Dismiss us with Thy blessing	J. Hart	30
Early, my God, without delay	I. Watts	10
Eternal Spirit, we confess	I. Watts	146
Far from my heavenly home	H. F. Lyte	258
Father, hear our humble claim	Wesleyan	299
Father of eternal grace	J. Montgomery	276
Father of love, our guide	W. J. Irons	263
Father of love, Thy grace bestow		344
Father of mercies, condescend	T. Morrell	383
Father of mercies, in Thy	Miss Steele	379
Father of mercies, send Thy	P. Doddridge	292
Father, whate'er of earthly bliss	Miss Steele	242
For all Thy Saints	Hymns An. & Mod.	262
For a season called to part	J. Newton	45
Forever with the Lord	J. Montgomery	420
For the beauty of the earth	J. Pierpont	460
Forsake me not, O Lord	Tr. by Alexander	270
From all that dwell below the	I. Watts	61
From Egypt's bondage come	T. Kelly	449
From every stormy wind that	H. Stowell	287
From fleeting pleasures, and abiding		160
From Greenland's icy mountains	R. Heber	369
Gently, Lord, O gently lead us	T. Hastings	199
Give me the wings of faith to	I. Watts	436
Glorious things of Thee are	J. Newton	327
Glory to Thee, my God, this	T. Ken	29
God bless our native land	J. S. Dwight	405
God is love, his mercy	J. Bowring	84
God is the refuge of His saints	I. Watts	64
God moves in a mysterious	Wm. Cowper	76
Go forward, Christian	Sullivan's Coll.	465
Grace, 'tis a charming sound	P. Doddridge	247
Gracious Saviour, gentle	Church Hymns	452
Gracious Spirit, love divine	J. Stocker	155
Great God, how infinite art Thou	I. Watts	75
Great God of nations	Church Hymns	403
Great God, we sing that	P. Doddridge	389
Great Shepherd of Thine Israel	I. Watts	333
Great Shepherd of Thy people		321
Guide me, O Thou Great	W. Williams	254
Hail, sacred truth whose	J. Buttress	379
Hail to the Lord's anointed	J. Montgomery	371
Hail to the Prince of life	P. Doddridge	127
Happy the souls to Jesus joined	C. Wesley	284
Hark, a voice divides the sky	C. Wesley	424
Hark, hark, my soul, angelic	F. W. Faber	445
Hark how the choral song of heaven		432
Hark, ten thousand harps and	T. Kelly	143
Hark, the glad sound, the	P. Doddridge	96
Hark, the herald angels sing	C. Wesley	93
Hark, what mean those holy	J. Cawood	90
Hasten, Lord, the glorious	Miss Auber	375
Heal me, O my Saviour, heal	G. Thring	162
Hear what God the Lord	J. Montgomery	204
Hear what the voice from heaven	I. Watts	441
Heavenly Father, from	Church Hymns	453
Heavenly Father, sovereign	Montgomery	156
Here, Lord of life and light	L. Bacon	382
Here, O my Lord, I see Thee	H. Bonar	353
High in the heavens, eternal	I. Watts	67
Holy Father, send Thy blessing		469
Holy, holy, holy, Lord God	R. Heber	23
Holy Saviour, from Thy throne		123
Holy Spirit, Lord of	Robert of France	144
How blest, from bonds of care		394
How bright these glorious	W. Cameron	438
How firm a foundation, ye saints	Kirkham	269
How gentle God's commands	Doddridge	186
How long, O Lord our God	H. Bonar	337
How long, O Lord our Saviour	H. Bonar	319
How oft, alas, this wretched	Miss Steele	170
How pleased and blest was I	I. Watts	22
How precious is the book	J. Fawcett	377
How shall the young secure	I. Watts	378
How sweetly flowed the	J. Bowring	103
How sweet the Name of Jesus	J. Newton	216
How sweet to leave the world	T. Kelly	43
How swift the torrent rolls	P. Doddridge	422
How vain is all beneath the	Pratt's Coll.	414
I heard the voice of Jesus say	H. Bonar	178
I love Thy kingdom, Lord	T. Dwight	336
I love to hear the story		455
I love to steal awhile away	Mrs. Brown	31
I need Thee, precious Jesus		456
I think when I read that sweet	J. Luke	470
I would not live alway	W. A. Muhlenburg	427
If thou but suffer God to guide	Neumark	271
If through unruffled seas	A. Toplady	257
I'm not ashamed to own my	I. Watts	218
In humble supplication	Sullivan's Coll.	318
In stature grows the Holy	J. Chandler	100

INDEX OF FIRST LINES.

In the cross of Christ I glory..*J. Bowring.* 124
In the hour of trial..........*J. Montgomery.* 472
In the vineyard of our Father...*Epis. Coll.* 462
In Thy Name, O Lord..............*T. Kelly.* 51
Inspirer and Hearer of prayer...*A. Toplady.* 33
Into a desolate land........................ 474
It came upon the midnight......*E. H. Sears.* 92

Jehovah, God, Thy gracious........*I. Watts.* 70
Jerusalem, my happy home...*Old English.* 434
Jerusalem the golden............*Tr. by Neale.* 443
Jesus, and shall it ever be..........*J. Grigg.* 219
Jesus, Lord of life and glory...*J. Cummins.* 255
Jesus, Lover of my soul..........*C. Wesley.* 206
Jesus, Name all names above..*J. M. Neale.* 112
Jesus, Prince of life and....*Church Hymns.* 119
Jesus, Saviour, ever mild....*Church Hymns.* 454
Jesus shall reign where'er the......*I. Watts.* 368
Jesus, still lead on................*Zinzendorf.* 266
Jesus, take me for Thine own.................. 191
Jesus, tender Shepherd, hear me................ 475
Jesus, the very thought is sweet...*Bernard.* 221
Jesus, the very thought of Thee......*Bernard.* 215
Jesus, Thou art the sinner's...*R. Burnham.* 173
Jesus, Thou joy of loving..*Tr. by R. Palmer.* 220
Jesus, Thy Name our souls....*Ray Palmer.* 233
Jesus, to Thy table led......*Church Hymns.* 348
Jesus, we look to Thee............*C. Wesley.* 302
Jesus, where'er Thy people....*Wm. Cowper.* 306
Jesus, with Thy Church....*Church Hymns.* 347
Joy to the world, the Lord is......*I. Watts.* 95
Just as I am, without......*Charlotte Elliott.* 164

Lead, kindly light, amid...*J. H. Newman.* 256
Let me be with Thee, where......*C. Elliott.* 412
Let no bitter tears be shed...*Church Hymns.* 447
Let our songs of praise ascending.............. 91
Let saints below in concert sing...*C. Wesley.* 285
Lift up your heads, eternal...*Sullivan's Coll.* 141
Light of the lonely pilgrim's....*E. Denny.* 362
Light of the soul, O Saviour......*Breviary.* 235
Light of those whose dreary......*C. Wesley.* 88
Lo, the day of rest declineth...*C. Robbins.* 48
Lo, the voice of Jesus........................ 473
Lo, what a glorious sight..........*I. Watts.* 360
Lord, as to Thy dear cross we flee...*Gurney.* 237
Lord, at this closing hour........*E. T. Fitch.* 39
Lord, dismiss us with Thy blessing..*Smyth.* 50
Lord God of hosts, by all adored.............. 57
Lord God, we worship Thee.*Sullivan's Coll.* 399
Lord, I believe, Thy power I own,*Wreford.* 240
Lord, I hear that showers......*Miss Codner.* 202
Lord, in the morning thou shalt...*I. Watts.* 18
Lord, in this, Thy mercy's day..*J. Williams.* 161
Lord, in Thy great, Thy glorious.*Miss Steele.* 234

Lord, it belongs not to my care..*R. Baxter.* 415
Lord, lead the way the Saviour.*W. Croswell.* 290
Lord, let me know mine end.................. 417
Lord of our life, and God of our salvation.. 340
Lord of the worlds above..........*I. Watts.* 20
Lord, Thou wilt hear me when....*I. Watts.* 320
Lord, to Thee alone we turn..*Sullivan's Coll.* 208
Lord, we come before Thee..*W. Hammond.* 301
Lord, when beside the grave we mourn...... 428
Lord, when I quit this earthly stage.*I. Watts.* 413
Lord, when we bend before Thy....*Carlyle.* 171
Lord, while for all mankind we....*Wreford.* 391
Love divine, all love excelling...*C. Wesley.* 205

Majestic sweetness sits enthroned...*Stennett.* 217
March, march onward........*Sullivan's Coll.* 459
May the grace of Christ our...*J. Newton.* 50-51
My country, 'tis of thee.........*S. F. Smith.* 406
My dear Redeemer, and my Lord..*I. Watts.* 102
My faith looks up to Thee......*Ray Palmer.* 209
My God, accept my heart........*Lyra Cathol.* 182
My God, and is Thy table spread..*Doddridge.* 345
My God, how endless is Thy love...*I. Watts.* 26
My God, how wonderful Thou art....*Faber.* 72
My God, is any hour so sweet......*C. Elliott.* 307
My God, my Father, blissful Name....*Steele.* 71
My God, my Father, while I stray...*Elliott.* 267
My God, the covenant of Thy...*Doddridge.* 339
My Jesus, as Thou wilt...*Lyra Germanica.* 280
My only Saviour, when I feel.................. 332
My opening eyes with rapture see..*I. Watts.* 28
My Saviour bids me come..........*C. Wesley.* 324
My soul, be on Thy guard..........*G. Heath.* 295
My spirit, on Thy care............*H. F. Lyte.* 261
My times are in Thy hand............*Lloyd.* 259

Nearer, my God, to Thee......*Miss Adams.* 238
No change of time shall ever shock...*Kirke.* 62
Nor eye hath seen, nor ear..........*I. Watts.* 437
Not all the blood of beasts............*I. Watts.* 110
Now God be with us for the..*C. Winkworth.* 52
Now is the accepted time..........*J. Dobell.* 325
Now thank we all our God....*German Coll.* 400

O bless the Lord, my soul..........*I. Watts.* 79
O bow Thine ear, eternal One.................. 380
O cease, my wandering soul........*Doane.* 188
O Christ, our hope.......*Tr. by J. Chandler.* 132
O Christ, Thou bright and morning star..... 210
O Christ, with each returning.*Latin Hymn.* 7
O come, all ye faithful........................ 87
O come, and mourn with me..*F. W. Faber.* 106
O come, loud anthems let us sing........*Tate.* 58
O could I find from day to day...*Cleaveland.* 243
O could I speak the matchless....*S. Medley.* 213

INDEX OF FIRST LINES.

O day of rest and gladness.. *C. Wordsworth.* 2
O for a closer walk with God. *Wm. Cowper.* 151
O for a heart to praise my God... *C. Wesley.* 225
O for a thousand tongues to sing.. *C. Wesley.* 236
O for the death of those... ... *Ch. Psalmody.* 418
O Fount of good, to own Thy love............ 293
O God, beneath Thy guiding... *L. Bacon.* 402
O God of Jacob, by whose hand.. *Doddridge.* 69
O God, our God, Thou shinest here.... *Gill.* 363
O God, our help in ages past........ *I. Watts.* 416
O God, unseen, yet ever near.... *E. Osler.* 350
O God, we praise Thee, and confess......... 73
O happy day that fixed............ *Doddridge.* 342
O Holy Ghost, Thou God.. *Hymnal Noted.* 331
O holy, holy, holy, Lord.. *J. W. Eastburn.* 56
O holy Lord our God......................... 384
O Jesus, crucified for man... *Sullivan's Coll.* 104
O Jesus, I have promised... *Sullivan's Coll.* 466
O Jesus, my Saviour, Thine agony. *German.* 283
O Jesus, our salvation...... *English Hymnal.* 114
O Lamb of God, still keep me......... *Deck.* 176
O Lord, accept our praise......... *Epis. Coll.* 38
O Lord and Master of us all... *J. Whittier.* 223
O Lord, another day is flown.. *H. K. White.* 320
O Lord, I would delight in Thee... *Ryland.* 181
O Lord of heaven, and earth.. *Wordsworth.* 298
O Lord, our carnal mind control............. 177
O Lord, Thy work revive...... *Mrs. Brown.* 316
O love divine, how sweet Thou art.. *Wesley.* 214
O love divine, that stooped... *O. W. Holmes.* 222
O Paradise, O Paradise......... *F. W. Faber.* 448
O praise our God to-day...... *H. W. Baker.* 296
O praise ye the Lord, prepare.......... *Tate.* 54
O sacred Head once....... *Tr. by Alexander.* 113
O Saviour, who didst come................ 228
O Spirit of the living God.. *J. Montgomery.* 359
O Son of man, and Son of God. *J. M. Neale.* 264
O Sun of righteousness, arise................ 358
O the sweet wonders of that cross.... *Watts.* 343
O Thou above all praise.... *J. Montgomery.* 81
O Thou, from whom all goodness.. *Hawies.* 179
O Thou, who by a star didst guide............ 99
O Thou, whom we adore......... *C. Wesley.* 364
O Thou, whose own vast temple.... *Bryant.* 381
O to be over yonder........ *Miss Armstrong.* 457
O what if we are Christ's.... *H. W. Baker.* 227
O where are kings and empires. *A. C. Coxe.* 335
O where shall rest be found... *Montgomery.* 185
On the mountain's top appearing... *T. Kelly.* 372
Onward, Christian soldiers...... *S. B. Gould.* 450
Once more the solemn season calls........... 396
One sweetly solemn thought.. *Phoebe Cary.* 419
One there is above all others,.... *J. Newton.* 197
Our blest Redeemer, ere He breathed.. *Lyte.* 157
Our children, Lord, in faith..... *Bickersteth.* 341

Our Father, God, whose rule....... *German.* 60
Our Father, through the coming year........ 392
Our heavenly Father calls.... *P. Doddridge.* 249
Our heavenly Father, hear.. *J. Montgomery.* 80
Our Helper, God, we bless Thy.. *Doddridge.* 390
Our Lord is risen from the dead.... *Wesley.* 130
Out of the deep I call....... *Sullivan's Coll.* 190

Pour down Thy Spirit, gracious.. *J. Newton.* 334
Praise, my soul, the King of heaven... *Lyte.* 85
Praise, O praise our God and King... *Trend.* 398
Praise the Lord, ye heavens... *Kempthorne.* 55
Praise to God, immortal praise... *Barbauld.* 397
Praise to Thee, Thou great Creator. *Fawcett.* 83
Prepare us, Lord, to view Thy cross......... 351
Prince of peace, control my will............ 277

Rejoice, the Lord is King......... *C. Wesley.* 138
Return, my soul, and sweetly rest... *Latrobe.* 232
Return, O wanderer, now return.... *Collyer.* 183
Revive Thy work, O Lord...... *A. Midlane.* 289
Rise, my soul, and stretch thy.. *R. Seagrave.* 407
Rock of ages, cleft for me....... *A. Toplady.* 200

Safely through another week.... *J. Newton.* 3
Saviour, again to Thy dear Name.. *Ellerton.* 41
Saviour and Lord of all............ *E. P. P.* 326
Saviour, blessed Saviour.... *Godfrey Thring.* 471
Saviour, breathe an evening...... *Edmeston.* 47
Saviour, like a shepherd lead us............. 451
Saviour, when in dust to Thee... *R. Grant.* 207
Saviour, who for us didst... *Sullivan's Coll.* 118
Saviour, whom I fain would love............ 120
Shall man, O God of life......... *T. Dwight.* 433
Shine, mighty God, on Zion shine.... *Watts.* 361
Sion's daughter, weep no more............... 122
Sleep thy last sleep.......... *E. A. Dayman.* 446
Soft and holy is the place...... *T. Hastings.* 313
Softly now the light of day... *G. W. Doane.* 44
Songs of praise the angels sang. *Montgomery.* 140
Soldiers of Christ, arise............ *C. Wesley.* 294
Soon may the last glad song arise............ 385
Sovereign of worlds, display Thy.. *Draper.* 386
Spirit divine, attend our prayer.... *A. Reed.* 148
Stand up, stand up for Jesus..... *S. Duffield.* 464
Stealing from the world away.. *Ray Palmer.* 300
Still with Thee, O my God..... *H. Bonar.* 36
Sun of my soul, Thou Saviour dear... *Keble.* 42
Sweet is the work, O Lord...... *Miss Auber.* 15
Sweet is Thy mercy, Lord. *J. S. B. Monsell.* 189
Sweet the moments, rich in blessing... *Allen.* 196

Take my heart, O Father, take it............ 201
Tarry with me, O my Saviour...... *Ply. Coll.* 49
Teach me, my Lord and King.. *G. Herbert.* 253

INDEX OF FIRST LINES.   309

The day is gently sinking to... *Wordsworth.* 53	Wake, oh wake, ye weary..... *E. P. Parker.* 476
The day is past and gone......... *J. Leland.* 37	Wake the song of jubilee.......... *L. Bacon.* 374
The day of resurrection....... *Tr. by Neale.* 129	We are dying day by day... *Church Hymns.* 425
The golden gates are lifted up................. 131	We bless Thee for Thy peace, O God....... 265
The harvest dawn is near... *Bishop Burgess.* 187	We come to sing Thy praise... *H. P. Haven.* 305
The head that once was crowned.. *T. Kelly.* 134	We come to Thee, dear Saviour...... *Faber.* 461
The heavens declare Thy glory... *I. Watts.* 330	We give Thee but Thine own.. *W. W. How.* 393
The homeland, O the homeland.... *Haweis.* 442	We love the place, O God...................... 17
The King of love my Shepherd is.... *Baker.* 278	We sinners, Lord, with earnest..... *Bernard.* 172
The Lord be with us as we bend............. 32	Weary of earth, and laden with. *J. S. Stone.* 168
The Lord be with us now..................... 304	Welcome, delightful morn........ *Hayward.* 21
The Lord is great, ye hosts of heaven....... 68	Welcome, sweet day of rest........ *I. Watts.* 14
The Lord my Shepherd is......... *I. Watts.* 252	What are these in bright array. *Montgomery.* 439
The morning light is breaking.. *S. F. Smith.* 370	What grace, O Lord, and beauty.. *E. Denny.* 98
The Spirit in our hearts.. *H. W. Onderdonk.* 184	What shall I a sinner do.. *Lyra Germanica.* 159
The way is long and dreary...... *A. Proctor.* 169	What shall I render to my God... *I. Watts.* 241
Thee we adore, O unseen Saviour. *Woodford.* 354	When all Thy mercies, O my God.. *Addison.* 78
There is a blessed home.......... *H. Baker.* 281	When cold our hearts, and far from Thee... 309
There is a fountain filled with.. *W. Cowper.* 174	When His salvation bringing........ *J. King.* 463
There is a land of pure delight.... *I. Watts.* 435	When I can read my title clear... *I. Watts.* 175
There is an hour of peaceful rest... *Tappan.* 440	When I survey the wondrous cross... *Watts.* 105
Thine earthly Sabbaths, Lord... *Doddridge.* 8	When in that tremendous... *Tr. by Stanley.* 430
Thine forever, God of love..., *Mrs. Maude.* 121	When my last hour is close. *Tr. by Bowring.* 429
This is the day of light .... *J. Ellerton.* 35	When our heads are bowed with.. *Milman.* 423
This is the day the Lord hath made.. *Watts.* 5	When overwhelmed with grief.... *I. Watts.* 260
Thou art the way, to Thee alone.... *Doane.* 101	When sins and fears prevailing... *Miss Steele.* 231
Thou dear Redeemer, dying Lamb. *Cennick.* 224	When streaming from the eastern. *Shrubsole.* 24
Thou from whom we never part............. 46	When Thou, my righteous Judge... *Shirley.* 431
Thou glorious Sun of Righteousness......... 9	Where Thy saints in glory.. *Church Hymns.* 426
Thou Holy Spirit, Lord of grace..... *Latin.* 149	While my Redeemer's near...... *Miss Steele.* 250
Thou Saviour, from Thy throne.... *Palmer.* 286	While Thee I seek, protecting... *Williams.* 77
Thou who didst on Calvary bleed.... *Burns.* 194	While with ceaseless course..... *J. Newton.* 388
Though faint, yet pursuing.. *Eng. Bap. Coll.* 273	Who is this that comes from Edom... *Kelly.* 142
Thus far the Lord has led me on.... *Watts.* 25	Who trusts in God, a strong abode. *German.* 279
Time is winging us away............. *Burton.* 408	Why should the children of a King.. *Watts.* 152
'Tis midnight, and on Olive's brow. *Tappan.* 107	With angel voices blending... *E. P. Parker.* 97
'Tis my happiness below...... *Wm. Cowper.* 192	With all my powers of heart....... *I. Watts.* 63
To Christ, the Prince of...... *Tr. by Caswell.* 111	With broken heart, and contrite...... *Elvin.* 166
To-day the Saviour calls........................ 310	With joy we hail the sacred... *Miss Auber.* 11
To God, the only wise............ *I. Watts.* 82	With joy we lift our eyes......... *T. Jervis.* 16
To heaven I lift my waiting eyes.. *I. Watts.* 74	
To our Redeemer's glorious Name... *Steele.* 19	Ye choirs of new Jerusalem.................... 135
To Thee our God we fly...... *Eng. Hymnal.* 404	Ye Christian heralds, go proclaim............ 357
Together with these symbols, Lord.......... 349	Ye nations round the earth, rejoice.. *Watts.* 59
Triumphant Zion, lift thine head. *Doddridge.* 329	Your harps, ye trembling saints. *A. Toplady.* 248
Unshaken as the sacred hill........ *I. Watts.* 239	Zion, ope thy gates of beauty...... *German.* 1
Unveil thy bosom, faithful tomb... *I. Watts.* 410	Zion stands with hills surrounded.. *T. Kelly.* 373

INDEX OF TUNES.

		Author.	Page.
Abbey	C. M.	Scotch.	106
Adeste Fideles	5s and 6s.	John Reading.	79
Adoration	11s and 8s.	J. Henley.	68
Advent Hymn	L. M., 6 lines.	Ch. Gounod.	78
Afton	12s and 11s.	Scotch.	103
Agnus	Irregular.		296
Alexander	6, 7, 6s.	Chorale.	185
Alexandria	C. M.		171, 220
Almsgiving	8s and 4.	J. B. Dykes.	200
Amsterdam	7s and 6s.	James Nares.	252
Angels of Jesus	11, 10.	W. H. Monk.	276
Angels of Jesus		J. Barnby.	277
Anselm	7s and 6s.	J. Barnby.	275
Arden	C. M.	E. P. Parker.	97, 136
Ariel	C. P. M.	L. Mason.	157
Arlington	C. M.	Dr. Arne.	134, 205
Art thou Weary	8, 5, 8, 3.	W. H. Monk.	211
Aspiration	C. M.	E. P. Parker.	212
Austria	8s and 7s.	J. Haydn.	61, 214
Avon	C. M.	H. Wilson.	72, 119, 138
Balerma	C. M.	Spanish.	210
Banner	6s and 5s.	A. Sullivan.	286
Barby	C. M.	Wm. Tansur.	170
Bartholomew	C. M.	Italian.	270
Bedford	C. M.	Dr. Wheal.	243
Behold the Lamb	6s, 4, 8s, 4.	E. P. Parker.	96
Benevento	7s.	S. Webbe.	150, 241
Bera	L. M.	J. E. Gould.	167, 253
Bethany	6s and 4s.	L. Mason.	169
Bethesda	H. M.	M. Greene.	250
Beulah	7s.	E. Ives.	271
Blondel	8s and 7s.	Arr. fr. Schumann.	149
Bowdoin Square	C. M.	Vogler.	228
Boylston	S. M.	L. Mason.	195

INDEX OF TUNES.

		AUTHOR.	PAGE.
Calm	S. M.	Handel Pond.	180
Calvary	P. M.		93
Cassel	7s.	German.	124
Cecilia	8, 7, Iambic.	J. B. Dykes.	190
Chester	L. M.	Arr. fr. Schumann.	161, 263
Christmas	C. M.	Handel.	84
Christmas Carol		E. P. Parker.	300
Christmas Hymn	P. M.	Arranged.	85
Cœna Domini	8, 8, 7.	J. Baptiste Calkin.	226
Communion	L. M.	Dr. Garrett.	223
Confession	7, 7, 6, 7, 7, 8.	German Chorale.	127
Comfort	11s and 10s.	E. P. Parker.	192
Coronation	C. M.	Holden.	109
Coventry	C. M.	English.	37
Crüger	6, 7, 6, 7, 6, 6.	German Chorale.	247
Daily Praise	8s and 7s.	German Tune.	295
Daily Work	8s, 7s and 4.	E. P. P.	290
Dalston	S. P. M	A. Williams.	42
Dawn	S. M.	E. P. Parker.	140, 258
Dayspring	S. M.	J. Barnby.	50, 92
Dedham	C. M.	Wm. Gardiner.	107, 218
Denfield	C. M.	Glaser.	73, 132
Dennis	S. M.	Nageli.	51, 203
Denton	S. M.	V. C. Taylor.	244
Dorrnance	8s and 7s.	I. B. Woodbury.	148
Dover	S. M.	English Melody.	199
Duke Street	L. M.	J. Hatton.	104, 242
Dundee	C. M.	Scotch Psalter.	70, 245
Easter Song	8s and 7s.	German.	301
Eastlake	7s.	German Melody.	99
Edom	8s and 7s.	Ch. Gounod.	113, 215
Elias	7s.	Arr. fr. Costa's "Eli."	143
Elliott	8s and 4.	Arranged.	128
Elyria	7s.	Cherubini.	121
Ein Feste Burg	8, 7, 6, 8.	Martin Luther.	112
Ernan	L. M.	L. Mason.	116, 160
Evan	C. M.	Havergal.	159
Evening Hymn	L. M.	Tallis.	47

INDEX OF TUNES.

		AUTHOR.	PAGE.
Evening Prayer............................			299
Eventide.................................	10s.	W. H. Monk.	52, 227
Ewing	7s and 6s.	A. Ewing.	274
Fatherland................................	5, 5, 8, 8, 5.	German.	182
Federal Street............................	L. M.	H. K. Oliver.	89
Frederick................................	11s.	Kingsley.	262
For a Child..............................	7s.		278
Gardner.................................	8s and 7s.	Lord Mornington.	76, 102
Germania................................	7s and 6s.	E. P. Parker.	95, 135, 209
Germany	L. M.	Beethoven.	254
Gloria	7s.	Mendelssohn.	83
Golden Hill..............................	S. M.	A. Chapin.	202
Gorton..................................	S. M.	Beethoven.	164, 257
Grace...................................	S. M.	J. Barnby.	141
Greenville...............................	8s and 7s.	J. J. Rousseau.	80
Greenwood	S. M.	J. E. Sweetser.	38
Hamburg	L. M.	Gregorian.	129
Hamden	8s, 7s and 4.	L. Mason.	176
Harvest Home............................	7s.	G. J. Elvey.	248
Harwell.................................	8s, 7s and 4.	L. Mason.	114
Hatton	7s.	E. P. Parker.	189, 260
Hebron	L. M.	L. Mason.	45, 194
Herald..................................	L. M. 6 ls.	Penfield.	44
Herold..................................	8s and 7s.	Herold.	144
Holland	L. M.	Mendelssohn.	166
Holley..................................	7s.	Geo. Hews.	55, 201
Hollingside..............................	7s.	J. B. Dykes.	151
Homeland	7s and 6s.	Arthur Sullivan.	273
Horton..................................	7s.	X. S. Von Wartensee.	142
Hosanna to Jesus.........................	7s and 6s.	Arranged.	291
Hursely	L. M.	Mozart.	54, 255
Hymn...................................	C. M.	Mod. Harp.	162
Intercession	8s and 7s.	E. S. Carter.	224
Into a Desolate Land.....................	Irregular.		299
Italian Hymn............................	6s and 4s.	Giardini.	123
Invocation	6s and 4s.	E. P. Parker.	118

		Author.	Page.
Jerusalem	C. M.	Old English.	268
Jesus, Pray for Me	6s and 5s.	Old Song.	298
Jesus, Tender Shepherd	8, 7, 8, 7.		299
Judgment Hymn	8, 8, 7.	Martin Luther.	64, 264
Kreüznach	7s and 6s.	German.	293
Lancaster	C. M.	Dr. S. Howard.	108
Lanesboro'	C. M.	English Melody.	36
Langran	10s.	J. Langran.	53, 130
Langton	S. M.	C. Streatfield.	139
Lenox	H. M.	J. Edson.	91
Lischer	P. M.	German.	41
Litany of our Saviour	Irregular.		101
Lyons	10, 10, 11, 10.	J. F. Haydn.	60
Lyte Chant		E. P. Parker.	59
March Onward	7s.	E. P. Parker.	287
Marlow	C. M.	English.	193, 225
Martyn	7s.	S. B. Marsh.	151
Mear	C. M.	Welsh Melody.	86
Mercy			98
Meribah	C. P. M.	L. Mason.	266
Messengers	C. M.	Mendelssohn.	158
Millais	S. M.	German.	110
Miss. Chant	L. M.	Ch. Zeüner.	62, 229, 249
Miss. Hymn	7s and 6s.	L. Mason.	234
Monkland	7s.	W. H. Monk.	111
Morning Hymn	L. M.	J. B. Dykes.	46
Morning Star	8, 6, 8, 6, 6.	German Chorale.	155
Mornington	S. M.	Lord Mornington.	178
Naomi	C. M.	L. Mason.	170
National Hymn	6s and 4s.	English.	251
Naumann	8, 6, 8, 8, 6.	J. Naumann.	272
Nearer to Thee	6s and 4s.	Wm. H. Monk.	169
Neumark	9, 8, 9, 8, 8, 8.	German Chorale.	186
Newman	P. M.	E. P. Parker.	177
Newton	7s.	L. Mason.	32
Nicea	Irregular.	J. B. Dykes.	43

INDEX OF TUNES.

		Author.	Page.
Northfield	C. M.		230
Nottingham	C. M.	J. Clarke.	133
Nuremburg	7s.	German Air.	237, 246
O Jesus, Saviour	6s.	Dr. Layriz.	193
O Sacred Head	7s and 6s.	German Chorale.	94
Old Hundred	L. M.	French Psalter.	65
Olivet	6s and 4s.	L. Mason.	154
Olmutz	S. M.	Gregorian.	93, 174, 219
Onward, Christian Soldiers	6s and 5s.	English.	281
Over Yonder	P. M.	Arranged.	285
Paradise	P. M.	J. Barnby.	279
Park Street	L. M.	Venua.	63, 267
Peterboro	C. M.	R. Harrison.	269
Pilgrimage	P. M.	A. Sullivan.	280
Playford	L. M.	J. Playford.	216
Pleyel's Hymn	7s.	Pleyel.	207
Portuguese Hymn	P. M.	John Reading.	184
Praise Him	8s, 7s.	E. S. Carter.	77
Prayer for Peace	11s and 5.	English.	221
Proctor	P. M.	Dr. Stainer.	131
Psalm of Praise	7s.	E. P. Parker.	288
Ramoth	7s.	J. Baptiste Calkin.	153
Redhead	7s.	R. Redhead.	100, 265
Rest	6s.	English.	191
Resurrection	7s and 6s.	George Cooper.	105
Robinson	11s.	Arranged.	187
Rockingham	L. M.	L. Mason.	88, 222
Rock of Ages	7s.	Dr. Hastings.	146
Rosefield	7s.	Dr. Malan.	206
Russian Hymn	L. M.	Russian Nat. Hymn.	67
Sanctuary	8s and 7s.	German.	30
Saviour and Lord of All	6s and 5s.		213
Saviour, Blessed Saviour	6s and 5s.	J. Pitts.	297
Schumann	S. M.	Schumann.	165, 259
Sears	C. M.	A. Sullivan.	82
Seymour	7s.	Weber.	188
Sicilian Hymn	8s and 7s.	Italian.	57

		Author.	Page.
Silver Street	S. M.	Isaac Smith.	198
Spanish Hymn	7s.	Spanish Melody.	156
Solemn Litany	7s.	Arr. fr. Herold.	152
Song of Children	C. M.	Arranged.	294
South Church	8s and 7s.	E. P. Parker.	147
Southwell	C. M.	Dr. Irons.	71
Stand up for Jesus	7s and 6s.	German.	292
Stanley	C. M.	Mozart.	48, 163, 256
State Street	S. M.	J. C. Woodman.	39
Stephen's	C. M.	Wm. Jones.	33, 196
Stockwell	8s and 7s.	D. Jones.	145
Sullivan	7s.	A. Sullivan.	126
Supplication	7, 7, 7, 6.	A. Sullivan.	261, 283
St. Agnes	C. M.	J. B. Dykes.	137, 181
St. Andrew	8s.		49
St. Ann's	C. M.	Dr. Croft.	117, 168, 218
St. Bride	S. M.	Dr. Howard.	179
St. Clement's Hymn	10s and 6.	Goudimel.	125
St. Cross	L. M.	J. B. Dykes.	90
St. Cuthbert	8s and 4.	J. B. Dykes.	122
St. Helena	S. M.	W. H. Monk.	74
St. Martin's	C. M.	Wm. Tansur.	231
St. Michael's	S. M.	John Day's Psalt.	75, 172, 232
St. Oswald	8s and 7s.	J. B. Dykes.	56
St. Peter	C. M.	A. R. Reinagle.	197
St. Philip	7s.	English.	126
St. Thomas	S. M.	Wm. Tansur.	120, 173, 208
Tallis		Tallis.	47
The Saviour's Call	6s and 4.		205
The Last Sleep	4s and 6s.	J. Barnby.	278
Trinity	C. M.	J. Barnby.	87
Troyte Chant		Troyte.	122, 183
The Story of Love	7s and 6s.	Geo. F. Root.	284
Uxbridge	L. M.	L. Mason.	233
Vesper Chant		E. P. Parker.	58
Vesper Hymn	8s, 7s, and 4.		282
Veni Sancte	7s.	J. Knecht.	115

		Author.	Page.
Ward...............................	L. M.	Scotch.	66
Wareham..........................	L. M.	J. Knapp.	34, 217
Warwick............................	C. M.	Stanley.	40
Watchful...........................	7s.		182
We Come to Thee...............	P. M.	E. P. Parker.	289
Webb	7s and 6s.	G. J. Webb.	31, 235
Welton..............................	L. M.	Dr. Malan.	204
Wilmot..............................	7s.	Weber.	81
Winchester........................	L. M.	German.	35
Windsor............................	C. M.	Kirby.	69
Zion...................................	8s, 7s, and 4.	Thomas Hastings.	236

INDEX OF CHANTS, CREEDS, &c.

Apostles and Nicene Creeds.................	29	
Burial Chant....................................	Dr. Blow..28	
Commandments...............................	24	
Blessed be the Lord God....................	{ H. Wilson (1). Dr. Nares (2). M. Luther (3). J. Goss (5).	 6
Christ, our Passover...........................	23	
Gloria in Excelsis..............................	16	
God be Merciful...............................	{ Jacobs (1). E. P. Parker (2) Flintoff (3). J. F. Harris (4).	 8
He is Despised.................................	Flintoff...... 22	
It is a Good Thing.............................	{ Henry Wilson. Henry Wilson.	21

INDEX OF CHANTS, CREEDS, &c. 317

Kyrie Eleison...............................	E. P. Parker.........................52
Kyrie Eleison...............................	27
Lord's Prayer	 1
My Soul doth Magnify...............	Downes. 13
O be Joyful.................................	{ E. P. Parker (3)......................... 4 { J. Hopkins (5).
O, Come let us Sing..................	{ Hayes (1). { Randall (2).......................... 2 { Beethoven (3). { Aldrich (4).
Offertory Sentences...................	26
O, All ye Works of the Lord.....	B. Tours 51
O, Saviour of the World...........	Flintoff......................................14
Out of the Depths......................	Woodward.................................. 1
Praise the Lord..........................	Spohr (2)...................................10
Sing Alleluia Forth....................	E. P. Parker..............................17
Te Deum Laudamus..................	...................................18 and 19
Therefore with Angels..............	20
Therefore with Angels..............	Henry Wilson...........................21

SELECTIONS

FROM

HOLY SCRIPTURE,

(And chiefly from the Book of Psalms,)

FOR USE IN

RESPONSIVE READINGS

IN THE

Church, Social Meeting, or Sunday-School.

LESSON 1.

PSALMS 1, 8, 13.

BLESSED is the man that walketh not in the counsel of the ungodly, nor standeth in the way of sinners, nor sitteth in the seat of the scornful.

2 But his delight is in the law of the LORD; and in his law doth he meditate day and night.

3 And he shall be like a tree planted by the rivers of water, that bringeth forth his fruit in his season; his leaf also shall not wither; and whatsoever he doeth shall prosper.

4 The ungodly are not so: but are like the chaff which the wind driveth away.

5 Therefore the ungodly shall not stand in the judgment, nor sinners in the congregation of the righteous.

6 For the LORD knoweth the way of the righteous: but the way of the ungodly shall perish.

O LORD our Lord, how excellent is thy name in all the earth! who hast set thy glory above the heavens.

2 Out of the mouth of babes and sucklings hast thou ordained strength because of thine enemies, that thou mightest still the enemy and the avenger.

3 When I consider thy heavens, the work of thy fingers, the moon and the stars, which thou hast ordained;

4 What is man, that thou art mindful of him? and the son of man, that thou visitest him?

5 For thou hast made him a little lower than the angels, and hast crowned him with glory and honour.

6 Thou madest him to have dominion over the works of thy hands; thou hast put all things under his feet:

7 All sheep and oxen, yea, and the beasts of the field;

8 The fowl of the air, and the fish of the sea, and whatsoever passeth through the paths of the seas.

9 O LORD our Lord, how excellent is thy name in all the earth!

HOW long wilt thou forget me, O Lord? forever? How long wilt thou hide thy face from me?

2 How long shall I take counsel in my soul, having sorrow in my heart daily? How long shall mine enemy be exalted over me?

3 Consider and hear me, O LORD my GOD: lighten mine eyes, lest I sleep the sleep of death;

4 Lest mine enemy say, I have prevailed against him; and those that trouble me rejoice when I am moved.

5 But I have trusted in thy mercy; my heart shall rejoice in thy salvation.

6 I will sing unto the Lord, because he hath dealt bountifully with me.

LESSON 2.

Psalms 16, 19.

PRESERVE me, O God: for in thee do I put my trust.

2 O my soul, thou hast said unto the Lord, Thou art my Lord: my goodness extendeth not to thee;

3 But to the saints that are in the earth, and to the excellent, in whom is all my delight.

4 Their sorrows shall be multiplied that hasten after another god: their drink offerings of blood will I not offer, nor take up their names into my lips.

5 The Lord is the portion of mine inheritance and of my cup: thou maintainest my lot.

6 The lines are fallen unto me in pleasant places; yea, I have a goodly heritage.

7 I will bless the Lord, who hath given me counsel: my reins also instruct me in the night seasons.

8 I have set the Lord always before me: because he is at my right hand, I shall not be moved.

9 Therefore my heart is glad, and my glory rejoiceth: my flesh also shall rest in hope.

10 For thou wilt not leave my soul in hell; neither wilt thou suffer thine Holy One to see corruption.

11 Thou wilt shew me the path of life: in thy presence is fullness of joy; at thy right hand there are pleasures for evermore.

THE heavens declare the glory of God; and the firmament sheweth his handywork.

2 Day unto day uttereth speech, and night unto night sheweth knowledge.

3 There is no speech nor language, where their voice is not heard.

4 Their line is gone out through all the earth, and their words to the end of the world. In them hath he set a tabernacle for the sun,

5 Which is as a bridegroom coming out of his chamber, and rejoiceth as a strong man to run a race.

6 His going forth is from the end of the heaven, and his circuit unto the ends of it: and there is nothing hid from the heat thereof.

7 The law of the Lord is perfect, converting the soul: the testimony of the Lord is sure, making wise the simple.

8 The statutes of the Lord are right, rejoicing the heart: the commandment of the Lord is pure, enlightening the eyes.

9 The fear of the LORD is clean, enduring for ever: the judgments of the LORD are true and righteous altogether.

10 More to be desired are they than gold, yea, than much fine gold: sweeter also than honey and the honeycomb.

11 Moreover by them is thy servant warned: and in keeping of them there is great reward.

12 Who can understand his errors? cleanse thou me from secret faults.

13 Keep back thy servant also from presumptuous sins; let them not have dominion over me: then shall I be upright, and I shall be innocent from the great transgression.

14 Let the words of my mouth, and the meditation of my heart, be acceptable in thy sight, O LORD, my strength, and my redeemer.

LESSON 3.

PSALMS 23, 24, 25: 1–14.

THE LORD is my shepherd; I shall not want.

2 He maketh me to lie down in green pastures: he leadeth me beside the still waters.

3 He restoreth my soul: he leadeth me in the paths of righteousness for his name's sake.

4 Yea, though I walk through the valley of the shadow of death, I will fear no evil: for thou art with me; thy rod and thy staff they comfort me.

5 Thou preparest a table before me in the presence of mine enemies: thou anointest my head with oil; my cup runneth over.

6 Surely goodness and mercy shall follow me all the days of my life: and I will dwell in the house of the LORD for ever.

THE earth is the LORD'S, and the fullness thereof; the world, and they that dwell therein.

2 For he hath founded it upon the seas, and established it upon the floods.

3 Who shall ascend into the hill of the LORD? or who shall stand in his holy place?

4 He that hath clean hands, and a pure heart; who hath not lifted up his soul unto vanity, nor sworn deceitfully.

5 He shall receive the blessing from the LORD, and righteousness from the God of his salvation.

6 This is the generation of them that seek him, that seek thy face, O Jacob.

7 Lift up your heads, O ye gates; and be ye lifted up, ye everlasting doors; and the King of glory shall come in.

8 Who is this King of glory? The LORD strong and mighty, the LORD mighty in battle.

9 Lift up your heads, O ye gates; even lift them up, ye everlasting doors; and the King of glory shall come in.
10 Who is this King of glory? The LORD of hosts, he is the King of glory.

UNTO thee, O LORD, do I lift up my soul.
  2 O my God, I trust in thee: let me not be ashamed, let not mine enemies triumph over me.
  3 Yea, let none that wait on thee be ashamed: let them be ashamed which transgress without cause.
  4 Shew me thy ways, O LORD; teach me thy paths.
  5 Lead me in thy truth, and teach me: for thou art the God of my salvation; on thee do I wait all the day.
  6 Remember, O LORD, thy tender mercies and thy lovingkindnesses; for they have been ever of old.
  7 Remember not the sins of my youth, nor my transgressions: according to mercy remember thou me for thy goodness' sake, O LORD.
  8 Good and upright is the LORD: therefore will he teach sinners in the way.
  9 The meek will he guide in judgment: and the meek will he teach his way.
  10 All the paths of the LORD are mercy and truth unto such as keep his covenant and his testimonies.
  11 For thy name's sake, O LORD, pardon mine iniquity; for it is great.
  12 What man is he that feareth the LORD? him shall he teach in the way that he shall choose.
  13 His soul shall dwell at ease; and his seed shall inherit the earth.
  14 The secret of the LORD is with them that fear him; and he will shew them his covenant.

LESSON 4.

PSALMS 27, 34.

THE LORD is my light and my salvation, whom shall I fear? the LORD is the strength of my life; of whom shall I be afraid?
  2 When the wicked, even mine enemies and my foes, came upon me to eat up my flesh, they stumbled and fell.
  3 Though a host should encamp against me, my heart shall not fear: though war should rise against me, in this will I be confident.
  4 One thing have I desired of the LORD, that will I seek after; that I may dwell in the house of the LORD all the days of my life, to behold the beauty of the LORD, and to inquire in his temple.
  5 For in the time of trouble he shall hide me in his pavilion: in the secret of his tabernacle shall he hide me; he shall set me up upon a rock.
  6 And now shall mine head be lifted up above mine enemies round about me:

therefore will I offer in his tabernacle sacrifices of joy; I will sing, yea, I will sing praises unto the Lord.

7 Hear, O Lord, when I cry with my voice: have mercy also upon me, and answer me.

8 When thou saidst, Seek ye my face; my heart said unto thee, Thy face, Lord, will I seek.

9 Hide not thy face far from me; put not thy servant away in anger: thou hast been my help; leave me not, neither forsake me, O God of my salvation.

10 When my father and my mother forsake me, then the Lord will take me up.

11 Teach me thy way, O Lord, and lead me in a plain path, because of mine enemies.

12 Deliver me not over unto the will of mine enemies: for false witnesses are risen up against me, and such as breathe out cruelty.

13 I had fainted, unless I had believed to see the goodness of the Lord in the land of the living.

14 Wait on the Lord: be of good courage, and he shall strengthen thine heart: wait, I say, on the Lord.

I WILL bless the Lord at all times: his praise shall continually be in my mouth.

2 My soul shall make her boast in the Lord: the humble shall hear thereof, and be glad.

3 O magnify the Lord with me, and let us exalt his name together.

4 I sought the Lord, and he heard me, and delivered me from all my fears.

5 They looked unto him, and were lightened: and their faces were not ashamed.

6 This poor man cried, and the Lord heard him, and saved him out of all his troubles.

7 The angel of the Lord encampeth round about them that fear him, and delivereth them.

8 O taste and see that the Lord is good: blessed is the man that trusteth in him.

9 O fear the Lord, ye his saints: for there is no want to them that fear him.

10 The young lions do lack, and suffer hunger: but they that seek the Lord shall not want any good thing.

11 Come, ye children, hearken unto me: I will teach you the fear of the Lord.

12 What man is he that desireth life, and loveth many days, that he may see good?

13 Keep thy tongue from evil, and thy lips from speaking guile.

14 Depart from evil, and do good; seek peace, and pursue it.

15 The eyes of the Lord are upon the righteous, and his ears are open unto their cry.

16 The face of the Lord is against them that do evil, to cut off the remembrance of them from the earth.

17 The righteous cry, and the Lord heareth, and delivereth them out of all their troubles.

18 The LORD is nigh unto them that are of a broken heart; and saveth such as be of a contrite spirit.

19 Many are the afflictions of the righteous; but the LORD delivereth him out of them all.

20 He keepeth all his bones: not one of them is broken.

21 Evil shall slay the wicked: and they that hate the righteous shall be desolate.

22 The LORD redeemeth the soul of his servants: and none of them that trust in him shall be desolate.

LESSON 5.

PSALMS 36, 37, 1–8 and 23–37.

THE transgression of the wicked saith within my heart, that there is no fear of God before his eyes.

2 For he flattereth himself in his own eyes, until his iniquity be found to be hateful.

3 The words of his mouth are iniquity and deceit: he hath left off to be wise, and to do good.

4 He deviseth mischief upon his bed; he setteth himself in a way that is not good; he abhorreth not evil.

5 Thy mercy, O LORD, is in the heavens; and thy faithfulness reacheth unto the clouds.

6 Thy righteousness is like the great mountains; thy judgments are a great deep: O LORD, thou preservest man and beast.

7 How excellent is thy lovingkindness, O God! therefore the children of men put their trust under the shadow of thy wings.

8 They shall be abundantly satisfied with the fatness of thy house; and thou shalt make them drink of the river of thy pleasures.

9 For with thee is the fountain of life: in thy light shall we see light.

10 O continue thy lovingkindness unto them that know thee; and thy righteousness to the upright in heart.

11 Let not the foot of pride come against me, and let not the hand of the wicked remove me.

12 There are the workers of iniquity fallen: they are cast down, and shall not be able to rise.

FRET not thyself because of evil doers, neither be thou envious against the workers of iniquity.

2 For they shall soon be cut down like the grass, and wither as the green herb.

3 Trust in the LORD, and do good; so shalt thou dwell in the land, and verily thou shalt be fed.

4 Delight thyself also in the Lord; and he shall give thee the desires of thine heart.

5 Commit thy way unto the Lord; trust also in him; and he shall bring it to pass.

6 And he shall bring forth thy righteousness as the light, and thy judgment as the noonday.

7 Rest in the Lord, and wait patiently for him: fret not thyself because of him who prospereth in his way, because of the man who bringeth wicked devices to pass.

23 The steps of a good man are ordered by the Lord: and he delighteth in his way.

24 Though he fall, he shall not be utterly cast down: for the Lord upholdeth him with his hand.

25 I have been young, and now am old; yet have I not seen the righteous forsaken, nor his seed begging bread.

26 He is ever merciful, and lendeth; and his seed is blessed.

27 Depart from evil, and do good; and dwell for evermore.

28 For the Lord loveth judgment, and forsaketh not his saints; they are preserved for ever: but the seed of the wicked shall be cut off.

29 The righteous shall inherit the land, and dwell therein for ever.

30 The mouth of the righteous speaketh wisdom, and his tongue talketh of judgment.

31 The law of his God is in his heart; none of his steps shall slide.

32 The wicked watcheth the righteous, and seeketh to slay him.

33 The Lord will not leave him in his hand, nor condemn him when he is judged.

34 Wait on the Lord, and keep his way, and he shall exalt thee to inherit the land: when the wicked are cut off, thou shalt see it.

35 I have seen the wicked in great power, and spreading himself like a green bay tree.

36 Yet he passed away, and, lo, he was not: yea, I sought him, but he could not be found.

37 Mark the perfect man, and behold the upright: for the end of that man is peace.

LESSON 6.

Psalms 39, 40.

I SAID, I will take heed to my ways, that I sin not with my tongue: I will keep my mouth with a bridle, while the wicked is before me.

2 I was dumb with silence, I held my peace, even from good; and my sorrow was stirred.

3 My heart was hot within me; while I was musing the fire burned: then spake I with my tongue,

4 Lord, make me to know mine end, and the measure of my days, what it is; that I may know how frail I am.

5 Behold, thou hast made my days as a hand-breadth; and mine age is as nothing before thee: verily every man at his best state is altogether vanity.

6 Surely every man walketh in a vain shew: surely they are disquieted in vain: he heapeth up riches, and knoweth not who shall gather them.

7 And now, Lord, what wait I for? my hope is in thee.

8 Deliver me from all my transgressions: make me not the reproach of the foolish.

9 I was dumb, I opened not my mouth; because thou didst it.

10 Remove thy stroke away from me: I am consumed by the blow of thine hand.

11 When thou with rebukes dost correct man for iniquity, thou makest his beauty to consume away like a moth: surely every man is vanity.

12 Hear my prayer, O Lord, and give ear unto my cry; hold not thy peace at my tears: for I am a stranger with thee, and a sojourner, as all my fathers were.

13 O spare me, that I may recover strength, before I go hence, and be no more.

I WAITED patiently for the Lord; and he inclined unto me, and heard my cry.

2 He brought me up also out of a horrible pit, out of the miry clay, and set my feet upon a rock, and established my goings.

3 And he hath put a new song in my mouth, even praise unto our God; many shall see it, and fear, and shall trust in the Lord.

4 Blessed is that man that maketh the Lord his trust, and respecteth not the proud, nor such as turn aside to lies.

5 Many, O Lord my God, are thy wonderful works which thou hast done, and thy thoughts which are to us-ward: they cannot be reckoned up in order unto thee: if I would declare and speak of them, they are more than can be numbered.

6 Sacrifice and offering thou didst not desire; mine ears hast thou opened: burnt offering and sin offering hast thou not required.

7 Then said I, Lo, I come: in the volume of the book it is written of me,

8 I delight to do thy will, O my God: yea, thy law is within my heart.

9 I have preached righteousness in the great congregation: lo, I have not refrained my lips, O Lord, thou knowest.

10 I have not hid thy righteousness within my heart; I have declared thy faithfulness and thy salvation: I have not concealed thy lovingkindness and thy truth from the great congregation.

11 Withhold not thou thy tender mercies from me, O Lord: let thy lovingkindness and thy truth continually preserve me.

12 For innumerable evils have compassed me about: mine iniquities have taken hold upon me, so that I am not able to look up: they are more than the hairs of mine head: therefore my heart faileth me.

13 Be pleased, O Lord, to deliver me: O Lord, make haste to help me.

14 Let them be ashamed and confounded together that seek after my soul to destroy it; let them be driven backward and put to shame that wish me evil.

15 Let them be desolate for a reward of their shame that say unto me, Aha, aha.

16 Let all those that seek thee rejoice and be glad in thee: let such as love thy salvation say continually, The Lord be magnified.

17 But I am poor and needy; yet the Lord thinketh upon me: thou art my help and my deliverer; make no tarrying, O my God.

LESSON 7.

Psalms 42, 46, 47.

AS the hart panteth after the water brooks, so panteth my soul after thee, O God.

2 My soul thirsteth for God, for the living God: when shall I come and appear before God?

3 My tears have been my meat day and night, while they continually say unto me, Where is thy God?

4 When I remember these things, I pour out my soul in me: for I had gone with the multitude, I went with them to the house of God, with the voice of joy and praise, with a multitude that kept holyday.

5 Why art thou cast down, O my soul? and why art thou disquieted in me? hope thou in God: for I shall yet praise him for the help of his countenance.

6 O my God, my soul is cast down within me: therefore will I remember thee from the land of Jordan, and of the Hermonites, from the hill Mizar.

7 Deep calleth unto deep at the noise of thy waterspouts: all thy waves and thy billows are gone over me.

8 Yet the Lord will command his lovingkindness in the daytime, and in the night his song shall be with me, and my prayer unto the God of my life.

9 I will say unto God my rock, Why hast thou forgotten me? why go I mourning because of the oppression of the enemy?

10 As with a sword in my bones, mine enemies reproach me; while they say daily unto me, Where is thy God?

11 Why art thou cast down, O my soul? and why art thou disquieted within me? hope thou in God: for I shall yet praise him, who is the health of my countenance, and my God.

GOD is our refuge and strength, a very present help in trouble.

2 Therefore will not we fear, though the earth be removed, and though the mountains be carried into the midst of the sea;

3 Though the waters thereof roar and be troubled, though the mountains shake with the swelling thereof.

4 There is a river, the streams whereof shall make glad the city of God, the holy place of the tabernacles of the Most High.

5 God is in the midst of her; she shall not be moved: God shall help her, and that right early.

6 The heathen raged, the kingdoms were moved: he uttered his voice, the earth melted.

7 The LORD of hosts is with us; the God of Jacob is our refuge.

8 Come, behold the works of the LORD, what desolations he hath made in the earth.

9 He maketh wars to cease unto the end of the earth; he breaketh the bow, and cutteth the spear in sunder; he burneth the chariot in the fire.

10 Be still, and know that I am God: I will be exalted among the heathen, I will be exalted in the earth.

11 The LORD of hosts is with us; the God of Jacob is our refuge.

O CLAP your hands, all ye people; shout unto God with the voice of triumph.

2 For the LORD most high is terrible; he is a great King over all the earth.

3 He shall subdue the people under us, and the nations under our feet.

4 He shall choose our inheritance for us, the excellency of Jacob whom he loved.

5 God is gone up with a shout, the LORD with the sound of a trumpet.

6 Sing praises to God, sing praises: sing praises unto our King, sing praises.

7 For God is the King of all the earth: sing ye praises with understanding.

8 God reigneth over the heathen: God sitteth upon the throne of his holiness.

9 The princes of the people are gathered together, even the people of the God of Abraham: for the shields of the earth belong unto God: he is greatly exalted.

LESSON 8.

PSALMS 51, 56.

HAVE mercy upon me, O God, according to thy lovingkindness: according unto the multitude of thy tender mercies blot out my transgressions.

2 Wash me thoroughly from mine iniquity, and cleanse me from my sin.

3 For I acknowledge my transgressions: and my sin is ever before me.

4 Against thee, thee only, have I sinned, and done this evil in thy sight; that thou mightest be justified when thou speakest, and be clear when thou judgest.

5 Behold, I was shapen in iniquity; and in sin did my mother conceive me.

6 Behold, thou desirest truth in the inward parts: and in the hidden part thou shalt make me to know wisdom.

7 Purge me with hyssop, and I shall be clean: wash me, and I shall be whiter than snow.

8 Make me to hear joy and gladness; that the bones which thou hast broken may rejoice.

9 Hide thy face from my sins, and blot out all mine iniquities.

10 Create in me a clean heart, O God; and renew a right spirit within me.

11 Cast me not away from thy presence; and take not thy Holy Spirit from me.

12 Restore unto me the joy of thy salvation; and uphold me with thy free Spirit.

13 Then will I teach transgressors thy ways; and sinners shall be converted unto thee.

14 Deliver me from bloodguiltiness, O God, thou God of my salvation: and my tongue shall sing aloud of thy righteousness.

15 O Lord, open thou my lips; and my mouth shall shew forth thy praise.

16 For thou desirest not sacrifice; else would I give it: thou delightest not in burnt offering.

17 The sacrifices of God are a broken spirit: a broken and a contrite heart, O God, thou wilt not despise.

18 Do good in thy good pleasure unto Zion: build thou the walls of Jerusalem.

19 Then shalt thou be pleased with the sacrifices of righteousness, with burnt offering and whole burnt offering: then shall they offer bullocks upon thine altar.

BE merciful unto me, O God: for man would swallow me up; he fighting daily oppresseth me.

2 Mine enemies would daily swallow me up: for they be many that fight against me, O thou Most High.

3 What time I am afraid, I will trust in thee.

4 In God I will praise his word: in God I have put my trust; I will not fear what flesh can do unto me.

5 Every day they wrest my words: all their thoughts are against me for evil.

6 They gather themselves together, they hide themselves, they mark my steps, when they wait for my soul.

7 Shall they escape by iniquity? in thine anger cast down the people, O God.

8 Thou tellest my wanderings: put thou my tears into thy bottle: are they not in thy book?

9 When I cry unto thee, then shall mine enemies turn back: this I know; for God is for me.

10 In God will I praise his word: in the Lord will I praise his word.

11 In God have I put my trust: I will not be afraid what man can do unto me.

12 Thy vows are upon me, O God: I will render praises unto thee.

13 For thou hast delivered my soul from death: wilt not thou deliver my feet from falling, that I may walk before God in the light of the living?

LESSON 9.

Psalms 61, 62: 5-12, 63: 1-8.

HEAR my cry, O God; attend unto my prayer.
2 From the end of the earth will I cry unto thee, when my heart is overwhelmed: lead me to the rock that is higher than I.
3 For thou hast been a shelter for me, and a strong tower from the enemy.
4 I will abide in thy tabernacle for ever: I will trust in the covert of thy wings.
5 For thou, O God, hast heard my vows: thou hast given me the heritage of those that fear thy name,
6 Thou wilt prolong the king's life: and his years as many generations.
7 He shall abide before God for ever: O prepare mercy and truth, which may preserve him.
8 So will I sing praise unto thy name for ever, that I may daily perform my vows.

MY soul, wait thou only upon God, for my expectation is from him.
6 He only is my rock and my salvation: he is my defence; I shall not be moved.
7 In God is my salvation and my glory: the rock of my strength, and my refuge, is in God.
8 Trust in him at all times: ye people, pour out your heart before him: God is a refuge for us.
9 Surely men of low degree are vanity, and men of high degree are a lie: to be laid in the balance, they are altogether lighter than vanity.
10 Trust not in oppression, and become not vain in robbery: if riches increase, set not your heart upon them.
11 God hath spoken once; twice have I heard this; that power belongeth unto God.
12 Also unto thee, O Lord, belongeth mercy: for thou renderest to every man according to his work.

O GOD, thou art my God; early will I seek thee: my soul thirsteth for thee, my flesh longeth for thee in a dry and thirsty land, where no water is;
2 To see thy power and thy glory, so as I have seen thee in the sanctuary.
3 Because thy lovingkindness is better than life, my lips shall praise thee.
4 Thus will I bless thee while I live; I will lift up my hands in thy name.
5 My soul shall be satisfied as with marrow and fatness; and my mouth shall praise thee with joyful lips:
6 When I remember thee upon my bed, and meditate on thee in the night watches.

7 Because thou hast been my help, therefore in the shadow of thy wings will I rejoice.

8 My soul followeth hard after thee: thy right hand upholdeth me.

LESSON 10.

Psalms 65, 72.

PRAISE waiteth for thee, O God, in Zion: and unto thee shall the vow be performed.

2 O thou that hearest prayer, unto thee shall all flesh come.

3 Iniquities prevail against me: as for our transgressions, thou shalt purge them away.

4 Blessed is the man whom thou choosest, and causest to approach unto thee, that he may dwell in thy courts: we shall be satisfied with the goodness of thy house, even of thy holy temple.

5 By terrible things in righteousness wilt thou answer us, O God of our salvation; who art the confidence of all the ends of the earth, and of them that are afar off upon the sea:

6 Which by his strength setteth fast the mountains; being girded with power:

7 Which stilleth the noise of the seas, the noise of their waves, and the tumult of the people.

8 They also that dwell in the uttermost parts are afraid at thy tokens: thou makest the outgoings of the morning and evening to rejoice.

9 Thou visitest the earth, and waterest it: thou greatly enrichest it with the river of God, which is full of water: thou preparest them corn, when thou hast so provided for it.

10 Thou waterest the ridges thereof abundantly: thou settlest the furrows thereof: thou makest it soft with showers: thou blessest the springing thereof.

11 Thou crownest the year with thy goodness; and thy paths drop fatness.

12 They drop upon the pastures of the wilderness: and the little hills rejoice on every side.

13 The pastures are clothed with flocks; the valleys also are covered over with corn; they shout for joy, they also sing.

GIVE the king thy judgments, O God, and thy righteousness unto the king's son.

2 He shall judge thy people with righteousness, and thy poor with judgment.

3 The mountains shall bring peace to the people, and the little hills, by righteousness.

4 He shall judge the poor of the people, he shall save the children of the needy, and shall break in pieces the oppressor.

5 They shall fear thee as long as the sun and moon endure, throughout all generations.

6 He shall come down like rain upon the mown grass. as showers that water the earth.

7 In his days shall the righteous flourish; and abundance of peace so long as the moon endureth.

8 He shall have dominion also from sea to sea, and from the river unto the ends of the earth.

9 They that dwell in the wilderness shall bow before him; and his enemies shall lick the dust.

10 The kings of Tarshish and the isles shall bring presents: the kings of Sheba and Seba shall offer gifts.

11 Yea, all kings shall fall down before him: all nations shall serve him.

12 For he shall deliver the needy when he crieth; the poor also, and him that hath no helper.

13 He shall spare the poor and needy, and shall save the souls of the needy.

14 He shall redeem their soul from deceit and violence: and precious shall their blood be in his sight.

15 And he shall live, and to him shall be given of the gold of Sheba: prayer also shall be made for him continually; and daily shall he be praised.

16 There shall be a handful of corn in the earth upon the top of the mountains; the fruit thereof shall shake like Lebanon: and they of the city shall flourish like grass of the earth.

17 His name shall endure for ever: his name shall be continued as long as the sun: and men shall be blessed in him: all nations shall call him blessed.

18 Blessed be the LORD God, the God of Israel, who only doeth wondrous things.

19 And blessed be his glorious name for ever: and let the whole earth be filled with his glory. Amen, and Amen.

LESSON 11.

PSALMS 84, 85.

HOW amiable are thy tabernacles, O LORD of hosts!

2 My soul longeth, yea, even fainteth for the courts of the LORD: my heart and my flesh crieth out for the living God.

3 Yea, the sparrow hath found a house, and the swallow a nest for herself, where she may lay her young, even thine altars, O LORD of hosts, my King, and my God.

4 Blessed are they that dwell in thy house: they will be still praising thee.

5 Blessed is the man whose strength is in thee; in whose heart are the ways of them,

6 Who passing through the valley of Baca make it a well; the rain also filleth the pools.

7 They go from strength to strength, every one of them in Zion appeareth before God.

8 O Lord God of hosts, hear my prayer: give ear, O God of Jacob.

9 Behold, O God our shield, and look upon the face of thine anointed.

10 For a day in thy courts is better than a thousand. I had rather be a doorkeeper in the house of my God, than to dwell in the tents of wickedness.

11 For the Lord God is a sun and shield: the Lord will give grace and glory: no good thing will he withhold from them that walk uprightly.

12 O Lord of hosts, blessed is the man that trusteth in thee.

LORD, thou hast been favourable unto thy land: thou hast brought back the captivity of Jacob.

2 Thou hast forgiven the iniquity of thy people; thou hast covered all their sin.

3 Thou hast taken away all thy wrath: thou hast turned thyself from the fierceness of thine anger.

4 Turn us, O God of our salvation, and cause thine anger toward us to cease.

5 Wilt thou be angry with us forever? wilt thou draw out thine anger to all generations?

6 Wilt thou not revive us again: that thy people may rejoice in thee?

7 Shew us thy mercy, O Lord, and grant us thy salvation.

8 I will hear what God the Lord will speak: for he will speak peace unto his people, and to his saints: but let them not turn again to folly.

9 Surely his salvation is nigh them that fear him; that glory may dwell in our land.

10 Mercy and truth are met together; righteousness and peace have kissed each other.

11 Truth shall spring out of the earth; and righteousness shall look down from heaven.

12 Yea, the Lord shall give that which is good; and our land shall yield her increase.

13 Righteousness shall go before him; and shall set us in the way of his steps.

LESSON 12.

Psalms 86, 89, 1-18.

BOW down thine ear, O Lord, hear me: for I am poor and needy.

2 Preserve my soul; for I am holy: O thou my God, save thy servant that trusteth in thee.

3 Be merciful unto me, O Lord: for I cry unto thee daily.

4 Rejoice the soul of thy servant: for unto thee, O Lord, do I lift up my soul.

5 For thou, Lord, art good, and ready to forgive; and plenteous in mercy unto all them that call upon thee.

6 Give ear, O Lord, unto my prayer; and attend to the voice of my supplications.

7 In the day of my trouble I will call upon thee: for thou wilt answer me.

8 Among the gods there is none like unto thee, O Lord; neither are there any works like unto thy works.

9 All nations whom thou hast made shall come and worship before thee, O Lord; and shall glorify thy name.

10 For thou art great, and doest wondrous things: thou art God alone.

11 Teach me thy way, O Lord; I will walk in thy truth: unite my heart to fear thy name.

12 I will praise thee, O Lord my God, with all my heart: and I will glorify thy name for evermore.

13 For great is thy mercy toward me: and thou hast delivered my soul from the lowest hell.

14 O God, the proud are risen against me, and the assemblies of violent men have sought after my soul; and have not set thee before them.

15 But thou, O Lord, art a God full of compassion, and gracious, longsuffering, and plenteous in mercy and truth.

16 O turn unto me, and have mercy upon me; give thy strength unto thy servant, and save the son of thine handmaid.

17 Shew me a token for good; that they which hate me may see it, and be ashamed: because thou, Lord, hast holpen me, and comforted me.

I WILL sing of the mercies of the Lord for ever: with my mouth will I make known thy faithfulness to all generations.

2 For I have said, Mercy shall be built up for ever: thy faithfulness shalt thou establish in the very heavens.

3 I have made a covenant with my chosen, I have sworn unto David my servant,

4 Thy seed will I establish for ever, and build up thy throne to all generations.

5 And the heavens shall praise thy wonders, O Lord: thy faithfulness also in the congregation of the saints.

6 For who in the heaven can be compared unto the Lord? who among the sons of the mighty can be likened unto the Lord?

7 God is greatly to be feared in the assembly of the saints, and to be had in reverence of all them that are about him.

8 O Lord God of hosts, who is a strong Lord like unto thee? or to thy faithfulness round about thee?

9 Thou rulest the raging of the sea: when the waves thereof arise, thou stillest them.

10 Thou hast broken Rahab in pieces, as one that is slain; thou hast scattered thine enemies with thy strong arm.

11 The heavens are thine, the earth also is thine: as for the world and the fulness thereof, thou hast founded them.

12 The north and the south thou hast created them: Tabor and Hermon shall rejoice in thy name.

13 Thou hast a mighty arm: strong is thy hand, and high is thy right hand.

14 Justice and judgment are the habitation of thy throne: mercy and truth shall go before thy face.

15 Blessed is the people that know the joyful sound: they shall walk, O Lord, in the light of thy countenance.

16 In thy name shall they rejoice all the day: and in thy righteousness shall they be exalted.

17 For thou art the glory of their strength: and in thy favour our horn shall be exalted.

18 For the Lord is our defence; and the Holy One of Israel is our King.

LESSON 13.

Psalms 90, 91.

LORD, thou hast been our dwellingplace in all generations.

2 Before the mountains were brought forth, or ever thou hadst formed the earth and the world, even from everlasting to everlasting, thou art God.

3 Thou turnest man to destruction; and sayest, Return, ye children of men.

4 For a thousand years in thy sight are but as yesterday when it is past, and as a watch in the night.

5 Thou carriest them away as with a flood; they are as a sleep: in the morning they are like grass which groweth up.

6 In the morning it flourisheth, and groweth up; in the evening it is cut down, and withereth.

7 For we are consumed by thine anger, and by thy wrath are we troubled.

8 Thou hast set our iniquities before thee, our secret sins in the light of thy countenance.

9 For all our days are passed away in thy wrath: we spend our years as a tale that is told.

10 The days of our years are threescore years and ten; and if by reason of strength they be fourscore years, yet is their strength labour and sorrow; for it is soon cut off, and we fly away.

11 Who knoweth the power of thine anger? even according to thy fear, so is thy wrath.

12 So teach us to number our days, that we may apply our hearts unto wisdom.

13 Return, O Lord, how long? and let it repent thee concerning thy servants.

14 O satisfy us early with thy mercy; that we may rejoice and be glad all our days.

15 Make us glad according to the days wherein thou hast afflicted us, and the years wherein we have seen evil.

16 Let thy work appear unto thy servants, and thy glory unto their children.

17 And let the beauty of the LORD our God be upon us: and establish thou the work of our hands upon us; yea, the work of our hands establish thou it.

HE that dwelleth in the secret place of the Most High shall abide under the shadow of the Almighty.

2 I will say unto the LORD, He is my refuge and my fortress: my God; in him will I trust.

3 Surely he shall deliver thee from the snare of the fowler, and from the noisome pestilence.

4 He shall cover thee with his feathers, and under his wings shalt thou trust: his truth shall be thy shield and buckler.

5 Thou shalt not be afraid for the terror by night; nor for the arrow that flieth by day;

6 Nor for the pestilence that walketh in darkness; nor for the destruction that wasteth at noonday.

7 A thousand shall fall at thy side, and ten thousand at thy right hand; but it shall not come nigh thee.

8 Only with thine eyes shalt thou behold and see the reward of the wicked.

9 Because thou hast made the LORD, which is my refuge, even the Most High, thy habitation;

10 There shall no evil befall thee, neither shall any plague come nigh thy dwelling.

11 For he shall give his angels charge over thee, to keep thee in all thy ways.

12 They shall bear thee up in their hands, lest thou dash thy foot against a stone.

13 Thou shalt tread upon the lion and adder: the young lion and the dragon shalt thou trample under feet.

14 Because he hath set his love upon me, therefore will I deliver him: I will set him on high, because he hath known my name.

15 He shall call upon me, and I will answer him: I will be with him in trouble; I will deliver him, and honour him.

16 With long life will I satisfy him, and shew him my salvation.

LESSON 14.

PSALMS 93, 95, 96.

THE LORD reigneth, he is clothed with majesty; the LORD is clothed with strength, wherewith he hath girded himself: the world also is stablished, that it cannot be moved.

2 Thy throne is established of old: thou art from everlasting.

3 The floods have lifted up, O Lord, the floods have lifted up their voice; the floods lift up their waves.

4 The Lord on high is mightier than the noise of many waters, yea, than the mighty waves of the sea.

5 Thy testimonies are very sure: holiness becometh thine house, O Lord, for ever.

O COME, let us sing unto the Lord: let us make a joyful noise to the Rock of our salvation.

2 Let us come before his presence with thanksgiving, and make a joyful noise unto him with psalms.

3 For the Lord is a great God, and a great King above all gods.

4 In his hand are the deep places of the earth: the strength of the hills is his also.

5 The sea is his, and he made it: and his hands formed the dry land.

6 O come, let us worship and bow down: let us kneel before the Lord our maker.

7 For he is the Lord our God; and we are the people of his pasture, and the sheep of his hand.

O SING unto the Lord a new song: sing unto the Lord, all the earth.

2 Sing unto the Lord, bless his name; shew forth his salvation from day to day.

3 Declare his glory among the heathen, his wonders among all people.

4 For the Lord is great, and greatly to be praised: he is to be feared above all gods.

5 For all the gods of the nations are idols: but the Lord made the heavens.

6 Honour and majesty are before him: strength and beauty are in his sanctuary.

7 Give unto the Lord, O ye kindreds of the people, give unto the Lord glory and strength.

8 Give unto the Lord the glory due unto his name: bring an offering, and come into his courts.

9 O worship the Lord in the beauty of holiness: fear before him, all the earth.

10 Say among the heathen that the Lord reigneth: the world also shall be established that it shall not be moved: he shall judge the people righteously.

11 Let the heavens rejoice, and let the earth be glad; let the sea roar, and the fulness thereof.

12 Let the field be joyful, and all that is therein: then shall all the trees of the wood rejoice

13 Before the Lord: for he cometh, for he cometh to judge the earth: he shall judge the world with righteousness, and the people with his truth.

LESSON 15.

Psalms 102: 16-28, 103.

WHEN the Lord shall build up Zion, he shall appear in his glory.
17 He will regard the prayer of the destitute, and not despise their prayer.
18 This shall be written for the generation to come: and the people which shall be created shall praise the Lord.
19 For he hath looked down from the height of his sanctuary; from heaven did the Lord behold the earth;
20 To hear the groaning of the prisoner; to loose those that are appointed to death.
21 To declare the name of the Lord in Zion, and his praise in Jerusalem;
22 When the people are gathered together, and the kingdoms, to serve the Lord.
23 He weakened my strength in the way; he shortened my days.
24 I said, O my God, take me not away in the midst of my days: thy years are throughout all generations.
25 Of old hast thou laid the foundation of the earth: and the heavens are the work of thy hands.
26 They shall perish, but thou shalt endure: yea, all of them shall wax old like a garment; as a vesture shalt thou change them, and they shall be changed:
27 But thou art the same, and thy years shall have no end.
28 The children of Thy servants shall continue, and their seed shall be established before thee.

BLESS the Lord, O my soul: and all that is within me, bless his holy name.
2 Bless the Lord, O my soul, and forget not all his benefits:
3 Who forgiveth all thine iniquities; who healeth all thy diseases;
4 Who redeemeth thy life from destruction; who crowneth thee with lovingkindness and tender mercies;
5 Who satisfieth thy mouth with good things; so that thy youth is renewed like the eagle's.
6 The Lord executeth righteousness and judgment for all that are oppressed.
7 He made known his ways unto Moses, his acts unto the children of Israel.
8 The Lord is merciful and gracious, slow to anger, and plenteous in mercy.
9 He will not always chide: neither will he keep his anger for ever.
10 He hath not dealt with us after our sins; nor rewarded us according to our iniquities.
11 For as the heaven is high above the earth, so great is his mercy toward them that fear him.
12 As far as the east is from the west, so far hath he removed our transgressions from us.
13 Like as a father pitieth his children, so the Lord pitieth them that fear him.

14 For he knoweth our frame; he remembereth that we are dust.

15 As for man, his days are as grass: as a flower of the field, so he flourisheth.

16 For the wind passeth over it, and it is gone; and the place thereof shall know it no more.

17 But the mercy of the LORD is from everlasting to everlasting upon them that fear him, and his righteousness unto children's children;

18 To such as keep his covenant, and to those that remember his commandments to do them.

19 The LORD hath prepared his throne in the heavens; and his kingdom ruleth over all.

20 Bless the LORD, ye his angels, that excel in strength, that do his commandments, hearkening unto the voice of his word.

21 Bless ye the LORD, all ye his hosts; ye ministers of his, that do his pleasure.

22 Bless the LORD, all his works in all places of his dominion: bless the LORD, O my soul.

LESSON 16.

PSALMS 107: 1-8, 111, 113, 117.

O GIVE thanks unto the LORD, for he is good: for his mercy endureth for ever.

2 Let the redeemed of the LORD say so, whom he hath redeemed from the hand of the enemy;

3 And gathered them out of the lands, from the east, and from the west, from the north, and from the south.

4 They wandered in the wilderness in a solitary way; they found no city to dwell in.

5 Hungry and thirsty, their soul fainted in them.

6 Then they cried unto the LORD in their trouble, and he delivered them out of their distresses.

7 And he led them forth by the right way, that they might go to a city of habitation.

8 Oh that men would praise the LORD for his goodness, and for his wonderful works to the children of men!

PRAISE ye the LORD. I will praise the LORD with my whole heart, in the assembly of the upright, and in the congregation.

2 The works of the LORD are great, sought out of all them that have pleasure therein.

3 His work is honourable and glorious: and his righteousness endureth for ever.

4 He hath made his wonderful works to be remembered: the LORD is gracious and full of compassion.

5 He hath given meat unto them that fear him: he will ever be mindful of his covenant.

6 He hath shewed his people the power of his works, that he may give them the heritage of the heathen.

7 The works of his hands are verity and judgment; all his commandments are sure.

8 They stand fast for ever and ever, and are done in truth and uprightness.

9 He sent redemption unto his people: he hath commanded his covenant for ever: holy and reverend is his name.

10 The fear of the LORD is the beginning of wisdom: a good understanding have all they that do his commandments: his praise endureth for ever.

PRAISE ye the LORD. Praise, O ye servants of the LORD, praise the name of the LORD.

2 Blessed be the name of the LORD from this time forth and for ever more.

3 From the rising of the sun unto the going down of the same the LORD'S name is to be praised.

4 The LORD is high above all nations, and his glory above the heavens.

5 Who is like unto the LORD our God, who dwelleth on high,

6 Who humbleth himself to behold the things that are in heaven, and in the earth!

7 He raiseth up the poor out of the dust, and lifteth the needy out of the dunghill;

8 That he may set him with princes, even with the princes of his people.

9 He maketh the barren woman to keep house, and to be a joyful mother of children. Praise ye the LORD.

LESSON 17.

PSALMS 116, 118: 14–29

I LOVE the LORD, because he hath heard my voice and my supplications.

2 Because he hath inclined his ear unto me, therefore will I call upon him as long as I live.

3 The sorrows of death compassed me, and the pains of hell gat hold upon me: I found trouble and sorrow.

4 Then called I upon the name of the LORD; O LORD, I beseech thee, deliver my soul.

5 Gracious is the LORD, and righteous; yea, our God is merciful.

6 The LORD preserveth the simple: I was brought low, and he helped me.

7 Return unto thy rest, O my soul; for the LORD hath dealt bountifully with thee.

8 For thou hast delivered my soul from death, mine eyes from tears, and my feet from falling.
9 I will walk before the LORD in the land of the living.
10 I believed, therefore have I spoken: I was greatly afflicted:
11 I said in my haste, All men are liars.
12 What shall I render unto the LORD for all his benefits toward me?
13 I will take the cup of salvation, and call upon the name of the LORD.
14 I will pay my vows unto the LORD now in the presence of all his people.
15 Precious in the sight of the LORD is the death of his saints.
16 O LORD, truly I am thy servant; I am thy servant, and the son of thine handmaid: thou hast loosed my bonds.
17 I will offer to thee the sacrifice of thanksgiving, and will call upon the name of the LORD.
18 I will pay my vows unto the LORD now in the presence of all his people.
19 In the courts of the LORD's house, in the midst of thee, O Jerusalem, Praise ye the LORD.

THE LORD is my strength and song, and is become my salvation.
15 The voice of rejoicing and salvation is in the tabernacles of the righteous: the right hand of the LORD doeth valiantly.
16 The right hand of the LORD is exalted: the right hand of the LORD doeth valiantly.
17 I shall not die, but live, and declare the works of the LORD.
18 The LORD hath chastened me sore: but he hath not given me over unto death.
19 Open to me the gates of righteousness: I will go into them, and I will praise the LORD:
20 This gate of the LORD, into which the righteous shall enter.
21 I will praise thee: for thou hast heard me, and art become my salvation.
22 The stone which the builders refused is become the head stone of the corner.
23 This is the LORD's doing; it is marvellous in our eyes.
24 This is the day which the LORD hath made; we will rejoice and be glad in it.
25 Save now, I beseech thee, O LORD: O LORD, I beseech thee, send now prosperity.
26 Blessed be he that cometh in the name of the LORD: we have blessed you out of the house of the LORD.
27 God is the LORD, which hath shewed us light: bind the sacrifice with cords, even unto the horns of the altar.
28 Thou art my God, and I will praise thee: thou art my God, I will exalt thee.
29 O give thanks unto the LORD; for he is good: for his mercy endureth for ever.

LESSON 18.

Psalm 119: 1-16, 41-48, 73-80.

BLESSED are the undefiled in the way, who walk in the law of the Lord.
2 Blessed are they that keep his testimonies, and that seek him with the whole heart.
3 They also do no iniquity: they walk in his ways.
4 Thou hast commanded us to keep thy precepts diligently.
5 O that my ways were directed to keep thy statutes!
6 Then shall I not be ashamed, when I have respect unto all thy commandments.
7 I will praise thee with uprightness of heart, when I shall have learned thy righteous judgments.
8 I will keep thy statutes: O forsake me not utterly.
9 Wherewithal shall a young man cleanse his way? by taking heed thereto according to thy word.
10 With my whole heart have I sought thee: O let me not wander from thy commandments.
11 Thy word have I hid in my heart, that I might not sin against thee.
12 Blessed art thou, O Lord: teach me thy statutes.
13 With my lips have I declared all the judgments of thy mouth.
14 I have rejoiced in the way of thy testimonies, as much as in all riches.
15 I will meditate in thy precepts, and have respect unto thy ways.
16 I will delight myself in thy statutes: I will not forget thy word.
41 Let thy mercies come also unto me, O Lord, even thy salvation, according to thy word.
42 So shall I have wherewith to answer him that reproacheth me: for I trust in thy word.
43 And take not the word of truth utterly out of my mouth; for I have hoped in thy judgments.
44 So shall I keep thy law continually for ever and ever.
45 And I will walk at liberty: for I seek thy precepts.
46 I will speak of thy testimonies also before kings, and will not be ashamed.
47 And I will delight myself in thy commandments, which I have loved.
48 My hands also will I lift up unto thy commandments, which I have loved; and I will meditate in thy statutes.
73 Thy hands have made me and fashioned me: give me understanding, that I may learn thy commandments.
74 They that fear thee will be glad when they see me; because I have hoped in thy word.
75 I know, O Lord, that thy judgments are right, and that thou in faithfulness hast afflicted me.

76 Let, I pray thee, thy merciful kindness be for my comfort, according to thy word unto thy servant.

77 Let thy tender mercies come unto me, that I may live: for thy law is my delight.

78 Let the proud be ashamed; for they dealt perversely with me without a cause: but I will meditate in thy precepts.

79 Let those that fear thee turn unto me, and those that have known thy testimonies.

80 Let my heart be sound in thy statutes; that I be not ashamed.

LESSON 19.

Psalm 119, 97-112: 130-136: 169-176.

O HOW love I thy law! it is my meditation all the day.

98 Thou through thy commandments hast made me wiser than mine enemies: for they are ever with me.

99 I have more understanding than all my teachers: for thy testimonies are my meditation.

100 I understand more than the ancients, because I keep thy precepts.

101 I have refrained my feet from every evil way, that I might keep thy word.

102 I have not departed from thy judgments; for thou hast taught me.

103 How sweet are thy words unto my taste! yea, sweeter than honey to my mouth.

104 Through thy precepts I get understanding: therefore I hate every false way.

105 Thy word is a lamp unto my feet, and a light unto my path.

106 I have sworn, and I will perform it, that I will keep thy righteous judgments.

107 I am afflicted very much: quicken me, O Lord, according unto thy word.

108 Accept, I beseech thee, the freewill offerings of my mouth, O Lord, and teach me thy judgments.

109 My soul is continually in my hand: yet do I not forget thy law.

110 The wicked have laid a snare for me: yet I erred not from thy precepts.

111 Thy testimonies have I taken as a heritage for ever: for they are the rejoicing of my heart.

112 I have inclined mine heart to perform thy statutes always, even unto the end.

130 The entrance of thy words giveth light; it giveth understanding unto the simple.

131 I opened my mouth, and panted: for I longed for thy commandments.

132 Look thou upon me, and be merciful unto me, as thou usest to do unto those that love thy name.

133 Order my steps in thy word: and let not any iniquity have dominion over me.

134 Deliver me from the oppression of man: so will I keep thy precepts.

135 Make thy face to shine upon thy servant; and teach me thy statutes.
136 Rivers of waters run down mine eyes, because they keep not thy law.
169 Let my cry come near before thee, O Lord: give me understanding according to thy word.
170 Let my supplication come before thee: deliver me according to thy word.
171 My lips shall utter praise, when thou hast taught me thy statutes.
172 My tongue shall speak of thy word: for all thy commandments are righteousness.
173 Let thine hand help me; for I have chosen thy precepts.
174 I have longed for thy salvation, O Lord; and thy law is my delight.
175 Let my soul live, and it shall praise thee; and let thy judgments help me.
176 I have gone astray like a lost sheep: seek thy servant; for I do not forget thy commandments.

LESSON 20.

Psalms 121, 122, 123.

I WILL lift up mine eyes unto the hills, from whence cometh my help.
2 My help cometh from the Lord, which made heaven and earth.
3 He will not suffer thy foot to be moved: he that keepeth thee will not slumber.
4 Behold, he that keepeth Israel shall neither slumber nor sleep.
5 The Lord is thy keeper: the Lord is thy shade upon thy right hand.
6 The sun shall not smite thee by day, nor the moon by night.
7 The Lord shall preserve thee from all evil: he shall preserve thy soul.
8 The Lord shall preserve thy going out and thy coming in from this time forth, and even for evermore.

I WAS glad when they said unto me, Let us go into the house of the Lord.
2 Our feet shall stand within thy gates, O Jerusalem.
3 Jerusalem is builded as a city that is compact together:
4 Whither the tribes go up, the tribes of the Lord, unto the testimony of Israel, to give thanks unto the name of the Lord.
5 For there are set thrones of judgment, the thrones of the house of David.
6 Pray for the peace of Jerusalem: they shall prosper that love thee.
7 Peace be within thy walls, and prosperity within thy palaces.
8 For my brethren and companions' sakes, I will now say, Peace be within thee.
9 Because of the house of the Lord our God I will seek thy good.

UNTO thee lift I up mine eyes, O thou that dwellest in the heavens.
2 Behold, as the eyes of servants look unto the hand of their masters, and

as the eyes of a maiden unto the hand of her mistress; so our eyes wait upon the Lord our God, until that he have mercy upon us.

3 Have mercy upon us, O Lord, have mercy upon us: for we are exceedingly filled with contempt.

4 Our soul is exceedingly filled with the scorning of those that are at ease, and with the contempt of the proud.

LESSON 21.
Psalms 126, 127, 130.

THEY that trust in the Lord shall be as mount Zion, which cannot be moved, but abideth for ever.

2 As the mountains are round about Jerusalem, so the Lord is round about his people from henceforth even for ever.

3 For the rod of the wicked shall not rest upon the lot of the righteous; lest the righteous put forth their hands unto iniquity.

4 Do good, O Lord, unto those that be good, and to them that are upright in their hearts.

5 As for such as turn aside unto their crooked ways, the Lord shall lead them forth with the workers of iniquity: but peace shall be upon Israel.

WHEN the Lord turned again the captivity of Zion, we were like them that dream.

2 Then was our mouth filled with laughter, and our tongue with singing: then said they among the heathen, The Lord hath done great things for them.

3 The Lord hath done great things for us; whereof we are glad.

4 Turn again our captivity, O Lord, as the streams in the south.

5 They that sow in tears shall reap in joy.

6 He that goeth forth and weepeth, bearing precious seed, shall doubtless come again with rejoicing, bringing his sheaves with him.

BLESSED is every one that feareth the Lord; that walketh in his ways.

2 For thou shalt eat the labour of thine hands: happy shalt thou be, and it shall be well with thee.

3 Thy wife shall be as a fruitful vine by the sides of thine house: thy children like olive plants round about thy table.

4 Behold, that thus shall the man be blessed that feareth the Lord.

5 The Lord shall bless thee out of Zion: and thou shalt see the good of Jerusalem all the days of thy life.

6 Yea, thou shalt see thy children's children, and peace upon Israel.

OUT of the depths have I cried unto thee, O Lord.

2 Lord, hear my voice: let thine ears be attentive to the voice of my supplications.

3 If thou, Lord, shouldest mark iniquities, O Lord, who shall stand?
4 But there is forgiveness with thee, that thou mayest be feared.
5 I wait for the Lord, my soul doth wait, and in his word do I hope.
6 My soul waiteth for the Lord more than they that watch for the morning.
7 Let Israel hope in the Lord: for with the Lord there is mercy, and with him is plenteous redemption.
8 And he shall redeem Israel from all his iniquities.

LESSON 22.

Psalms 132: 8-16, 133, 134, 138.

ARISE, O Lord, into thy rest; thou and the ark of thy strength.
9 Let thy priests be clothed with righteousness, and let thy saints shout for joy.
10 For thy servant David's sake turn not away the face of thine anointed.
11 The Lord hath sworn in truth unto David; he will not turn from it; Of the fruit of thy body will I set upon thy throne.
12 If thy children will keep my covenant and my testimony that I shall teach them, their children shall also sit upon thy throne for evermore.
13 For the Lord hath chosen Zion; he hath desired it for his habitation.
14 This is my rest for ever: here will I dwell; for I have desired it.
15 I will abundantly bless her provision: I will satisfy her poor with bread.
16 I will also clothe her priests with salvation: and her saints shall shout aloud for joy.

BEHOLD, how good and how pleasant it is for brethren to dwell together in unity!
2 It is like the precious ointment upon the head, that ran down upon the beard, even Aaron's beard: that went down to the skirts of his garments;
3 As the dew of Hermon, and as the dew that descended upon the mountains of Zion: for there the Lord commanded the blessing, even life for evermore.

BEHOLD, bless ye the Lord, all ye servants of the Lord, which by night stand in the house of the Lord.
2 Lift up your hands in the sanctuary, and bless the Lord.
3 The Lord that made heaven and earth bless thee out of Zion.

I WILL praise thee with my whole heart: before the gods will I sing praise unto thee.
2 I will worship toward thy holy temple, and praise thy name for thy lovingkindness and for thy truth: for thou hast magnified thy word above all thy name.
3 In the day when I cried thou answeredst me, and strengthenedst me with strength in my soul.

4 All the kings of the earth shall praise thee, O Lord, when they hear the words of thy mouth.

5 Yea, they shall sing in the ways of the Lord: for great is the glory of the Lord.

6 Though the Lord be high, yet hath he respect unto the lowly: but the proud he knoweth afar off.

7 Though I walk in the midst of trouble, thou wilt revive me: thou shalt stretch forth thine hand against the wrath of mine enemies, and thy right hand shall save me.

8 The Lord will perfect that which concerneth me: thy mercy, O Lord, endureth for ever; forsake not the works of thine own hands.

LESSON 23.

Psalms 139, 143.

O LORD, thou hast searched me, and known me.

2 Thou knowest my downsitting and mine up-rising, thou understandest my thought afar off.

3 Thou compassest my path and my lying down, and art acquainted with all my ways.

4 For there is not a word in my tongue, but lo, O Lord, thou knowest it altogether.

5 Thou hast beset me behind and before, and laid thine hand upon me.

6 Such knowledge is too wonderful for me; it is high, I cannot attain unto it.

7 Whither shall I go from thy Spirit? or whither shall I flee from thy presence?

8 If I ascend up into heaven, thou art there: if I make my bed in hell, behold, thou art there.

9 If I take the wings of the morning, and dwell in the uttermost parts of the sea;

10 Even there shall thy hand lead me, and thy right hand shall hold me.

11 If I say, Surely the darkness shall cover me; even the night shall be light about me.

12 Yea, the darkness hideth not from thee; but the night shineth as the day: the darkness and the light are both alike to thee.

13 For thou hast possessed my reins: thou hast covered me in my mother's womb.

14 I will praise thee; for I am fearfully and wonderfully made: marvellous are thy works; and that my soul knoweth right well.

15 My substance was not hid from thee, when I was made in secret, and curiously wrought in the lowest parts of the earth.

16 Thine eyes did see my substance, yet being unperfect; and in thy book all my members were written, which in continuance were fashioned, when as yet there was none of them.

17 How precious also are thy thoughts unto me, O God! how great is the sum of them!
18 If I should count them, they are more in number than the sand: when I awake, I am still with thee.
19 Surely thou wilt slay the wicked, O God: depart from me therefore, ye bloody men.
20 For they speak against thee wickedly, and thine enemies take thy name in vain.
21 Do not I hate them, O LORD, that hate thee? and am not I grieved with those that rise up against thee?
22 I hate them with perfect hatred: I count them mine enemies.
23 Search me, O God, and know my heart: try me, and know my thoughts:
24 And see if there be any wicked way in me, and lead me in the way everlasting.

HEAR my prayer, O LORD, give ear to my supplications: in thy faithfulness answer me, and in thy righteousness.
2 And enter not into judgment with thy servant: for in thy sight shall no man living be justified.
3 For the enemy hath persecuted my soul; he hath smitten my life down to the ground; he hath made me to dwell in darkness, as those that have been long dead.
4 Therefore is my spirit overwhelmed within me; my heart within me is desolate.
5 I remember the days of old; I meditate on all thy works; I muse on the work of thy hands.
6 I stretch forth my hands unto thee: my soul thirsteth after thee, as a thirsty land.
7 Hear me speedily, O LORD; my spirit faileth: hide not thy face from me, lest I be like unto them that go down into the pit.
8 Cause me to hear thy lovingkindness in the morning; for in thee do I trust: cause me to know the way wherein I should walk; for I lift up my soul unto thee.
9 Deliver me, O LORD, from mine enemies: I flee unto thee to hide me.
10 Teach me to do thy will; for thou art my God: thy Spirit is good; lead me into the land of uprightness.
11 Quicken me, O LORD, for thy name's sake: for thy righteousness' sake bring my soul out of trouble.
12 And of thy mercy cut off mine enemies, and destroy all them that afflict my soul: for I am thy servant.

LESSON 24.

Psalms 145, 146.

I WILL extol thee, my God, O King; and I will bless thy name for ever and ever.

2 Every day will I bless thee; and I will praise thy name for ever and ever.

3 Great is the Lord, and greatly to be praised; and his greatness is unsearchable.

4 One generation shall praise thy works to another, and shall declare thy mighty acts.

5 I will speak of the glorious honour of thy majesty, and of thy wondrous works.

6 And men shall speak of the might of thy terrible acts: and I will declare thy greatness.

7 They shall abundantly utter the memory of thy great goodness, and shall sing of thy righteousness.

8 The Lord is gracious, and full of compassion; slow to anger, and of great mercy.

9 The Lord is good to all: and his tender mercies are over all his works.

10 All thy works shall praise thee, O Lord; and thy saints shall bless thee.

11 They shall speak of the glory of thy kingdom, and talk of thy power;

12 To make known to the sons of men his mighty acts, and the glorious majesty of his kingdom.

13 Thy kingdom is an everlasting kingdom, and thy dominion endureth throughout all generations.

14 The Lord upholdeth all that fall, and raiseth up all those that be bowed down.

15 The eyes of all wait upon thee, and thou givest them their meat in due season.

16 Thou openest thine hand, and satisfiest the desire of every living thing.

17 The Lord is righteous in all his ways, and holy in all his works.

18 The Lord is nigh unto all them that call upon him, to all that call upon him in truth.

19 He will fulfill the desire of them that fear him: he also will hear their cry, and will save them.

20 The Lord preserveth all them that love him: but all the wicked will he destroy.

21 My mouth shall speak the praise of the Lord: and let all flesh bless his holy name for ever and ever.

PRAISE ye the Lord. Praise the Lord, O my soul.

2 While I live will I praise the Lord: I will sing praises unto my God while I have any being.

3 Put not your trust in princes, nor in the son of man, in whom there is no help.
4 His breath goeth forth, he returneth to his earth; in that very day his thoughts perish.
5 Happy is he that hath the God of Jacob for his help, whose hope is in the LORD his God:
6 Which made heaven, and earth, the sea, and all that therein is: which keepeth truth for ever:
7 Which executeth judgment for the oppressed: which giveth food to the hungry. The LORD looseth the prisoners:
8 The LORD openeth the eyes of the blind: the LORD raiseth them that are bowed down: the LORD loveth the righteous:
9 The LORD preserveth the strangers; he relieveth the fatherless and widow: but the way of the wicked he turneth upside down.
10 The LORD shall reign for ever, even thy God, O Zion, unto all generations. Praise ye the LORD.

LESSON 25.

PSALMS 147, 148.

PRAISE ye the LORD: for it is good to sing praises unto our God; for it is pleasant; and praise is comely.
2 The LORD doth build up Jerusalem: he gathereth together the outcasts of Israel.
3 He healeth the broken in heart, and bindeth up their wounds.
4 He telleth the number of the stars; he calleth them all by their names.
5 Great is our LORD, and of great power: his understanding is infinite.
6 The LORD lifteth up the meek: he casteth the wicked down to the ground.
7 Sing unto the LORD with thanksgiving; sing praise upon the harp unto our God:
8 Who covereth the heaven with clouds, who prepareth rain for the earth, who maketh grass to grow upon the mountains.
9 He giveth to the beast his food, and to the young ravens which cry.
10 He delighteth not in the strength of the horse: he taketh not pleasure in the legs of a man.
11 The LORD taketh pleasure in them that fear him, in those that hope in his mercy.
12 Praise the LORD, O Jerusalem; praise thy God, O Zion.
13 For he hath strengthened the bars of thy gates; he hath blessed thy children within thee.
14 He maketh peace in thy borders, and filleth thee with the finest of the wheat.
15 He sendeth forth his commandment upon earth: his word runneth very swiftly.

16 He giveth snow like wool: he scattereth the hoar frost like ashes.

17 He casteth forth his ice like morsels: who can stand before his cold?

18 He sendeth out his word, and melteth them: he causeth his wind to blow, and the waters flow.

19 He sheweth his word unto Jacob, his statutes and his judgments unto Israel.

20 He hath not dealt so with any nation: and as for his judgments, they have not known them. Praise ye the LORD.

PRAISE ye the LORD. Praise ye the LORD from the heavens: praise him in the heights.

2 Praise ye him, all his angels: praise ye him, all his hosts.

3 Praise ye him, sun and moon: praise him, all ye stars of light.

4 Praise him, ye heavens of heavens, and ye waters that be above the heavens.

5 Let them praise the name of the LORD: for he commanded, and they were created.

6 He hath also stablished them for ever and ever: he hath made a decree which shall not pass.

7 Praise the LORD from the earth, ye dragons, and all deeps:

8 Fire, and hail; snow, and vapour; stormy wind fulfilling his word:

9 Mountains, and all hills; fruitful trees, and all cedars:

10 Beasts, and all cattle; creeping things, and flying fowl:

11 Kings of the earth, and all people; princes, and all judges of the earth:

12 Both young men, and maidens; old men, and children:

13 Let them praise the name of the LORD: for his name alone is excellent; his glory is above the earth and heaven.

14 He also exalteth the horn of his people, the praise of all his saints; even of the childen of Israel, a people near unto him. Praise ye the LORD.

LESSON 26.

From "The PROVERBS."

MY son, hear the instruction of thy father, and forsake not the law of thy mother.

2 For they shall be an ornament of grace unto thy head, and chains about thy neck.

3 My son, if sinners entice thee, consent thou not.

4 Walk not thou in the way with them: refrain thy foot from their path.

5 My son, forget not my law; but let thy heart keep my commandments.

6 For length of days, and long life, and peace, shall they add to thee.

7 Let not mercy and truth forsake thee; bind them about thy neck; write them upon the table of thine heart.

8 So shalt thou find favour and good understanding in the sight of God and man.

9 Trust in the Lord with all thine heart, and lean not unto thine own understanding.

10 In all thy ways acknowledge him, and he shall direct thy paths.

11 My son, despise not thou the chastening of the Lord; neither be weary of his correction.

12 For whom the Lord loveth he correcteth; even as a father the son in whom he delighteth.

13 The path of the just is as the shining light, that shineth more and more unto the perfect day.

14 Keep thine heart with all diligence, for out of it are the issues of life.

15 I love them that love me, and those that seek me early shall find me.

16 Now therefore, hearken unto me, O ye children; for blessed are they that keep my ways.

LESSON 27.

Isaiah 12, 55.

O LORD, I will praise thee: though thou wast angry with me, thine anger is turned away, and thou comfortedst me.

2 Behold, God is my salvation; I will trust, and not be afraid: for the Lord Jehovah is my strength and song; he also is become my salvation.

3 Therefore with joy shall ye draw water out of the wells of salvation.

4 And in that day shall ye say, Praise the Lord, call upon his name, declare his doings among the people, make mention that his name is exalted.

5 Sing unto the Lord; for he hath done excellent things: this is known in all the earth.

6 Cry out, and shout, O thou inhabitant of Zion: for great is the Holy One of Israel in the midst of thee.

HO, every one that thirsteth, come ye to the waters, and he that hath no money; come ye, buy, and eat; yea, come, buy wine and milk without money and without price.

2 Wherefore do ye spend money for that which is not bread? and your labor for that which satisfieth not? hearken diligently unto me, and eat ye that which is good, and let your soul delight itself in fatness.

3 Incline your ear, and come unto me: hear, and your soul shall live; and I will make an everlasting covenant with you, even the sure mercies of David.

4 Seek ye the Lord while he may be found: call ye upon him while he is near.

5 Let the wicked forsake his way, and the unrighteous man his thoughts: and

let him return unto the LORD, and he will have mercy upon him; and to our God, for he will abundantly pardon.

6 For my thoughts are not your thoughts, neither are your ways my ways, saith the LORD.

7 For as the heavens are higher than the earth, so are my ways higher than your ways, and my thoughts than your thoughts.

LESSON 28.

"SONG OF THE THREE CHILDREN."

BLESSED art thou, O LORD God of our fathers: and to be praised and magnified for ever:

2 And blessed is thy glorious and holy name: and to be praised and magnified for ever.

3 O all ye works of the LORD, bless ye the LORD: praise him and magnify him for ever.

4 O all ye angels of the LORD, bless ye the LORD: praise him and magnify him for ever.

5 O ye heavens, bless ye the LORD: praise him and magnify him for ever.

6 O all ye powers of the LORD, bless ye the LORD: praise him and magnify him for ever.

7 O ye sun and moon, bless ye the LORD: praise him and magnify him for ever.

8 O ye stars of heaven, bless ye the LORD: praise him and magnify him for ever.

9 O ye showers and dew, bless ye the LORD: praise him and magnify him for ever.

10 O ye winds of God, bless ye the LORD: praise him and magnify him for ever.

11 O ye fire and heat, bless ye the LORD: praise him and magnify him for ever.

12 O ye winter and summer, bless ye the LORD: praise him and magnify him for ever.

13 O ye dews and frosts, bless ye the LORD: praise him and magnify him for ever.

14 O ye light and darkness, bless ye the LORD: praise him and magnify him for ever.

15 O let the earth bless the LORD: yea, let it praise him and magnify him for ever.

16 O ye mountains and hills, bless ye the LORD: praise him and magnify him for ever.

17 O all ye things that grow on the earth, bless ye the Lord: praise him and magnify him for ever.

18 O ye fountains, bless ye the Lord: praise him and magnify him for ever.

19 O ye seas and rivers, bless ye the Lord: praise him and magnify him for ever.

20 O all ye fowls of the air, bless ye the Lord: praise him and magnify him for ever.

21 O all ye beasts and cattle, bless ye the Lord: praise him and magnify him for ever.

22 O ye children of men, bless ye the Lord: praise him and magnify him for ever.

23 O ye priests of the Lord, bless ye the Lord: praise him and magnify him for ever.

24 O ye servants of the Lord, bless ye the Lord: praise him and magnify him for ever.

25 O ye spirits and souls of the righteous, bless ye the Lord: praise him and magnify him for ever.

26 O ye holy and humble men of heart, bless ye the Lord: praise him and magnify him for ever.

27 O give thanks unto the Lord, because he is gracious: for his mercy endureth for ever.

28 O all ye that worship the Lord, bless the God of gods; praise him and give him thanks: for his mercy endureth forever.

LESSON 29.

Matthew 5: 1-10, 7: 7-27.

AND seeing the multitudes, he went up into a mountain: and when he was set, his disciples came unto him:

2 And he opened his mouth, and taught them, saying,

3 Blessed are the poor in spirit: for theirs is the kingdom of heaven.

4 Blessed are they that mourn: for they shall be comforted.

5 Blessed are the meek: for they shall inherit the earth.

6 Blessed are they which do hunger and thirst after righteousness: for they shall be filled.

7 Blessed are the merciful: for they shall obtain mercy.

8 Blessed are the pure in heart: for they shall see God.

9 Blessed are the peacemakers: for they shall be called the children of God.

10 Blessed are they which are persecuted for righteousness' sake: for theirs is the kingdom of heaven.

ASK, and it shall be given you; seek, and ye shall find; knock, and it shall be opened unto you.

8 For every one that asketh receiveth: and he that seeketh findeth; and to him that knocketh it shall be opened.

9 Or what man is there of you, whom if his son ask bread, will he give him a stone?

10 Or if he ask a fish, will he give him a serpent?

11 If ye then, being evil, know how to give good gifts unto your children, how much more shall your Father which is in heaven give good things to them that ask him?

12 Therefore all things whatsoever ye would that men should do to you, do ye even so to them: for this is the law and the prophets.

NOT every one that saith unto me, LORD, LORD, shall enter into the kingdom of heaven; but he that doeth the will of my Father which is in heaven.

22 Many will say to me in that day, LORD, LORD, have we not prophesied in thy name? and in thy name have cast out devils? and in thy name done many wonderful works?

23 And then will I profess unto them, I never knew you: depart from me, ye that work iniquity.

24 Therefore whosoever heareth these sayings of mine, and doeth them, I will liken him unto a wise man, which built his house upon a rock:

25 And the rain descended, and the floods came, and the winds blew, and beat upon that house; and it fell not: for it was founded upon a rock.

26 And every one that heareth these sayings of mine, and doeth them not, shall be likened unto a foolish man, which built his house upon the sand:

27 And the rain descended, and the floods came, and the winds blew, and beat upon that house; and it fell; and great was the fall of it.

LESSON 30.

1st COR. 13. 1st JOHN 4: 7–13.

THOUGH I speak with the tongues of men and of angels, and have not charity, I am become as sounding brass, or a tinkling cymbal.

2 And though I have the gift of prophecy, and understand all mysteries, and all knowledge; and though I have all faith, so that I could remove mountains, and have not charity, I am nothing.

3 And though I bestow all my goods to feed the poor, and though I give my body to be burned, and have not charity, it profiteth me nothing.

4 Charity suffereth long, and is kind; charity envieth not; charity vaunteth not itself, is not puffed up,

5 Doth not behave itself unseemly, seeketh not her own, is not easily provoked, thinketh no evil;

6 Rejoiceth not in iniquity, but rejoiceth in the truth;

7 Beareth all things, believeth all things, hopeth all things, endureth all things.

8 Charity never faileth: but whether there be prophecies, they shall fail; whether there be tongues, they shall cease; whether there be knowledge, it shall vanish away.

9 For we know in part, and we prophesy in part.

10 But when that which is perfect is come, then that which is in part shall be done away.

11 When I was a child, I spake as a child, I understood as a child, I thought as a child: but when I became a man, I put away childish things.

12 For now we see through a glass, darkly; but then face to face: now I know in part; but then shall I know even as also I am known.

13 And now abideth faith, hope, charity, these three; but the greatest of these is charity.

BELOVED, let us love one another: for love is of God; and every one that loveth is born of God, and knoweth God.

8 He that loveth not, knoweth not God; for God is love.

9 In this was manifested the love of God towards us, because that God sent his only begotten Son into the world, that we might live through him.

10 Herein is love, not that we loved God, but that he loved us, and sent his Son to be the propitiation for our sins.

11 Beloved, if God so loved us, we ought also to love one another.

12 No man hath seen God at any time. If we love one another, God dwelleth in us, and his love is perfected in us.

13 Hereby know we that we dwell in him and he in us, because he hath given us of his spirit.

LESSON 31.

REV. 7: 9–17, 21: 22–27.

AFTER this I beheld, and, lo, a great multitude which no man could number, of all nations, and kindreds, and people, and tongues, stood before the throne, and before the Lamb, clothed in white robes, and palms in their hands;

10 And cried with a loud voice, saying, Salvation to our God which sitteth upon the throne, and unto the Lamb.

11 And all the angels stood round about the throne and about the elders and the four beasts, and fell before the throne on their faces, and worshipped God, saying,

12 Amen: Blessing, and glory, and wisdom, and thanksgiving, and honour, and power, and might, be unto our God for ever and ever. Amen.

13 And one of the elders answered, saying unto me, What are these which are arrayed in white robes? and whence came they?

14 And I said unto him, Sir, thou knowest. And he said unto me, These are they which came out of great tribulation, and have washed their robes, and made them white in the blood of the Lamb.

15 Therefore are they before the throne of God, and serve him day and night in his temple: and he that sitteth on the throne shall dwell among them.

16 They shall hunger no more, neither thirst any more; neither shall the sun light on them, nor any heat.

17 For the Lamb which is in the midst of the throne shall feed them, and shall lead them unto living fountains of waters: and God shall wipe away all tears from their eyes.

AND I saw no temple therein: for the Lord God Almighty and the Lamb are the temple of it.

23 And the city had no need of the sun, neither of the moon, to shine in it: for the glory of God did lighten it, and the Lamb is the light thereof.

24 And the nations of them that are saved shall walk in the light of it: and the kings of the earth do bring their glory and honour into it.

25 And the gates of it shall not be shut at all by day: for there shall be no night there.

26 And they shall bring the glory and honour of the nations into it.

27 And there shall in no wise enter into it anything that defileth, neither worketh abomination, or maketh a lie: but they which are written in the Lamb's book of life.

HOLY, holy, holy, Lord God Almighty, which was, and is, and is to come.

2 Thou art worthy, O Lord, to receive glory, and honour, and power: for thou hast created all things, and for thy pleasure they are, and were created.

WORTHY is the Lamb that was slain, to receive power, and riches, and wisdom, and strength, and honour, and glory, and blessing.

2 Blessing, and honour, and glory, and power, be unto him that sitteth upon the throne, and unto the Lamb for ever and ever.

LESSON 32.

Te Deum Laudamus.

WE praise thee, O God; we acknowledge thee to be the Lord.
2 All the earth doth worship thee, the Father everlasting.
3 To thee all angels cry aloud; the heavens, and all the powers therein.
4 To thee cherubim and seraphim continually do cry:
5 Holy, Holy, Holy, Lord God of Sabaoth;
6 Heaven and earth are full of the majesty of thy glory.
7 The glorious company of the Apostles praise thee.
8 The goodly fellowship of the Prophets praise thee.
9 The noble army of Martyrs praise thee.
10 The Holy Church throughout all the world doth acknowledge thee,
11 The Father, of an infinite majesty;
12 Thine adorable, true, and only Son;
13 Also the Holy Ghost, the Comforter.
14 Thou art the King of glory, O Christ;
15 Thou art the everlasting Son of the Father.
16 When thou tookest upon thee to deliver man, thou didst humble thyself to be born of a Virgin.
17 When thou hadst overcome the sharpness of death, thou didst open the kingdom of heaven to all believers.
18 Thou sittest at the right hand of God, in the glory of the Father.
19 We believe that thou shalt come to be our Judge:
20 We therefore pray thee, help thy servants, whom thou hast redeemed with thy precious blood:
21 Make them to be numbered with thy saints, in glory everlasting.
22 O Lord, save thy people, and bless thine heritage:
23 Govern them and lift them up forever.
24 Day by day we magnify thee;
25 And we worship thy Name ever, world without end.
26 Vouchsafe, O Lord, to keep us this day without sin.
27 O Lord, have mercy upon us, have mercy upon us.
28 O Lord, let thy mercy be upon us, as our trust is in thee.
29 O Lord, in thee have I trusted; let me never be confounded.

www.ingramcontent.com/pod-product-compliance
Lightning Source LLC
Chambersburg PA
CBHW031846220426
43663CB00006B/512